Introduction to Quechua

Language of the Andes

SECOND EDITION

Cover photograph: Wool wall hanging from the Peruvian town of San Pedro de Cajas, known for the excellence of its foot loomed tapestries.

First edition

© 1999 NTC/Contemporary Publishing Group, Inc.

Second edition

© 2007 JUDITH NOBLE AND JAIME LACASA

All Rights Reserved.

No part of this publication may be reproduced, stored in a retrieval system, or transmitted, in any form or by any means, electronic, mechanical, photocopying, recording, or otherwise, without the written permission of the author.

This edition published by
Dog Ear Publishing
4010 W. 86th Street, Ste H
Indianapolis, IN 46268

www.dogearpublishing.net

ISBN: 978-160844-154-9

This book is printed on acid-free paper.

Printed in the United States of America

Introduction to Quechua

Language of the Andes

SECOND EDITION

JUDITH NOBLE

JAIME LACASA

To our highly esteemed teachers,
George Urioste
the late Joaquín Herrero
Xavier Albó

Table of Contents

PREFACE xiii

Section I: The Quechua Language

    A. Origins 1

    B. Geographical Extension 1

    C. Quipus 2

    D. Written Quechua 2

    E. Characteristics 2

    F. The Quechua Used in This Work 3

    G. The Sounds of Quechua 4

        1. Generalities 4

        2. Quechua Vowels 4

        3. Vowel Sound Changes 4

        4. Characters of the Quechua Alphabet and Their Pronunciation 5

        5. Pronunciation Guide 5

        6. Stress and Accentuation 7

Section II: Model Sentences

CHAPTER 1

    A. Greetings and Responses [Model Sentences 1-8] 9

    B. Introductions and Responses [9-10] 12

    C. Asking and Telling People's Names [11-13] 12

    D. Asking and Telling What Other People Do or Are, and Telling What You Are or Do [14-18] 14

    E. Pointing Out and Identifying People [19-21] 18

    F. Asking About and Telling Where People Are From [22-27] 23

    G. Ending a Conversation and Saying Good-bye [28-30] 25

CHAPTER 2

    A. Attracting Someone's Attention [Model Sentences 1-8]   37

    B. Asking and Answering Some Useful Questions [9-29]   39

CHAPTER 3

    A. Social Courtesies [Model Sentences 1-13]   57

    B. Ways to Cope in a Conversation [14-29]   64

CHAPTER 4

    A. Where People Are From/Live/Stay [Model Sentences 1-6]   75

    B. Where People Are Going and Where They Are Coming From [7-10]   78

    C. Family [11-18]   79

    D. What People Do for a Living [19-28]   82

    E. Knowing People, Places, Information, and Skills [29-38]   85

CHAPTER 5

    A Asking and Telling About the Location of People, Places, and Things [Model Sentences 1-7]   91

    B. Asking and Telling About Transportation [8-30]   95

    C. Asking for Some Travel Help [31-37]   99

    D. Offering and Getting Help, and Expressing the Need for Help [38-50]   101

CHAPTER 6

    A. What Things Are [Model Sentences 1-12]   117

    B. To Whom Things Belong [13-24]   121

    C. From Whom or From Where Things Are [25-29]   127

    D. For Whom Things Are [30-31]   128

    E. What Things Are Made Of [32-35]   130

F. What Things Are Used For [36-41]   132

CHAPTER 7
　A. Describing Cities, Towns, and Terrain by Characteristics or Traits [Model Sentences 1-10]   137
　B. Describing Things by Size, Distance, Weight, and Fit [11-21]   139
　C. Describing Things by Age, Appearance, and Color [22-32]   142
　D. Describing Things by Taste and Smell [33-38]   144
　E. Describing Things by Price and Value [39-48]   145
　F. Describing Things by Quality [49-50]   149
　G. Describing Things by Ease and Difficulty [51-52]   149

CHAPTER 8
　A. Asking and Telling People's Names [Model Sentences 1-5]   151
　B. Asking, Telling, and Pointing Out Who Someone Is [6-13]   154
　C. Identifying People by Job, Role, or Position [14-15]   155
　D. Identifying People by What They Are Doing [16-17]   156
　E. Identifying People by Relationship [18-25]   158

CHAPTER 9
　A. Describing People by Physical Characteristics [Model Sentences 1-3]   163
　B. Describing People by Age [4-5]   164
　C. Describing People by Condition - Health and Feelings [6-32]   165
　D. Describing People and Things by Making Comparisons [33-37]   173

CHAPTER 10
　A. The Time of Day [Model Sentences 1-13]   183
　B. The Day of the Week [14-16]   188
　C. The Month of the Year [17-19]   189

D. Dates [20-23]   189

CHAPTER 11

A. The Time, Day, Date, or General Time Period of an Event [Model Sentences 1-13]   195

B. The Duration of an Event [14-18]   200

C. The Frequency of an Event [19-20]   202

D. How Long Something Has Been Happening [21-22]   202

E. How Long Ago Something Happened [23-24]   202

F. The Weather [25-41]   203

CHAPTER 12

A. Asking and Telling What Is Going On/Happening, Went On/Happened [1-2]   214

B. Asking and Telling How Something Happened to Different People [3-4]   214

C. Wondering What To Do and Responding [5-7]   215

D. Asking What People Are Doing, When Present, with No Idea of What Is Going On, and Responding to Those Questions [8-9]   216

E. Asking and Telling What Activity People Do [10-13]   217

F. Asking and Telling What Activity People Are Doing [14-15]   218

G. Asking and Telling What Activity People Did [16-17]   218

H. Asking and Telling What Activity People Will Do [18-19]   218

I. Asking and Telling What Activity People Would Do [20-21]   219

J. Asking and Telling What People Are Doing the Way That They Are Doing Something [22-23]   220

K. Asking "What For" and "Why," and Telling "To (Activity)" and "Because" [24-27]   220

L. Asking and Telling How Something Is Done [28-30]   223

M. Asking and Telling When Something Will Happen or When Something Happens or Happened With Respect to Another Action [31-33]   224

CHAPTER 13

    A. Wants, Being Glad, Being Sad [Model Sentences 1-16] 229

    B. Wonder and Surprise [17-20] 234

    C. Likes and Dislikes [21-28] 236

    D. Forgetting [29-30] 236

    E. Obligation [31-37] 239

    F. Intention [38-42] 241

    G. Ability [43-53] 242

CHAPTER 14

    A. Direct Commands [Model Sentences 1-3] 249

    B. "Let's" Commands [4-6] 251

    C. Indirect Commands [7-8] 253

    D. Warning [9-10] 254

    E. Condition with "If" [11-13] 255

Section III: Quechua Grammar Notes

1. Postpositions with the Function of Prepositions 261
2. Plural of Nouns 262

    A. Formation of the plural of nouns with **-kuna** or with **-s** 262

    B. Emphatic **-ni-** with plural nouns formed with **-s** 262

    C. Position of affixes with plural nouns formed with **-kuna** 262

3. Adjectives 263
4. Possession 263

    A. Quechua for "my," "your," and the like 263

    B. Quechua for "of," " 's," and "s'" 264

    C. Quechua for "mine," "of mine," "yours," "of yours," and the like 265

    D. Quechua for "to have" 266

5. Cardinal Numbers 269

6. Ordinal Numbers 272

7. Negation 273

8. Questions 273

9. Diminutives 274

    A. The most authentic and common diminutive endings 274

    B. Additional diminutive suffixes 275

10. Model for Simple Verbs 277

11. Introduction to Complex Verbs 288

12. Verbs Expressing Action or State of Being In Progress (Progressive Verbs) 290

13. Verbs Expressing Transformation of the Subject from One State to Another 291

14. Verbs Expressing Transition of the Subject from One Condition or Situation to Another 293

15. Model for Verbs Expressing Obligation 294

16. Model for Verbs that Include (Pronominally) the Verbal Object "Me" 300

17. Model for Verbs that Include (Periphrastically and Pronominally) the Verbal Object "Us" 304

18. Model for Verbs that Include (Pronominally) the Verbal Object "You (One Person)" 309

19. Model for Verbs that Include (Periphrastically and Pronominally) the Verbal Object "You (More Than One Person)" 313

20. Model for Verbs that Include (Only Periphrastically) the Verbal Objects "Him," "Her," and "Them" 318

21. Model for Verbs in which the Subject and the Object are the Same (Reflexive Verbs) 319

QUECHUA-ENGLISH VOCABULARY 321

ENGLISH-QUECHUA VOCABULARY 357

Preface

This book provides speakers of English with a basic working knowledge of Quechua. The general language of the former Inca Empire, Quechua is used today by over six million people in the portion of the Andean region of South America extending from southern Colombia through Ecuador, Peru, and Bolivia to northwestern Argentina and northern Chile.

The influence of the Quechua language and the culture of its speakers, both past and present, is experienced in varying degrees in the present-day life of this region. In some areas, the farther one moves from urban centers, the more one finds Quechua to predominate, to the point of encountering speakers of this tongue who are not conversant in Spanish. Any traveler, student, researcher or business person interested in the Andean countries will find this book helpful in communicating with Quechua speakers and, to some extent, in understanding the culture of the area.

The book is divided into three sections. The first is a brief introduction to the Quechua language, primarily focusing on spelling and pronunciation. As is pointed out, there is no universally accepted Quechua alphabet, that is, no uniformly adopted way of transcribing the sounds of what basically is a spoken language. The majority of works dealing with Quechua have been and are written by and for speakers of Spanish, which naturally has influenced spelling decisions. In this book a fairly common alphabet is used. However, since it addresses speakers of English, the authors have opted to write an "**h**" for the rasping, guttural, and, from some Quechuaphone areas, soft sounds that others may write anywhere in a word as "**j**" (which has an "h" sound in Spanish, the Spanish "*h*" being silent), internally or finally as "**kk**," or when the final sound in a word as "**c**" or "**q**."

The second section, the body of the work, consists of fourteen chapters of Model Sentences, often in question-and-answer pairs. These offer a means of communicating on different topics covering a variety of needs and situations. A quick perusal of the fairly detailed Table of Contents provides a good overview of this. The Model Sentences, their literal translations, also included, and their frequent Expansions are more than just tools for handling specific situations. They provide a means for understanding the grammatical structures and how to incorporate different vocabulary in the models given, thus allowing the application of the sentences and their structure to other situations and subjects.

The third section contains notes on a few important grammatical topics, with model verb conjugations at the end.

The book concludes with Quechua-English and English-Quechua vocabularies. These include many more words than those found in the Model Sentence section, thus making it possible to broaden the scope and usefulness of those sentences and their Expansions.

Given the geographical extension and the regional variants in the Quechuaphone world, terms and expressions different from those found here can be encountered.

It is the hope of the authors that this book will help the user feel more comfortable when encountering speakers of Quechua, and will provide an avenue for gaining an insight into their language and culture.

J.N.
J.L.
Emeriti
Iowa State University

Section I
The Quechua Language

A. Origins

Quechua or Kechua, which in that language can be found spelled **Kechua, Khechua, Kj'eschua, Kkechuwa, Kichua, Qheshwa, Qhëshwa**, and **Quichua**, was the general language of the Inca Empire, which existed in its historical (post-legendary) period from 1438, under Pachacuteh Yupanki (Pachacuti Yupanqui) (ruled 1438-1471), to 1533, then under Ataw Wallpa (Atahuallpa) (ruled 1527-1533).

Apparently Quechua, or **qheshwa simi**, originally was the language spoken in pre-Incan times by the people, **qheshwa runa**, of the temperate highland valleys, **qheshwakuna**, of present-day central southern Peru, west of the city of Cuzco. The Inca royalty had their own private language, which some believe was Chimú. However, in their expansion of the Empire, the Incas adopted **qheshwa simi** as their language of colonization, and its use extended throughout the Empire, coexisting with or replacing local languages. It later was used throughout the territory of the former Inca Empire and beyond by Spanish missionaries and administrators. The Spanish were the ones who gave this language a name, calling it both "*quechua*," in reference to the region and its people from whom the language was adopted by the Incas, and later, **runa simi**, "people's speech," to distinguish it from their own language, **kastilla simi**, "Castilian speech."

B. Geographical Extension

At the time of its maximum expansion under the eleventh Inca, Wayna Qhapah Inka (Huayna Capac) (1493-1527), the Inca Empire extended some 3,000 miles, from the **Anqas Mayu** (today, the *Río Azul*, Blue River) in present day southern Colombia to the **Maulli Mayu** (today, the *Río Maule*, Maule River) in central Chile, and from the Pacific Ocean to the eastern slopes of the Andes Mountains.

Today, Quechua, or **runa simi** ("people's speech"), is the most widely spoken of the indigenous tongues surviving in the Americas. Six to ten million people in the Andean area from southern Colombia through Ecuador, Peru, and Bolivia, to northwestern Argentina and northern Chile use Quechua as their everyday language. (The figures vary depending upon what is understood to define a speaker of the language.) The cultural influence of Quechua and its speakers is seen in varying degrees throughout the region.

Quechua is a co-official language with Spanish in Peru, with Spanish and Shuar in Ecuador, and with Spanish and Aymara (the other of the Quechumaran language group) in Bolivia. Aymara is spoken by close to one and a half million people in the area around Lake Titicaca, which lies partly in southern Peru and partly in northwestern Bolivia.

In the urban centers of the southern Peruvian Andes and in the central Bolivian valleys, one encounters Spanish-Quechua bilingualism, with Spanish culture dominating. In the surrounding rural areas, while this bilingualism still exists, the Quechua culture traits prevail. In the more outlying areas, Quechua predominates in both language and culture.

C. Quipus

For the pre-Inca and Inca speakers of Quechua, their language was not a written one. They did have, however, elaborate quipus (**khipukuna**) with which accounting and administrative notes were kept, information was preserved, poetry was recorded, and messages were sent. Quipus are generally considered a mnemonic device, and by some, something of an a-graphic writing system. They consisted of a single, main cord from which were hung a series of knotted strings of different lengths, and at times of different colors. Quipus were made and deciphered by official scholars and historians trained for such (**khipukamayohkuna**).

D. Written Quechua

The Spaniards, who arrived in Peru in 1531 with Francisco Pizarro (1478-1541), were the first to devise a spelling system for and to write Quechua. They employed the Spanish alphabet as much as possible to record the sounds of the language. For those that were not similar to Spanish ones, writers created their own orthographic designations. To this day there is no real agreement on spelling; there is no universally accepted alphabet, in spite of the few that have been recognized as official by different bodies.

E. Characteristics

Quechua is an extremely agglutinative language, that is, by addition of infixes and suffixes to a word or its root, a new word is created. Infixes, used primarily with verbs, provide nuances or modifications to the meaning of the original word. Suffixes are used primarily to conjugate verbs and, with other parts of speech, to show the grammatical function of the word in the sentence. Thus, one

Quechua word can contain many elements and convey a thought that may take a phrase or sentence to express in another language. For example:

> **¡Aparichimpullawaychehña!** Please bring it to me right away (addressing more than one person).
> **¡Apa-ri-chi-m-pu-lla-wa-ycheh-ña!**
> *Carry-please-make-in this direction[Please bring]-it-just-to me-[command marker addressing more than one person]-right away!*

> **chimpachinakuy** for one to go to the other side of a stream, being helped by the offered hand of the one staying behind, and then offering his or her hand to help the other person across
> **chimpa-chi-naku-y**
> *go to the other side of something that one is facing and that is difficult to reach, as in the opposite bank of a river, irrigation ditch, gully-(make what the meaning of the verb is)-each other-(infinitive marker, "to)*

Since the time of the Spaniards who first studied the language, Quechua has been considered to be well developed and very expressive. In its structure, it is strikingly regular, precise, and logical, although it does have some noticeable exceptions.

In 1985, in part as a reaction to what the *Washington Post* called our national language illiteracy, the United States Department of Education published a list of the 169 languages whose knowledge was considered critical for the promotion of scientific research, as well as for national security and economic interests. Quechua was one of them.

F. The Quechua Used in This Work

The Quechua used in this book is basically the one labeled by Cerrón-Palomino "Norteño-Sureño C," a sub-group of the "Norteño-Sureño" group of Quechua dialects. Included in this sub-group are the Ayacucho and Cuzco dialects of Peru, and Bolivian, Argentinean, and Chilean Quechua.[1] This has been selected in the belief that it provides the best avenue for a basic introduction to understanding and communicating in the language.

---

[1] Rodolfo Cerrón-Palomino. El quechua: una mirada de conjunto. Documento de Trabajo No. 42. Lima: Universidad Nacional Mayor de San Marcos, Centro de investigación de lingüistica aplicada. 1980. p. 8.

G. The Sounds of Quechua

1. GENERALITIES

As was mentioned above, the Quechua language had no graphic writing system, and therefore no alphabet. Spaniards, the first to transcribe Quechua with Latin letters, and other subsequent students of the language had to devise a graphic system to represent its sounds. Today there is no universally accepted alphabet, and individual writers often are found to have created their own. Further complicating the spelling issue are the pronunciation variations found in different regions and among different speakers of Quechua. This contributes to the great variety that can be found in the way in which Quechua words are written.

Quechua is first a spoken language rather than a written one and, as indicated above, variations in pronunciation can be heard.

2. QUECHUA VOWELS

The Quechua language has five vowel sounds. The primary three are **a**, **i**, and **u**. The two secondary vowel sounds, represented here by **e** and **o** (some write them **ë** and **ö**), are not found with the degree of frequency of the other vowel sounds. Speakers of the northern and southernmost Quechuaphone areas do not use them at all.

3. VOWEL SOUND CHANGES

In the Quechuaphone areas where the secondary vowels **e** and **o** are used (primarily in southern Peru and in Bolivia), an **i** and a **u** can become **e** and **o** respectively. These changes, indicated in this book by [**i** > **e**] and [**u** > **o**], occur when words are altered by the addition of certain suffixes (letters or syllables attached to the end of a word) or by certain infixes (syllables inserted in the middle of a word). The possibility of encountering these vowel changes must be kept in mind when dealing with Quechua from different areas, especially when consulting dictionaries.

The **i** and the **u** are replaced by **e** and **o** respectively in some areas only when followed, and in other areas when followed or preceded, by a suffix or infix beginning with **q**, **qh**, **q'**; **nq**, **rq**, or **h**.

4. Characters of the Quechua Alphabet and Their Pronunciation

The Quechua alphabet used in this book, the official one established in 1975, is given here. Letters in parentheses are found only in borrowed words.
a, (b), ch, chh, ch', (d), e, (f), (g), h, i, k, kh, k', l, ll, m, n, ñ, o, p, ph, p', q, qh, q', r, s, t, th, t', u, w, y

Quechua speakers of Ecuador, northern Peru, and northern Argentina do not use the **chh, ch'; kh, k'; ph, p'; qh, q'**, or **th, t'** sounds. They use a simple **c, k, p, q,** or **t** sound respectively for each of the preceding pairs.

5. Pronunciation Guide

a	like "a" of *"father"*
(b)	only in borrowings; like an English "b"
ch	similar to the "ch" in *"church,"* but without the puff of breath that can accompany the English "ch"
chh	a **ch** followed by a strong **h**
ch'	like the **ch** sound, but with the opening at the throat closed then opened at the end of the utterance, causing a kind of popping sound
(d)	only in borrowings; like an English "d"
e	a range of sounds similar to those in the English *"tin"* and *"ten."* For a final **e**, some writers use an **i** instead.
(f)	only in borrowings; like an English "f." Some speakers use an **h** sound instead.
(g)	only in borrowings. When initial, much like the English "g," but with no puff of breath. When between two vowels, a liquid sound, much as in the English *"Agatha."* Some speakers use a more familiar sound instead, or just omit it.
h	except in the consonant combinations with **h** that are found in the alphabet, **ch, chh, kh, ph, qh, th,** and **sh,** usually a rasping sound. When the **h** sound is before a consonant or at the end of a word, the opening at the throat is completely closed. While here this guttural sound is written as an **h**, some writers use **q**, and others use designations such as **c, j,** or **kk** for it. Quechua speakers of Ecuador, northern Peru, and northern Argentina omit the **h** sound or use a softer sound similar to that in the English *"how."*
i	like "ee" of English *"leek"*
k	similar to the "k" sound in *"speak,"* which does not have a strong puff of breath
kh	like the "k" sound of *"cup"* followed by a strong **h**
k'	like the **k** sound, but with the opening at the throat closed then opened at the end of the utterance, causing a kind of clicking or popping sound

l	similar to the English "l," but with the tip of the tongue against the back of the upper teeth. The **l** sound did not originally exist in Quechua, but arose from the Spanish "*ll*" or "*r*." Thus some modern writers use **ll** or **r** instead of **l**.
ll	except when followed by a consonant, much like the "lli" in the English *"William."* When followed by a consonant, the pronunciation is naturally forced to be "yl."
m	much like the English "m"
n	other than when followed by a **k** sound, much like the English "n" except the front of the tongue is pressed against the back of the upper teeth. When followed by a **k** sound, like the "n" in the "ng" of the English word *"wing."*
ñ	much like the "ny" of English *"canyon"*
o	a range of sounds similar to those in the English *"put"* and *"fork."* Some Quechua speakers, principally those of Ecuador, northern Peru, and northern Argentina, do not use any sound represented here by **o**.
p	like the "p" of English *"speak,"* that is, with no puff of breath
ph	like the "p" of English *"pin"* followed by a strong **h**; much like a strong "f" sound but with the lip position of a "p." In some Quechuaphone areas, especially that of Cuzco, a **ph** is pronounced more like an "f."
p'	like the "p" of English *"pin,"* but with the opening at the throat closed so that as the **p'** is pronounced the air that was compressed in the mouth produces something of a popping effect
q	a "k" sound somewhat similar to but farther back in the mouth than the "k" in the English word *"sulk,"* and usually with no strong puff of breath. To get an idea of how this sound is formed, a suggestion has been to depress the tongue with an index finger and then say a word such as *"cocoa."*
qh	like the **q** sound followed by a strong **h**
q'	like the **q** sound, but with the opening at the throat closed then opened at the end of the utterance, causing a kind of clicking or popping sound
r	a soft, slightly buzzing sound similar to an "r" after a "z"; like the "z" in *"zoo,"* but with an "r" after it
s	similar to an English "s," but farther forward in the mouth and thus a softer sound
t	similar to an English "t," but without the puff of breath that usually accompanies it
th	like the **t** sound followed by a strong **h**
t'	formed like the **t** sound, but with the opening at the throat closed so that as the **t'** is pronounced the air that has been compressed in the mouth produces something of a popping effect
u	like "oo" of English *"soon,"* but the lips are never pursed as they can be in English, rather they are almost flat

w	the same sound as the Quechua **u**. For a final **w**, some writers use a **y** instead.
y	the same sound as the Quechua **i**

6. STRESS AND ACCENTUATION

With rare exception all words of more than one syllable are stressed on the next to the last syllable.
    r<u>u</u>na man, the man
    maypa-<u>cha</u>-chus when
When one or more affixes (infixes or suffixes) are added to a word, the stress shifts so as to be on the next to the last syllable of the new word.
    r<u>u</u>na man, the man
    ru<u>na</u>-pah for the man
    runa-<u>pah</u>-tah and for the man
    runa-pah-<u>tah</u>-lla and just (only) for the man
Quechua words that are not stressed on the next to the last syllable are stressed on the last one. Here these are written with an acute accent mark (´). Words that follow this stress pattern fall into several categories, which include most exclamatory words and nouns used when calling to someone.
    a) in exclamatory words
        ¡Atatáw! or **¡Atatáy!** Ouch!
    b) in directly addressing someone, when the suffix for "my", **-y**, is added.
        ta(y)ta father
        ta(y)ta-y my father (talking about him)
        ¡Ta(y)tá-y! My father! (calling to him)

Section II

Model Sentences and Their Expansions

Chapter 1

This chapter deals with

A. Greetings and Responses [Model Sentences 1-8]

B. Introductions and Responses [9-10]

C. Asking and Telling People's Names [11-13]

D. Asking and Telling What Other People Do or Are, and Telling What You Are or Do [14-18]

E. Pointing Out and Identifying People [19-21]

F. Asking About and Telling Where People Are From [22-27]

G. Ending a Conversation and Saying Good-bye [28-30]

A. GREETINGS AND RESPONSES

1. **¡Winus diyas!**[1] Good morning!/Good day!

2. **¡Winas tardis!** Good afternoon! (until around 6:00 P.M. or until dark)

3. **¡Winas nuchis!** Good evening! (from 6:00 P.M. on, or after dark)

Expansion A:

Greetings related to the time of day that may be used in areas where there is less contact with Spanish:

¡Allin p'unchaw! Good morning!/Good day!
¡Allin sukha! Good afternoon! (until around 6:00 P.M.)
¡Allin ch'isi! Good evening! (from 6:00 P.M. until dark)
¡Allin tuta! Good evening! (after dark)

Expansion B:

Greetings not related to the time of day and that show some formality or respect. At times the literal meaning of these greetings will dictate which is most appropriate for the situation.

¡Rima-yku-lla-yki, taytá-y! Good morning!/Good afternoon!/Good evening! (addressing a male) (somewhat formal)
Speak-(cordiality marker)-just(for emphasis)-I to you(one person), father/sir(somewhat formal)-my. *

¡Rima-yku-lla-yki, mamá-y! Good morning!/Good afternoon!/Good evening! (addressing a female) (informal)
Speak-(cordiality marker)-just(for emphasis)-I to you(one person), mother/ma'am(informal)-my.

*[Note: Here and throughout the book, the literal meaning of the Quechua is shown in italics.]

[Note that the greetings with **rima-** are more commonly used than those below.]

Napa-yku-lla-yki, taytá-y. Good morning!/Good afternoon!/Good evening! (addressing a male) (somewhat formal)
Greet-(cordiality marker)-just(for emphasis)-I (to) you(one person), father/sir(somewhat formal)-my.

Napa-yku-lla-yki, mamá-y. Good morning!/Good afternoon!/Good evening! (addressing a female) (informal)
Greet-(cordiality marker)-just(for emphasis)-I (to) you(one person), mother/ma'am(informal)-my.

Tupa-yku-lla-yki. Good morning!/Good afternoon!/Good evening!
Encounter/Meet-(cordiality marker)-just(for emphasis)-I (to) you(one person).

Chaski-yku-lla-yki. Good morning!/Good afternoon!/Good evening!
Receive-(cordiality marker)-just(for emphasis)-I (to) you(one person).

[Note: In all of the greetings above, **taytá-y** and **mamá-y** may be included or omitted. Any person's name or other form of address, such as **kamayoh**, "boss," followed by the **-y**, "my," (which is preceded by the euphonic infix **-ni-** if the sound of the word requires it) may also be included in any of the greetings.]

4. **¿Imaynalla(tah) kasanki?***,2,3,4 How are you (one person)?
   ¿Imayna-lla(-tah) kasa-nki?
   How-just(-and) be-you(one person)?

   *[Note: As is pointed out in Note 3 at the end of this chapter, anything in parentheses, such as the **-tah** here, is optional, and can be added merely for sound or to give clarity, emphasis, or more body to the statement.]

Expansion:

"How are you (one person)?"
"How are you (more than one person)?"

¿Imayna-lla(-tah) kasa-nki? How are you (one person)?
¿Imayna-lla(-tah) kasa-nki-cheh?[5] How are you (more than one person)?
How-just(-and) be-(dual marker for "you[more than one person]")?

---

5. **Alli(lla)npuni. ¿Qanrí?**[6,7,8,9] Very well. And you (one person)?
   Alli(-lla)-n-puni. ¿Qan-rí?
   Well(-just)-(euphonic particle)-very. You(one person)-and(with a contrastive nuance)?

Expansion A:

"And you (one person)?"
"And you (more than one person)?" with **alli**

Alli(-lla)-n-puni. ¿Qan-rí? Very well. And you (one person)?
Alli(-lla)-n-puni. ¿Qan-kuna-rí? Very well. And you (more than one person)?

Expansion B:

"And you (one person)?"
"And you (more than one person)?" with **waleh**

Waleh(-lla)-puni. ¿Qan-rí? Very well. And you (one person)?
Waleh(-lla)-puni. ¿Qan-kuna-rí? Very well. And you (more than one person)?

---

6. **Ñoqapas alli(lla)n.**[10,11] I'm fine, too.
   Ñoqa-pas alli(-lla)-n.
   I-also well(-just)-(euphonic particle

7. **Mana alli(lla)npunichu.**[12] Not very well.
   Mana alli(-lla)-n-puni-chu.
   Not well(-just)-(euphonic particle)-very-(negative marker).

Expansion:

Variants of the negative response "Not very well" (formed by beginning the phrase with **mana** or **ma**, "no," and ending the phrase with **-chu**)

<u>Mana</u> alli(-lla)-n-puni-<u>chu</u>. <u>Not</u> very well. OR
<u>Ma</u> alli(-lla)-n-puni-<u>chu</u>. <u>Not</u> very well.
Not well(-just)-(euphonic particle)-very-(negative marker).

<u>Mana</u> waleh(-lla)-puni-<u>chu</u>. <u>Not</u> very well. OR
<u>Ma</u> waleh(-lla)-puni-<u>chu</u>. <u>Not</u> very well.
Not well(-just)-very-(negative marker).

---

8. **Anchata phutikuni.** I'm very sorry.
   Ancha-ta phuti-ku-ni.
   Much-(adverb marker) sadden-self-I.

B. INTRODUCTIONS AND RESPONSES

9. **(Ñoqa) Pidru Kunturi(m) kani.**[13,14] I am Pedro Kunturi.
   (Ñoqa) Pidru Kunturi(-m) ka-ni.
   *(I) Pedro Kunturi(-particle of certainty or assurance) be-I. (The use of **ñoqa** gives more emphasis to "I" or more body to the statement.)*

10. **Anchata kusikuni rehsisuspa(y).** I am very glad to meet you (one person).
    Ancha-ta kusi-ku-ni rehsi-su-spa(-y).
    Much-(adverb marker) gladden-self-I know-you(one person; object of a gerund)-(invariable gerund marker, "-ing")(-my).

[Note: From here on, if not indicated to the contrary, any words or forms referring to "you" designate just one person.]

C. ASKING AND TELLING PEOPLE'S NAMES

11. **¿Ima(n) sutiyki?** What is your name?[15]
    ¿Ima(-n) suti-yki?
    What(-euphonic particle) name-your(one person)? ("Is" is understood.)

Expansion:

"What is his name?"
"What is her name?"

¿Ima(-n) suti-yki? What is your name?
¿Ima(-n) suti-n? What is his/her name?
What(-euphonic particle) name-his/her? ("Is" is understood.)

12. **Pidru(m) sutiy.** My name is Pedro.
    Pidru(-m) suti-y.
    Pedro(-particle of certainty or assurance) name-my. ("Is" is understood.)

Expansion:

"His name is . . ."
"Her name is . . ."
"This one's name is . . ."
"That one's name is . . ."
"That one's (over there) name is . . ."

Pidru(-m) suti-y. My name is Pedro.
Hwan(-mi) suti-n.[16] His name is Juan.
Mariya(-m) suti-n. Her name is Maria.

Kay-pata, Pidru(-m) suti-n. This one's name is Pedro.
This one-of, Pedro(-particle of certainty or assurance) name-his. ("Is" is understood.)
Chay-pata, Hwan(-mi) suti-n. That one's name is Juan.
That one-of, Juan(-particle of certainty or assurance) name-his. ("Is" is understood.)
Haqay-pata, Mariya(-m) suti-n. That one's (over there) name is Maria.
That one(over there)-of, Maria(-particle of certainty or assurance) name-her. ("Is" is understood.)

13. **¿Qanpatarí?** And yours?
    ¿Qan-pata-rí?
    You-of[Yours]-and(with a contrastive nuance)?

D. ASKING AND TELLING WHAT OTHER PEOPLE DO OR ARE, AND TELLING WHAT YOU ARE OR DO

14. **¿Imatah kanki?** What do you do?/What are you?
    ¿Ima-tah ka-nki?
    What-and be-you(one person)?

Expansion:

"What do you (one person) do?"
"What are you (one person)?"

"What do you (more than one person) do?"
"What are you (more than one person)?"

¿Ima-tah ka-nki? What do <u>you (one person)</u> do? What are <u>you (one person)</u>?

¿Ima-tah ka-nki-cheh? What do <u>you (more than one person)</u> do?/What are <u>you (more than one person)</u>?

---

15. **(Ñoqa) alumnu kani.**[17,18,19] I am a student (male).
    (Ñoqa) alumnu ka-ni.
    (I, added for emphasis) student(male) be-I. ("A" and "an" usually are understood.)

Expansion A:

I am (role, occupation, personal relationship)."

(Ñoqa) alumnu ka-ni. I am <u>a student (male)</u>.

<u>alumna</u> a student (female)

<u>midiku</u>[20,21] a doctor (physician) (male)
<u>midika</u> a doctor (physician) (female)

<u>maystru</u>[22] a teacher/professor (male)
<u>maystra</u> a teacher/professor (female) OR
<u>yacha-che-h</u> a teacher/professor[21] [sound change, -chi- > -che-] (For sound changes, see Section I: The Quechua Language [G. The Sounds of Quechua, 3. Vowel Sound Changes].)
know-make-the one who

<u>pure-h</u> a walker/traveler [**puri-** > **pure-**]
walk-the one who

Pidro-hpa amigu-n[23,24] a friend (male) of Pedro/Pedro's friend [**Pidru** > **Pidro**]
Pedro-of friend (male)-his ("A" is understood.)

Pidro-hpa amiga-n a friend (female) of Pedro/Pedro's friend [**Pidru** > **Pidro**]
Pedro-of friend (female)-his ("A" is understood.) OR

Pidro-hpa atillcha-n[23,24] a friend of Pedro/Pedro's friend [**Pidru** > **Pidro**]

Pidro-hpa masi-n a companion of Pedro/Pedro's companion [**Pidru** > **Pidro**]
Pedro-of companion-his ("A" is understood.)

Pidro-hpa pure-h-masi-n a traveling companion of Pedro/Pedro's traveling companion [**Pidru** > **Pidro, puri-** > **pure-**]
Pedro-of walk-the one who-companion-his

Expansion B:

"We (excluding the person or persons addressed) are (roles, occupations, personal relationships)."[25]

(Ñoqa) alumnu ka-ni. I am a student (male).

(Ñoqayku) alumnu-s ka-yku. We are students (males or male[s] and female[s]).
(We[excluding the person(s) addressed]) student-s(males or male[s] and female[s]) be-we(excluding the person[s] addressed).

[Note: From now on, unless indicated to the contrary, any words or forms referring to "we" exclude the person or persons addressed.]

alumna-s students (females)

midiku-s doctors (physicians) (males)
midika-s doctors (physicians) (females)

maystru-s teachers/professors (males)
maystra-s teachers/professors (females) OR
yacha-che-h-kuna[26] teachers/professors [**-chi-** > **-che-**]
know-make-the one who-(plural marker/designating more than one)[the ones who]

pure-h-kuna walkers/travelers [**puri-** > **pure-**]
walk-the one who-(plural marker)

Pidro-hpa amigu-s-ni-n[26,27,28] friends (males or male[s] and female[s]) of Pedro/Pedro's friends [**Pidru** > **Pidro**]
Pedro-of friend-s(males or male[s] and female[s])-(euphonic particle)-his

Pidro-hpa amiga-s-ni-n friends (females) of Pedro/Pedro's friends [**Pidru** > **Pidro**]
Pedro-of friend(female)-s-(euphonic particle)-his OR

Pidro-hpa atillcha-n-kuna[26,29] friends of Pedro/Pedro's friends [**Pidru** > **Pidro**]
Pedro-of friend-his-(plural marker) OR

Pidro-hpa atillcha-s-ni-n friends of Pedro/Pedro's friends [**Pidru** > **Pidro**]
Pedro-of friend-s-(euphonic particle)-his

Pidro-hpa masi-n-kuna companions of Pedro/Pedro's companions [**Pidru** > **Pidro**]
Pedro-of companion-his-(plural marker) OR

Pidro-hpa masi-s-ni-n companions of Pedro/Pedro's companions [**Pidru** > **Pidro**]
Pedro-of companion-s-(euphonic particle)-his

Pidro-hpa pure-h-masi-n-kuna traveling companions of Pedro/Pedro's traveling companions [**Pidru** > **Pidro, puri-** > **pure-**]
Pedro-of walk-the one who-companion-his-(plural marker) OR

Pidro-hpa pure-h-masi-s-ni-n traveling companions of Pedro/Pedro's traveling companions [**Pidru** > **Pidro, puri-** > **pure-**]
Pedro-of walk-the one who-companion-s-(euphonic particle)-his

16. **¿Ima qanrí?** And what do you do?/And what are you?
    ¿Ima qan-rí?
    What-you(one person)-and(with a contrastive nuance)? ("Are" is understood.)

Expansion:

"And what do you (one person) do?"
"And what are you (one person)?"

"And what do you (more than one person) do?"
"And what are you (more than one person)?"

¿Ima qan-rí? And what do <u>you (one person)</u> do?/And what are <u>you (one person)</u>?

¿Ima qan-kuna-rí? And what do <u>you (more than one person)</u> do?/And what are <u>you (more than one person)</u>? *("Are" is understood.)*

17. **¿Ima payrí?** And what does he/she do?/And what is he/she?
    ¿Ima pay-rí?
    What-he/she-and(with a contrastive nuance)? ("Is" is understood.)

Expansion:

"And what does he do?"
"And what is he?"

"And what does she do?"
"And what is she?"

"And what do they do?"
"And what are they?"

¿Ima pay-rí? And what does he/she do?/And what is he/she?
¿Ima-tah pay? And what does he/she do?/And what is he/she?
What-and(with a contrastive nuance) he/she? ("Is" is understood.)

¿Ima pay-kuna-rí? And what do they do?/And what are they?
What he/she-(plural marker)[they]-and(with a contrastive nuance)? ("Are" is understood.)

¿Ima-tah pay-kuna? And what do they do?/And what are they?
What-and(with a contrastive nuance) he/she-(plural marker)[they]? ("Are" is understood.)

¿Ima-tah pay-kuna (ka-nku)? And what do they do?/And what are they?
What-and(with a contrastive nuance) he/she-(plural marker)[they] (be-they)?

¿Ima-tah ka-nku? And what do they do?/And what are they?
What-and(with a contrastive nuance) be-they?

---

18. **Pay alumnu.**[30] He is a student.
    He student. ("Is" and "a" are understood.)

Expansion:

"They are (roles, occupations, personal relationships)."

Pay alumnu. He is a student.

Pay-kuna alumnu-s (ka-nku). They are students (males or male[s] and female[s]).
He/She-(plural marker)[They] student-s(males or male[s] and female[s]) (be-they).

Pidro-hpa masi-n-kuna[31] companions of Pedro/Pedro's companions
   [Pidru > Pidro]
Pedro-of companion-his-(plural marker) OR
Pidro-hpa masi-s-ni-n companions of Pedro/Pedro's companions
   [Pidru > Pidro]
Pedro-of companion-s-(euphonic particle)-his

E. POINTING OUT AND IDENTIFYING PEOPLE

19. **¿Pi(tah) chay wayna?** Who is that young man?
¿Pi(-tah) chay wayna?
Who(-and) that young man? ("Is" is understood.)

Expansion A:

Pointing out and asking who "this," "that," "these," and "those" people are

¿Pi(-tah) kay wayna? Who is this young man?

chay wayna that young man
haqay wayna that young man (over there)

¿Pi-kuna(-tah) kay wayna-kuna (ka-nku)?[32,33] Who are these young men?
Who-(plural marker)(-and) these young man-(plural marker)[men] (be-they)? OR
¿Pi-kuna(-tah) kay wayna-s (ka-nku)? Who are these young men?
Who-(plural marker)(-and) these young man-s[men] (be-they)?

chay wayna-kuna those young men OR
chay wayna-s those young men

haqay wayna-kuna those young men (over there) OR
haqay wayna-s those young men (over there)

Expansion B:

Pointing out and asking who men, women, and youngsters are

¿Pi(-tah) chay wayna? Who is that young man?

chay sipas that young woman OR
chay warmicha that young woman
chay pallacha that young lady

chay runa that person (usually a male)
chay qhari that man
chay wiraqocha that man/that gentleman

chay warmi that woman
chay palla that lady

chay wamra that boy/that young man (10-14 years old)
chay wamira that girl/that young woman/that young lady (10-14 years old)

chay yoqalla that boy
chay imilla that girl

chay wawa that little boy/that little girl/that baby

¿**Pi-kuna(-tah) chay wayna-kuna (ka-nku)?** Who are those young men?
Who-(plural marker)(-and) those young man-(plural marker)[men] (be-they)? OR
¿**Pi-kuna(-tah) chay wayna-s (ka-nku)?** Who are those young men?
Who-(plural marker)(-and) those young man-s[men] (be-they)?

chay sipas-kuna those young women OR
chay warmicha-kuna those young women OR
chay warmicha-s those young women

chay pallacha-kuna those young ladies OR
chay pallacha-s those young ladies

chay runa-kuna those people (usually males) OR
chay runa-s those people (usually males)

chay qhari-kuna those men OR
chay qhari-s those men

chay wiraqocha-kuna those men/those gentlemen OR
chay wiraqocha-s those men/those gentlemen

chay warmi-kuna those women OR
chay warmi-s those women

chay palla-kuna those ladies OR
chay palla-s those ladies

chay wamra-kuna those boys/those young men (10-14 years old) OR
chay wamra-s those boys/those young men (10-14 years old)

chay wamira-kuna those girls/those young women/those young ladies (10-14 years old) OR
chay wamira-s those girls/those young women/those young ladies (10-14 years old)

chay yoqalla-kuna those boys OR
chay yoqalla-s those boys

chay imilla-kuna those girls OR
chay imilla-s those girls

chay wawa-kuna those little boys/those little girls/those babies OR
chay wawa-s those little boys/those little girls/those babies

20. **Chay wayna(qa), Pidru.**[35] That young man is Pedro.
Chay wayna(-qa), Pidru.
That young man(-emphatic particle), Pedro. ("Is" is understood.)

Expansion:

Pointing out and telling who "this," "that," "these," and "those" people are

Kay, Pidru. This is Pedro.
This one, Pedro. ("Is" is understood.)
Chay, Pidru. That is Pedro
That one, Pedro. ("Is" is understood.)
Haqay, Pidru. That one (over there) is Pedro.
That one(over there), Pedro. ("Is" is understood.)

Kay wayna(-qa), Pidru. This young man is Pedro.
Chay wayna(-qa), Pidru. That young man is Pedro.
Haqay wayna(-qa), Pidru. That young man (over there) is Pedro.

Kay-kuna, Pidru(-pis) Ruwirtu-pis (ka-nku).[34] These are Pedro and Roberto.
This-(plural marker)[These], Pedro(-and) Roberto-and (be-they).
Chay-kuna, Pidru(-pis) Ruwirtu-pis (ka-nku). Those are Pedro and Roberto.
Haqay-kuna, Pidru(-pis) Ruwirtu-pis (ka-nku). Those (over there) are Pedro and Roberto.

Kay wayna-kuna(-qa), Pidru(-pis) Ruwirtu-pis (ka-nku). These young men are Pedro and Roberto.
These young man-(plural marker)[men](-emphatic particle), Pedro(-and) Roberto-and (be-they).

Chay wayna-kuna(-qa), Pidru(-pis) Ruwirtu-pis (ka-nku). Those young men are Pedro and Roberto.
Haqay wayna-kuna(-qa), Pidru(-pis) Ruwirtu-pis (ka-nku). Those young men (over there) are Pedro and Roberto.

---

21. **Chay runa(qa), amiguy Pidru.** That man is my friend Pedro.
    Chay runa(-qa), amigu-y Pidru.
    That man(-emphatic particle), friend-my Pedro. ("Is" is understood.)

Expansion:

"That man is my friend."
"That man is your friend."
"That man is his/her/its friend." and so on

"Those men are my friends."
"Those men are your friends."
"Those men are his/her/its friends." and so on

Chay runa(-qa), amigu-y Pidru. That man is my friend Pedro.

Chay runa(-qa), amigu-y. That man is my friend. OR
Chay runa(-qa), atillcha-y. That man is my friend.

Chay runa(-qa), amigu-yki. That man is your (one person) friend. OR
Chay runa(-qa), atillcha-yki. That man is your (one person) friend.

Chay runa(-qa), amigu-n. That man is his/her/its friend. OR
Chay runa(-qa), atillcha-n. That man is his/her/its friend.

Chay runa(-qa), amigu-yku. That man is our (excluding the person[s] addressed) friend.
Chay runa(-qa), atillcha-yku. That man is our (excluding the person[s] addressed) friend.

Chay runa(-qa), amigu-ncheh.[36] That man is our (including the person[s] addressed) friend. OR
Chay runa(-qa), atillcha-ncheh. That man is our (including the person[s] addressed) friend.

Chay runa(-qa), amigu-ykicheh.[37] That man is your (more than one person) friend. OR
Chay runa(-qa), atillcha-ykicheh. That man is your (more than one person) friend.

Chay runa(-qa), amigu-nku. That man is their friend. OR
Chay runa(-qa), atillcha-nku. That man is their friend.

Chay runa-kuna(-qa), amigu-s-ni-y (ka-nku).[38] Those men are my friends. OR
Chay runa-kuna(-qa), atillcha-y-kuna (ka-nku). Those men are my friends.

Chay runa-kuna(-qa), amigu-s-ni-yki (ka-nku). Those men are your (one person) friends. OR
Chay runa-kuna(-qa), atillcha-yki-kuna (ka-nku). Those men are your (one person) friends.

Chay runa-kuna(-qa), amigu-s-ni-n (ka-nku). Those men are his/her/its friends. OR
Chay runa-kuna(-qa), atillcha-n-kuna (ka-nku). Those men are his/her/its friends.

Chay runa-kuna(-qa), amigu-s-ni-yku (ka-nku). Those men are our (excluding the person[s] addressed) friends (males or male[s] and female[s]). OR
Chay runa-kuna(-qa), atillcha-yku-kuna (ka-nku). Those men are our (excluding the person[s] addressed) friends.

Chay runa-kuna(-qa), amigu-s-ni-ncheh (ka-nku). Those men are our (including the person[s] addressed) friends. OR
Chay runa-kuna(-qa), atillcha-ncheh-kuna (ka-nku). Those men are our (including the person[s] addressed) friends.

Chay runa-kuna(-qa), amigu-s-ni-ykicheh (ka-nku). Those men are your (more than one person) friends (males or male[s] and female[s]). OR
Chay runa-kuna(-qa), atillcha-ykicheh-kuna (ka-nku). Those men are your (more than one person) friends.

Chay runa-kuna(-qa), amigu-s-ni-nku (ka-nku).* Those men are their friends (males or male[s] and female[s]). OR
Chay runa-kuna(-qa), atillcha-nku-kuna (ka-nku). Those men are their friends.

*[Note: From now on, the optional plural formed with an **-s** (see Note 25) will seldom be used.]

F. ASKING ABOUT AND TELLING WHERE PEOPLE ARE FROM

22. **¿Maymanta(n) kanki?** Where are you from?
    ¿May-manta(-n) ka-nki?
    Where-from(-euphonic particle) be-you?

Expansion:

"Where are you (one person) from?"
"Where are you (more than one person) from?"

¿May-manta(-n) ka-nki? Where are <u>you (one person)</u> from?
¿May-manta(-n) ka-nki-cheh? Where are <u>you (more than one person)</u> from?
Where-from(-euphonic particle) be-(dual marker for "you[more than one person]")?

23. **Istadus Unidusmanta(n) kani.**[39] I am from the United States.
    Istadus Unidus-manta(-n) ka-ni.
    States United-from(-euphonic particle) be-I. ("The" is understood.)

Expansion:

"I am from . . ."
"We are from . . ."

Istadus Unidus-manta(-n) ka-<u>ni</u>. <u>I</u> am from the United States.
Istadus Unidus-manta(-n) ka-<u>yku</u>. <u>We</u> are from the United States.
States United-from(-euphonic particle) be-we(excluding the person[s] addressed). ("The" is understood.)

24. **¿Maymanta(n) payrí?** And where is he/she from?
    ¿May-manta(-n) pay-rí?
    Where-from(-euphonic particle) he/she-and(with a contrastive nuance)? ("Is" is understood.)

Expansion:

"Where is he from?"
"Where is she from?"
"Where are they from?"

¿May-manta(-n) <u>pay</u>-rí? And where is <u>he/she</u> from?

¿May-manta(-n) <u>pay</u>? Where is <u>he/she</u> from?

¿**May-manta(-n) pay-kuna**? Where are they from? OR
¿**May-manta(-n) ka-nku**? Where are they from? OR
¿**May-manta(-n) pay-kuna (ka-nku)**? Where are they from?

25. **(Pay) Limamanta(n).**[40] He/She is from Lima.
    (Pay) Lima-manta(-n).
    (He/She) Lima-from(-euphonic particle). ("Is" is understood.)

Expansion:

"He is from . . ."
"She is from . . ."
They are from . . ."

(Pay) Lima-manta(-n). He/She is from Lima.
(Pay-kuna) Lima-manta(-n) (ka-nku). They are from Lima.

26. ¿**Limamanta(n) kankichu?**[41] Are you from Lima?
    ¿Lima-manta(-n) ka-nki-chu?
    Lima-from(-euphonic particle) be-you(one person)-(question marker)?

Expansion:

Asking if different people are from Lima

¿**Lima-manta(-n) ka-nki-chu?** Are you (one person) from Lima?
¿**Lima-manta(-n) ka-nki-cheh-chu?** Are you (more than one person) from Lima?

¿**Lima-manta(-n) pay-chu?** Is he/she from Lima?
¿**Lima-manta(-n) pay-kuna-chu?** Are they from Lima? OR
¿**Lima-manta(-n) ka-nku-chu?** Are they from Lima? OR
¿**Lima-manta(-n) pay-kuna (ka-nku)-chu?** Are they from Lima?

27. **Mana Limamanta(n) kanichu, Qosqomanta(n).**[42] I'm not from Lima; I'm from Cuzco.
    Mana Lima-manta(-n) ka-ni-chu, Qosqo-manta(-n).
    Not Lima-from(-euphonic particle) be-I-(negative marker), Cuzco-from(-euphonic particle).

G. ENDING A CONVERSATION AND SAYING GOOD-BYE

28. **Allillanña.** That's all.
    Alli-lla-n-ña.
    Well-just-(euphonic particle)-already.

29. **Uh ratukama.** See you later/in a little while.
    Uh ratu-kama.
    One/A little while-until.

Expansion:

Other ways to say "good-bye"

Uh ratu-kama. See you <u>later</u>/in <u>a little while</u>.
Chhika(-n)-kama. See you <u>later</u>./Until <u>later</u>.
A little(-euphonic particle)-until.
Sukha-kama. See you <u>this afternoon</u>.
Afternoon-until.
Ch'isi-kama. See you <u>this evening</u>.
Evening-until.
Tuta-kama. See you <u>tonight</u>.
Night (after dark)-until.
Q'aya-kama. See you <u>tomorrow</u>.
Tomorrow-until.
Q'aya-kama-lla. See you <u>tomorrow</u>.
Tomorrow-until-just.
Paqarin-kama. See you <u>tomorrow morning</u>.
Early morning-until.
Uh kuti-kama. See you <u>another time</u>.
One time/Another time-until.
Dumingu-kama.[43] See you <u>Sunday</u>.
Sunday-until.
Tupa-na-ncheh-kama. <u>So long./Good-bye</u>.
Meet-(future infinitive marker)[Meeting (in the future)]-our(including the person[s] addressed)-until.

---

30. **¡Adiyús!** Good-bye!
    (From the Spanish *adiós*, "good-bye." This word keeps the Spanish stress pattern and written accent. Note that it is an exception to the Quechua stress pattern.)

NOTES

1. **¡Winus diyas!**, **¡Winas tardis!** and **¡Winas nuchis!** are adaptations of Spanish greetings, and are those generally used in and near urban areas.

2. Infixes and suffixes, like the **-lla-** here, are very common in Quechua. Two or more of these particles are often used in one word. Quechua infixes and suffixes serve different purposes. Some are optional, added for the sound or nuance they bring. Some are used to give emphasis. Some serve other functions, such as to indicate who is doing the action to whom. Others show the subject of a verb, that is, who is performing the action, and some particles add the meaning of a preposition (such as "from" and "until"). In this book, to make it easier to decipher compound words and constructions, the Model Sentences are presented with both a normal and a hyphenated version, and the Expansions always have the hyphenated version.

3. Anything in parentheses, such as the **-tah** here, is optional, and can be added merely for sound or to give clarity, emphasis, or more body to the statement.

4. There are two verbs that mean "to be," **ka-y** and **ka-sa-y**. For the sake of simplicity, in this book we write **ka-sa-y** as **kasa-y**.

   Regional differences in pronunciation and spelling, as well as personal preference in usage of these, often are found in Quechua. The infix **-sa-** in the verb **ka-sa-y/kasa-y**, also used in other verbal constructions, has the variants **-chka-**, **-sha-**, **-shka-**, **-ska-**, **-skia-**, **-sia-**, and **-sya-**.

   The form **kasa-nki**, "you (one person) are," "you (one person) are being," is from **kasa-y**, "to be," which literally means "to being," the **-sa-** adding the idea of "-ing."

   While **ka-y** and **kasa-y** can be used interchangeably, in this book forms of **kasa-y** are used with conditions or situations, such as in the question, **¿Imayna-lla(-tah) kasa-nki?** "How are you (one person)?" and with location. The verb **ka-y** is used for identifying and for giving characteristics, traits, and qualities.

5. As was pointed out in the preceding note, regional differences in pronunciation and spelling, as well as personal preference in usage of these, often are found in Quechua. The **-cheh** in the verb ending for "you (more than one person)," **-nki-cheh**, is also found in some other constructions. It should be noted that **-cheh** has the variants **-chej**, **-chih**, **-chij**, **-chik**, and **-chis**.

6. **Alli**, "well," "good," usually has a euphonic **-n** attached to it: **alli-n**. As is done with many bi-syllabic words ending in **-n**, if **-lla** is affixed, it goes between the root word and the euphonic **-n**. Compare:
Alli-n p'unchaw. "Good morning."/"Good day."
alli-lla-n, "just fine"

7. The **-n**, an apocopation of the suffix **-min** (see Note 13 below), here is a euphonic particle that cannot be translated literally.

8. A variant of **qan**, "you (one person)," is **qam**.

9. The suffix **-rí**, "and," is used in a question with a contrastive nuance: "How are you?" "Very well. And you?" **¿Qan-rí?**

10. Regional variants of **ñoqa**, "I," are **ñuqa**, **noqa**, and **nuqa**.

11. A regional variant of **-pas**, "also," is **-pis**.

12. Note the way the negative construction is formed.
Alli(-lla)-n-puni. Very well.
Mana alli(-lla)-n-puni**-chu**. Not very well.

13. A note of certainty or assurance can be added to a word by attaching to it **-min** or its apocopated variants **-mi**, **-m** (as seen here), or **-n**.

 The forms **-m** and **-n** are attached to words ending in a vowel, and **-mi** to words ending in a consonant. The suffix **-min** can be attached to either, but also is less used than **-mi**, **-m**, or **-n**.

 The particles **-mi**, **-m**, and **-n** are used more frequently in Peru and Ecuador than in Bolivia.

 Both **-min** and **-n** can have additional uses. For example:
 When **-min** is used in a question, it adds a note of curiosity or doubt, as in
¿Ima-min? What is it? (showing some curiosity or doubt)
What-(particle used in a question to show some curiosity or doubt)?
 The third variant of **-min**, **-n**, can be used merely as a euphonic particle, as was seen above in Model Sentence 5 (and Note 7)
Alli(lla)npuni. Very well.
Alli(-lla)-n-puni.
Well(-just)-(euphonic particle)-very.
or **-n** can express emphasis, as will be seen later in Model Sentence 11 of Chapter 2.
Mana(n), (ñoqa) mana kastillanuta rimanichu. No, I don't speak Spanish.
Mana(-n), (ñoqa) mana kastillanu-ta rima-ni-chu.

No(-emphatic particle), (I) not Spanish-(direct object marker) speak-I-(negative marker).

14. **Ka-ni**, "I am," is from **ka-y**, "to be," which literally means "be-to." To show who the subject of any verb is, the **-y**, "to," which is the infinitive ending or marker, is removed and an appropriate ending is added. For example: **ka-y**, "to be"; **ka-ni** "I am"; **ka-nki** "you (one person) are"; **ka-nki-cheh** "you (more than one person) are."

    Since the ending of the verb changes according to who the subject is, it usually is not necessary to express "I," "you," and so on. For emphasis, however, the subject can be included, and you can say, for example: **ñoqa ka-ni** "I am"; **qan ka-nki** "you (one person) are"; **qan-kuna ka-nki-cheh** "you (more than one person) are."

15. The third-person singular of **ka-y**, "to be," **ka-n**, with its meanings "he is," "she is," and "it is," is never expressed. **Ka-n** is used only with the meanings "there is" or "there are."

16. For **-mi**, see Note 13.

17. Quechua really does not have the articles "the," "a," and "an." At times, the idea of "a" or "an" is needed to place emphasis on what follows. Then **uh** or one of its regional variants **uj**, **uk**, **huh**, **huk** or **hoq** ("a," "an"; "one") is used. Therefore, in sentences such as "I am a student," "a" can be expressed or merely understood. Compare:

    (Ñoqa) alumnu ka-ni. "I am a student (male)"
    (Ñoqa) uh alumnu ka-ni. "I am a <u>student</u> (male)."

18. The words for many roles, jobs, or professions can be found adapted from the Spanish. Here we have **alumnu**, "student" (a male), from the Spanish *alumno*. A female student is **alumna** (from the Spanish *alumna*). A real Quechua word for "student" is **yacha-ko-h** [**-ku-** > **-ko-**], which literally means "know-(for)self-the one who." The Spanish adaptation is more commonly used.

19. Many names of roles, jobs, and professions borrowed from Spanish indicate a male or a female by their ending, **-u** for a male, and **-a** for a female.

    Quechua, like English, pays no attention to gender (masculine, feminine, or neuter). Quechua words designating roles, jobs, and professions are considered to refer to a male. To specify that they refer to a female, they are preceded by **warmi**, "female," as in **warmi yacha-ko-h** [**-ku-** > **-ko-**], "female student," literally "female know-(for)self-the one who." Compare:

    awa-h weaver (generally considered to refer to a male)
    warmi awa-h weaver (a female)

To emphasize reference to a male, **qhari** precedes the noun.
awa-h weaver (generally considered to refer to a male)
qhari awa-h weaver (emphasizing that the weaver is a male)
However it should be noted that Quechua, again like English, has gender nouns, that is, nouns designating people that denote the natural gender of the person(s) to whom they refer, such as **sipas**, "young woman," and **wayna**, "young man."

20. Two real Quchua words for "doctor (physician)" are **hampi-kama-yoh**, "the one with healing/curing skill," literally, "cure/medicine/remedy-skill-with," and **hampe-h** [**hampi-** > **-hampe-** (from **hampi-y**, "to heal, to cure, to prescribe remedies")],"the one who heals," literally "heal/cure/prescribe remedies-the one who."

21. **Midiku** comes from Spanish *médico* (doctor [physician]). Note the Quechua pattern of stress is followed, **midiku**, not the Spanish one of *médico*. This is also true for other words with a similar Spanish accent pattern, such as **mikaniku**, from *mecánico* (mechanic).

22. The word **maystru**, "teacher" (from the Spanish *maestro*), is used for males. For females, in addition to **maystra** (from the Spanish *maestra*), in many places, when referring to the person, **siñurita** (from the Spanish *señorita*, "young lady") is used. A real Quechua word for "teacher" is **yacha-che-h** [**-chi-** > **-che-**], which literally means "know-make-the one who."

23. The word **amigu**, "friend" (a male), and its counterpart **amiga**, "friend" (a female), are borrowings from Spanish. Real Quechua words for "friend" are **atillcha**, **masi**, and **kumpa**.

24. Note the Quechua dual possessive construction in **Pidro-hpa amigu-n** (OR **Pidro-hpa atillcha-n**), "Pedro-of friend-his" [**Pidru** > **Pidro**].
    Possession shown by "of," " 's," and "s' " is indicated by means of the postpositional (prepositional) endings **-h**, **-hta**, **-hpa**, or **-hpata** affixed to nouns ending in a vowel, and by **-pa** or **-pata** for nouns ending in a consonant. For example:
    Pidro-h *Pedro-of*: of Pedro, Pedro's [**Pidru** > **Pidro**]
    Pidro-hta *Pedro-of*: of Pedro, Pedro's
    Pidro-hpa *Pedro-of*: of Pedro, Pedro's
    Pidro-hpata *Pedro-of*: of Pedro, Pedro's
    Pidro-h amigu-n *Pedro-of friend-his*: a friend of Pedro, Pedro's friend
    Pidro-hta amigu-n *Pedro-of friend-his*: a friend of Pedro, Pedro's friend

> **Pidro-hpa amigu-n** *Pedro-of friend-his*: a friend of Pedro, Pedro's friend
> **Pidro-hpata amigu-n** *Pedro-of friend-his*: a friend of Pedro, Pedro's friend
> (OR
> **Pidro-h atillcha-n** *Pedro-of friend-his*: a friend of Pedro, Pedro's friend
> **Pidro-hta atillcha-n** *Pedro-of friend-his*: a friend of Pedro, Pedro's friend
> **Pidro-hpa atillcha-n** *Pedro-of friend-his*: a friend of Pedro, Pedro's friend
> **Pidro-hpata atillcha-n** *Pedro-of friend-his*: a friend of Pedro, Pedro's friend)
>
> **Hwan-pa** *Juan-of*: of Juan, Juan's
> **Hwan-pata** *Juan-of*: of Juan, Juan's
>
> **Hwan-pa masi-n** *Juan-of companion-his*: a companion of Juan, Juan's companion
> **Hwan-pata masi-n** *Juan-of companion-his*: a companion of Juan, Juan's companion

[Note: For the plural of common nouns, as in "friend<u>s</u>," "companion<u>s</u>," see Note 26 below. For possessive constructions with plural nouns, as in "friend<u>s</u> <u>of his</u>," companion<u>s</u> <u>of his</u>, see Note 29 below.]

25. Quechua has a different form for "we" and its accompanying verb, depending on whether the person addressed is included or excluded. Compare:
    > **(Ñoqayku) alumnu-s ka-yku.** We (excluding the person[s] addressed) are students (males or male[s] and female[s]).
    > *(We[excluding the person(s) addressed]) student-s(males or male[s] and female[s]) be-we(excluding the person[s] addressed).*
    >
    > **(Ñoqancheh) alumnu-s ka-ncheh.** We (including the person[s] addressed) are students (males or male[s] and female[s]).
    > *(We[including the person(s) addressed]) student-s(males or male[s] and female[s]) be-we(including the person[s] addressed).*

    Here, we are dealing only with the "we" that excludes the one being spoken to.

26. The real Quechua way of forming the plural (designation of more than one) of nouns is by adding **-kuna** to the singular.
    > **yacha-che-h** a teacher/professor [**-chi-** > **-che-**]
    > *know-make-the one who*

> **yacha-che-h-kuna** teachers/professors [**-chi-** > **-che-**]
> *know-make-the one who-(plural marker/designating more than one)[the ones who]*
>
> **pure-h** the one who walks; walker/traveler
> **pure-h-kuna** the ones who walk; walkers/travelers
>
> **masi** companion
> **masi-kuna** companions
>
> **atillcha** friend
> **atillcha-kuna** friends

However, if the noun is a borrowing from Spanish, the Spanish way of forming the plural by adding an **-s** usually is used.

> **alumnu** student (male)
> **alumnu-s** students (males or male[s] and female[s])
>
> **amigu** friend (male)
> **amigu-s** friends (males or male[s] and female[s])
>
> **amiga** friend (female)
> **amiga-s** friends (females)

In some areas, mainly in Bolivia, **-kuna** is used only to form the plural of words ending in a consonant, and **-s** is used to form the plural of words ending in a vowel, whether or not they are borrowings from Spanish. Compare:

> Most places other than Bolivia:
> **atillcha** friend
> **atillcha-kuna** friends
>
> **masi** companion
> **masi-kuna** companions
>
> In Bolivia:
> **atillcha** friend
> **atillcha-s** friends
> **masi** companion
> **masi-s** companions

27. The euphonic infix **-ni-** is required between a word ending in a consonant and a following affixed infix or suffix that is a single consonant, as is the case here, or that begins with a **y** or a double consonant combination not found in the alphabet.

28. It has been pointed out above (see Note 26) that in some Quechuaphone areas, through the influence of Spanish, an **-s** is or can be used to form the plural of words ending in a vowel. However, the true Quechua

function of a final **-s** (affixed to a word ending in a vowel) and of its equivalent **-si** (affixed to a word ending in a consonant) is to indicate that what is being said is second-hand information, conveying the idea of "they say (that)," "it is said (that)," "I have heard but am not sure (that)," "someone said (that)," and the like. The word to which either of these suffixes is attached is the element of the sentence on which the emphasis is placed. Compare:

> **amigu-s** friends (males or male[s] and female[s]) OR they say (that) a friend
> *friend-s(males or male[s] and female[s]) OR friend-(second-hand information marker) ("A" is understood.)*

> **Uh amigu-s hamu-n.** They say (that) a friend is coming (emphasis on "friend").
> *A friend-(second-hand information marker) come-he/she.*
> **Uh amigu hamu-n-si.** They say (that) a friend is coming (emphasis on "is coming").
> *A friend come-he/she-(second-hand information marker).*

> **Pidru-s suti-n.** I have heard but am not sure (that)/Someone said (that) his name is Pedro.
> *Pedro-(second-hand information marker) name-his. ("Is" is understood.)*

29. In a plural formed with **-s**, any possessive ("my," "your," "his," "her," "its," etc. [see Note 37 below]) follows the **-s** and the required euphonic infix **-ni-** (see Note 27 above). However, if the plural is formed with **-kuna**, the possessive goes before the **-kuna**.

    (The examples below have the Quechua possessive construction that includes both "Pedro's" and "his." It is the placement of "his," which in this case is not used in the English equivalent of these phrases, that is the focal point of this note.) Compare:

    > **Pidro-hpa amigu-s-ni-n** friends (males or male[s] and female[s]) of Pedro/Pedro's friends [**Pidru > Pidro**]
    > *Pedro-of friend-s(males or male[s] and female[s])-(euphonic particle)-his*
    > **Pidro-hpa amiga-s-ni-n** friends (females) of Pedro/Pedro's friends [**Pidru > Pidro**] OR
    > **Pidro-hpa atillcha-s-ni-n** friends of Pedro/Pedro's friends [**Pidru > Pidro**]
    > *Pedro-of friend-s-(euphonic particle)-his*

    > AND
    > **Pidro-hpa atillcha-n-kuna** friends of Pedro/Pedro's friends [**Pidru > Pidro**]

Pedro-of friend-his-(plural marker)

Compare:

Pidro-hpa masi-s-ni-n companions of Pedro/Pedro's companions [**Pidru > Pidro**]
Pedro-of companion-s-(euphonic particle)-his

AND

Pidro-hpa masi-n-kuna companions of Pedro/Pedro's companions [**Pidru > Pidro**]
Pedro-of companion-his-(plural marker))

Compare:

Pidro-hpa pure-h-masi-s-ni-n traveling companions of Pedro/Pedro's traveling companions [**Pidru > Pidro, puri- > pure-**]
Pedro-of walk-the one who-companion-s-(euphonic particle)-his

AND

Pidro-hpa pure-h-masi-n-kuna traveling companions of Pedro/Pedro's traveling companions [**Pidru > Pidro, puri- > pure-**]
Pedro-of walk-the one who-companion-his-(plural marker)

30. Here, and often above, it has been noted that "is" is understood. This is because the present tense verb form of **ka-y**, "to be," for the subjects "he," "she," and "it," **ka-n**, unless this form has the special meaning "there is," "there are," is never used. Note that for all other verbs, the form for "he," "she," and "it" is used.

31. See Note 26.

32. Note that the plural of **pi**, "who," is formed with **-kuna**:
    ¿**Pi?** Who (one person)?
    ¿**Pi-kuna?** Who (more than one person)?

33. See Note 26.

34. **Kay**, when followed by a noun (thus being an adjective), means both "this" and "these"; **kay wayna**, "this young man"; **kay wayna-kuna**, "these young men."

    But, when **kay** stands alone (thus being a pronoun), it adds **-kuna** for the plural, "these"; **kay**, "this," "this one"; **kay-kuna**, "these."

    The same is true for **chay**, "that," "those," and **haqay**, "that (over there)" and "those (over there)."

35. The particle **-qa** is used to place emphasis upon an item or topic under discussion or consideration. Model Sentence 19 poses the question ¿**Pi(-**

tah) **chay wayna?"** "Who is that young man?" (with "is" being understood). This introduces the topic of "that young man." The reply here, **Chay wayna(-qa), Pidru,** "That young man is Pedro" (with "is" being understood), has the optional emphatic **-qa**, which, if used, intensifies the connection of the answer with the question.

36. The possessive affix **-ncheh,** "our (including the person[s] addressed)," has several variants: **-nchej, -nchih, -nchij, -nchik,** and **-nchis**.

37. The possessive affix **-ykicheh,** "your (more than one person)," has several variants: **-ykichej, -ykichih, -ykichij, -ykichik,** and **-ykichis**.

38. As was pointed out in Note 29 above, with a plural noun formed with **-kuna**, any possessive adjective (see below) goes between the noun and the **-kuna**. However, if the plural is formed with **-s**, the word order is as follows: noun / **-s** / required euphonic infix **-ni-** / possessive adjective.

    -y my
    -yki your (one person)
    -n his/her
    -yku our (excluding the person[s] addressed)
    -ncheh (or one of its variants, **-nchej, -nchih, -nchij, -nchik, -nchis**) our (including the person[s] addressed)
    -ykicheh (or one of its variants, **-ykichej, -ykichih, -ykichij, -ykichik, -ykichis**) your (more than one person)
    -nku their

Compare:
    amigu-s-ni-y my friends
    friend-s(males or male[s] and female[s])-(euphonic particle)-my
    OR
    atillcha-y-kuna my friends
    friend-my-(plural marker)

    masi-s companions
    companion-s
    masi-s-ni-n his companions
    companion-s-(euphonic particle)-his
    masi-n-kuna his companions
    companion-his-(plural marker)

39. The names of countries are Quechuasized Spanish names. For example, **Istadus Unidus** is from the Spanish *Estados Unidos*, "United States." Other examples, some of which have written accents, following the Spanish pattern, are **Alimanya** (Germany), **Awstralya** (Australia), **Hapún** (Japan), **Inlatira** (England), **Kanadá** (Canada), and **Swisia** (Sweden).

40. **Lima**, Lima: Capital of the Department of Lima and of Peru. Founded by Francisco Pizarro in 1535, with the name Ciudad de los Reyes, "City of the Kings (the three Wise Men)," because its site was selected January 5, the eve of the day of the Festival of the Magi (the three Wise Men). The city subsequently was called Lima, an apparent corruption of Rimac, the name of the small river on whose banks it lies.

41. A question that does not begin with an interrogative word such as "how?" "who?" "where?" must have the question marker **-chu**, which usually is affixed to the main verb.

42. **Qosqo**, Cuzco: Known as **pacha pupu**, "navel of the earth," "navel of the universe," and as **qhapah llahta**, "illustrious city." Capital of the Inca Empire, supposedly founded in the 11th century by Manco Capac (**Manku Qhapah**). Taken by the Spaniards, under Francisco Pizarro, in 1533. Present-day capital of the Department of Cuzco, Peru. Located at the foot and just south of the majestic ancient Inca fortress, Sacsahuaman (**Sahsaywaman**).

    (Interestingly, there are the verbs **qosqo-y**, "to go Cuzco," and **qosqo-ku-y**, "to arrive at Cuzco," "to enter the city of Cuzco." There also are other verbs such as **lima-y**, "to go to Lima," and **llahta-y**, "to go to town".)

43. Today practically everywhere in the Quechua-speaking world, the days of the week are adaptations of the Spanish names for them: **lunis** (Monday), **martis** (Tuesday), **mirkulis** (Wednesday), **huywis** (Thursday), **wirnis** (Friday), **sawaru** (Saturday), **dumingu** (Sunday). The first day of the week in the Hispanic world, which includes the Quechuaphone area, is Monday.

SECTION II

Model Sentences and Their Expansions

Chapter 2

This chapter deals with
A. Attracting Someone's Attention [Model Sentences 1-8]
B. Asking and Answering Some Useful Questions [9-29]

A. ATTRACTING SOMEONE'S ATTENTION

1. ¡**Uyariy!**[1] Listen! (addressing one person)
   ¡Uyari-y!
   Listen-(command marker addressing one person)!

Expansion:

"Listen!" (addressing one person)
"Listen!" (addressing more than one person)

¡**Uyari-y!** Listen! (addressing one person)
¡**Uyari-y-cheh!** Listen! (addressing more than one person)
Listen-(dual command marker addressing more than one person)!

2. ¡**Siñura!** Ma'am! (formal)

3. ¡**Siñur!** Sir! (formal)

4. ¡**Tayta!** Sir! (somewhat formal)

5. ¡**Mama!** Ma'am! (informal)

6. ¡**Tata!** Sir! (informal) (shortened form of ¡**Tayta!**)

Expansion:

Variants on ways to address people to attract their attention

¡**Siñurá-y!**[2,3] Ma'am! (formal)

Ma'am-my!
¡Siñur-ní-y! Sir! (formal)
Sir-(euphonic particle)-my)!
¡Taytá-y! Sir! (somewhat formal)
Sir-my!
¡Mamá-y! Ma'am! (informal)
Ma'am-my!
¡Tatá-y! Sir! (informal)
Sir-my!
¡Wiraqocha! Sir! (quite formal, used only by native speakers of Quechua when addressing urban residents or foreigners)[4,5]

[Note: In the Quechua culture, it is customary for a person to repeat any greeting to each individual of a group whom he or she considers to be of higher status.]

7. **¡Yaw!** Hey!/Say there! (very informal)

Expansion:

Additional ways of attracting attention

¡Yaw-kuna! Hey!/Say there! (addressing more than one person) (very informal)
Hey/Say there-(plural marker)!
¡Yu! Hey!/Say there! (very informal)
¡Chuy! Hey!/Say there! (very informal)

8. **¡Wawqéy!** Brother! (very friendly)
¡Wawqé-y!
Brother(of a male)-my!

Expansion:

Additional ways of attracting the attention of specific people
¡Wayna! Young man!
¡Sipas! Young lady!
¡Wamra! Boy!
Young man (10-14 years old)!
¡Wamira! Girl!
Young woman (10-14 years old)!

¡Wawá-y! (Little) boy!/(Little) girl!; My boy!/My girl!
Boy/Girl-my!

B. ASKING AND ANSWERING SOME USEFUL QUESTIONS

9. **¿Kastillanuta rimankichu?**[6] Do you speak Spanish?
   ¿Kastillanu-ta rima-nki-chu?
   Castilian/Spanish-(direct object marker) speak-you(one person)-(question marker)?[7]

Expansion A:

Regional variants of "Do you speak?"

¿Kastillanu-ta **rima**-nki-chu? Do you <u>speak</u> Spanish? (used more in Ecuador, Peru, and northern Argentina)
¿Kastillanu-ta **parla**-nki-chu?[8] Do you <u>speak</u> Spanish? (used mainly in Bolivia)

Expansion B:

Languages

¿Kastillanu-ta rima-nki-chu? Do you speak <u>Spanish</u>?

Qheshwa Quechua OR
Runasimi Quechua
People speech[9]

Inles (Inlis) English (language)
Aliman German (language)
Hapunis Japanese (language)
Swiku (language)

10. **Arí, uh pisichallata rimani.**[10] Yes, I speak just a little.
    Arí, uh pisi-cha-lla-ta rima-ni.
    Yes, a little-(diminutive marker)-just-(direct object marker) speak-I.

Expansion

Various affirmative responses to "Do you speak . . .?"

Arí. Yes.
Arí, uh pisi-cha-lla-ta rima-ni. Yes, I speak <u>just a little</u>.
Arí, ñoqa uh pisi kastillanu-ta rima-ni. Yes, I speak <u>a little Spanish</u>.
Yes, a little Spanish-(direct object marker) speak-I.

Ñoqa <u>uh pisi qheshwa-ta</u> rima-ni. I speak <u>a little Quechua</u>.
I a little Quechua-(direct object marker) speak-I.
Ñoqa <u>kastillanu-ta</u> rima-ni. I speak <u>Spanish</u>.
Ñoqa <u>runasimi-ta</u> rima-ni. I speak <u>Quechua</u>.
Ñoqa <u>inles-ta</u> rima-ni. I speak <u>English</u>.

11. **Mana(n), (ñoqa) mana kastillanuta rimanichu.**[11] No, I don't speak Spanish.
    Mana(-n), (ñoqa) mana kastillanu-ta rima-ni-chu.
    No(-emphatic particle), (I) not Spanish-(direct object marker) speak-I-(negative marker).

Expansion:

Various negative responses to "Do you speak . . .?"

Mana. <u>No</u>.
Mana(-n). <u>No</u>. (more emphatic or more polite)
Mana(-n), (ñoqa) mana kastillanu-ta rima-ni-chu. <u>No</u>, I do<u>n't</u> speak Spanish.
Ñoqa mana(-n) kastillanu-ta rima-ni-chu. I do<u>n't</u> speak Spanish.

12. **¿Imata(n) munanki?** What do you want?
    ¿Ima-ta(-n) muna-nki?
    What-(direct object marker)(-euphonic particle) want-you(one person)?

Expansion:

How to ask what different people want

¿Ima-ta(-n) muna-<u>nki</u>? What do <u>you (one person)</u> want?
¿Ima-ta(-n) muna-<u>n</u>? What does <u>he/she</u> want?
¿Ima-ta(-n) muna-<u>nki-chch</u>? What do <u>you (more than one person)</u> want?
¿Ima-ta(-n) muna-<u>nku</u>? What do <u>they</u> want?

¿Ima-ta(-n) <u>Pidru</u> muna-<u>n</u>? What <u>does Pedro</u> want?
¿Ima-ta(-n) <u>Pidru(-pis) Mariya-pis</u> muna-<u>nku</u>? What <u>do Pedro and Maria</u> want?
What-(direct object marker)(-euphonic particle) Pedro(-and) Maria-and want-they?

13. **Unuta munani.** I want water
    Unu-ta muna-ni.
    Water-(direct object marker) want-I.

Expansion A:

Different people wanting water

Unu-ta muna-ni. I want water.

muna-nki you (one person) want
muna-n he/she wants
muna-yku we (excluding the person[s] addressed) want
muna-ncheh we (including the person[s] addressed) want
muna-nki-cheh you (more than one person) want
muna-nku they want

Expansion B:

"I want (different things)."

Unu-ta muna-ni. I want water.
Water-(direct object marker) want-I.

Yaku water (regional variant)

Uhya-na unu drinking water
Drink"-able"[drinkable] water
Mikhu-na[12] something to eat/food
Eat"-able"[edible]
Uhya-na something to drink/a drink
Drink"-able"
Mikhu-y to eat
Eat-to(infinitive marker, "to")
Uhya-y to drink
Drink-to(infinitive marker, "to")
Mikhuy (eating)/food (something edible)[13]
Uhyay (drinking)/a drink (something drinkable)

Expansion C:

"anything (to) . . . "
"something (to) . . . "

Unu-ta muna-ni. I want water. OR
Yaku-ta muna-ni. I want water.

Ima(-lla)-ta-pas anything/something
Thing(-just)-(direct object marker)-any

Ima mikhuna(-lla)-ta-pas anything/something to eat
Thing eat"-able"[edible](-just)-(direct object marker)-any
Ima uhyana(-lla)-ta-pas anything/something to drink
Thing drink"-able"[drinkable](-just)-(direct object marker)-any

Expansion D:

"I want (something) to (direction/destination)."

Unu-ta muna-ni. I want water. OR
Yaku-ta muna-ni. I want water.

[Note: In the substitutions below, the direct object marker, **-ta**, goes with the first element ("ticket," "bus," "to go").]

Uh wulitu-ta Ururu-ta[14] a ticket to Oruro
A ticket-(direct object marker) Oruro-to
Uh wulitu-ta Ururu-man[15] a ticket to Oruro
A ticket-(direct object marker) Oruro-to/toward/headed for/in the direction of

Awtuwus-ta Lima-ta a/the bus to Lima
Bus-(direct object marker) Lima-to ("A" and "the" are understood.)
Awtuwus-ta Lima-man a/the bus to/toward/headed for Lima
Bus-(direct object marker) Lima-to/toward/headed for/in the direction of ("A" and "the" are understood.)

Ururu-ta ri-y-ta to go to Oruro
Oruro-to go-(infinitive marker, "to")-(direct object marker)
Ururu-man ri-y-ta to go to/toward/headed for Oruro
Oruro-to/toward/headed for/in the direction of go-(infinitive marker, "to")-(direct object marker)

14. **¿Unu kanchu?**[16,17] Is there water?
    ¿Unu ka-n-chu?
    Water be-it[there is]-(question marker)?

15. **Arí, (unu) kan.** Yes, there is (water).
    Arí, (unu) ka-n.
    Yes, (water) be-it[there is].

Expansion:

Variants of "Yes, there is."/"Yes, there is some."

Arí, (unu) **ka-n**. Yes, there is (water).
Arí, (unu) **ka-n**(-mi). Yes, there is (water).
Yes, (water) be-it[there is](-particle of certainty or assurance).

Arí, **ka-n**(-mi). Yes, there is./Yes, there is some.
Yes, be-it[there is](-particle of certainty or assurance).
Arí, **tia-n**(-mi). Yes, there is./Yes, there is some.
Arí, **tiya-n**(-mi).[18] Yes, there is./Yes, there is some.

16. **Mana(n), mana (unu) kanchu.** No, there isn't (any) (water)./No, there isn't any./No, there is none/(no water).
    Mana(-n), mana (unu) ka-n-chu.
    No(-emphatic particle), not (water) be-it[there is]-(negative marker).

Expansion:

Variants of "There isn't."/"There isn't any."

Mana(-n), mana (unu) ka-n-chu. No, there isn't (any) (water)./No, there isn't any./No, there is none/(no water).
Mana(-n), mana ka-n-chu. No, there isn't./No, there isn't any.
No(-emphatic particle), not be-it[there is]-(negative marker).

Mana(-n) ka-n-chu. There isn't./There isn't any.
Mana(-n) tia-n-chu. There isn't./There isn't any.
Mana(-n) tiya-n-chu. There isn't./There isn't any.

17. **Mana(n) q'oñi unu kanchu, ichaqa chiri unu kan(mi).** There isn't (any) hot water, but there is cold water./There is no hot water, but there is cold water.
    Mana(-n) q'oñi unu ka-n-chu, ichaqa chiri unu ka-n(-mi).
    Not(-emphatic particle) hot water be-it[there is]-(negative marker), but cold water be-it[there is](-particle of certainty or assurance).

18. **¿Kaynehpi uh mikhuywasichu kan?**[19,20] Is there a restaurant around here?
    ¿Kay-neh-pi uh mikhuy-wasi-chu ka-n?
    Here-around-in/at an eating-house-(question marker) be-it[there is]?

Expansion A:

"around here"
"around there (nearby)"
"around there (farther away)"

¿Kay-neh-pi uh mikhuy-wasi-chu ka-n? Is there a restaurant <u>around here</u>?

Chay-neh-pi <u>around there (nearby)</u>
Haqay-neh-pi <u>around there (farther away)</u>

Expansion B:
Businesses and other establishments

¿Kay-neh-pi <u>uh mikhuy-wasi</u>-chu ka-n? Is there <u>a restaurant</u> around here?

puñuy-wasi <u>hotel/hostel, and the like</u>
sleep-house OR
samana-wasi <u>hotel/hostel, and the like</u>
place to rest-house

mikhuna qhatu-wasi <u>grocery store</u>
food market-house

plasa <u>market</u> OR
mirkadu[21] <u>market</u> OR
qhatu <u>market</u>

wutika <u>pharmacy</u> OR
hampi-wasi <u>pharmacy</u>
remedy/medicine-house
uspital <u>hospital</u> OR
hampi-na-wasi <u>hospital</u>
cure/heal-(marker to designate the place where the action expressed by the verb stem to which it is attached usually takes place)-house OR
onqo-h-kuna wasi <u>hospital</u>
be sick-the one who-(plural marker)[the ones who]-house

ilisya <u>church</u> OR
Tiyus-pa wasi-n <u>church</u>
God-of house-his

Expansion C:
Person who plies a given trade

¿Kay-neh-pi <u>uh mikhuy-wasi</u>-chu ka-n? Is there <u>a restaurant</u> around here?

sapatiru shoemaker OR
chhichay-kama-yoh shoemaker OR
shoe making-skill-with
phapa(tu)-kama-yoh shoemaker, shoe repairman
shoe-skill-with

pharmasiyutika pharmacist (female) OR
pharmasiyutiku pharmacist (male) OR
hampi-rante-h pharmacist
remedy/medicine-sell-the one who

midika doctor (female), physician (female) OR
midiku doctor (male), physician (male) OR
hampi-kama-yoh doctor, physician
remedy/medicine-skill-with

---

19. **¿Maynehpi uh bañu kan?** Where is there a latrine/bathroom?
    ¿May-neh-pi uh bañu ka-n?
    Where-around-in/at a bathroom be-it[there is]?

Expansion A:

Various terms for "bathroom," "lavatory," "restroom," "water closet," and "toilet," that may be used in and near urban areas

¿May-neh-pi uh bañu ka-n? Where is there a latrine/bathroom?

uh pincha a bathroom, lavatory, restroom, water closet, toilet
uh ritriti a bathroom, lavatory, restroom, water closet, toilet
uh mayllaku a lavatory (place to wash hands) or
uh mahchhiku a lavatory (place to wash hands)

Expansion B:

Terms and phrases that may be used in a very rural location with no bathroom facilities

¿May-neh-pi uh bañu ka-n? Where is there a latrine/bathroom?

uh aka-wasi an outhouse
uh hisp'ay-wasi an outhouse

uh hisp'a-na[22] a place to urinate
*a urinate-(marker to designate the place where the action expressed by
   the verb stem to which it is attached usually takes place)*

¿**May-pi hisp'a(-ku)-y-man?** Where could I urinate?
Where-in/at urinate(-self)-(dual marker for "I could")?

aka defecate (from **aka-y**, "to defecate")

Expansion C:
Ways to ask for a place where one can do different kinds of washing

¿**May-neh-pi uh bañu ka-n?** Where is there a latrine/bathroom?

uh t'ahsay-kama a laundry
a washing (of clothes or anything else that can absorb water)-exclusively
uh kiti t'ahsana a washing place (on the bank of a river, etc.) for clothes, hair, or anything else that can absorb water
a place where the washing of clothes, hair, or anything else that can absorb water is done
uh t'ahsakuna a wash basin or sink where one can wash clothes, hair, or anything else that can absorb water
a wash basin for washing clothes, hair, or anything else that can absorb water

uh mayllakuna a wash basin or sink where one can wash up or wash anything that cannot absorb water
a wash basin for washing up or for washing anything that cannot absorb water OR
uh mahchhikuna a wash basin or sink where one can wash up or wash anything that cannot absorb water
a wash basin for washing up or for washing anything that cannot absorb water

uh armakuna a place to bathe; a hot spring, baths

20. ¿**Puñuna ñoqapah kanchu?**[23] Is there a bed for me?
    ¿Puñuna ñoqa-pah ka-n-chu?
    Bed I-for be-it[there is]-question marker? ("A" is understood.)

21. **Arí. Puñuna qanpah kan.** Yes, There is a bed for you.
    Arí. Puñuna qan-pah ka-n.
    Yes. Bed you-for be-it[there-is]. ("A" is understood.)

Expansion:
"There is a bed for ..."

Puñuna qan-pah ka-n. There is a bed for you.
ñoqa-pah for me

ñoqayku-pah for us (excluding the person[s] addressed)
ñoqancheh-pah[24] for us (including the person[s] addressed)

qan-pah for you (one person)
qan-kuna-pah for you (more than one person)

pay-pah for him/for her/for it
pay-kuna-pah for them

Hwan-pah for Juan
Hwan-pah(-pis) Pidru-pah-pis for Juan and Pedro
Juan-for(-and) Pedro-for-and

tukuy(-ni)-yku-pah for all of us (excluding the person[s] addressed)
all(-euphonic particle)-our(excluding the person[s] addressed)-for
tukuy(-ni)-ncheh-pah for all of us (including the person[s] addressed)
all(-euphonic particle)-our(including the person[s] addressed)-for

22. **¿Ima(lla)pas ñoqapah kanchu?** Is there anything/something for me?
¿Ima(-lla)-pas ñoqa-pah ka-n-chu?
Thing(-just)-any I-for[for me] be-it[there is]-(question marker)?

Expansion:

"Is there (something)?"
"Are there (things)?"

¿Ima(-lla)-pas ñoqa-pah ka-n-chu? Is there anything/something for me?

Ima mikhuna(-lla)-pas anything/something to eat
Thing food(-just)-any
Ima uhyana(-lla)-pas anything/something to drink

Uh karta qan-pah a letter for you
A letter you(one person)-for
Karta-s qan-pah* any letters for you
Letter-s you(one person)-for

*[Note: **Ka-n** means both "there is" and "there are," so **¿Karta-s ka-n-chu?** means "Are there letters?" and **¿Karta-s qan-pah ka-n-chu?**, "Are there any letters for you?"]

Uh qellqa(laqhe) a letter
A something written(leaf/sheet)
Uh qellqa(laqhe) qan-pah a letter for you
A something written(leaf/sheet) you(one person)-for
Qellqa(laqhe)-kuna qan-pah any letters for you
Something written(leaf/sheet)-(plural marker)[written things/(written leaves/sheets)] you(one person)-for

23. **Arí. Uh karta qanpah kan(mi).** Yes. There is a letter for you.
    Arí. Uh karta qan-pah ka-n(-mi).
    Yes. A letter you(one person)-for be-it[there is](-particle of certainty or assurance).

Expansion:

"There is a letter for you."
"There are letters for you."
"There are many things for you.

Uh karta qan-pah ka-n(-mi). Yes. There is a letter for you.

Uh qellqa(laqhe) a letter
A something written(leaf/sheet)

Karta-s letters OR
Qellqa(laqhe)-kuna letters
Something written(leaf/sheet)-(plural marker)[written things/(written leaves/sheets)]

Imaymana many things

24. **Mana ima kanchu.** There isn't anything./There is nothing.
    Mana ima ka-n-chu.
    No thing be-it[there is]-(negative marker).

Expansion A:

"There isn't anything."/"There is nothing."

Mana ima ka-n-chu. There isn't anything./There is nothing.

Ni ima not anything/nothing
Not even thing

Expansion B:

Things that there aren't

Mana ima ka-n-chu. There is<u>n't anything.</u>/There is <u>nothing</u>.

Ni ima <u>not anything/nothing</u>
Not even thing

Mana ima mikhuna(-lla)-pas <u>nothing to eat</u>
Mana ima uhyana(-lla)-pas <u>nothing to drink</u>

Mana karta <u>no letter</u> OR
Mana qellqa(laqhe) <u>no letter</u>
No something written(leaf/sheet)

Mana karta-s <u>no letters</u> OR
Mana qellqa(laqhe)-kuna <u>no letters</u>
No something written(leaf/sheet)-(plural marker)[written things/(written leaves/sheets)]

25. **¿Pichári kaypi kan?**[25] Is there anybody/somebody here?
    ¿Pi-chá-ri kay-pi ka-n?
    Who-(marker expressing doubt or lack of knowledge)-and/then(prolonging the question without adding any specific meaning) here-in/at be-it[there is]?

26. **Arí, kaypi pipas kan(mi).** Yes, there is someone here.
    Arí, kay-pi pi-pas ka-n(-mi).
    Yes, here-in/at who-any[someone] be-it[there is](-particle of certainty or assurance).

Expansion:

"There is someone here."
"There are some people here."

Kay-pi pi-pas ka-n(-mi). There is <u>someone</u> here.

uh-kuna [are] <u>some people</u>
one-(plural marker)[some]

27. **Mana(n), kaypi mana pipas kanchu.** No, there isn't anybody/anyone here. No, there is nobody/no one here.
    Mana(-n), kay-pi mana pi-pas ka-n-chu.
    *No(-emphatic particle), here-in/at not who-any[**mana pi-pas** = nobody/no one] be-it[there is]-(negative marker).*

Expansion:

Variant of "There isn't anybody/anyone."/"There is nobody/no one."

Mana(-n), (kay-pi) mana pi-pas ka-n-chu. No, there is<u>n't</u> <u>anybody/anyone</u> (here)./No, there is <u>nobody/no one</u> (here).

<u>ni-pi</u> no one/not anybody/not anyone
not even who

---

28. **¿Limamanchu kay kamiyun rin?** Does this truck go to Lima?
     ¿Lima-man-chu kay kamiyun ri-n?
     Lima-to/toward/in the direction of-(question marker) this truck go-it?

Expansion:

Variant of "truck"

¿Lima-man-chu kay <u>kamiyun</u> ri-n? Does this <u>truck</u> go to Lima?

tañu rampana truck
flat litter

---

29. **¿Limapi kay awtuwus sayanqachu?** Will this bus stop in Lima?
     ¿Lima-pi kay awtuwus saya-nqa-chu?
     Lima-in this bus stop-it will-(question marker)?

NOTES

1. The ending for a command to one person is the same as that of the infinitive of the verb (the "to" form of a verb). Context in writing or tone of voice distinguishes one from another:
    uyari-y to listen
    ¡Uyari-y! Listen! (addressing one person)
    The ending for a command to more than one person is **-y-cheh**.
    ¡Uyari-y-cheh! Listen! (addressing more than one person)

2. In calling someone's attention, if the possessive suffix **-y**, "my," is added to a noun, the last syllable of the word is stressed. However, if **-y**, "my," is added to the end of a noun that is not used to attract attention, the stress remains on the next to the last syllable, and thus no accent mark is used in writing. Compare:
    siñura "lady"
    ¡Siñura! "Ma'am!" (formal)

      siñura-y "my lady"
      ¡**Siñurá-y!** "Lady!", "Ma'am!" (formal)
And compare:
      kumpari compadre, pal
      ¡**Kumpari!** "Compadre!", "Pal!"
      kumpari-y "my compadre", "my pal"
      ¡**Kumparí-y!** "Compadre!", "Pal!"

3. The use of **-y**, "my," adds warmth or a degree of friendliness to shorten social distance.
      ¡**Siñurá-y!** Ma'am! (formal)
      Lady-my!
      ¡**Siñur-ní-y!** Sir! (formal)
      Lord-(euphonic particle)-my!

A greater degree of warmth or affection can be brought to a few nouns by adding **-y**, "my," to their diminutive form.
      ¡**Mama!** Ma'am! (informal)
      (Mom)/Ma'am!
      ¡**Mamá-y!** Ma'am!, My lady! (informal)
      (Mom-my)/Ma'am!
      ¡**Mamitá-y!** Ma'am! (informal, with a greater degree of friendliness)
      (Mommy-my)/Ma'am!

      ¡**Tata!** Sir! (informal)
      (Dad)/Sir!
      ¡**Tatá-y!** Sir!, My lord! (informal)
      (Dad-my)/Sir!
      ¡**Tatitú-y!** Sir! (informal, with a greater degree of friendliness)
      (Daddy-my)/Sir!

      ¡**Wawa!** Baby!/Child!/(Little) boy!/(Little) girl!
      ¡**Wawá-y!** My baby!/My child!/My (little) boy!/My (little) girl!
      ¡**Wawitá-y!** My little baby!/My little child!/My little boy!/My little girl! (with a greater degree of affection)
      Baby little-my!

For more on diminutives, see number 9. Diminutives, in Section III: Quechua Grammar Notes.

4. **Wiraqocha** (Viracocha), also known as **T'ehsi Wiraqocha**, **Pachakuteh** and **Qhon**, was the Incas' primary deity, the World Creator. The name **Wiraqocha** was also taken by **Ripah Yupanki Inca**, the eighth and last Lord of Cuzco, whose son, **Pachakuteh** (Pachacuti) (ruled 1438-1471) was the first Inca emperor.

5. The female parallel to **Wiraqocha**, usually used just in referring to a person, not in addressing someone, is **Wiraqocha-h warmi-n**, literally "Wiraqocha-of woman-his."

6. Remember that a question that begins with an interrogative word, such as **¿Imayna?**, "How?"; **¿Ima?**, "What?"; **¿Mayqen?**, "Which?"; **¿Pi?**, "Who?"; and so on, does not use **-chu**. If there is no interrogative word to formulate the question, as is the case here, **-chu** is needed. It usually is affixed to the main verb of the question. Compare:

    ¿Kastillanu-ta rima-nki-chu? Do you speak Spanish? (emphasis on "you")
    Castilian/Spanish-(direct object marker) speak-you(one person)-(question marker)?

    ¿Kastillanu-ta-chu rima-nki? Do you speak Spanish? (emphasis on "Spanish")
    Castilian/Spanish-(direct object marker)-(question marker) speak-you(one person)?

    [Note: Any question that can be answered with yes or no will need **-chu** in it; any that must be answered otherwise will not use **-chu**.]

7. One of the functions of the suffix **-ta** is to indicate that the word to which it is affixed is the direct object of the verb, the person or thing that answers the question "who?" or "what?" is affected by the action of the verb. Here, "what" you speak is Spanish. Thus "Spanish" is the direct object of "speak."

8. There are two verbs for "to speak," **rima-y** and **parla-y**. The latter is a borrowing from the old Spanish *parlar*, and is the one commonly used in Bolivia.

9. **Runasimi** is from **runa**, "man," "people," and **simi**, "language," "tongue." It can be found written as one word, as here, or as two words, **runa simi**.

10. **Pisi** means "little (in amount)." **Pisi-cha** and **pisi-situ** are diminutive forms meaning "very little," "a little bit." (The **situ** in the latter construction is an adaptation of the Spanish diminutive ending *-ito*.) For more on diminutives, see number 9. Diminutives, in Section III: Quechua Grammar Notes.

11. The suffix **-n** found here in **mana(-n)** is a variant of the suffix **-min** (see Notes 7 and 13 in Chapter 1). While the **-n** is often used also as a euphonic particle, in some cases it could be considered either euphonic or emphatic. In this book, due to the context of the construction, with the word **mana** it is designated as emphatic.

12. The suffix **-na** (or infix **-na-**), which is affixed to the stem of a verb (the infinitive, the "to" form, minus the final **-y**), has several functions and therefore meanings. Here it is used to form a noun that designates the thing used to fulfill the action expressed by the verb stem to which it is attached.

> **mikhu-y** to eat
> *eat-to*
> **mikhu-na** something to eat, something edible, food

> **uhya-y** to drink
> *drink-to*
> **uhya-na** something to drink, something drinkable, a drink

[Note: After this Expansion, this **-na** will not be separated from any verb stem to which it is affixed. For example, **mikhu-na** will be written **mikhuna**.]

13. Often the infinitive, the "to" form, of a Quechua verb is also a noun (nominalized infinitive). Although the infinitive and noun are identical in form and meaning in Quechua, the English translation will differ according to whether the word is used as a noun or a verb. Here, for the sake of clarity, a distinction is made between the two. A hyphen is used with the verb to separate the verb root from its infinitive marker **-y** ("to"). In spoken Quechua, of course, and in written Quechua where hyphens are not used, context will dictate if the word is a verb or a noun. Compare:

> **mikhu-y** to eat
> *eat-to*
> **mikhuy** eating; food (something edible)

> **uhya-y** to drink
> *drink-to*
> **uhyay** drinking; a drink (something drinkable)

14. **Ururu**, Oruro: Capital of the Department of Oruro, Bolivia. Founded in 1604. Formerly capital of the country. Mining center. Altitude:12,119 feet above sea level. About 120 miles south-southeast of La Paz, the present-day seat of the executive and legislative branches of the Bolivian government. (The judicial branch is in Sucre.)

15. The suffix **-man** means "toward," "to." The suffix **-ta**, usually used to indicate the direct object of a verb, can also meant "to." Some speakers make a distinction between **-man** and **-ta**, using **-man** only for "toward," "in the direction of," "headed to," and **-ta** for "to," indicating reaching the place designated. Compare:

> **Ururu-man ri-n.** He/She/It goes, is going, to/toward Oruro (in that direction).

Ururu-ta ri-n. He/She/It goes, is going, to Oruro (arrival there expected).

Of course, context can dictate the meaning of **-man**, for a ticket **Ururu-man** obviously would be one to take the traveler all the way to Oruro, not just in that direction.

In this book, **-ta** and **-man** are used interchangeably.

16. **Ka-n**, "there is," "there are," is from **ka-y**, "to be," "for there to be." **Ka-n** also has the meaning "is," but with this meaning it always is omitted and just understood, as has frequently been pointed out before. Compare:
    Pidru suti-y. My name is Pedro.
    Pedro name-my. ("Is" is understood.)
    Unu ka-n. There is water.
    Water be-it[there is].

17. Compare:
    Unu-ta muna-ni. I want water.
    AND
    ¿Unu ka-n-chu? Is there water?
    Unu ka-n. There is water.

    In the first sentence, "water" is the direct object of "want" because it tells "what" I want, so the direct object marker **-ta** is affixed to **unu**. However, forms of "to be" and "for there to be," as in the one that means "there is" and "there are," do not take a direct object. Thus, in the second and third examples there is no **-ta** with **unu**.

18. Personal or regional preference dictates which of the three ways to say "there is" and "there are," **ka-n** (from **ka-y**), **tia-n** (from **tia-y**), or **tiya-n** (from **tiya-y**), is used.

19. Note that here the question marker, **-chu**, rather than following the verb, is placed after the phrase for "restaurant" in order to place emphasis on that. Compare:
    ¿Kay-neh-pi uh mikhuy-wasi ka-n-chu? Is there a restaurant around here?
    ¿Kay-neh-pi uh mikhuy-wasi-chu ka-n? Is there a restaurant around here?

20. Compare the following:
    kay here
    kay-pi here, (in/at) here (much more commonly used than **kay** alone)
    here-in/at
    kay-neh-pi around here
    here-around-in/at

Words and phrases denoting location usually have attached to them some suffix such as **-pi**, "in/at," as seen here. (See Note 7 of Chapter 5.)

21. **Plasa** and **mirkadu** are from the Spanish *plaza*, meaning "town square," and *mercado*, "market." To refer to places or things found in metropolitan areas or to places or things that appeared after the arrival of the Spaniards, such as post offices and railroad stations, take and adapt a Spanish word.

22. As was pointed out above, the suffix **-na** (or infix **-na-**), which is affixed to the stem of a verb (the infinitive, the "to" form, minus the final **-y**), has several functions and therefore meanings. Here, it is used to form a word that designates the place where the action expressed by the verb stem to which it is attached usually takes place. For example:
    hisp'a-y to urinate
    hisp'a-na place to urinate, latrine, bathroom, lavatory, restroom, water closet, toilet

    mikhu-y to eat
    mikhu-na place to eat, dining room [Note that **mikhu-na** (or **mihuna**) can have this meaning as well as that of "food."]
    From here on, this **-na** will not be separated from any verb stem to which it is affixed. For example, **hisp'a-na** will be **hisp'ana**.

23. Note that **puñuna**, "bed," is **puñu-na**, "sleep-(marker to designate the place where the action expressed by the verb stem to which it is attached usually takes place)," based on the stem of **puñu-y**, "to sleep."

24. If more than one person is involved but each person has or is using only one of the items under consideration, the singular form of the word for that item is used. However, if people are to share one item, a word for "a" or "an," **uh** or one of its variants, is used with the noun designating the item. Compare:
    Puñuna ñoqancheh-pah ka-n. There are beds for us (including the person[s] addressed). (Each person has a bed.)
    Uh puñuna ñoqancheh-pah ka-n. There is a bed for us (including the person[s] addressed). (Two people share one bed.).]

25. This **-ri** adds the idea of an "and" or "then" that prolongs a statement or question without adding any specific meaning of its own. "And who is there here?" or "Then who is there here?" is the idea of ¿**Pi-chá-ri kay-pi ka-n.?** "Is there anybody/somebody here?"

SECTION II
Model Sentences and Their Expansions

Chapter 3

This chapter deals with
A. Social Courtesies [Model Sentences 1-13]
B. Ways to Cope in a Conversation [14-29]

A. SOCIAL COURTESIES

1. **Allichu.** Please. (idiomatic)

   ### Expansion:
   Various ways to say "Please"

   Allichu. Please.
   Ama hina-chu ka-wah. Please.
   Not(used in prohibitions in conjunction with a form of the conditional) thus-(negative marker) be-you(one person) would.
   Ama hina ka-y-chu. Please.
   Not(used in commands) thus be-(command marker addressing one person)-(negative marker).

2. **Anchata agradisiyki.**[1] I thank you very much.
   Ancha-ta agradisi-yki.
   Much-(adverb marker) thank-I (to) you(one person).

   ### Expansion A:
   Various ways to thank people
   Ancha-ta agradisi-yki. I <u>thank</u> you (addressing one person) very much.

Ancha-ta agradisi-yki-cheh.[2] I thank you (addressing more than one person) very much.
Much-(adverb marker) thank-(dual maker for "I (to) you[more than one person]").

Ancha-ta sonqo(n)cha thank
Much-(adverb marker)grateful for a favor[thank]
Ancha-ta sullpa thank
Much-(adverb marker) thank
Alli-cha thank
Good-make(what the noun or adjective to which it is attached is)
Alli-cha-pu[3] thank for it
Good-make(what the noun or adjective to which it is attached is)-it

Diyus paga-pu-so-nqa.[4] Thank you (addressing one person). (for a favor) [-su- > -so-]
God pay/reward-it-(dual marker for "He will [to]) you[one person]").
Diyus paga-pu-so-nqa-cheh.[5] Thank you (addressing more than one person). (for a favor) [-su- > -so-]
God pay/reward-it-(triple marker for "He will [to] you[more than one person]").

¡Sullpa! Thanks!

Expansion B:

Ways to thank people for different things or actions

Ancha-ta agradisi-yki. I thank you (addressing one person) very much.
Ancha-ta agradisi-yki tukuy ima-rayku. I thank you (addressing one person) very much for everything.
Much-(adverb marker) thank-I (to) you(one person) all thing-for/because of.

wulitu-rayku for the ticket
ticket-for/because of ("The" is understood.)
yanapa-yki-rayku for your help
help-your(one person)-for/because of

Ancha-ta agradisi-yki-cheh. I thank you (addressing more than one person) very much.
Much-(adverb marker) thank-(dual marker for "I [to] you[more than one person]").

Ancha-ta agradisi-yki-cheh tukuy ima-rayku. I thank you (addressing more than one person) very much for everything.
Much-(adverb marker) thank-(dual marker for "I [to] you[more than one person]") all thing-for/because of.

<u>yanapa-ykicheh-rayku</u> for your (more than one person) help
help-your(more than one person)-for/because of

3. **Mana imamanta.** You're welcome.
   Mana ima-manta.
   No thing-from.

Expansion:

Various ways to say "You're welcome."

Mana ima-manta. You're welcome.
Ni ima-manta. You're welcome.
No thing-from.
Hina-lla-ta-pis. You're welcome.
Thus-just-(adverb marker)-any.

---

4. **Pantasqa kasani.** I am mistaken.
   Panta-sqa kasa-ni.
   Mistake-(past participle marker, "-ed")[Mistaken] be-I.

Expansion:

"I am mistaken."
"We are mistaken."

Panta-sqa kasa-<u>ni</u>. <u>I</u> am mistaken.
Panta-sqa kasa-<u>yku</u>. <u>We (excluding the person[s] addressed)</u> are mistaken.
Mistake-(past participle marker, "-ed")[Mistaken] be-we(excluding the person[s] addressed).

---

5. **Ama manchakuychu.** Don't worry (addressing one person).
   Ama mancha-ku-y-chu.
   Not(used in a command) worry-self-(command marker addressing one person)-(negative marker).

Expansion:

Various ways to tell people not to worry.

Ama mancha-ku-y-chu. Don't worry (addressing one person).
Ama mancha-ku-y-cheh-chu. Don't worry (addressing more than one person).

Ama chay-manta-qa mancha-ku-y-chu. Don't worry about that (addressing one person).
Not(used in a command) that-about-(emphatic particle) worry-self-(command marker addressing one person)-(negative marker).
Ama chay-manta-qa mancha-ku-y-cheh-chu. Don't worry about that (addressing more than one person).
Not(used in a command) that-about-(emphatic particle) worry-selves-(dual command marker addressing more than one person)-(negative marker).

6. **Allillan.** Fine.
Alli-lla-n.
Well-just-(euphonic particle).

Expansion:

Various ways to say "Fine."

Alli-lla-n. Fine.
Alli-lla-n-chu. Fine, that's all.
Well-just-(euphonic particle)-(negative marker, added to convey, in conjunction with -lla-, the idea of "that's all").

Waleh-lla. Fine.
Fine-just.
Waleh-lla puni. Very fine./Very well.
Fine-just very.

7. **Panpachaway.**[6,7] Excuse me (apologizing to one person).
Panpa-cha-wa-y.
Flat-make(what the noun or adjective is to which it is attached is)-to me-(command marker addressing one person).

Expansion:

Variants of
"Excuse me (apologizing)."
"Excuse us (apologizing)."

Panpa-cha-wa-y. Excuse me (apologizing to one person).

Panpa-cha-wa-y-cheh. Excuse me (apologizing to more than one person).
Flat-make(what the noun or adjective is to which it is attached is)-to me-(dual command marker addressing more than one person).

Panpa-cha-wa-yku-y.[8] Excuse us (apologizing to one person).
Flat-make(what the noun or adjective is to which it is attached is)-(dual marker for "to us [excluding the person[s] addressed]")-(command marker addressing one person).

Panpa-cha-wa-yku-y-cheh. Excuse us (apologizing to more than one person).
Flat-make(what the noun or adjective is to which it is attached is)-(dual marker for "to us [excluding the person[s] addressed ")-(dual command marker addressing more than one person).

8. **Pasachillaway, mamáy.** Excuse me, ma'am. (used in asking permission, as in stepping in front of someone)
Pasa-chi-lla-wa-y, mamá-y.
Pass-make(what the meaning of the verb is)-just-me-(command marker addressing one person), lady-my.

Expansion:

Variants of
"Excuse me (asking permission)."
"Excuse us (asking permission)."

Pasa-chi-lla-wa-y, mamá-y. Excuse me, ma'am. (used in asking permission, as in stepping in front of someone)
Pasa-chi-lla-wa-y-cheh. Excuse me (addressing more than one person). (used in asking permission, as in stepping in front of someone)

Pasa-chi-lla-wa-yku-y. Excuse us (addressing one person). (used in asking permission, as in stepping in front of someone)
Pasa-chi-lla-wa-yku-y-cheh. Excuse us (addressing more than one person). (used in asking permission, as in stepping in front of someone)

9. **¿Wasiykiman yaykuymanchu?** Could I come in your (one person) house?
¿Wasi-yki-man yayku-y-man-chu?
House-your(one person)-to/toward enter-(dual marker for "I could")-(question marker)?

Expansion:

Requesting permission for you and/or your companion(s) to go into someone's house.

¿Wasi-yki-man yayku-y-man-chu? Could I come in your (one person) house?

¿Wasi-ykicheh-man yayku-y-man-chu? Could I come in your (more than one person) house?
House-your(more than one person)-to/toward enter-(dual marker for "I could")-(question marker)?

¿Wasi-yki-man yayku-yku-man-chu? Could we come in your (one person) house?
House-your(one person)-to/toward enter-(dual marker for "we[excluding the person(s) addressed] could")-(question marker)?

¿Wasi-ykicheh-man yayku-yku-man-chu? Could we come in your (more than one person) house?
House-your(more than one person)-to/toward enter-(dual marker for "we[excluding the person(s) addressed] could")-(question marker)?

10. **Imamanaqa.** Why not?/Of course!
Ima-mana-qa.
What-not-certainly.

11. **Walehlla. Yaykumullay.** Fine. Come in (addressing one person).
Waleh-lla. Yayku-mu-lla-y.
Fine-just. Enter-in this direction[Come in]-just-(command marker addressing one person).

Expansion:

Various ways to say "Come in!"

Waleh-lla. Yayku-mu-lla-y. Fine. Come in (addressing one person).
Waleh-lla. Yayku-mu-lla-y-cheh. Fine. Come in (addressing more than one person).

¡Pasa-ku-y! Come in (addressing one person)!
Pass-self-(command marker addressing one person)!
¡Pasa-ku-y-cheh! Come in (addressing more than one person)!
Pass-selves-(dual command marker addressing more than one person)!

¡Pasa-ka-mu-y! Come in (addressing one person)! [-ku- > -ka-]
Pass-(self)-in this direction[Come in]-(command marker addressing one person)!

¡**Pasa-ka-mu-y-cheh**! Come in (addressing more than one person)! [**-ku- > -ka-**]
Pass-(selves)-in this direction[Come in]-(dual command marker addressing more than one person)!

12. **Allichu, uh ratulla suyay.** Please wait a minute/moment (addressing one person).
    Allichu, uh ratu-lla suya-y.
    Please, a little while-just wait-(command marker addressing one person).

Expansion:

"Please, wait a minute/moment (addressing one person)."
"Please, wait a minute/moment (addressing more than one person)."

Allichu, uh ratu-lla suya-y. Please, wait a minute/moment (addressing one person).
Please, a little while-just wait-(command marker addressing one person).

Allichu, uh ratu-lla suya-y-cheh. Please, wait a minute/moment (addressing more than one person).
Please, a little while-just wait-(dual command marker addressing more than one person).

---

13. **Tiarikuy.**[9,10] Please, sit down (addressing one person).
    Tia-ri-ku-y.
    Sit-(particle that softens the request/"please")-self-(command marker addressing one person).

Expansion:

"Please, sit down (addressing one person)."
"Please, sit down (addressing more than one person)."

Tia-ri-ku-y. Please, sit down (addressing one person).
Sit-(particle that softens the request/"please")-self-(command marker addressing one person).

Tia-ri-ku-y-cheh. Please, sit down (addressing more than one person).
Sit-(particle that softens the request/"please")-selves-(dual command marker addressing more than one person).

B. WAYS TO COPE IN A CONVERSATION

14. **¿Runasimita rimankichu?** Do you speak Quechua?
    Runasimi-ta rima-nki-chu?
    Man speech[Quechua]-(direct object marker) speak-you(one person)-(question marker)?

Expansion:
Asking if different people speak Quechua

¿Runasimi-ta rima-nki-chu? Do you (one person) speak Quechua?

rima-n he/she speaks
rima-nki-cheh you (more than one person) speak
rima-nku they speak

---

15. **Arí, uh pisichallata rimani.** Yes, I speak just a little.
    Arí, uh pisi-cha-lla-ta rima-ni.
    Yes, a little-(diminutive marker)-just-(direct object marker) speak-I.

Expansion:
Telling that different people speak just a little

Uh pisi-cha-lla-ta rima-ni. I speak just a little.

rima-nki you (one person) speak
rima-n he/she speaks
rima-yku we (excluding the person[s] addressed) speak
rima-ncheh we (including the person[s] addressed) speak
rima-nki-cheh you (more than one person) speak
rima-nku they speak

---

16. **Mana(n). (Ñoqa) mana runasimita rimanichu. Inles(lla)ta rimani.**
    No. I don't speak Quechua. I just speak English.
    Mana(-n). (Ñoqa) mana runasimi-ta rima-ni-chu. Inles(-lla)-ta rima-ni.
    No(-emphatic particle). (I) not Quechua-(direct object marker) speak-I-(negative marker). English(-just)-(direct object marker) speak-I.

Expansion:
Mana(n). (Ñoqa) mana runasimita rimanichu. Inles(lla)ta rimani.
No. I don't speak Quechua. I just speak English.

Aliman German

Hapunis Japanese
Inles (Inlis) English
Kastillanu Spanish
Swiku Swedish

---

17. **Runasimita yachakusani.**[11] I am learning Quechua.
    Runasimi-ta yacha-ku-sa-ni.
    Quechua-(direct object marker) know-for self[learn]-(progressive marker, "-ing")[learning]-I.

18. **¡Allichu, allillanmanta rima(wa)y!** Please, speak slowly (to me)!
    ¡Allichu, alli-lla-n-manta rima(-wa)-y!
    Please, good-just-(euphonic particle)-(adverb marker)[well] speak(-to me)-(command marker addressing one person)!

Expansion:

Some other ways to ask someone to speak slowly

¡Allichu, <u>alli-lla-n-manta</u> rima(-wa)-y! Please, speak <u>slowly</u> (to me)!
¡Allichu, <u>alli-lla-n-manta</u> rima-y! Please, speak <u>slowly</u>!
Please, good-just-(euphonic particle)-(adverb marker)[well] speak-(command marker addressing one person)!

¡Allichu, <u>alli-lla-n-wan</u> rima(-wa)-y! Please, speak <u>slowly</u> (to me)!
Please, good-just-(euphonic particle)-with speak(-to me)-(command marker addressing one person)!
¡Allichu, <u>alli-lla-n-wan</u> rima-y! Please, speak <u>slowly</u>!
Please, good-just-(euphonic particle)-with speak-(command marker addressing one person)!

---

19. **Allichu, uhtawan ni(wa)y.** Please, repeat (to me).
    Allichu, uh-ta-wan ni(-wa)-y.
    Please, one-(marker for number of times)-with[again] say/tell(-to me)-(command marker addressing one person).

Expansion:

Other ways to ask someone to repeat

Allichu, <u>uh-ta-wan</u> ni(-wa)-y. Please, repeat (to me)./Please tell (me) <u>again</u>.
Allichu, <u>wateh(manta)</u> ni(-wa)-y. Please, repeat (to me)./Please tell (me) <u>again</u>.
Please, again say/tell(-to me)-(command marker addressing one person).

Allichu, simi-kuna-yki-ta <u>uh-ta-wan</u> ni(-wa)-y. Please, repeat your words (to me)./Please say your words (to me) <u>again</u>.
Please, word-(plural marker)-your(one person)-(direct object marker) one-(marker for number of times)-with[again] say/tell(-to me)-(command marker addressing one person).

Allichu, simi-kuna-yki-ta <u>wateh(manta)</u> ni(-wa)-y. Please, repeat your words (to me)./Please say your words (to me) <u>again</u>.
Please, word-(plural marker)-your(one person)-(direct object marker) again say/tell(-to me)-(command marker addressing one person).

20. **(Ñoqa) simisniykita mana hap'inichu.** I don't understand you.
(Ñoqa) simi-s-ni-yki-ta mana hap'i-ni-chu.
(I) word-s-(euphonic particle)-your(one person)-(direct object marker) not grasp-I-(negative marker).

Expansion:

Other ways to say "I don't understand you."

(Ñoqa) <u>simi-s</u>-ni-yki-ta mana hap'i-ni-chu. I don't understand you.
(I) <u>word-s</u>-(euphonic particle)-your(one person)-(direct object marker) not grasp-I-(negative marker). OR

(Ñoqa) <u>simi-kuna</u>-ni-yki-ta mana hap'i-ni-chu. I don't understand you.
(I) <u>word-(plural marker)</u>-(euphonic particle)-your(one person)-(direct object marker) not grasp-I-(negative marker).

(Ñoqa) <u>palawra-s</u>-ni-yki-ta mana hap'i-ni-chu.[12] I don't understand you.
(I) <u>word-s</u>-(euphonic particle)-your(one person)-(direct object marker) not grasp-I-(negative marker).

21. **¿Imata nisan?** What is he/she saying?
¿Ima-ta ni-sa-n?
What-(direct object marker) say-(progressive marker, "-ing")-he/she?

Expansion:

Asking what different people are saying
¿Ima-ta ni-sa-<u>n</u>? What is <u>he/she</u> saying?

ni-sa-<u>nku</u> are <u>they</u> saying
ni-sa-<u>nki</u> are <u>you (one person)</u> saying
ni-sa-<u>nki-cheh</u> are <u>you (more than one person)</u> saying

22. **Mana yachanichu.** I don't know.
    Mana yacha-ni-chu.
    Not know-I-(negative marker).

23. **Imata nisasqan mana yachanichu.** I don't know what he/she is saying.
    Ima-ta ni-sa-sqa-n mana yacha-ni-chu.
    What-(direct object marker) say-(progressive marker, "-ing")-(particle to form the passive [or past] participle for the present and past, used in a construction that in English is introduced by a relative pronoun, often "what," "that," or "which," when the verb denotes what someone or something did or is doing)-his/her[here, showing who is doing the saying, "he/she"] not know-I-(negative marker).

Expansion:

"I don't know <u>what he/she is saying</u>."
"I don't know <u>what he/she said/has said</u>."
"I don't know <u>what he/she will say</u>."

<u>**Ima-ta ni-sa-sqa-n**</u> mana yacha-ni-chu. I don't know <u>what he/she is saying</u>.

<u>**Ima-ta ni-sa-sqa-n**</u> What he/she said/has said
What-(direct object marke)r say-(progressive marker, "-ing")-(particle to form the passive [or past] participle for the present and past, used in a construction that in English is introduced by a relative pronoun, often "what," "that," or "which," when the verb denotes what someone or something did or is doing)-his/her[here, showing who said/has said, "he/she"]

<u>**Ima-ta ni-sa-na-n**</u> What he/she will say
What-(direct object marke)r say-(progressive marker, "-ing")-(particle to form the passive [or past] participle for the future, used in a construction that in English is introduced by a relative pronoun, often "what," "that," or "which," when the verb denotes what someone or something will do)-his/her[here, showing who will say, "he/she"]

[Note: In these constructions (relative clause constructions), the one performing the action is indicated by a possessive particle affixed to the verb. If the one who is doing the action is to be clarified or emphasized, the appropriate noun or subject pronoun, with **-pah**, "for," attached precedes the verb, as in these examples:
<u>**Ima-ta pay-pah ni-sa-na-n**</u> What **he/she** will say
<u>**Ima-ta Maria-pah ni-sa-na-n**</u> What **Maria** will say]

24. **¿Ima kastillanupi tutahpata sutin?** How do you say **tuta** ("night") in Spanish?/What is **tuta** ("night") in Spanish?
¿Ima kastillanu-pi tuta-hpata suti-n?
*What Castilian/Spanish-in **tuta**-of name-its? ("Is" is understood.)*

Expansion:

Asking what different things mean in another language

¿Ima kastillanu-pi tuta-hpata suti-n? How do you say **tuta** ("night") in Spanish?/What is **tuta** ("night") in Spanish?

mayo-hpata mayu ("river") [**mayu > mayo**]
mayu("river")-of
mikhu-y-pata ("to eat") mikhu-y ("to eat") [Remember that with any word or phrase that ends in a consonant, a following "of" must be expressed without the "**h**": **-pa** or **-pata**.]
eat-(infinitive marker, "to")-of

¿Ima qheshwa-pi *noche*-hpata suti-n? How do you say *noche* ("night") in Quechua?

río-**hpata** ("river") *río* ("river")
río("river")-of
comer-**pata** ("to eat") *comer* ("to eat") [Remember that with any word or phrase that ends in a consonant, a following "of" must be expressed without the "**h**": **-pa** or **-pata**.]
comer("to eat")-of

---

25. **Kastillanupi tutaqa *noche*.** In Spanish, **tuta** means/is *noche* ("night").
Kastillanu-pi tuta-qa *noche*.
*Spanish-in **tuta**-(emphatic particle) noche. ("Is" is understood.)*

26. **¿Ima kaypata sutin?** What do you call this?
¿Ima kay-pata suti-n?
What this-of name-its? ("Is" is understood.)

Expansion:

How to ask what things that are pointed out are called in Quechua
¿Ima kay-pata suti-n? What do you call this?
¿Ima qheshwa-pi kay-pata suti-n? What do you call this in Quechua?
What Quechua-in this-of name-its? ("Is" is understood.)

chay that (nearby)
haqay that (over there)

¿Ima **kay-kuna**-hpata suti-n/suti-nku?[13] What do you call these?
What this-(plural marker)[these]-of name-its/name-their? ("Is" is understood.)

¿Ima qheshwa-pi **kay-kuna**-hpata suti-n/suti-nku? What do you call these in Quechua?
What Quechua-in this-(plural marker)[these]-of name-its/name-their? ("Is" is understood.)

chay-kuna those (nearby)
haqay-kuna those (over there)

27. **Kaypata pirwa sutin.** This is called a barn.
Kay-pata pirwa suti-n.
This-of barn name its. ("Is" is understood.)

Expansion:
How to tell what different things are called in Quechua

Kay-pata pirwa suti-n. This is called a barn.
Qheshwa-pi kay-kuna-hpata pirwa suti-n/suti-nku. In Quechua these are called barns.
Quechua-in this-(plural marker)[these]-of barn name-its/name-their. ("Is" is understood.)

chay-kuna those (nearby)
haqay-kuna those (over there)

28. ¿Ima "Winas nuchis" **niyta munan?** What does **Winas nuchis** mean?
¿Ima "Winas nuchis" ni-y-ta muna-n?
What "Winas nuchis" say-(infinitive marker, "to")-(direct object marker) want-it?

29. **Chay,** "Good evening" **niyta munan.** That means "good evening."
Chay, "Good evening" ni-y-ta muna-n.
That, "Good evening" say-(infinitive marker, "to")-(direct object marker) want-it.

NOTES

1. Quechua has some special verbal forms that include in them the personal object pronouns "(to) me," "(to) us," "(to) you (one person)," and "(to) you (more than one person)." In this Model Sentence,
Ancha-ta agradisi-yki. I thank you very much.

Much-(adverb marker) thank-I (to) you(one person),
as is seen in the literal translation, the ending **-yki** conveys the idea of "I (to) you (one person)." For more on this, see number 18. Model for Verbs that Include (Pronominally) the Verbal Object "You (One Person)," in Section III: Quechua Grammar Notes.

2. As was pointed out in Note 1 above, Quechua has some special verbal forms that include in them the personal object pronouns "(to) me," "(to) us," "(to) you (one person)," and "(to) you (more than one person)." In this Model Sentence,

   Ancha-ta agradisi-yki-cheh. I thank you (addressing more than one person) very much.
   Much-(adverb marker) thank-(dual maker for "I (to) you[more than one person]"),

   as is seen in the literal translation, the ending **-yki-cheh** conveys the idea of "I (to) you (more than one person)." For more on this, see number 19. Model for Verbs that Include (Periphrastically and Pronominally) the Verbal Object "You (More Than One Person)," in Section III: Quechua Grammar Notes.

3. As was pointed out in Note 1 above, Quechua has some special verbal forms that include in them the personal object pronouns "(to) me," "(to) us," "(to) you (one person)," and "(to) you (more than one person)." They have the same form for both direct and indirect objects. (See the following note for explanation of direct and indirect.)

   [Note: Direct objects answer the question "whom?" or "what?" in relationship to the verb, while indirect objects answer the question "to whom?" or "for whom?" For instance, in Chapter 5 we find the following two sentences.

   Allichu, midiku-man pusa-wa-y. Please, take me to a/the doctor (addressing one person).
   ("Me" answers the question "whom" is to be taken, thus showing it is a direct object.)
   Allichu, unu-ta qo-wa-y. Please, give me water (addressing one person).
   ("Me answers the question "to whom" the "water" (the direct object) is to be given, thus showing it is an indirect object.)]

   When one of these verbal constructions is used with the person being the indirect object, if the direct object "it" or "them" is also to be included, the infix **-pu-** ("it," "them") is added after the verb stem. (For these dual pronomial constructions, see number 11. Introduction to Complex Verbs in Section III: Quechua Grammar Notes.)

   Alli-cha-yki. (I) thank you.

> *Good-make(what the noun or adjective to which it is attached is)-I (to) you(one person).*
> **Alli-cha-pu-yki.** (I) thank you for it.
> *Good-make(what the noun or adjective to which it is attached is)-it-I (to) you(one person).*

4. As was pointed out in Note 1 above, Quechua has some special verbal forms that include in them the objects "(to) me," "(to) us," "(to) you (one person)," and "(to) you (more than one person)." Here the **-so-nqa** conveys the idea of "Him to you (one person)." For more on these constructions, see number 18. Model for Verbs that Include (Pronominally) the Verbal Object "You (One Person)" in Section III: Quechua Grammar Notes.

5. As seen in Note 4 above, the **-so-nqa** construction conveys the idea of "Him to you (one person)." Here we have a triple marker **-so-nqa-cheh** for "He will (to) you (more than one person)." See number 19. Model for Verbs that Include (Periphrastically and Pronominally) the Verbal Object "You (More Than One Person)" in Section III: Quechua Grammar Notes.

6. Here the particle **-cha** is affixed to a noun to create a verb that indicates the making of or filling with what is indicated by that noun. For example:
   wasi house; **wasi-cha-y** to make/build a house
   t'uru mud; **t'uru-cha-y** to make mud; to fill with mud

   Panpa-cha-wa-y, "Excuse me," used in apologizing, as an idiomatic expression that comes from **panpa**, "plain," "level land," "flat land."
   Panpa-cha-wa-y therefore means "make (it) flat for me," referring to flattening, leveling the wrong thing that I may have done, thus making it disappear.

7. When the object of a verb is "me," **-wa-** is affixed to the stem of the verb. (As will be pointed out later, there are two exceptions in the placement of **-wa-**. It is preceded by the direct object "it," "them", **-pu-**, and may be preceded by the progressive marker ["-ing"], **-sa-**. See number 16. Model for Verbs that Include [Pronominally] Verbal Object "Me," in Section III: Quechua Grammar Notes.)

8. When the object of a verb is "us (excluding the person[s] addressed)," **-wa-** is affixed to the stem of simple verb, in the appropriate form, for "we (excluding the person[s] addressed)." Similarly, if the object is "us (including the person[s] addressed," **-wa-** is affixed to the stem of simple verb, in the appropriate form, for "we (including the person[s] addressed)."

9. You will remember that the verb **tia-y** and its variant **tiya-y** used impersonally mean "for there to be," as in
>**Unu ti(y)a-n(-mi).** There is water.
>*Water be-it[there is](-particle of certainty or assurance).*

The reflexive form of these two verbs, which have **-ku-**, "self," "selves," between the stem and the "to" ending, **-y**, **tia-ku-y**, and **tiya-ku-y**, can mean "to sit," "to reside," "to live," or, by extension, "to stay," as in
>**Ti(y)a-ri-ku-y.** Please, sit down (addressing one person).
>*Sit-(particle that softens the request/"please")-self-(command marker addressing one person).*
>**Uh llahta-pi ti(y)a-ku-ni.** I live in a town.
>*A town-in reside/live-self-I.*
>**Chay util-pi ti(y)a-ku-ni.** I'm staying at that hotel.
>*That hotel-in/at stay-self-I.*

10. Compare **-ri-** and **-rí**:
The infix **-ri-**, which has no accent, is used with a verb to soften a request, adding the concept of "please."
>**Tiya-ri-ku-y.** Please, sit down (addressing one person).
>*Sit-(particle that softens the request/"please")-self-(command marker addressing one person).*

The suffix **-rí**, which has an accent, means "and," with a contrastive nuance.
>**Pidru(-m) suti-y. ¿Qan-pata-rí?** My name is Pedro. And yours?
>*Pedro(-particle of certainty or assurance) name-my. You-of[Yours]-and(with a contrastive nuance)? ("Is" is understood.)*

11. A verb can be made progressive by adding the equivalent of English "-ing," **-sa-** or its variants **-chka-**, **-sha-**, **-shka-**, **-ska-**, **-skia-**, **-sia-**, and **-sya-**. (In this book **-sa-** is used for simplicity.)

A progressive form places emphasis on an action in progress. See number 12. Verbs Expressing Action or State of Being in Progress (Progressive Verbs) in Section III: Quechua Grammar Notes. Compare:
>**Yacha-ku-ni.** I learn.
>*Know-for self-I.*
>**Yacha-ku-sa-ni.** I am learning.
>*Know-for-self-(progressive marker, "-ing")-I.*

And in sentence 21, we have
>**¿Ima-ta ni-sa-n?** What is he/she saying?

What-(direct object marker) say-(progressive marker, "-ing")-he/she?

Compare that with

¿Ima-ta ni-n? What does he/she say?
What-(direct object marker) say-he/she?

12. Instead of **simi-s** or **simi-kuna**, one can hear **palawra-s**, a borrowing from the Spanish for "word," *palabra*.

13. In this and similar questions and answers, instead of **suti-nku**, "their name," **suti-n**, "its name," is often used.

SECTION II

Model Sentences and Their Expansions

Chapter 4

> This chapter deals with topics for small talk (for talking with someone on a bus, with someone in a village, and the like)
>
> A. Where People Are From/Live/Stay [Model Sentences 1-6]
> B. Where People Are Going and Where They Are Coming From [7-10]
> C. Family [11-18]
> D. What People Do for a Living [19-28]
> E. Knowing People, Places, Information, and Skills [29-38]

A. WHERE PEOPLE ARE FROM/LIVE/STAY

1. **¿Maymanta kanki?** Where are you from?
   ¿May-manta ka-nki?
   Where-from be-you(one person)?

Expansion:

"Where are you from?"
"Where are you (more than one person) from?"

¿May-manta ka-nki? Where are <u>you (one person)</u> from?
¿May-manta ka-nki-cheh? Where are <u>you (more than one person)</u> from?
Where-from be-you(more than one person)?

---

2. **Perumanta kani.** I am from Peru.
   Peru-manta ka-ni.
   Peru-from be-I.

Expansion:

"We are from . . ."
"I am from . . ., and/but he/she is from . . ."
We are from . . ., and/but they are from . . . "

Peru-manta ka-ni. I am from Peru.
Peru-manta ka-yku. We are from Peru.
Peru-from be-we(excluding the person[s] addressed).

(Ñoqa) Peru-manta ka-ni, pay-rí Wuliwya-manta. I am from Peru, and/but he/she is from Bolivia.
(I) Peru-from be-I, he/she-and(with a contrastive nuance)/but Bolivia-from. ("Is" is understood.)

(Ñoqayku) Peru-manta ka-yku, pay-kuna-rí Ikwadur-manta (ka-nku). We are from Peru, and/but they are from Ecuador.
(We[excluding the person(s) addressed]) Peru-from be-we(excluding the person[s] addressed), he/she-(plural marker)[they] and(with a contrastive nuance)/but Ecuador-from (be-they).

---

3. **¿Maypi tiakunki?**[1] Where do you live?
   ¿May-pi tia-ku-nki?
   Where-in/at live/reside-self-you(one person)?

4. **Uh llahtapi tiakuni.** I live in a town
   Uh llahta-pi tia-ku-ni.
   A town-in live/reside-self-I.

Expansion:

Where people live

Uh llahta-pi tia-ku-ni. I live in a town.

Uh hatun llahta-pi in a city
A large town-in

Kay llahta-pi in this town
This town-in
Kay-pi here
Here-in/at
Kay-pe-qa here (with emphasis) [**-pi-** > **-pe-**]
Here-in/at-(emphatic particle)

5. **¿Maypi tiakunki?** Where are you staying? (This question is identical to number 3 above, where it has the meaning "Where do you live?" Context will dictate the meaning.)
¿May-pi tia-ku-nki?
Where-at stay-self-you(one person)?

Expansion:

"Where are you staying?"
"Where are you (more than one person) staying?

¿May-pi tia-ku-nki? Where are <u>you (one person)</u> staying?
¿May-pi tia-ku-nki-cheh? Where are <u>you (more than one person)</u> staying?

---

6. **Chay utilpi tiakuni.** I'm staying at that hotel.
Chay util-pi tia-ku-ni.
That hotel-in/at stay-self-I.

Expansion A:

"I'm staying at that hotel."
"We're staying at that hotel."

Chay util-pi tia-ku-<u>ni</u>. <u>I</u>'m staying at that hotel.
Chay util-pi tia-ku-<u>yku</u>. <u>We</u>'re staying at that hotel.
That hotel-in/at stay-selves-we(excluding the person[s] addressed).

Expansion B:

Places where people are staying

<u>Chay</u> <u>util-pi</u> tia-ku-ni. I'm staying <u>at that hotel</u>.
<u>Chay</u> <u>util-pi</u> tia-ku-yku. We're staying <u>at that hotel</u>.

<u>Chay</u> <u>tampu-wasi-pi</u> at that hotel
<u>Chay</u> <u>qorpachana-wasi-pi</u> at that hotel

Pidro-hpa-pi at Pedro's [**Pidru** > **Pidro**]
Pedro-of-at
Amigu-s-ni-y-pa-pi at my friends' (males or male[s] and female[s]) (house)
Friend-s(males or male[s] and female[s])-(euphonic particle)-my-of-in/at ("House" is understood.)

Amigu-s-ni-yko-hpa-pi at our friends' (males or male[s] and female[s]) (house) [-yku- > -yko-]
Friend-s(males or male[s] and female[s])-(euphonic particle)-our(excluding the person[s] addressed)-of-in/at ("House" is understood.)
Llahta-pi in (a/the) town

B. WHERE PEOPLE ARE GOING AND WHERE THEY ARE COMING FROM

7. **¿Mayman risanki?** Where are you going?
   ¿May-man ri-sa-nki?
   Where-/to/toward go-(progressive marker, "-ing")-you(one person)?

8. **Sukriman risani.**[2] I am going to Sucre.
   Sukri-man ri-sa-ni.
   Sucre-to/toward go-(progressive marker, "-ing")-I.

Expansion A:

Telling that different people or things are going to Sucre.

Sukri-man ri-sa-ni. I am going to Sucre.
Sukri-man ri-sa-nki. You (one person) are going to Sucre.
Sukri-man ri-sa-n. He/She/It is going to Sucre.
Sukri-man ri-sa-yku. We (excluding the person[s] addressed) are going to Sucre.
Sukri-man ri-sa-ncheh. We (including the person[s] addressed) are going to Sucre.
Sukri-man ri-sa-nki-cheh. You (more than one person) are going to Sucre.
Sukri-man ri-sa-nku. They are going to Sucre.

Expansion B:

"I am going to (different places)."
"I am going (in different directions)."

Sukri-man ri-sa-ni. I am going to Sucre.

Hwan-pa-man to Juan's
Juan-of-to/toward

Orqo-kuna-man to the mountains/to the hills
Mountain/hill-[plural marker]-to/toward ("The" is understood.)
Hawa-man outside
Outside-to/toward
Ukhu-man inside
Interior-to/toward

9. **¿Maymanta hamusanki?** Where are you coming from?
   ¿May-manta hamu-sa-nki?
   Where-from come-(progressive marker, "-ing")-you(one person)?

10. **Ururumanta hamusarqani.** I just came from Oruro.
    Ururu-manta hamu-sa-rqa-ni.
    Oruro-from come-(progressive marker, "-ing")-did(which with progressive -sa- can give the idea of "just did")-I.

C. FAMILY

11. a. **¿Warmiyoh kankichu?**[3] (to a man) Are you married?
       ¿Warmi-yoh ka-nki-chu?
       Woman/Wife-with be-you(one person)-(question marker)?

    b. **¿Qosayoh kankichu?** (to a woman) Are you married?
       ¿Qosa-yoh ka-nki-chu?
       Husband-with be-you(one person)-(question marker)?

12. a. **Arí, warmiyoh kani.** (a man speaking) Yes, I am married.
       Arí, warmi-yoh ka-ni.
       Yes, woman/wife-with be-I.

    b. **Arí, qosayoh kani.** (a woman speaking) Yes, I am married.
       Arí, qosa-yoh ka-ni.
       Yes, husband-with be-I.

13. a. **¿Wawqeyoh kankichu?** (to a male) Do you have a brother?
       ¿Wawqe-yoh ka-nki-chu?
       Brother(of a male)-with be-you(one person)-(question marker)? ("A" is understood.)

    b. **¿Turayoh kankichu?** (to a female) Do you have a brother?
       ¿Tura-yoh ka-nki-chu?
       Brother(of a female)-with be-you(one person)-(question marker)? ("A" is understood.)

14. a. **Arí. Uh wawqeyoh kani.**[4] (a male speaking) Yes. I have a brother.
    Arí. Uh wawqe-yoh ka-ni.
    Yes. A brother(of a male)-with be-I.

    b. **Arí. Uh turayoh kani.** (a female speaking) Yes. I have a brother.
    Arí. Uh tura-yoh ka-ni.
    Yes. A brother(of a female)-with be-I.

Expansion:

Brothers and sisters

Arí. Uh wawqe-yoh ka-ni. (a male speaking) Yes. I have a brother.

Wawqe-kuna brothers (a male speaking)
Brother-(plural marker) OR
Wawqe-s-ni brothers (a male speaking)
Brother-s-(euphonic particle required before the following -y)

Uh pana a sister (a male speaking)
Pana-kuna sisters (a male speaking)
Sister-(plural marker) OR
Pana-s-ni sisters (a male speaking)
Sister-s-(euphonic particle required before the following -y)

Uh tura a brother (a female speaking)
Yura-kuna brothers (a female speaking)
Brother-(plural marker) OR
Tura-s-ni brothers (a female speaking)
Brother-s-(euphonic particle required before the following -y)

Uh ñaña a sister (a female speaking)
Ñaña-kuna sisters (a female speaking)
Sister-(plural marker) OR
Ñaña-s-ni sisters (a female speaking)
Sister-s-(euphonic particle required before the following -y)

---

15. a. **Mana(n). Mana uh wawqeyoh kanichu.** (a male speaking) No. I don't have a brother.
    Mana(-n). Mana uh wawqe-yoh ka-ni-chu.
    No(-emphatic particle). Not a brother(of a male)-with be-I-(negative marker).

b. **Mana(n). Mana uh turayoh kanichu.** (a female speaking) No. I
don't have a brother.
Mana(-n). Mana uh tura-yoh ka-ni-chu.
*No(-emphatic particle). Not a brother(of a female)-with be-I-
(negative marker).*

16. ¿**Wawasniyoh kankichu?** Do you have children (male[s] and
female[s])?
¿Wawa-s-ni-yoh ka-nki-chu?
*Child-s[Children]-(euphonic particle required before the following -y)-
with be-you(one person)-(question marker)?*

Expansion:

Sons and daughters

¿**Wawa-s-ni-yoh ka-nki-chu?** Do you have children (male[s] and
female[s])? OR
¿**Wawa-kuna-yoh ka-nki-chu?** Do you have children (male[s] and
female[s])?
*Child-(plural marker)[Children]-with be-you(one person)-(question
marker)?*

Uh churi a son (speaking to a male)
A son(of a male)
Churi-kuna sons (speaking to a male)
Son(of a male)-(plural marker) OR
Churi-s-ni sons (speaking to a male)
Son(of a male)-s-(euphonic particle required before the following -y)

Uh ususi a daughter (speaking to a male)
A daughter(of a male)
Ususi-kuna daughters (speaking to a male)
Daughter(of a male)-(plural marker) OR
Ususi-s-ni daughters (speaking to a male)
*Daughter(of a male)-s-(euphonic particle required before the following -
y)*

Uh (qhari) wawa a son (speaking to a female)
A (male) child(of a female)
(Qhari) wawa-kuna sons (speaking to a female)
(Male) child(of a female)-(plural marker)[children] OR
(Qhari) wawa-s-ni sons (speaking to a female)
*(Male) child(of a female)-s[children]-(euphonic particle required before
the following -y)*

> **Uh (warmi) wawa** a daughter (speaking to a female)
> *A (female) child(of a female)*
> **(Warmi) wawa-kuna** daughters (speaking to a female)
> *(Female) child(of a female)-(plural marker)[children]*
> **(Warmi) wawa-s-ni** daughters (speaking to a female)
> *(Female) child(of a female)-s[children]-(euphonic particle required before the following -y)*

17. **¿Hayk'a wawayoh kanki?**[5] How many children do you have?
    ¿Hayk'a wawa-yoh ka-nki?
    How many child-with be-you(one person)?

18. a. **Tawa wawayoh kani. Iskay churiyoh(pis) iskay ususiyohpis kani.** (a male speaking) I have four children. I have two sons and two daughters.
    Tawa wawa-yoh ka-ni. Iskay churi-yoh(-pis) iskay ususi-yoh-pis ka-ni.
    Four child-with be-I. Two son(of a male)-with(-and) two daughter(of a male)-with-and be-I.

    b. **Tawa wawayoh kani. Iskay qhari wawayoh(pis) iskay warmi wawayohpis kani.** (a female speaking) I have four children. I have two sons and two daughters.
    Tawa wawa-yoh ka-ni. Iskay qhari wawa-yoh(-pis) iskay warmi wawa-yoh-pis ka-ni.
    Four child-with be-I. Two-(dual construction for "son" of a female)-with(-and) two-(dual construction for "daughter" of a female)-with-and be-I.

D. WHAT PEOPLE DO FOR A LIVING

19. **¿Imapim llank'anki?** What is your work (field work/manual work/traditional work of the Quechua people)?
    ¿Ima-pi-m llank'a-nki?
    What-in/at-(particle of certainty or assurance) work-you(one person)?

20. **¿Imapim trawahanki?**[6] What is your work (all other work)?
    ¿Ima-pi-m trawaha-nki?
    What-in/at-(particle of certainty or assurance) work-you(one person)?

21. **¿Imatam ruakunki?**[7] What do you do for a living?
    ¿Ima-ta-m rua-ku-nki?
    What-(direct object marker)-(particle of certainty or assurance) do-for self-you(one person)?

Expansion:

Different ways to ask what different people do for a living

¿Ima-ta-m rua-ku-nki? What do <u>you (one person)</u> do for a living?
¿Ima-ta-m rua-ku-nki-cheh? What do <u>you (more than one person)</u> do for a living?
¿Ima-ta-m rua-ku-n? What does <u>he/she</u> do for a living?
¿Ima-ta-m rua-ku-nku? What do <u>they</u> do for a living?

¿Ima-tah ruana-yki? What is <u>your (one person)</u> job/occupation?
What-and occupation-your(one person)? ("Is" is understood.)
¿Ima-tah ruana-ykicheh? What is <u>your (more than one person)</u> job/occupation?
¿Ima-tah ruana-n? What is <u>his/her</u> job/occupation?
¿Ima-tah ruana-nku? What is <u>their</u> job/occupation?

22. **¿(H)allp'a llank'ahchu kanki?** Are you a farmer?
    ¿(H)allp'a llank'a-h-chu ka-nki?
    Soil/Earth/Land work-the one who-(question marker) be-you(one person)?

23. **Arí. (H)allp'a llank'ah (kani).** Yes. I am a farmer.
    Arí. (H)allp'a llank'a-h (ka-ni).
    Yes. Soil/Earth/Land work-the one who (be-I). (For the English translation above, "a" is understood.)

Expansion A:

"I am (job, profession, occupation)."

(H)allp'a llank'a-h ka-ni. I am a <u>farmer</u>. ("A" is understood.)

Awa-h <u>weaver</u>
Weave-the one who
Miche-h <u>herder</u> [**michi-** > **miche-**]
Herd-the one who
Qhoya-runa <u>miner</u>
Mine-man
Alwañil <u>bricklayer, stone mason</u> OR
Perqa-kama-yoh <u>bricklayer, stone mason</u>
Wall-skill-with

Expansion B:
"I am/He is a farmer. // We/They are farmers."

(Ñoqa) (h)allp'a llank'a-h ka-ni. I am a farmer.

(Ñoqayku) (h)allp'a llank'a-h-kuna ka-yku. We (excluding the person[s] addressed) are farmers.
(We[excluding the person(s) addressed]) soil/earth/land work-the one who-(plural marker) be-we(excluding the person[s] addressed).

(Ñoqancheh) (h)allp'a llank'a-h-kuna ka-ncheh. We (including the person[s] addressed) are farmers.
(We[including the person(s) addressed]) soil/earth/land work-the one who-(plural marker) be-we(including the person[s] addressed).

(Pay) (h)allp'a llank'a-h. He/She is a farmer.
(He/She) soil/earth/land work-the one who. ("Is" is understood.)

(Pay-kuna) (h)allp'a llank'a-h-kuna (ka-nku). They are farmers.
(He/She-[plural marker][They]) soil/earth/land work-the one who-(plural marker) (be-they).
---

24. **¿Maypim llank'anki?** Where do you work (farm)?
¿May-pi-m llank'a-nki?
Where-in/at-(particle of certainty or assurance) work-you(one person)?

25. **Chahraypi llank'ani.** I work on my farm.
Chahra-y-pi llank'a-ni.
Farm-my-on/at work-I.

26. **¿Maypim trawahanki?** Where do you work (all other work)?
¿May-pi-m trawaha-nki?
Where-in/at-(particle of certainty or assurance) work-you(one person)?

27. **Uh ufisinapi trawahani.** I work in an office.
Uh ufisina-pi trawaha-ni.
An office-in/at work-I.

28. **¿Pipah trawahanki?** Whom do you work for?
¿Pi-pah trawaha-nki?
Who-for[For whom] work-you(one person)?

E. KNOWING PEOPLE, PLACES, INFORMATION, AND SKILLS

29. **¿Amiguyta Riguwirtu Mamani rehsinkichu?** Do you know my friend Rigoberto Mamani?
    ¿Amigu-y-ta Riguwirtu Mamani rehsi-nki-chu?
    Friend(a male)-my-(direct object marker) Rigoberto Mamani know-you(one person)-(question marker)?

30. **Arí, payta rehsini.** Yes, I know him.
    Arí, pay-ta rehsi-ni.
    Yes, he-(direct object marker)[him] know-I.

31. **Mana(n), amiguykita mana rehsinichu.** No, I don't know your friend.
    Mana(-n), amigu-yki-ta mana rehsi-ni-chu.
    No(-emphatic particle), friend(a male)-your(one person)-(direct object marker) not know-I-(negative marker).

32. **¿Llahtayta rikunkichu?**[8,9] Do you know my town/city/country?
    ¿Llahta-y-ta riku-nki-chu?
    Town/City/Country-my-(direct object marker) see/have seen[know]-you(one person)-(question marker)?

Expansion:

"Do you know (a place)?"

¿Llahta-y-ta riku-nki-chu? Do you know <u>my town/city/country</u>?/Have you seen <u>my town/city/country</u>?

Ñan-ta qhocha-ta the road to the lake
Road-(direct object marker) lake-to ("The" is understood.)

---

33. **Mana(n), mana rikunichu.** No, I do not know it.
    Mana(-n), mana riku-ni-chu.
    No(-emphatic particle), not know-I-(negative marker). ("It" is understood.)

34. **¿Rikuchipuwankimanchu?** Would you show it to me?
    ¿Riku-chi-pu-wa-nki-man-chu?
    See-make(what the meaning of the verb is)[Show]-it-to me-(dual marker for "you[one person] would")-(question marker)?

Expansion:

"Would you (one person) show it to me?"

"Would you (more than one person) show it to me?

¿Riku-chi-pu-wa-<u>nki-man</u>-chu? Would you (one person) show it to me?

¿Riku-chi-pu-wa-<u>nki-cheh-man</u>-chu? Would you (more than one person) show it to me?

See-make(what the meaning of the verb is)[Show]-it-to me-(triple marker for "you[more than one person] would")-(question marker)?

35. **¿Hayk'ah kay awtuwus llohsenqa? ¿Yachankichu?** When will this bus leave? Do you know? [**llohsi-** > **llohse-**]
¿Hayk'ah kay awtuwus llohse-nqa? ¿Yacha-nki-chu?
When this bus leave-it will? Know-you(one person)-(question marker)?

Expansion:

Knowing information

¿Hayk'ah <u>kay awtuwus llohse-nqa</u>? ¿Yacha-nki-chu? When <u>will this bus leave</u>? Do you know?

chay awtuwus hamo-nqa that bus will come [**hamu-** > **hamo-**]
that bus come-it will
chay awtuwus chaya-mo-nqa that bus will arrive here [**-mu-** > **-mo-**]
that bus arrive-in this direction-it will
chay awtuwus chaya-nqa that bus will arrive there
that bus arrive-it will ("There" is understood.)

chay awtuwus kuti-mo-nqa that bus will return here [**-mu-** > **-mo-**]
that bus return-in this direction-it will
chay awtuwus kute-nqa that bus will return there [**kuti-** > **kute-**]
that bus return-it will ("There" is understood.)

kicha-nqa-nku they will open
open-(dual marker for "they will")
wisk'a-nqa-nku they will close
close-(dual marker for "they will")

36. **Mana yachanichu.** I don't know.
Mana yacha-ni-chu.
Not know-I-(negative marker).

37. **¿Awayta yachankichu?** Do you know how to weave?
¿Awa-y-ta yacha-nki-chu?
Weave-(infinitive marker, "to")-(direct object marker) know-you(one person)-(question marker)?

38. **¿Yachachiwankimanchu?*** Would you show me how?
¿Yacha-chi-wa-nki-man-chu?
Know-make(what the meaning of the verb is)[Teach/Show how]-me-(dual marker for "you[one person] would")-(question marker)?

*[Note: There are two verb endings for the conditional "you (one person) would," **-nki-man** and **-wah**, and for "you (more than one person) would," **-nki-cheh-man** and **-wah-cheh**. The endings **-wah** and **-wah-cheh** are more common, but when the conditional ending is preceded by the infix **-wa-**, as is seen here, or by **-su-**, **-nki-man** and **-nki-cheh-man** are used instead. See number 10. Model for Simple Verbs in Section III: Quechua Grammar Notes.]

NOTES

1. Remember that the verb **tia-y** and its variant **tiya-y** give the forms **tia-n** and **tiya-n**, "there is" and "there are." As was mentioned in Chapter 3, in the reflexive forms of these two verbs, **tia-ku-y** and **tiya-ku-y** (which have **-ku-**, "self," "selves," between the stem and the "to" ending, **-y**), mean "to sit," "to reside," "to live," or, by extension, "to stay."

2. **Sukri**, Sucre: Capital of the Department of Chuquisaca and judicial capital of Bolivia. (The legislative and executive branches of the government are in La Paz.) Founded in 1538, by order of Francisco Pizarro. Originally named Charcas, later Chuquisaca, and then La Plata. Finally, the name was changed to Sucre in 1840, in honor of the first constitutional president of Bolivia, Antonio José de Sucre. Altitude: 9,331 feet above sea level. About 320 miles southeast of La Paz, the city generally considered the capital of Bolivia.

3. The Quechua **-yoh**, "with," conveys the idea of "has," while **-wan**, "with," means "accompanied by." Compare:

    ¿Warmi-yoh ka-nki-chu? Are you (addressing a male) married? This really means "Are you with/Do you have a wife?"
    Woman/Wife-with be/have-you(one person)-(question marker)? ("A" is understood.)

    ¿Warmi-wan ri-sa-nki-chu? Are you going with (accompanied by) the/a woman?
    Woman-with/accompanied by go-(progressive marker, "-ing")-you(one person)-(question marker)? ("The" or "A" are understood.)

Note that "Are you going with your wife?" is the same as the preceding question with "your" added.

¿Warmi-yki-wan-ri-sa-nki-chu? Are you going with your wife?
Woman/Wife-your(one person)-with/accompanied by go-(progressive marker, "-ing")-you(one person)-(question marker)?

(When words ending in **i** are followed by **-yki**, "your (one person)," or **-ykichech**, "your (more than one person)," the **y** may be silent in speech and dropped in writing. Thus, **warmi-yki** could be **warmi-ki**.)

4. Note that **uh** is used in this answer. This places emphasis on the idea of "a" or "one." "I have a brother," "I have one brother."

5. With "how many," **hayk'a**, and with numbers, a following noun is singular rather than plural.

    ¿Hayk'a wawa-yoh ka-nki? How many children do you have?
    How many child-with be-you(one person)?

    Tawa wawa-yoh ka-ni. Iskay churi-yoh(-pis) iskay ususi-yoh-pis ka-ni. (a male speaking) I have four children. I have two sons and two daughters. (a male speaking)
    Four child-with be-I. Two son(of a male)-with(-and) two daughter(of a male)-with-and be-I.

6. The verb **trawaha-y** comes from the Spanish *trabajar*, "to work." Note that the Quechua verb for "to work," **llank'a-y**, refers more to farming, while the one from Spanish is used for all other kinds of work.

7. There are variants, **rua-y**, **rura-y**, and **ruwa-y**, "to do," that are identical in meaning and usage. Personal or regional preference will dictate the one that is used.

8. Note that a present-tense verb, such as **riku-nki** here, in addition to its habitual present-tense meaning, such as "you see," can also have a present-perfect translation, "you have seen."

9. The different verbs meaning "to know" have specific uses.
    Rehsi-y is used for knowing people.
    ¿Amigu-y-ta rehsi-nki-chu? Do you know my friend (a male)?
    Friend(a male)-my-(direct object marker) know-you(one person)-(question marker)?

    Riku-y, "to see," is used for knowing, being familiar with a place.
    ¿Llahta-y-ta riku-nki-chu? Do you know/Do you see/Have you seen my town/city/country?

Town/City/Country-my-(direct object marker) see/have seen[know]-you(one person)-(question marker)?

Yacha-y is used for knowing information, as is seen in the question of 35:

¿Hayk'ah kay awtuwus llohse-nqa? ¿<u>Yacha-nki-chu</u>? When will this bus leave? <u>Do you know</u>? [**llohsi-** > **llohse-**]

When this bus leave-it will? Know-you(one person)-(question marker)?

SECTION II

Model Sentences and Their Expansions

Chapter 5

This chapter deals with

A. Asking and Telling About the Location of People, Places, and Things [Model Sentences 1-7]

B. Asking and Telling About Transportation [8-30]

C. Asking for Some Travel Help [31-37]

D. Offering and Getting Help, and Expressing the Need for Help [38-50]

A. ASKING AND TELLING ABOUT THE LOCATION OF PEOPLE, PLACES, AND THINGS

1. **¿Maypi(tah) tatayki (kasan)?**[1] Where is your father?
   ¿May-pi(-tah) tata-yki (kasa-n)?
   Where-in/at(-and) father-your(one person) (be-he)?

Expansion A:

"Where is your father?"
"Where is your mother?"
"Where are your parents?"

¿May-pi(-tah) tata-yki (kasa-n)? Where is your father?
Where-in/at(-and) father-your(one person) (be-he)?
¿May-pi(-tah) mama-yki (kasa-n)? Where is your mother?
Where-in/at(-and) mother-your(one person) (be-she)?

¿May-pi(-tah) tata-mama-yki kasa-nku? Where are your parents?
Where-in/at(-and) father-mother[parents]-your(one person) be-they?
¿May-pi(-tah) tata-mama-yki (kasa-n)?[2] Where are your parents?
Where-in/at(-and) father-mother[parents]-your(one person) (be-he/she])?

Expansion B:

Where is your . . . ?"

¿May-pi(-tah) <u>tata-yki</u> (kasa-n)? Where is <u>your father</u>?

amigu-yki Nikulas your friend Nicholas
llama-yki[3] your llama
q'epi-yki[4] your "q'epi" (bundle or piece of luggage)
wasi-yki your house

tata-ykicheh your (more than one person) father
amigu-ykicheh Nikulas your (more than one person) friend Nicholas
llama-ykicheh your (more than one person) llama
wasi-ykicheh your (more than one person) house

Expansion C:

"Where are your . . . ?"

¿May-pi(-tah) <u>tata-mama-yki</u> kasa-nku? Where are <u>your parents</u>?

amigu-s-ni-yki[5] your friends (males or male[s] and female[s])
friend-s-(euphonic particle)-your(one person)
llama-yki-kuna[5] your llamas
llama-your(one person)-(plural marker)
q'epi-yki-kuna your "q'epis" (bundles or pieces of luggage)
wasi-yki-kuna your houses

amigu-s-ni-ykicheh your (more than one person) friends (males or male[s] and female[s])
friend-s-(euphonic particle)-your(more than one person)
llama-ykicheh-kuna your (more than one person) llamas
llama-your(more than one person)-(plural marker)
q'epi-ykicheh-kuna your (more than one person) "q'epis" (bundles or pieces of luggage)
wasi-ykicheh-kuna your (more than one person) houses

2. **Mana yachanichu maypi kasan.** I don't know where he is.
   Mana yacha-ni-chu may-pi kasa-n.
   Not know-I-(negative marker) where-in/at be-he.

Expansion:

"I don't know where he/she is."
"I don't know where they are."

Mana yacha-ni-chu may-pi kasa-n. I don't know where <u>he/she</u> is.
Mana yacha-ni-chu may-pi kasa-nku. I don't know where <u>they</u> are.

3. **Tatay kaypi (kasan).** My father is here.
   Tata-y kay-pi (kasa-n).
   Father-my here-in/at (be-he).

Expansion A:

"My (different people) are/are not here."

Tata-y <u>kay-pi</u> (kasa-n). My mother is <u>here</u>.
Mama-y <u>kay-pi</u> (kasa-n). My mother is <u>here</u>.
Tata-mama-y <u>kay-pi</u> kasa-nku. My parents are <u>here</u>.
Father-mother[Parents]-my here-in/at be-they.

mana <u>kay-pi-chu</u> not here
not here-in/at-(negative marker)

Expansion B:

Telling different places someone is

Tata-y <u>kay-pi</u> (kasa-n). My father is <u>here</u>.

kay-neh-pi around here
here-around-in/at
haqay-pi over there
(over) there-in/at
llahta-pi-rah still in town
town-in/at-still
sach'a-sach'a-pi[6] in the woods
tree-tree[woods, forest]-in/at ("The" is understood.)
wasi ukhu-pi[7] inside the house
house inside-in/at ("The" is understood.)
wasi hawa-pi outside the house
house outside-in/at ("The" is understood.)
Hwan-pa-pi at Juan's (house)
Juan-of-in/at ("House" is understood.)

4. **¿Maypi(tah) uh mikhuywasi kan?**[8] Where is there a restaurant?
   ¿May-pi-(-tah) uh mikhuy-wasi ka-n?
   Where-in/at(-and) an eating-house be-it[there is]?

5. **Kaypi uh kan(mi).** There is one here.
Kay-pi uh ka-n(-mi).
Here-in/at one be-it[there is](-particle of certainty or assurance).

Expansion:

"There is one (location)."

Kay-pi uh ka-n(-mi). There is one <u>here</u>.

Iskwiyla-hpa ñawpaqe-n-pi <u>across the street from the school</u>
School-of front-its-in/at ("The" is understood.)
Uspital qaylla-pi <u>near the hospital</u>
Hospital near-in/at ("The" is understood.) OR
Uspital sispa <u>near the hospital</u>
Hospital near ("The" is undersood.)

6. **¿Maypi(tah) q'epiyta saqeyman?** Where could I leave my "q'epi?"
¿May-pi(-tah) q'epi-y-ta saqe-y-man?
Where-in/at(-and) "q'epi"-my-(direct object marker) leave-(dual marker for "I could")?

Expansion A:

Asking where I could do different things
¿May-pi(-tah) <u>q'epi-y-ta saqe-y-man</u>? Where could I <u>leave my "q'epi"</u>?

Replace the underlined portion above with the stem of the verb (the infinitive minus **-y** [the infinitive ("to") ending]).

mikhu-y <u>to eat</u>
puñu-y <u>to sleep</u>
hisp'a-y <u>to urinate</u>
wulitu-ta ranti-y <u>to buy a ticket</u>
ticket-(direct object marker) buy(-(infinitve marker, "to") ("A" is understood.)
unu-ta tinku-y <u>to find water</u>
water-(direct object marker) find-(infinitive marker, "to")
tuta-ntin-ta qhepa-ku-y <u>to stay all night</u>
night-whole-during(with a period of time) stay-self-(infinitive marker, "to")

Expansion B:

Asking where different people could leave my "q'epi"

¿**May-pi(-tah) q'epi-y-ta saqe-y-man?** Where <u>could I</u> leave my "q'epi?"

-wah OR **-nki-man** <u>could you (one person)</u>
-n-man <u>could he/she/it</u>
-yku-man <u>could we (excluding the person[s] addressed)</u>
(-su)-ncheh-man <u>could we (including the person[s] addressed)</u>
-wah-cheh OR **-nki-cheh-man** <u>could you (more than one person)</u>
-nku-man <u>could they</u>

[Note: All these conditional verb forms can mean both "could" and "would." Context dictates which English word is better.]

[Note also that **-man** is a marker for the conditional verb forms. With the exception of the form for "I," where **-y** instead of **-ni** is the personal marker, the all other conditional endings are like or have an option that is like those of the present tense with the conditional marker **-man** added.]

[Of the two forms for "you (one person) could/would" and "you (more than one person) could/would," **-wah** and **-wah-cheh** are more common, but when the conditional ending is preceded by the infix **-wa-** or **-su-**, the endings **-nki-man** and **-nki-cheh-man** are used instead.]

7. **Mayllapipis.** Anywhere./Any place./Any old place.
   May-lla-pi-pis.
   Where-just-in/at-any/any old.

Expansion:

Variant of "anywhere"

May-lla-pi-pis. Anywhere./Any place./Any old place.
Mayqen laru-pi-pis. Anywhere./Any place./Any old place.
Any old place-in/at-any old.

B. ASKING AND TELLING ABOUT TRANSPORTATION

8. ¿**Kay tiana ch'usahchu kasan?** Is this seat unoccupied?
   ¿Kay tiana ch'usah-chu kasa-n?
   This seat unoccupied/empty-(question marker) be-it?

9. **Ashkha runa awtuwuspi sayasqa kasanku.** Many people are standing on the bus.
Ashkha runa awtuwus-pi saya-sqa kasa-nku.
Many people/persons bus-on stand-(past participle marker, "-ed")[stood] be-they. ("The" is understood.)

Expansion:

"Many people are standing[stood]."
"Many people are sitting[seated] on the ground."

Ashkha runa <u>awtuwus-pi saya-sqa</u> kasa-nku. Many people are <u>standing on the bus</u>.

<u>panpa-pi tia-ku-sqa</u> <u>sitting on the ground</u>
ground-on seat-selves-(past participle marker, "-ed")[seated] ("The" is understood.)

---

10. **Kaypi ashkha runa tian.** There are many people here.
Kay-pi ashkha runa tia-n.
Here-in/at many people/persons be-it[there are].

11. **¿Maymanta chay awtuwus hamusan?** Where is that bus coming from?
¿May-manta chay awtuwus hamu-sa-n?
Where-from that bus come-(progressive marker, "-ing")-it?

12. **Unsiya llahtamanta hamusan.**[9] It is coming from Uncía.
Unsiya llahta-manta hamu-sa-n.
Uncía town/city-from come-(progressive marker, "-ing")-it.

13. **¿Mayman kay awtuwus risan? ¿Ururumanchu?** Where is this bus going? To Oruro?
¿May-man kay awtuwus ri-sa-n? ¿Ururu-man-chu?
Where-to/toward this bus go-(progressive marker, "-ing")-it? Oruro-to/toward-(question marker)?

Expansion A:

Ways to ask "to where" something or someone is going

¿<u>May-man</u> kay awtuwus ri-sa-n? <u>Where</u> is this bus going?

<u>May-ta</u>[10] <u>Where</u>
Where-to (arrival there assumed)

Expansion B:

"Where is this bus going?"
"Where does this bus go?"

¿May-man kay awtuwus **ri-sa-n**? Where <u>is</u> this bus <u>going</u>?
¿May-man kay awtuwus **ri-n**? Where <u>does</u> this bus <u>go</u>?

14. **Ikaman risan.**[11] It is going to Ica.
    Ika-man ri-sa-n.
    Ica-to/toward go-(progressive marker, "-ing")-it.

15. **¿Maymanta Limaman awtuwus llohsin?** Where does the bus for Lima leave from?
    ¿May-manta Lima-man awtuwus llohsi-n?
    Where-from Lima-to/toward bus leave-it? ("The" is understood.)

16. **Kaymanta(qa) llohsin.** It leaves from (right) here.
    Kay-manta(-qa) llohsi-n.
    Here-from(-"right," emphatic particle) leave-it.

17. **¿Uh awtuwus Ururu(n)ta rinchu?** Does a bus go through Oruro?
    ¿Uh awtuwus Ururu(-n)ta ri-n-chu?
    A bus Oruro-through go-it-(question marker)?

18. **¿Ima llahta(n)ta kay awtuwus rin?** What town does this bus go through?
    ¿Ima llahta(-n)ta kay awtuwus ri-n?
    What town-through this bus go-it?

19. **¿Kay awtuwus Ururumanchu rin?** Does this bus go to Oruro?
    ¿Kay awtuwus Ururu-man-chu ri-n?
    This bus Oruro-to/toward-(question marker) go-it?

20. **¿Ayak'uchuman awtuwus kaypichu (kasan)?**[12] Is the bus to Ayacucho here?
    ¿Ayak'uchu-man awtuwus kay-pi-chu (kasa-n)?
    Ayacucho-to/toward bus here-in/at-(question marker) (be-it)? ("The" is understood.)

21. **Arí. Kaypi (kasan).** Yes. It's here.
    Arí. Kay-pi (kasa-n).
    Yes. Here-in/at (be-it).

22. **Mana(n). Mana kaypichu (kasan).** No. It isn't here.
    Mana(-n). Mana kay-pi-chu (kasa-n).
    No(-emphatic particle). Not here-in/at-(negative marker) (be-it).

23. **¿Karuchu Ururu llahta (kasan)?** Is the city of Oruro far?
    ¿Karu-chu Ururu llahta (kasa-n)?
    Far-(question marker) Oruro town/city (be-it)? ("The" is understood.)

24. **Mana(n). Mana karuchu. Kaypi ancha sispa (kasan).** No. It's not far. It's very near here.
    Mana(-n). Mana karu-chu. Kay-pi ancha sispa (kasa-n).
    No(-emphatic particle). Not far-(negative marker). Here-in/at very near (be-it).

Expansion:

Indicating proximity

Kay-pi ancha sispa (kasa-n). It's <u>very near here</u>.

Ancha karu very far
Very far
Kay-pi sispa near here
Here-in/at near
Kay-manta karu far from here
Here-from far

Qhochapanpa sispa[13] near Cochabamba
Cochabamba near
Qhochapanpa-manta karu far from Cochabamba
Cochabamba-from far

---

25. **¿Maypi(tah) awtuwus sayan?** Where does the bus stop?
    ¿May-pi(-tah) awtuwus saya-n?
    Where-in/at(-and) bus stop-it? ("The" is understood.)

26. **¿Ima llahtapi awtuwus sayan?** What town does the bus stop in?
    ¿Ima llahta-pi awtuwus saya-n?
    What town-in/at bus stop-it? ("The" is understood.)

27. **Arikipapi sayan.**[14] It stops in Arequipa.
    Arikipa-pi saya-n.
    Arequipa-in/at stop-it.

28. **Allichu, ¿kaychu Urupanpa?**[15] Please, is this Urubamba?
    Allichu, ¿kay-chu Urupanpa?
    Please, this-(question marker) Urubamba? ("Is" is understood.)

29. **Allichu, kaypi sayay.** Please, stop here.
    Allichu, kay-pi saya-y.
    Please, here-in/at stop-(command marker addressing one person).

30. **Allichu, Ururuta chayahtincheh willaway.** Please, tell me when we get to Oruro.
Allichu, Ururu-ta chaya-hti-ncheh willa-wa-y.
Please, Oruro-to/at arrive-(variable gerund marker, "-ing," used when the subject of the gerund is different from that of the main verb)-our(including the person[s] addressed) inform-me-(command marker addressing one person).

C. ASKING FOR SOME TRAVEL HELP

31. **Chinkasqa kasani.** I am lost.
Chinka-sqa kasa-ni.
Lose-(past participle marker, "-ed")[Lost] be-I.

32. **¿Awtuñanta Ururuman rikuchiwankimanchu?** Could you show me the roadway to Oruro?
¿Awtu-ñan-ta Ururu-man riku-chi-wa-nki-man-chu?
Auto-road-(direct object marker) Oruro-to/toward see-make(what the meaning of the verb is)[show]-me-(dual marker for "you[one person]could")-(question marker)? ("The" is understood.)

33. **Arí. Ñoqawan hamuy. Rikuchisayki.**[16] Yes. Come with me. I will show you.
Arí. Ñoqa-wan hamu-y. Riku-chi-sayki.
Yes. I-with come-(command marker addressing one person). See-make(what the meaning of the verb is)[show]-I will (to) you(one person).

34. **¿Pitah chayta pusawanqari?** And who will guide me there?
¿Pi-tah chay-ta pusa-wa-nqa-ri?
Who-and there-to lead-me-he/she will-and/then(prolonging the question without adding any specific meaning)?

Expansion:

"Who will guide (different people) there?"[17]

¿Pi-tah chay-ta <u>pusa-wa-nqa</u>-ri? And who <u>will guide me</u> there?

<u>pusa-wa-sahku</u> <u>will guide us (excluding the person[s] addressed)</u>
lead-(dual marker for "he/she will us[excluding the person(s) addressed]")

pusa-wa-su-n(cheh) will guide us (including the person[s] addressed)
lead-(triple marker for "he/she will us[including the person(s) addressed]")

pusa-so-nqa will guide you (one person) [-su- > -so-]
lead-(dual marker for "he/she will you[one person]")
pusa-so-nqa-cheh will guide you (more than one person) [-su- > -so-]
lead-(triple marker for "he/she will you[more than one person]")

pay-ta puso-nqa will guide him/her [-su- > -so-]
he/she-(direct object marker)[him/her] lead-he/she will
pay-kuna-ta puso-nqa will guide them [-su- > -so-]
he/she-(plural marker)[they]-(direct object marker)[them] lead-he/she will

35. **Ñoqaqa chayta pusasayki.** I (with emphasis) will guide you there.
    Ñoqa-qa chay-ta pusa-sayki.
    I-(emphatic particle) there-to lead-I will you(one person).

Expansion:

"(Different people) will guide you there."
"(Different people) will guide you (more than one person) there."

Ñoqa-qa chay-ta pusa-sayki.[18] I (with emphasis) will guide you (one person) there.
Ñoqa-qa chay-ta pusa-sayki-cheh. I (with emphasis) will guide you (more than one person) there.
I-(emphatic particle) there-to lead-(dual marker for "I will you[more than one person]").

Ñoqayku chay-ta pusa-sayki. We will guide you (one person) there.
We(excluding the person[s] addressed) there-to lead-we will you(one person).
Ñoqayku chay-ta pusa-sayki-cheh. We will guide you (more than one person) there.
We(excluding the person[s] addressed) there-to lead-(dual marker for "we will you[more than one person]").

Pay chay-ta pusa-so-nqa. He/She will guide you (one person) there. [-su- > -so-]
He/She there-to lead-(dual marker for "he/she will you[one person]").
Pay chay-ta pusa-so-nqa-cheh. He/She will guide you (more than one person) there. [-su- > -so-]
He/She there-to lead-(triple marker for "he/she will you[more than one person]").

Pay-kuna chay-ta pusa-**so-nqa-nku**. They will guide you (one person) there. [-**su**- > -**so**-]
He/She-(plural marker)[They] there-to lead-(triple marker for "they will you[one person]").

Pay-kuna chay-ta pusa-**so-nqa-cheh**. They will guide you (more than one person) there. [-**su**- > -**so**-]
He/She-(plural marker)[They] there-to lead-(triple marker for "they will you[more than one person]").

36. **¿Pitah pusamuwanqari?** Then who will guide me back?
    ¿Pi-tah pusa-mu-wa-nqa-ri?
    Who-and lead-in this direction-me-he/she will-and/then(prolonging the question without adding any specific meaning)?

37. **Ñoqaqa pusamusayki.** I (with emphasis) will guide you back.
    Ñoqa-qa pusa-mu-sayki.
    I-(emphatic particle) lead-in this direction-I will you(one person).

D. OFFERING AND GETTING HELP, AND EXPRESSING THE NEED FOR HELP

38. **¿Imata munanki?** What do you want?
    ¿Ima-ta muna-nki?
    What-(direct object marker) want-you(one person)?

39. **Qatata munani.** I want a blanket.
    Qata-ta muna-ni.
    Blanket-(direct object marker) want-I. ("A" is understood.)

Expansion:

Different things someone may want

Qata-ta muna-ni. I want a blanket.

Yanapa-ta help
Help-(direct object marker)
Sama-y-ta to rest
Rest-(infinitive marker, "to")-(direct object marker)
Ima uhyana(-lla)-ta-pas anything/something to drink
Thing drinkable(-just)-(direct object marker)-any

40. **Allichu. ¡Yanapariway!** Please. Help me, please (addressing one person)!
Allichu. ¡Yanapa-ri-wa-y!
Please. Help-(particle that softens the request/"please")-me-(command marker addressing one person)!

Expansion:

Asking one or more persons for help

¡Yanapa-ri-<u>wa-y</u>! Help <u>me</u>, please <u>(addressing one person)</u>!
¡Yanapa-ri-<u>wa-y-cheh</u>! Help <u>me</u>, please <u>(addressing more than one person)</u>!

¡Yanapa-ri-<u>wa-yku</u>! Help <u>us</u>, please <u>(addressing one or more than one person)</u>!
Help-(particle that softens the request/"please")-(dual marker for "us[in a command, excluding the person(s) addressed]")!

41. **Allichu, yanapata(n) kachamuy.** Please, send help (addressing one person).
Allichu, yanapa-ta(-n) kacha-mu-y.
Please, help-(direct object marker)(-emphatic particle) send-in this direction-(command marker addressing one person).

Expansion A:

"Please, (requesting something for oneself from one and more than one person)."

Allichu, <u>yanapa-ta(-n)</u> <u>kacha-mu-y</u>. Please, <u>send help (addressing one person)</u>.

<u>idiku-man</u> <u>pusa-wa-y</u> take me to a/the doctor (addressing one person)
doctor-to/toward guide/lead/take-me-(command marker addressing one person)
<u>unu-ta</u> <u>qo-wa-y</u> give me water (addressing one person)
water-(direct object marker) give-(to) me-(command marker addressing one person)
<u>unu-ta</u> <u>apa-mu-wa-y</u> bring me water (addressing one person)
water-(direct object marker) carry/take-in this direction[bring]-(to) me-(command marker addressing one person)

q'epi-y-ta yuya-pu-wa-y[19] watch my "q'epi" for me (addressing one person)
"q'epi"/bundle/luggage-my-(direct object marker) think about/pay attention to-it-for me-(command marker addressing one person)
kay-ta(-m) ñoqa-pah hap'i-y[20] hold this for me (addressing one person)
this-(direct object marker)(-particle of certainty or assurance) I-for[for me] grab/take/seize/hold-(command marker addressing one person)

Allichu, yanapa-ta(-n) kacha-mu-y-cheh. Please, send help (addressing more than one person).

midiku-man pusa-wa-y-cheh take me to a/the doctor (addressing more than one person)
doctor-to/toward guide/lead/take-me-(dual command marker addressing more than one person)
unu-ta qo-wa-y-cheh give me water (addressing more than one person)
water-(direct object marker) give-(to) me-(dual command marker addressing more than one person)
unu-ta apa-mu-wa-y-cheh bring me water (addressing more than one person)
water-(direct object marker) carry/take-in this direction[bring]-(to) me-(dual command marker addressing more than one person)
q'epi-y-ta yuya-pu-wa-y-cheh watch my "q'epi" for me (addressing more than one person)
"q'epi"/bundle/luggage-my-(direct object marker) think about/pay attention to-it-for me-(command marker addressing more than one person)
kay-ta(-m) ñoqa-pah hap'i-y-cheh hold this for me (addressing more than one person)
this-(direct object marker)(-particle of certainty or assurance) I-for[for me] grab/take/seize/hold-(dual command marker addressing more than one person)

Expansion B:

"Please, (requesting something for oneself and others from one and more than one person)."

Allichu, yanapa-ta(-n) kacha-mu-y. Please, send help (addressing one person).

midiku-man pusa-wa-yku take us (excluding the person[s] addressed) to a/the doctor (addressing one or more than one person)
doctor-to/toward guide/lead/take-(dual command marker for " us[excluding the person(s) addressed]")

unu-ta qo-wa-yku give us (excluding the person[s] addressed) water (addressing one or more than one person)
water-(direct object marker) give-(dual comand marker for "[to] us[excluding the person(s) addressed]")

unu-ta apa-mu-wa-yku bring us (excluding the person[s] addressed) water (addressing one or more than one person)
water-(direct object marker) carry/take-in this direction[bring]-(dual command marker for "[to] us[excluding the person(s) addressed]")

q'epi-yku-kuna-ta yuya-pu-wa-yku watch our (exculding the person[s] addressed) "q'epis" for us (addressing one or more than one person)
"q'epi"/bundle/luggage-our(excluding the person[s] addressed)-(plural marker)-(direct object marker) think about/pay attention to them-for us-(dual command marker for "for us[excluding the person(s) addressed]")

kay-ta(-m) ñoqayku-pah hap'i-y hold this for us (excluding the person[s] addressed) (addressing one person)
this-(direct object marker)(-particle of certainty or assurance) us(excluding the person[s] addressed)-for grab/take/seize/hold-(command marker addressing one person)

kay-ta(-m) ñoqayku-pah hap'i-y-cheh hold this for us (excluding the person[s] addressed) (addressing more than one person)
this-(direct object marker)(-particle of certainty or assurance) us(excluding the person[s] addressed)-for grab/take/seize/hold-(command marker addressing more than one person)

42. **Allichu, q'epiyta apayta yanapariway.** Please, help me carry my luggage (addressing one person).
Allichu, q'epi-y-ta apa-y-ta yanapa-ri-wa-y.
Please, luggage-my-(direct object marker) carry-(infinitive marker, "to")-(direct object marker) help-(particle that softens the request/"please")-me-(command marker addressing one person).

Expansion:

"Please, help me . . . (addressing one person)"
"Please, help me . . . (addressing more than one person)"

Allichu, q'epi-y-ta apa-y-ta yanapa-ri-wa-y. Please, help me carry my luggage (addressing one person).

Allichu, q'epi-y-ta apa-y-ta yanapa-ri-wa-y-cheh. Please, help me carry my luggage (addressing more than one person).

kamiyun-man lloq'a-y-ta to get on the truck (implying that it is difficult to do)
truck-to/toward get on/climb on[something that offers some difficulty]-(infinitive marker, "to")-(direct object marker) ("The" is understood.)
trin-man wicha-y-ta to get on the train (implying that it is not difficult to do)
train-to/toward go up[get on][something that does not offer difficulty]-(infinitive marker, "to")-(direct object marker) ("The" is understood.)
kamiyun-manta uray-ku-y-ta[21] to get off the truck
truck-from down-self[get (me) off]-(infinitive marker, "to")-(direct object marker) ("The" is understood.)

43. **K'irisqa kasani.** I am hurt.
    K'iri-sqa kasa-ni.
    Hurt-(past participle marker, "-ed")[Hurt] be-I.

Expansion:

"I am hurt."
"I am tired."
"I am thirsty."
"I am hungry."

K'iri-sqa kasa-ni. I am hurt.

Sayk'u-sqa tired
Ch'aki-sqa thirsty
Yarqa-sqa hungry

44. **¿Yanapawayta atinkichu?** Can you help me?/Are you able to help me?
    ¿Yanapa-wa-y-ta ati-nki-chu?
    Help-me-(infinitive marker, "to")-(direct object marker) can/able-you(one person)-(question marker)?

Expansion:

"Can you help me?"
"Are you able to help me?"
"Can you help us?"
"Are you able to help us?"

¿Yanapa-wa-y-ta ati-nki-chu? Can you (one person) help me?/Are you (one person) able to help me?

¿Yanapa-wa-y-ta ati-nki-cheh-chu? Can you (more than one person) help me?/Are you (more than one person) able to help me?

¿**Yanapa-y-ta ñoqayku-ta ati-nki-chu?**[22] Can you (one person) help us?/Are you (one person) able to help us?
Help-(infinitive marker, "to")-(direct object marker) we(excluding the person[s] addressed)-(direct object marker)[us] can/able-you(one person)-(question marker)?
¿**Yanapa-y-ta ñoqayku-ta ati-nki-cheh-chu?**[22] Can you (more than one person) help us?/Are you (more than one person) able to help us?

45. **Arí, atinipunim.** Yes, I certainly can.
Arí, ati-ni-puni-m.
Yes, can-I-(intensive marker, "certainly")-(particle of certainty or assurance).

Expansion:

"I certainly can."
"We certainly can."

Arí, ati-ni-puni-m. Yes, I certainly can.
Arí, ati-yku-puni-m. Yes, we certainly can.

46. **Mana(n). Anchata llakikuni. Mana atinichu.** No, I'm very sorry. I can't.
Mana(-n). Ancha-ta llaki-ku-ni. Mana ati-ni-chu.
No(-emphatic particle). Much-(adverb marker) suffer-self-I. Not can/able-I-(negative marker).

Expansion:

"No. I'm very sorry. I can't."
"No. We're very sorry. We can't."

Mana(-n). Ancha-ta llaki-ku-ni. Mana ati-ni-chu. No. I'm very sorry. I can't.
Mana(-n). Ancha-ta llaki-ku-yku. Mana ati-yku-chu. No. We're very sorry. We can't.

47. ¿**Yanapasuyta atinichu?** Can I help you?
¿Yanapa-su-y-ta ati-ni-chu?
Help-you(one person; object of an infinitive)-(infinitive marker, "to")-(direct object marker) can/able-I-(question marker)?

Expansion:

"Can I help you (one person)?"
"Can we help you (one person)?"
"Can I help you (more than one person)?"
"Can we help you (more than one person)?

¿**Yanapa-su-y-ta ati-ni-chu?** Can I help you (one person)?
¿**Yanapa-su-y-ta ati-yku-chu?** Can we help you (one person)?

¿**Yanapa-y-ta qan-kuna-ta ati-ni-chu?**[23] Can I help you (more than one person)?
Help-(infinitive marker, "to")-(direct object marker) you-(plural marker)-(direct object marker) can/able-I-(question marker)?

¿**Yanapa-y-ta qan-kuna-ta ati-yku-chu?** Can we help you (more than one person)?

48. ¿**Ninariyta yanapasuyta atinichu?** Can I help you to start the fire?
    ¿Nina-ri-y-ta yanapa-su-y-ta ati-ni-chu?
    Fire-(marker indicating "to start"/"to begin" to do the action indicated by the verb)-(infinitive marker, "to")-(direct object marker) help-you(one person; object of an infinitive)-(infinitive marker, "to")-(direct object marker) can/able-I-(question marker)? ("The" is understood.)

49. ¿**Pichari yanapawayta atin?** Can anyone help me?/Is anyone able to help me?
    ¿Pi-cha-ri yanapa-wa-y-ta ati-n?
    Who-(marker to show lack of knowledge or doubt)-(particle that softens the question)[Anyone] help-me-(infinitive marker, "to")-(direct object marker) can/able-he/she?

50. **Ñoqaqa yanapasayki.** I'll certainly help you.
    Ñoqa-qa yanapa-sayki.
    I-certainly help-I will you(one person).

NOTES

1. The verb **kasa-y**, "to be," is used in this book to indicate location (and situations and temporary conditions). While with the related verb **ka-y**, "to be," the third-person singular form with the meaning "he/she/it is" is never used, the third person singular of **kasa-y**, **kasa-n**, can be expressed.

2. With a plural subject, the verbs **ka-y** and **kasa-y** can be found used with either the third person singular, the "he/she/it" form: **ka-n** or **kasa-n**, or the third person plural, the "they" form: **ka-nku** or **kasa-nku**. This probably is due to influence of the form **ka-n** that means both "there is" and "there are." Compare:

> **¿May-pi(-tah) tata-mama-yki (kasa-n)?** Where are your parents?
> *Where-in/at(-and) father-mother-your(one person) (be-he/she)?*
> AND
> **¿May-pi(-tah) tata-mama-yki kasa-nku?** Where are your parents?
> *Where-in/at(-and) father-mother-your(one person) be-they?*

> **Kay-neh-pi uh mikhuy-wasi ka-n.** There is a restaurant around here.
> *Here-around-in/at an eating-house be-it[there is].*
> AND
> **Kay-neh-pi mikhuy-wasi-kuna ka-n.** There are restaurants around here.
> *Here-around-at eating-house-(plural marker) be-it[there are].*

> BUT
> **¿May-pi(-tah) tata-yki trawaha-n?** Where does your father work?
> *Where-in/at(-and) father-your(one person) work-he?*

> **¿May-pi(-tah) tata-mama-yki trawaha-nku?** Where do your father and mother/your parents work?
> *Where-in/at(-and) father-mother-your(one person) work-they?*

3. Llamas have been very important animals in the Andean region since pre-Hispanic times. Their surefootedness has contributed to their not being replaced as beasts of burden by the European imports of horses and donkeys. Llamas (**llama-kuna** or **llama-s**), along with alpacas (**allpaqa-kuna** or **allpaqa-s**), guanacos (**wanaku-kuna** or **wanaku-s**), and vicuñas (**wik'uña-kuna** or **wik'uña-s**), are lamoids, the South American members of the Camelidae family, to which the Asian and African camels also belong. Llamas and alpacas are domestic animals, while guanacos and vicuñas are wild. The largest of the lamoids, llamas reach a height of almost four feet at the shoulder. They are used primarily as beasts of burden, being able to carry some one hundred pounds. (They are never ridden.) If a llama is overloaded or tired, it will refuse to move, lie down, kick, hiss, and spit. Llamas are also used as sources of milk, meat, tallow for candles, and wool. Their wool, which usually is white

but at times black or brown, is coarser than and thus inferior to that of the alpaca. In addition, the dried dung of llamas is used for fuel.

4. A **q'epi** is a bundle made from a long piece of fabric and carried on a person's back. To ready the **q'epi**, the fabric is straightened out, what is to be carried is placed in the middle, and the fabric is folded over or rolled to secure the load. The ends of the fabric are gathered up, the load placed on the person's back, and the ends brought around to the front of the body, one over one shoulder and the other under the opposite arm, and then tied together. By extension, a **q'epi** can also be used to refer to a piece of luggage.

5. Remember (see Chapter 1, Note 29) that with a plural noun formed with **-kuna**, any possessive adjective goes between the noun and the **-kuna**. However, if the plural is formed with **-s**, the word order is as follows: noun / -s / required euphonic infix **-ni-** / possessive adjective. Compare:

> **amigu-s-ni-yki** your friends (males or male[s] and female[s])
> *friend-s-(euphonic particle)-your(one person)*

> **llama-yki-kuna** your llamas
> *llama-your(one person)-(plural marker)*

6. **Sach'a** means "tree (uncultivated)." The repetition of a noun gives a collective noun designating a group of the items indicated. Thus, **sach'a-sach'a** means "woods," "forest." Another example is from **rumi**, "stone," **rumi-rumi**, a "stony area."

    Similarly, descriptive adjectives can be repeated to emphasize the description.

> **puka-puka t'ika** a very red flower
> *red-red flower*

Demonstrative adjectives (**kay**, "this," **chay**, "that [nearby]," and **haqay**, "that [over there]") can be repeated to pluralize the noun to which they refer. This is a more poetic construction.

> **chay-chay q'omer sach'a** those green trees
> *that-that green tree*

Adverbs can be repeated to add the idea of "very" to their meaning.

> **Karu karu hamu-sa-ni.** I am coming from very far.
> *Far far[Very far] come-(progressing marker, "-ing")-I.*

7. Note that "inside" and many other words of location, such as "outside," are not used alone. They have some suffix to complete their meaning. For example:

> **ukhu-pi** inside (in/at inside)
> **hawa-pi** outside (in/at outside)

> **ukhu-man** inside (to/toward inside)

hawa-man outside (to/toward outside)

8. Compare the following questions, "Where is the . . .?" "Where is there a . . .?" and "Is there a . . .?"
   Asking for the location of a restaurant:
   ¿May-pi(-tah) mikhuy-wase-qa (kasa-n)? Where is <u>the</u> restaurant? [**wasi > wase**]
   Where-in/at(-and) eating-house-(emphatic particle, thus here conveying the idea of the nonexistent "the") (be-it)?
   Asking for the existence of a restaurant:
   ¿May-pi(-tah) <u>uh</u> mikhuy-wasi kan-n? Where is there <u>a</u> restaurant?
   Where-in/at(-and) an eating-house be-it[there is]?
   ¿Kay-neh-pi <u>uh</u> mikhuy-wasi-chu ka-n? Is there <u>a</u> restaurant around here?
   Here-around-in/at an eating-house-(question marker) be-it[there is]?

9. **Unsiya**, Uncía: Capital of the Bustillos Province, Department of Potosí, Bolivia. Mining center. About 50 miles south southeast of Oruro. Altitude: 12,864 feet above sea level.

10. Remember that some people make a clear distinction between **-man** and **-ta**, using **-man** for the idea of "to," "toward," "in the direction of," "headed for," and **-ta** for "to," with arrival at the place mentioned assumed.
    As was mentioned before, in this book **-man** and **-ta** can be found used interchangeably.

11. **Ika**, Ica: Capital of the Department of Ica, Peru, on the Ica River, 170 miles southeast of Lima. Founded in 1563.

12. **Ayak'uchu (aya-k'uchu,** "corner of the dead"), Ayacucho: In 1539, Francisco Pizarro, Viceroy of Peru, founded the city of Huamanga (also spelled Guamanga), about 200 miles southeast of Lima. Some seven miles from Huamanga, near the village of La Quinua, is a small plain where, in 1542, Cristóbal Vaca de Castro, who assumed the governorship of Peru following the assassination of Francisco Pizarro, defeated a rebellion led by Diego de Almago (the younger). As a result of this bloody battle, the plain was given the name of **Aya-k'uchu,** "Corner of the Dead." On December 9, 1824, one of the definitive battles for the independence of Peru was fought on this same plain. At this battle, the troops fighting for independence, under the leadership of Antonio José de Sucre (soon to be the first constitutional president of Bolivia), defeated the royalists, led by José de La Serna, Viceroy of Peru. In 1825, the name

of Huamanga was changed to **Ayak'uchu**. Today Ayacucho is the capital of the Province of Huamanga and of the Department of Ayacucho.

13. **Qhochapanpa (Qochapanpa)**, Cochabamba: Capital of Mercado Province and of the Department of Cochabamba, Bolivia, about 80 miles northeast of Oruro. Founded in 1574. Originally known as Oropeza.

14. **Ar(i)qhepa** or **Arikipa**, Arequipa: Capital of the Province and the Department of Arequipa, Peru, the second largest city of the country. Founded by Francisco Pizarro on the site of an Inca village, Arequipa is 470 miles southeast of Lima. The city, at 7,550 feet above sea level, is to the west of and at the foot of El Misti volcano (19,110 feet above sea level).

    There are differing theories about the origin of the name of the city. In the Aymara language, spoken by those on the other side of the volcano, the name was "ariqhepa" or "arikipa," from "ari," "sharp," and "qhepa" or "kipa," "behind," thus apparently meaning "(the place) behind the sharp (peak, the conical El Misti volcano)." On the other hand, Quechua legend has it that when the fourth Lord of Cuzco, Mayta Capac (**Mayta Qhapah**) and his entourage once passed through this valley, as they were looking for a place to camp, he was so moved by its beauty that he said, "**Ari qhepay**," "Yes, stay." (It is of interest to note that later, during the time of the Inca Empire, **Ariqhepa** was an important point on the route from Cuzco to the Pacific Ocean, and in future years, in colonial times, it would have a similar role in the route used from Bolivia to the Pacific.)

    Glauco Torres, in his *Lexicón Etnolectológico del Quichua Andino* (2002) lists **ariquipai,** *cubrirse de vegetación,* "to become covered with vegetation," a verb apparently derived from the characteristics of the area, and **ariquipa,** *cubierto de vegetación,* "covered with vegetation."

    Arequipa is often referred to as the "White City," due to the color of many of its buildings, which are constructed of blocks of white rock hewn from the white lava of the volcano.

15. **Urupanpa**, Urubamba: Mining town in the Department of Cuzco, Peru, 20 miles north of the city of Cuzco.

16. As has been pointed out before, there are verbal constructions that include the personal object pronouns "(to) me," "(to) you (one person)," "(to) us," "(to) you (more than one person)."

    In this sentence, **Riku-chi-sayki**, "I will show you (one person)," -**sayki** is one of the two endings for "I will (to) you (one person)." More examples of these various constructions will be seen in following sentences and Expansions.

For more on the verbal constructions "(*subject, verb*) (to) you (one person)," see number 18. Model for Verbs that Include (Pronominally) the Verbal Object "You (One Person)" in Section III: Quechua Grammar Notes.

17. As has been pointed out before, there are verbal constructions that include the personal object pronouns "(to) me," "(to) you (one person)," "(to) us," "(to) you (more than one person)."

    In the sentences in this expansion there are examples of each of these constructions, as well as those more regular ones that are used for the subjects "he/she/it" and "they."

    ¿**Pi-tah chay-ta pusa-wa-nqa-ri?** "And who will guide me there?" The object "me," **-wa-** is affixed to the stem of the verb of the simple verb forms.

    For more on this, see number 16. Model for Verbs that Include (Pronominally) the Verbal Object "Me" in Section III: Quechua Grammar Notes.

    ¿**Pi-tah chay-ta pusa-wa-sahku-ri?** "And who will guide us (excluding the person[s] addressed) there?" Here the object "us" is part of the meaning of this dual marker for "he/she/it will us (excluding the person[s] addressed)." The object "us (excluding the person[s] addressed)" is formed by affixing **-wa-** to the stem of the simple verb form, in the appropriate tense, for "we (excluding the person[s] addressed)." Similarly, if the object is "us (including the person[s] addressed," **-wa-** is affixed to the stem of the simple verb form, in the appropriate tense, for "we (including the person[s] addressed)."

    For more on this, see number 17. Model for Verbs that Include (Periphrastically and Pronominally) the Verbal Object "Us" in Section III: Quechua Grammar Notes.

    ¿**Pi-tah chay-ta pusa-wa-su-n(cheh)-ri?** "And who will guide us (including the person[s] addressed) there?" Much like the sentence above, here the object "us" is part of the meaning of this triple marker for "he/she/it will us (including the person(s) addressed)." The object "us (including the person[s] addressed)" is formed by affixing **-wa-** to the stem of the simple verb form, in the appropriate tense, for "we (including the person[s] addressed)." Similarly, if the object is "us (excluding the person[s] addressed," **-wa-** is affixed to the stem of the simple verb form, in the appropriate tense, for "we (excluding the person[s] addressed)."

For more on this, see number 17. Model for Verbs that Include (Periphrastically and Pronominally) the Verbal Object "Us" in Section III: Quechua Grammar Notes.

¿**Pi-tah chay-ta pusa-so-nqa-ri?** "And who will guide you (one person) there?" Here the object "you (one person)" is **-so-**, variant of **-su-**.

For more on the verbal constructions "(*subject, verb*) (to) you (one person), see number 18. Model for Verbs that Include (Pronominally) the Verbal Object "You (One Person)" in Section III: Quechua Grammar Notes.

¿**Pi-tah chay-ta pusa-so-nqa-cheh-ri?** "And who will guide you (more than one person) there?" Here the object "you (more than one person)" is part of the meaning of this triple marker for "he/she/it will you (more than one person)."

For more on the verbal constructions "(*subject, verb*) (to) you (one person)," see number 19. Model for Verbs that Include (Periphrastically and Pronominally) the Verbal Object "You (More Than One Person)" in Section III: Quechua Grammar Notes.

¿**Pi-tah chay-ta pusa pay-ta puso-nqa-ri?** And who will guide him/her there? Here the object is someone other than "me," "us," or "you." Therefore a simple periphrastic construction is used:"*he/she-(direct object marker)[him/her] lead-he/she will.*"

¿**Pi-tah chay-ta pusa pay-kuna-ta puso-nqa-ri?** And who will guide them there? As with the sentence above, the object is someone other than "me," us," or "you." Therefore a simple periphrastic construction is used: "*he/she-(plural marker)[they]-(direct object marker)[them] lead-he/she will.*"

18. This expansion has "I," "he/she," "we," and "they" will guide "you (one person)," and "you (more than one person)." For more on these complex verbal constructions, see:

for "(*subject, verb*) (to) you (one person)," number 18. Model for Verbs that Include (Pronominally) the Verbal Object "You (One Person)" in Section III: Quechua Grammar Notes,

for "(*subject, verb*) (to) you (more than one person)," number 19. Model for Verbs that Include (Periphrastically and Pronominally) the Verbal Object "You (More Than One Person)" in Section III: Quechua Grammar Notes.

19. The **-pu-**, "it," is a direct object pronoun, here referring to **q'epi**, which is the direct object. This redundancy, repeating the noun object (**q'epi**) in

pronoun form (**-pu-**), can occur when there also is an indirect object expressed in the verb construction, as is seen here with the **-wa-**.

> **Allichu, q'epi-y-ta yuya-pu-wa-y.** Please, watch my "q'epi" for me (addressing one person).
>
> *Please, "q'epi"/bundle/luggage-my-(direct object marker) think about/pay attention to-it-for me-(command marker addressing one person).*

20. In this Expansion the word "me" is both a direct object and an indirect object. Direct objects answer the question "whom?" or "what?" in relation to the verb, while indirect objects answer the question "to whom?" or "for whom?" Compare:

> **Allichu, midiku-man pusa-wa-y.** Please, take me to a/the doctor (addressing one person).
>
> ["Me" answers the question "whom" is to be taken, thus showing it is a direct object.]

AND

> **Allichu, unu-ta qo-wa-y.** Please, give me water (addressing one person).
>
> ["Me answers the question "to whom" the "water" (the direct object) is to be given, thus showing it is an indirect object.]

With "me" as an indirect object ("to me" and "for me" also are indirect object phrases), there are two possible constructions in Quechua. One is a pronominal construction with **-wa-** inserted before the verbal ending. The other is a periphrastic construction with the use of a postpositional (with the function of a prepositional) phrase, **ñoqa-pah**, "for me," literally "*I-for*" before the verb. The former is preferred. Compare:

> **Allichu, q'epi-y-ta yuya-pu-wa-y.** Please, watch my "q'epi" for me (addressing one person).
>
> *Please, "q'epi"/bundle/luggage-my-(direct object marker) think about/pay attention to-it-for me-(command marker addressing one person).*

AND

> **Allichu, kay-ta(-m) ñoqa-pah hap'i-y.** Please, hold this for me (addressing one person).
>
> *Please, this-(direct object marker)(-particle of certainty or assurance) I-for grab/take/seize/hold-(command marker addressing one person).*

21. In Quechua, verbs can be created by adding the infinitive marker "to," the suffix **-y**, to different parts of speech. Here the verb "to get off" is created from the adverb **uray**, "down." Thus we have **kamiyun-manta**

uray-ku-y, "to get off the truck," literally, "to down oneself from the truck."

22. **Ñoqayku**, "we" (excluding the person[s] addressed) and **ñoqancheh**, "we" (including the person[s] addressed), are used with the direct object marker, **-ta**, affixed, when "us" is the object of an infinitive, as is the case here with the infinitive **yanapa-y**, "to help," and its object **ñoqayku**, "us."

>¿<u>Yanapa-y-ta ñoqayku-ta</u> ati-nki-chu? Can you (one person) <u>help us</u>?/Are you (one person) able <u>to help us</u>?
>
>*Help-(infinitive marker, "to")-(direct object marker) we(excluding the person[s] addressed)-(direct object marker)[us] can/able-you(one person)-(question marker)?*
>
>¿<u>Yanapa-y-ta ñoqayku-ta</u> ati-nki-cheh-chu? Can you (more than one person) <u>help us</u>?/Are you (more than one person) able <u>to help us</u>?

However, if "us" is the object of a conjugated verb, a different construction must be used. (See number 17. Model for Verbs that Include [Periphrastically and Pronominally] the Verbal Object "Us" in Section III: Quechua Grammar Notes.)

23. Remember that the constructions for "me" and "us" as objects of an infinitive differed from each other.

>¿**Yanapa-wa-y-ta** ati-nki-chu? Can you help <u>me</u>?/Are you able to help <u>me</u>?
>
>BUT
>
>¿**Yanapa-y-ta ñoqayku-ta** ati-nki-chu? Can you help <u>us</u>?/Are you able to help <u>me</u>?

When "you" is the object of an infinitive, the construction pattern is similar, depending on whether the object is "you (one person)" or "you (more than one person)".

>¿**Yanapa-su-y-ta** ati-ni-chu? Can I help <u>you (one person)</u>?
>
>BUT
>
>¿**Yanapa-y-ta qan-kuna-ta** ati-ni-chu? Can I help <u>you (more than one person)</u>?

SECTION II

Model Sentences and Their Expansions

Chapter 6

> **This chapter deals with identifying things.**
> A. What Things Are [Model Sentences 1-12]
> B. To Whom Things Belong [13-24]
> C. From Whom or From Where Things Are [25-29]
> D. For Whom Things Are [30-31]
> E. What Things Are Made Of [32-35]
> F. What Things Are Used For [36-41]

A. WHAT THINGS ARE

1. **¿Ima(tah) kay?** What is this?
   ¿Ima(-tah) kay?
   What(-and) this? ("Is" is understood.)

Expansion:

Asking what things that are pointed out are

¿Ima(-tah) kay? What is <u>this</u>?

chay that
haqay that (over there)

¿Ima(-tah) kay-kuna (ka-nku)? What are <u>these (things)</u>?

chay-kuna those (things)
haqay-kuna those (things) (over there)

2. **Kayqa uh pirwa.**[1] This is a barn (an indigenous, rustic granary/barn).
   Kay-qa uh pirwa.
   This-(emphatic particle) a barn. ("Is" is understood.)

117

Expansion:
Different ways to tell what different things are

Kay-qa uh pirwa. This is a barn (an indigenous, rustic granary/barn).
Uh pirwa-qa. This is a barn.
A barn-(emphatic particle). ("This is" is understood.)
Kay, pirwa. This is a/the barn.
Kay, pirwa-qa. This is a/the barn.

Kay-kuna-qa pirwa-kuna (ka-nku). These are barns./These are the barns.
This-(plural marker)[These]-(emphatic particle) barn-(plural marker) (be-they). ("The" is understood.)
Pirwa-kuna-qa (ka-nku). These are barns./These are the barns.
Barn-(plural marker)-(emphatic particle) (be-they). ("These" is understood.)
Kay-kuna, pirwa-kuna (ka-nku). These are barns./These are the barns.
Kay-kuna, pirwa-kuna-qa (ka-nku). These are barns./These are the barns.

---

3. **¿Chayrí?** And that?
   ¿Chay-rí? And that?
   That-and(with a contrastive nuance)?

4. **Chayqa llahtay.** That's my town.
   Chay-qa llahta-y.
   That-(emphatic particle) town-my. ("Is" is understood.)

Expansion:
Telling what things are in response to a question asking what they are

Chay-qa llahta-y. That's my town.
Chay-kuna-qa llahta-kuna (ka-nku). Those are (the) towns.

Chay, llahta-y-qa.[2] That, it's my town.
That, town-my-(emphatic particle). ("Is" is understood.)
Chay-kuna, llahta-kuna-qa (ka-nku). Those, they're (the) towns.

---

5. **¿Ima(tah) chay llahtahpata sutin?** What is the name of that town?
   ¿Ima(-tah) chay llahta-hpata suti-n?
   What(-and) that town-of name-its? ("Is" and "the" are understood.)

Expansion:

"What is the name of . . .?"

¿Ima(-tah) <u>**chay llahta-hpata**</u> **suti-n?** What is the name <u>of that town?</u>
<u>**chay mayo-hpa** of that river</u> [**mayu** > **mayo**]
<u>**kay qhocha-hpa** of this lake</u>
<u>**haqay suyo-hpata** of that region, area; district or department (political division)</u> [**suyu** > **suyo**]

6. **¿Ima llahtahpata? ¿Chay llahtahpatachu? Punoqa. Chay llahtahpata Puno sutin.**[3] Of what town? Of that town? Puno. The name of that town is Puno.
   ¿Ima llahta-hpata? ¿Chay llahta-hpata-chu? Puno-qa. Chay llahta-hpata Puno suti-n.
   What town-of? That town-of-(question marker)? Puno-(emphatic particle). That town-of Puno name-its. ("The" and "is" are understood.)

7. **¿Ima kaypata sutin?** What do you call this?
   ¿Ima kay-pata suti-n?
   What this-of name-its? ("Is" is understood.)

Expansion:

"What do you call this?"
"What do you call these (things)?"

¿Ima kay-pata suti-n? What do you call this?
¿Ima kay-kuna-hpata suti-n/suti-nku?[4] What do you call these?
What this-(plural marker)[these]-of name-its/name-their? ("Is" is understood.) [Note that "name" rather than "names" is used even though this asks about more than one thing.]

8. **¿Mayqenpata? ¿Kaypatachu?** What? This? (in response to "What do you call this?")
   ¿Mayqen-pata? ¿Kay-pata-chu?
   Which-of? This-of-(question marker)?

Expansion:

"What? This?"; "What? These?" (in response to "What do you call this/these?")

¿Mayqen-pata? ¿Kay-pata-chu? What? This?

¿Mayqen-kuna-pata? ¿Kay-kuna-pata-chu? What (things)? These (things)?
Which-(plural marker)-of? This-(plural marker)[These]-of-(question marker)?

9. **Mana yachanichu.** I don't know.
Mana yacha-ni-chu.
Not know-I-(negative marker).

10. **Kaypata khirkinchu sutin.** This is called an armadillo.
Kay-pata khirkinchu suti-n.
This-of armadillo name-its. ("Is" is understood.)

Expansion:

"This is called . . ."
"Those are called . . ."

Kay-pata <u>khirkinchu</u> suti-n. This is called <u>an armadillo</u>.
Chay-kuna-hpa <u>khirkinchu</u> suti-n/suti-nku. Those are called <u>armadillos</u>.
That-(plural marker)[Those]-of armadillo name-its/name-their.

wisk'acha vizcacha
qowi guinea pig

11. **¿Chayqa allpaqachu?**[5] Is that an alpaca?
¿Chay-qa allpaqa-chu?
That-(emphatic particle) alpaca-(question marker)? ("Is" and "an" are understood.)

Expansion:

"Is that . . .?" "Is that . . . or . . .?"
"Are those . . .?" "Are those . . . or . . .?"

¿Chay-qa allpaqa-chu? Is that an alpaca?
¿Chay-qa allpaqa-chu llama-chu? Is that an alpaca or a llama?
That-(emphatic particle) alpaca-(question marker) llama-(question marker)? ("Is," "an," and "a" are understood.)

¿Haqay-kuna-qa allpaqa-kuna-chu (ka-nku)? Are those alpacas (over there)?
That(over there)-(plural marker)[Those(over there)]-(emphatic particle) alpaca-(plural marker)-(question marker) (be-they)?

¿Haqay-kuna-qa allpaqa-kuna-chu llama-kuna-chu (ka-nku)? Are those alpacas or llamas (over there)?

12. **Mana(n), mana allpaqachu, chay, llamaqa.** No, that's not an alpaca, that's a llama.
Mana(-n), mana allpaqa-chu, chay, llama-qa.
No(-emphatic particle), not alpaca-(negative marker), that, llama-(emphatic particle). ("Is," "an," and "a" are understood.)

B. TO WHOM THINGS BELONG

13. **¿Pehpata chay?** Whose is that? [**pi-** > **pe-**]
¿Pe-hpata chay?
Who-of that? ("Is" is understood.)

Expansion A:

"Whose is that?"
"Whose are those?"

¿Pe-hpata chay? Whose is that? [**pi-** > **pe-**]
¿Pe-hpata chay-qa? Whose is that (emphatic)? [**pi-** > **pe-**]
Who-of that-(emphatic particle)? ("Is" is understood.)
¿Pe-hpata chay-rí? And whose is that? [**pi-** > **pe-**]
Who-of that-and(with a contrastive nuance)? ("Is" is understood.)

¿Pe-hpata chay-kuna (ka-nku)? Whose are those? [**pi-** > **pe-**]
Who-of that-(plural marker)[those] (be-they)?
¿Pe-hpata chay-kuna-qa (ka-nku)? Whose are those (emphatic)? [**pi-** > **pe-**]
¿Pe-hpata chay-kuna-rí (ka-nku)? And whose are those? [**pi-** > **pe-**]

Expansion B:

"Whose . . . is that?" "Whose is that . . .?"
"Whose . . . are those?" "Whose are those . . .?"

¿Pe-hpata chay? Whose is that?
¿Pe-hpata chay llama? Whose llama is that?/Whose is that llama?

¿Pe-hpata chay-kuna (ka-nku)? Whose are those?
Who-of that-(plural marker)[those] (be-they)?

¿Pe-hpata chay llama-kuna (ka-nku)?[6] Whose llamas are those?/Whose are those llamas?

14. **Ñoqahpata.** Mine.
    Ñoqa-hpata.
    I-of[Mine].

15. **¿Qanpatachu kayqa?** Is this yours?
    ¿Qan-pata-chu kay-qa?
    You(one person)-of[Yours]-(question marker) this-(emphatic particle)? ("Is" is understood.)

16. **Mana(n). Chayqa mana ñoqahpatachu.** No. That isn't mine.
    Mana(-n). Chay-qa mana ñoqa-hpata-chu.
    No(-emphatic particle). That-(emphatic particle) not I-of[mine]-(negative marker). ("Is" is understood.)

17. **Chayqa paypata.** That is his/hers.
    Chay-qa pay-pata.
    That-(emphatic particle) he/she-of[his/hers]. ("Is" is understood.)

Expansion A:

"That is/Those are mine, yours, his, hers," and so on.

Chay-qa pay-pata. That is his/hers.
Chay-kuna-qa pay-pata (ka-nku). Those are his/hers.

ñoqa-hpata mine
qan-pata[7] yours (one person)
pay-pata his/hers/its
ñoqayko-hpata ours (excluding the person[s] addressed) [**ñoqayku** > **ñoqayko**]
ñoqancheh-pata ours (including the person[s] addressed)
qan-kuna-hpata yours (more than one person)
pay-kuna-hpata theirs

Expansion B:

"That is his/hers."
"That llama is his/hers."

"Those are his/hers."
"Those llamas are his/hers."

Chay-qa pay-pata. That is his/hers.
Chay llama-qa pay-pata.[8] That llama is his/hers.
That llama-(emphatic particle) he/she-of[his/hers]. ("Is" is understood.)

Chay-kuna-qa pay-pata (ka-nku). Those are his/hers.
Chay llama-kuna-qa pay-pata (ka-nku). Those llamas are his/hers.
Those llama-(plural marker)-(emphatic particle) he/she-of[his/hers] (be-they).

18. **¿Manachu qanpata?** Isn't it yours?
    ¿Mana-chu qan-pata?
    *Not-(question marker, which follows **mana** in a negative question) you(one person)-of[yours]? ("Is" and "it" are understood.)*

Expansion A:

"Isn't it yours?"
"Aren't they yours?"

¿Mana-chu qan-pata? Isn't it yours?
¿Mana-chu qan-pata (ka-nku)? Aren't they yours?
*Not-(question marker, which follows **mana** in a negative question) you(one person)-of[yours] be-they?*

Expansion B:

"Isn't this . . . yours?"
"Aren't these . . . yours?"

¿Mana-chu qan-pata? Isn't it yours?
¿Mana-chu kay llama qan-pata? Isn't this llama yours?
*Not-(question marker, which follows **mana** in a negative question) this llama you(one person)-of[yours]? ("Is" is understood.)*

¿Mana-chu qan-pata (ka-nku)? Aren't they yours?
¿Mana-chu kay llama-kuna qan-pata (ka-nku)? Aren't these llamas yours?
*Not-(question marker, which follows **mana** in a negative question) these llama-(plural marker) you(one person)-of[yours]?*

19. **Mana(n). Chayqa amiguypata.** No. That is my friend's (a male).
    Mana(-n). Chay-qa amigu-y-pata.
    No(-emphatic particle). That-(emphatic particle) friend(male)-my-of. ("Is" is understood.)

Expansion A:

"That is my/your (and so on) friend's."
"That is my/your (and so on) friends'."

Chay-qa amigu-y-pata. That is <u>my</u> friend's (a male).
Chay-qa amigu-s-ni-y-pata. That is <u>my</u> friends' (male or male[s] and female[s]).
That-(emphatic particle) friend-s(males or male[s] and female[s])-(euphonic particle)-my-of. ("Is" is understood.)

-y my
-yki your (one person)
-n his/her
-yku our (excluding the person[s] addressed)
-ncheh our (including the person[s] addressed)
-ykicheh your (more than one person)
-nku their

Expansion B:

"That's . . .'s."
"That's . . .('s) and . . .'s."

Chay-qa <u>amigu-y-pata</u>. That is <u>my friend's (a male)</u>.

Chay-qa <u>Akilina-hpata</u>. That is <u>Akilina's</u>.
That-(emphatic particle) Akilina-of. ("Is" is understood.)
Chay-qa <u>Akilina-hpata(-tah) Pidro-hpata-tah</u>.[9] That is <u>Akilina and Pedro's</u>. [**Pidru** > **Pidro**]
That-(emphatic particle) Akilina-of(-and) Pedro-of-and. ("Is" is understood.)

20. **Mana(n). Chayqa Akilinahpata amigunpata.** No. That is Akilina's friend's (a male).
    Mana(-n). Chay-qa Akilina-hpata amigu-n-pata.
    No(-emphatic particle). That-(emphatic particle) Akilina-of friend(male)-her-of. ("Is" is understood.)

Expansion:

"That is . . .'s/. . .'s."
"That is . . .'s/. . .s'."

Chay-qa Akilina-hpata amigu-n-pata. That is Akilina's friend's (a male).

Chay-qa Akilina-hpata amigu-s-ni-n-pata. That is Akilina's friends' (males or male[s] and female[s]).
That-(emphatic particle) Akilina-of friend-s(males or male[s] and female[s])-(euphonic particle)-her-of. ("Is" is understood.)

Chay-qa Akilina-hpata(-tah) Pidro-hpata-tah amigu-nko-hpata. That is Akilina and Pedro's friend's (a male). [**Pidru > Pidro, -nku- > -nko-**]
That-(emphatic particle) Akilina-of(-and) Pedro-of-and friend(male)-their-of. ("Is" is understood.)

Chay-qa Akilina-hpata(-tah) Pidro-hpata-tah amigu-s-ni-nko-hpata. That is Akilina and Pedro's friends' (males or male[s] and female[s]). [**Pidru > Pidro, -nku- > -nko-**]
That-(emphatic particle) Akilina-of(-and) Pedro-of-and friend(male)-(plural marker)-(euphonic particle)-their-of. ("Is" is understood.)

Chay-qa Hwan-pa wawqe-n-pata. That is Juan's brother's.
That-(emphatic particle) Juan-of brother(of a male)-his-of. ("Is" is understood.) OR

Chay-qa Hwan-pah wawqe-n-pata.[10] That is Juan's brother's.
That-(emphatic particle) Juan-of brother(of a male)-his-of. ("Is" is understood.)

21. **¿Paypatachu chay punchu?** Does that poncho belong to him/her?/Is that poncho his/hers?
Pay-pata-chu chay punchu?
He/She-of[His/Hers](question marker) that poncho? ("Is" is understood.)

Expansion A:

"Does that poncho belong to him/her?"
"Is that poncho his/hers?"

"Do those ponchos belong to him/her?"
"Are those ponchos his/hers?"

¿Pay-pata-chu chay punchu? Does that poncho belong to him/her?/Is that poncho his/hers?

¿Pay-pata-chu chay punchu-s (ka-nku)? Do those ponchos belong to him/her?/Are those ponchos his/hers?

Expansion B:

"Does that poncho belong to . . .?"
"Is that poncho (somebody's)?"

"Do those ponchos belong to . . .?"
"Are those ponchos (somebody's)?"

¿Pay-pata-chu chay punchu? Does that poncho <u>belong to him/her?</u>/Is that poncho <u>his/hers</u>?
¿Pay-pata-chu chay punchu-s (ka-nku)? Do those ponchos <u>belong to him/her?</u>/Are those ponchos <u>his/hers</u>?

Ñoqa-hpata belong to me/mine
Qan-pata belong to you/yours (one person)
Pay-pata belong to him, her, it/his, hers, its
Ñoqayko-hpata belong to us/ours (excluding the person[s] addressed) [ñoqayku > ñoqayko]
Ñoqancheh-pata belong to us/ours (including the person[s] addressed)
Qan-kuna-hpata belong to you/yours (more than one person)
Pay-kuna-hpata belong to them/theirs

22. **¿Ima punchu? ¿Haqayqachu?** What poncho? That one (over there)?
¿Ima punchu? ¿Haqay-qa-chu?
What poncho? That one(over there)-(emphatic particle)-(question marker)?

Expansion:

"What poncho?"
"What ponchos?"

"Which poncho?"
"Which ponchos?"

¿Ima punchu? What poncho?
¿Ima punchu-s? What ponchos?

¿Mayqen punchu? Which poncho?
¿Mayqen punchu-s? Which ponchos?

23. **Mana(n). Mana paypatachu.** No. It isn't his/hers.
Mana(-n). Mana pay-pata-chu.
No(-emphatic particle). Not he/she-of[his/hers]-(negative marker). ("It is" is understood.)

24. **Haqay runa puka ch'ulluyoh, paypata.** It belongs to that man (over there) with (wearing) the red cap.
Haqay runa puka ch'ullu-yoh, pay-pata.
That(over there) man red cap-with, he-of[his]. (In "It belongs to," literally "It is of," "It is" is understood.)

Expansion:

"It belongs to . . . (with a/the) . . ."

<u>Haqay</u> <u>runa</u> <u>puka</u> <u>ch'ullu-yoh,</u> **pay-pata.** It belongs to <u>that man (over there) with (wearing) the red cap.</u>

chay warmi anqas pullira-yoh that (nearby) woman with (wearing) the blue skirt
that(nearby) woman blue skirt-with ("The" is understood.)
sipas q'omer awayu-yoh the young woman with (wearing) the green shawl
young woman green shawl-with ("The" is understood.)
wayna q'epi-yoh that young man with (carrying) the "q'epi"
young man "q'epi"-with ("The" is understood.)
ch'ete piluta-yoh the boy with the ball [it's his ball]
boy ball-with ("The" is understood.)
chay qhari-kuna llama-kuna-wan[11] those men with (herding) the llamas
those male-(plural marker)[men] llama-(plural marker)-with ("The" is understood.)
chay warmi-kuna wawa-wan those women with (accompanying) the child
those woman-(plural marker)[women] child-with ("The" is understood.)

C. FROM WHOM OR FROM WHERE THINGS ARE

25. **¿Pimanta chay?** Who is that from?
¿Pi-manta chay?
Whom-from that? ("Is" is understood.)

26. **Llahtamasiymantaqa.** It's from my fellow townsman.
Llahta-masi-y-manta-qa.
Town-companion-my-from-(euphonic particle). ("It is" is understood.)

27. **¿Maymanta chay? ¿Ayak'uchumantachu?** Where is that from? From Ayacucho?
¿May-manta chay? Ayak'uchu-manta-chu?
Where-from that? Ayacucho-from-(question marker)? ("Is" is understood.)

Expansion:

"Where is that (. . .) from?"
"Where are those (. . .) from?"

¿May-manta chay? Where is <u>that</u> from?
¿May-manta <u>chay punchu</u>? Where is <u>that poncho</u> from?
Where-from that poncho? ("Is" is understood.)

¿May-manta <u>chay-kuna</u> (ka-nku)? Where are <u>those</u> from?
¿May-manta <u>chay punchu-s</u> (ka-nku)? Where are <u>those ponchos</u> from?

---

28. **¿Punchoqa Ayak'uchumantachu?** Is the poncho from Ayacucho?
 [punchu > puncho]
¿Puncho-qa Ayak'uchu-manta-chu?
Poncho-(emphatic particle) Ayacucho-from-(question marker)? ("Is" and "the" are understood.)

29. **Arí, Ayak'uchumantaqa.** Yes, it's from Ayacucho.
Arí, Ayak'uchu-manta-qa.
Yes, Ayacucho-from-(emphatic particle). ("It is" is understood.)

Expansion:

"It's from Ayacucho."
"They're from Ayacucho."

Ayak'uchu-manta-qa. It's from Ayacucho.
Ayak'uchu-manta-qa (ka-nku). They're from Ayacucho.
Ayacucho-from-(emphatic particle) (be-they).

D. FOR WHOM THINGS ARE

30. **¿Pipah chay?** Whom is that for?
¿Pi-pah chay?
Whom(one person)-for that? ("Is" is understood.)

Expansion:

Asking whom something is for

¿Pi-pah <u>chay</u>? Whom (one person) <u>is that</u> for?

¿Pi-pah? Whom (one person) <u>is it</u> for?
Whom-for? ("Is it" is understood.)
¿Pi-pah <u>chay-kuna (ka-nku)</u>? Whom (one person) <u>are those</u> for?
Whom-for that-(plural marker)[those] (be-they)?
¿Pi-pah <u>(ka-nku)</u>? Whom (one person) <u>are they</u> for?
Whom-for (be-they)?

¿Pi-kuna-pah? Whom (more than one person) <u>is it</u> for?
Whom-(plural marker)-for? ("Is it" is understood.)
¿Pi-kuna-pah <u>chay-kuna (ka-nku)</u>? Whom (more than one person) <u>are those</u> for?
Whom-(plural marker)-for that-(plural marker)[those] (be-they)?
¿Pi-kuna-pah <u>(ka-nku)</u>? Whom (more than one person) <u>are they</u> for?
Whom-(plural marker)-for (be-they)?

31. **Chayqa Pidrupah.** That's for Pedro.
    Chay-qa Pidru-pah.
    That-(emphatic particle) Pedro-for. ("Is" is understood.)

Expansion:

"That's for . . ."
"Those are for . . ."

Chay-qa <u>Pidru-pah.</u> That's <u>for Pedro</u>.
Chay-qa <u>Pidru-pah(-pis) Tirisa-pah-pis</u>. That is <u>for Pedro and Teresa</u>.
That-(emphatic particle) Pedro-for(-and) Teresa-for-and.

Chay-kuna-qa <u>Pidru-pah</u> (ka-nku). Those are <u>for Pedro</u>.
That-(plural marker)[Those]-(emphatic particle) Pedro-for (be-they).
Chay-kuna-qa <u>Pidru-pah(-pis) Tirisa-pah-pis</u> (ka-nku). Those are <u>for Pedro and Teresa</u>.
That-(plural marker)[Those]-(emphatic particle) Pedro-for(-and) Teresa-for-and (be-they).

E. WHAT THINGS ARE MADE OF

32. **¿Imamanta kay?** What is this made of?
    ¿Ima-manta kay?
    What-from/of this? ("Is made" is understood.)

Expansion:

"What is this made of?"
"What are these made of?"

¿Ima-manta kay? What is <u>this</u> made of?
¿Ima-manta kay-kuna (ka-nku)? What are <u>these</u> made of?
What-from/of this-(plural marker)[these] (be-they)? ("Made" is understood.)

---

33. **¿Qolqemantachu kayqa?** Is this made of silver?
    ¿Qolqe-manta-chu kay-qa?
    Silver-from/of-(question marker) this-(emphatic particle)? ("Is made" is understood.)

Expansion A:

"Is this made of silver?"
"Are these made of silver?"

¿Qolqe-manta-chu kay-qa? Is <u>this</u> made of silver?
¿Qolqe-manta-chu kay-kuna-qa (ka-nku)? Are <u>these</u> made of silver?
Silver-from/of-(question marker) this-(plural marker)[these]-(emphatic particle) (be-they)? ("Made" is understood.)

Expansion B:

"Is this ... made of ...?"
"Are these ... made of ...?"

¿Qolqe-manta-chu kay-qa? Is this made of silver?
¿Qolqe-manta-chu kay chipana-qa? Is this <u>bracelet</u> made of <u>silver</u>?
Silver-from/of-(question marker) this bracelet-(emphatic particle)? ("Is made" is understood.)

qori gold / **piñi** OR **wal(l)qa** necklace
millma wool / **chompa** sweater

¿**Qolqe-manta-chu kay-kuna-qa (ka-nku)?** Are these made of silver?
Silver-from/of-(question marker) this-(plural marker)[these]-(emphatic particle) (be-they)? ("Made" is understood.)

¿**Qolqe-manta-chu kay chipana-kuna-qa (ka-nku)?** Are these <u>bracelets</u> made of <u>silver</u>?
Silver-from/of-(question marker) these bracelet-(plural marker)-(emphatic particle) (be-they)? ("Made" is understood.)

<u>**qori**</u> gold / <u>**piñi-kuna**</u> OR <u>**wal(l)qa-kuna**</u> necklaces
<u>**millma**</u> wool / <u>**chompa-kuna**</u> sweaters

34. ¿**Kayqa qolqemantachu qorimantachu?**[12] Is this made of silver or of gold?
    ¿Kay-qa qolqe-manta-chu qori-manta-chu?
    This-(emphatic particle) silver-from/of-(question marker) gold-from/of-(question marker)? ("Is made" is understood.)

Expansion:

"Is this made of silver or of gold?"
"Are these made of silver or of gold?"

¿**Kay-qa <u>qolqe</u>-manta-chu <u>qori</u>-manta-chu?** Is this made of <u>silver</u> or of <u>gold</u>?
¿**Kay-kuna-qa <u>qolqe</u>-manta-chu <u>qori</u>-manta-chu (ka-nku)?** Are these made of <u>silver</u> or of <u>gold</u>?
This-(plural marker)[These]-(emphatic particle) silver-from/of-(question marker) gold-from/of-(question marker) (be-they)? ("Made" is understood.)

---

35. **Kay qolqemantaqa.** This is made of silver.
    Kay qolqe-manta-qa.
    This silver-from/of-(emphatic particle). ("Is made" is understood.)

Expansion A:

"This is made of silver."
"These are made of silver."

Kay <u>qolqe-manta-qa</u>. This is made <u>of silver</u>.
Kay-kuna <u>qolqe-manta-qa</u> (ka-nku). These are made <u>of silver</u>.

Expansion B:

"This . . . is made of silver."
"These . . . are made of silver."

Kay qolqe-manta-qa. This is made of silver.
Kay chipana qolqe-manta-qa. This bracelet is made of silver.
This bracelet silver-from/of-(emphatic particle). ("Is made" is understood.)

ch'ullu colorful native conical-shaped knit cap with ear flaps / **millma** wool

Kay chipana-kuna qolqe-manta-qa (ka-nku). These bracelets are made of silver.
These bracelet-(plural marker) silver-from/of-(emphatic particle) (be-they). ("Made" is understood.)

ushut'a-kuna sandals (rustic sandal) / **qara** leather

F. WHAT THINGS ARE USED FOR

36. **¿Imapah kay?** What is this (thing) for?
    ¿Ima-pah kay?
    What-for this? ("Is" is understood.)

Expansion:

"What is this (thing) for?"
"What are these (things) for?"

¿Ima-pah kay? What is this (thing) for?
¿Ima-pah kay-kuna (ka-nku)? What are these (things) for?

37. **¿Imachá?** What thing?
    ¿Ima-chá?
    What-(marker expressing doubt or lack of knowledge)?

Expansion:

"What thing??"
"What things?"

¿Ima-chá? What thing?
¿Ima-kuna-chá? What things?

38. **Chayqa.** That (thing).
    Chay-qa.
    That-(emphatic particle).

39. **Imapahchá.** I don't know what it is for./I don't know what it must be for.
    Ima-pah-chá.
    What-for-(marker expressing doubt or lack of knowledge). ("It is" and "It must be" are understood.)

40. **¿Imapah chay puka millma?** What is that red wool for?
    ¿Ima-pah chay puka millma?
    What-for that red wool? ("Is" is understood.)

41. **Uh punchuta awaypah.** To weave a poncho.
    Uh punchu-ta awa-y-pah.
    A poncho-(direct object marker) weave-(infinitive marker, "to")-for.

Expansion:

Asking and telling what different things are for

¿Ima-pah chay puka millma? What is that red wool for?
Uh punchu-ta awa-y-pah. To weave a poncho.
A poncho-(direct object marker) weave-(infinitive marker, "to")-for.

mat(h)i dried gourd (used as a drinking cup for maté)
Mat(h)i-y to drink maté or any other kind of tea-like infusion

chuwa deep plate (usually the bottom part of a gourd)
Qara-y to serve food
Serve food/feed-(infinitive marker, "to")

NOTES

1. A **pirwa**, in its strictest meaning, is a raised platform upon which bundles of corn stalks or sacks of grain, potatoes, or other agricultural products are piled in rows and tiers to keep them out of the reach of cattle and other large animals. By extension, the word can be applied to any rustic structure that serves to store agricultural products.

    A **q'awa** (dung) **pirwa** is a **pirwa** on which cow, horse, or llama dung is placed for drying or storing for subsequent use as fuel.

2. Compare the difference in emphasis in these two sentences.
    Chay-qa llahta. That's a/the town.
    Chay, llahta-qa. That, it's a/the town.

3. **Puno**, Puno: Capital of the Department of Puno, in Peru, located on the west bank of Lake Titicaca, in a predominantly Aymara speaking area. Puno is some 200 miles east northeast of Arequipa, and at 12,641 feet above sea level, is one of the two highest lacustrine ports of the world, the other being Guaqui, Bolivia, at the south end of Lake Titicaca. (Guaqui is 61 miles due west of La Paz.)

4. Remember that in Chapter 3, Model Sentence 26 and its Expansion we find

    ¿**Ima kay-pata suti-n?** What do you call this?
    What this-of name-its? ("Is" is understood.)
    ¿**Ima kay-kuna-hpata suti-n/suti-nku?** What do you call these?
    What this-(plural marker)[these]-of name-its/name-their? ("Is" is understood.)

    In reference to the second sentence, Note 13 in that chapter says, "In this and similar questions and answers, instead of **suti-nku**, 'their name,' **suti-n**, 'its name,' is often used."

    The Model Sentence dealt with here is the same as the second one above.

5. Alpacas, along with llamas, guanacos, and vicuñas, are the lamoids, the South American members of the Camelidae family, to which the Asian and African camels belong. Alpacas, domestic animals, are found in Peru and Bolivia. They grow to about the size of a sheep, standing some three feet tall at the shoulder. They are valued primarily for their silky lightweight wool, which is long, in one breed (**suri**) growing almost to the ground. In the time of the Inca Empire, members of the nobility wore robes made of alpaca wool. Alpacas are also used for meat. It should be noted that alpacas, like the other lamoids, spit when annoyed.

6. Compare:

    ¿**Pe-hpata chay?** Whose is that?
    ¿**Pe-hpata chay llama?** Whose llama is that?/Whose is that llama?
    AND
    ¿**Pe-hpata chay-kuna (ka-nku)?** Whose are those?
    ¿**Pe-hpata chay llama-kuna (ka-nku)?** Whose llamas are those?/Whose are those llamas?

7. Remember that there are variants of the suffix for "of," **-h**, **-hpa**, **-hta**, or **-hpata** used with a word ending in a vowel, and **-pa** or **-pata** with a word ending in a consonant.

8. Compare the following pairs of sentences. (The first of each pair uses pronominal possession, the second, adjectival possession.)

    Chay llama pay-pata. That llama is his/hers.

Chay-qa llama-n. That is his/her llama.

Chay llama-kuna pay-pata (ka-nku). Those llamas are his/hers.
Chay-kuna-qa llama-n-kuna (ka-nku). Those are his/her llamas.

9. In previous sentences with ". . . and . . .," **(-pis) . . . -pis** was used. The **(-tah) . . . -tah** seen here could just as well have been used. It should be noted, however, that with verbs, **(-tah) . . . -tah** is used. Compare:
   Akilina(-tah) Pidru-tah Akilina and Pedro OR
   Akilina(-pis) Pidru-pis Akilina and Pedro
   BUT
   Taki-nku(-tah) tusu-nku-tah. They sing and they dance.

10. As is seen in this pair of sentences, when **-pa**, "of," is affixed to a noun that is followed by a noun with a possessive, **-pah**, "for," may be used instead.

11. Remember that the two ways of saying "with," **-yoh** and **-wan**, convey different ideas: **-yoh** indicates the noun to which it is attached is owned by or is being worn by the person mentioned; **-wan** merely shows that the person has along with him or her the noun to which it is attached.

12. The expressions "(either) . . . or . . . " and "(neither) . . . nor":
    (1) In a question, "(either) . . . or . . . " is **. . .-chu. . .-chu**.
       Is this made (either) of silver or of gold?
       ¿Kay-qa qolqe-manta-chu qori-manta-chu kay-qa?
       This-(emphatic particle) silver-from/of-(question marker) gold-from/of-(question marker) this-(emphatic particle)? ("Is made" is understood.)
    (2) In a negative statement, "not . . . or . . ."/"(neither) . . . nor . . ." is
       mana(-tah). . .-chu mana(-tah). . .-chu or **ni(-tah). . .-chu ni(-tah). . .-chu**.
       This is not made of silver or gold./This is made neither of silver nor of gold.
       ¿Kay-qa mana(-tah) qolqe-manta-chu mana(-tah) qori-manta-chu.
       This-(emphatic particle) not(-and) silver-from/of-(negative marker) not(-and) gold from/of-(negative marker). ("Is made" is understood.) OR
       ¿Kay-qa ni(-tah) qolqe-manta-chu ni(-tah) qori-manta-chu.
       This-(emphatic particle) not(-and) silver-from/of-(negative marker) not(-and) gold from/of-(negative marker). ("Is made" is understood.)

(3) In an affirmative statement, "(either) . . . or . . ." is **. . .-chus. . .-chus**.

This is made of (either) silver or gold.
Kay-qa qolqe-manta-chus qori-manta-chus.
This-(emphatic particle) silver-from/of-either gold from/of-or. ("Is made" is understood.)

SECTION II
Model Sentences and Their Expansions

Chapter 7

This chapter deals with

A. Describing Cities, Towns, and Terrain by Characteristics or Traits [Model Sentences 1-10]

B. Describing Things by Size, Distance, Weight, and Fit [11-21]

C. Describing Things by Age, Appearance, and Color [22-32]

D. Describing Things by Taste and Smell [33-38]

E. Describing Things by Price and Value [39-48]

F. Describing Things by Quality [49-50]

G. Describing Things by Ease and Difficulty [51-52]

A. DESCRIBING CITIES, TOWNS, AND TERRAIN BY CHARACTERISTICS OR TRAITS

1. **¿Imaynatah Sukri? ¿K'achachu?** What is Sucre like? Beautiful?
   ¿Imayna-tah Sukri? ¿K'acha-chu?
   How-and Sucre? Beautiful-(question marker)? ("Is" is understood.)

Expansion:

"What is/was/are/were . . . like?"

¿Imayna-tah Sukri? What is <u>Sucre</u> like?
¿Imayna-tah Sukri ka-rqa? What was <u>Sucre</u> like?
How-and Sucre be-it did(past tense marker, which stands alone without an additional ending for "he," "she," and "it")?

<u>**chay**</u> that
<u>**chay**</u> <u>**ñan**</u> that road OR
<u>**chay**</u> <u>**yan**</u> that road

chay suyu that region
(h)allp'a the land
mayu the river

¿Imayna-tah chay ñan-kuna (ka-nku)? What are those roads like?
¿Imayna-tah chay ñan-kuna (ka-rqa-nku)? What were those roads like?

chay-kuna those
chay ñan-kuna those roads OR
chay yan-kuna those roads
chay suyu-kuna those regions
mayu-kuna the rivers

2. **Arí. Ancha k'acha. Sukri ñawpa llahta. Sukri runaqa qheshwata rimanku.** Yes. Very beautiful. Sucre is an old town. The people of Sucre speak Quechua.
   Arí. Ancha k'acha. Sukri ñawpa llahta. Sukri runa-qa qheshwa-ta rima-nku.
   Yes. Very beautiful. Sucre old(antique) town. ("Is" and "an" are understood.) Sucre people-(emphatic particle) Quechua-(direct object marker) speak-they. ("The" is understood.)

3. **Llahtaqa hatun.** The town/city is big.
   Llahta-qa hatun.
   Town/City-(emphatic particle) big. ("The" and "is" are understood.)

4. **Chay ñanqa ancha suni.** That road is very long.
   Chay ñan-qa ancha suni.
   That road-(emphatic particle) very long. ("Is" is understood.)

5. **Chay yanpi ashkha llink'u tian.**[1] That road has many curves.
   Chay yan-pi ashkha llink'u tia-n.
   That road-on many curve there be-it[there is/there are].

Expansion:

"That road has/had a lot of curves."
"Those roads have/had a lot of curves."

Chay yan-pi ashkha llink'u tia-n. That road has many curves.
Chay yan-pi ashkha llink'u tia-rqa. That road had many curves.

Chay yan-kuna-pi ashkha llink'u tia-n. Those roads have many curves.

<u>Chay yan-kuna-pi</u> ashkha llink'u tia-rqa. <u>Those roads</u> had many curves.

6. **Chay yanqa urayman rin.** That road goes downhill.
   Chay yan-qa uray-man ri-n.
   That road-(emphatic particle) down-to/toward go-it.

Expansion:

"That road goes downhill."
"That road goes uphill."

Chay yan-qa <u>uray</u>-man ri-n. That road goes <u>downhill</u>.
Chay yan-qa <u>pata</u>-man ri-n. That road goes <u>uphill</u>.
That road-(emphatic particle) up-to/toward go-it.

7. **¿Maypi chay yan wañun?** Where does that road end?
   ¿May-pi chay yan wañu-n?
   Where-in/at that road die-it?

8. **Chay yan orqoh patanpi wañun.** That road ends at the top of the hill.
   Chay yan orqo-h pata-n-pi wañu-n.
   That road hill-of top-its-at die-it. ("The" is understood.)

9. **¿Chhapuchhapuchu chay suyu?**[2] Is that area rough?
   ¿Chhapu-chhapu-chu chay suyu?
   Frayed border-frayed border[Rough]-(question marker) that region/area? ("Is" is understood.)

10. **Haqay mayu mahllumahllu.** That river is dangerous.
    Haqay mayu mahllu-mahllu.
    That river danger-danger[dangerous]. ("Is" is understood.)

B. DESCRIBING THINGS BY SIZE, DISTANCE, WEIGHT, AND FIT

11. **¿Ima chhikan Pidrohpata chahran?** What size is/How big is Pedro's farmland? [**Pidru** > **Pidro**]
    ¿Ima chhikan Pidro-hpata chahra-n?
    What size Pedro-of farmland-his? ("Is" is understood.)

Expansion:

Asking what size or how big things are

¿Ima chhikan Pidro-hpata chahra-n? What size is/How big is Pedro's farmland?
¿Ima chhikan Pidro-hpata chahra-n-kuna (ka-nku)? What size are/How big are Pedro's plots of farmland?
What size Pedro-of farmland-his-(plural marker) (be-they)?

¿Ima chhikan-tah? What size is it?/How big is it?
What size-and? ("Is it" is understood.)
¿Ima chhikan-tah (ka-nku)? What size are they?/How big are they?
What size-and (be-they)?

12. **Ancha hatun.** It is very big.
    Ancha hatun.
    Very big. ("It is" is understood.)

Expansion:

"It's (size)."
"They are (size)."

Ancha hatun. It is <u>very big</u>.
Ancha hatun (ka-nku). They are <u>very big</u>.

Ancha huch'uy very small, short
Ancha suni very long OR
Millay suni very long
Tahsa medium (size)

13. **Llaman uwiha chhikan.** His llama is the size of a sheep.
    Llama-n uwiha chhikan.
    Llama-his sheep size. ("Is," "the," and "of a" are understood.)

14. **¿Manachu llasa?** Isn't it heavy?
    Mana-chu llasa?
    *Not-(question marker, which follows **mana** in a negative question) heavy? ("Is it" is understood.)*

Expansion:

Asking if things are heavy or not

¿Mana-chu llasa? Isn't it heavy?
¿Mana-chu llasa (ka-nku)? Aren't they heavy?
*Not-(question marker, which follows **mana** in a negative question) heavy (be-they)?*

¿**Mana-chu llasa q'epi-yki?** Isn't your "q'epi" heavy?
*Not-(question marker, which follows **mana** in a negative question) heavy "q'epi"-your(one person)? ("Is" is understood.)*

¿**Mana-chu llasa q'epi-ykicheh (ka-nku)?**[3] Aren't your (more than one person) "q'epis" heavy?
*Not-(question marker, which follows **mana** in a negative question) heavy "q'epi"-your(more than one person) (be-they)?*

15. **Llasa, ¡a!** Heavy, yes!
    Llasa, ¡a!
    Heavy, certainly!

16. **Mana(n), uh chhikalla.** No, just a little.
    Mana(-n), uh chhika-lla.
    No(-emphatic particle), a little-just.

17. ¿**Hayk'an llasan?** How much does it weigh?
    ¿Hayk'a-n llasa-n?
    How much-(euphonic particle) weigh-it?

18. **Tawachunka kilu llasan.**[4] It weighs forty kilograms.
    Tawa-chunka kilu llasa-n.
    Four-ten[Forty] kilos weigh-it.

19. **Kay winay millay llasa uh llamapah.**[5] This load is too much/weighs too much for a llama.
    Kay winay millay llasa uh llama-pah.
    This load too heavy a llama-for. ("Is" is understood.)

20. **Kay mana kayman yaykunchu.** This does not fit here.
    Kay mana kay-man yayku-n-chu.
    This not here-into enter-it-(negative marker).

Expansion:

"That does/did/will not fit (in different places)."
"Those do/did/will not fit (in different places)."

Chay mana <u>kay-man</u> yayku-n-chu. That does not fit <u>here</u>.
Chay mana <u>kay-man</u> yayko-rqa-chu. That did not fit <u>here</u>. [**yayku-** > **yayko-**]
Chay mana <u>kay-man</u> yayko-nqa-chu. That will not/won't fit <u>here</u>. [**yayku-** > **yayko-**]

Chay-kuna mana <u>kay-man</u> yayku-nku-chu. Those do not fit <u>here</u>.

Chay-kuna mana <u>kay-man</u> yayko-rqa-nku-chu. Those did not fit <u>here</u>. [yayku- > yayko-]
Chay-kuna mana <u>kay-man</u> yayko-nqa-nku-chu. Those will not/won't fit <u>here</u>. [yayku- > yayko-]

<u>awtuwus-pa</u> <u>pata-n-pi</u> on the top of the bus
bus-of top-its-on
<u>kamiyun-pi</u> in/on the truck
truck-in/on
<u>q'epi-y-pi</u> in my "q'epi"
"q'epi"-my-in

21. **¿Hayk'a kilumitru Limakama?** How many kilometers is it to Lima?
     ¿Hayk'a kilumitru Lima-kama?
     How many kilometer Lima-over to/up to/down to/to? ("Is it" is understood.)

C. DESCRIBING THINGS BY AGE, APPEARANCE, AND COLOR

22. **¿Chay ch'uhlla mosohchu?** Is that hut new?
     ¿Chay ch'uhlla mosoh-chu?
     That hut new-(question marker)? ("Is" is understood.)

23. **Mana(n). Thanta.** No. It is old.
     Mana(-n). Thanta.
     No(-emphatic particle). Old/Used/Worn/Tattered. ("It is" is understood.)

Expansion:

Age of things

<u>Thanta</u>. It is <u>old/used/worn/ tattered.</u>
<u>Thanta</u> ka-nku. They are <u>old/used/worn/tattered.</u>
Old/used/worn/tattered be-they.

<u>Mawk'a</u> <u>old (deteriorated, out of style, in ruins)</u>
<u>Ñawpa</u> <u>old (historically)/antique</u>
<u>Inka-kuna</u> <u>pacha-manta</u> <u>from the time of the Incas</u> (There is no possessive in this construction; here two nouns are used together, as can be done in English with phrases such as "gold watch" and "straw hat.")
Inca-(plural marker) time-from ("The" and "of the" are understood.)

Tawa-pachah wata-yoh 400 years old
Four-hundred year-with
Mosoh new

---

24. **Haqay ancha sumah.** That is very beautiful.
    Haqay ancha sumah.
    That(over there) very beautiful. ("Is" is understood.)

25. **Kay q'omer llimp'eqa k'achitu.** This green color is pretty. [**llimp'i** > **llimp'e**]
    Kay q'omer llimp'e-qa k'achitu.
    This green color-(emphatic particle) pretty. ("Is" is understood.)

26. **¿Ima llimp'itah pullira?** What color is the skirt?
    ¿Ima llimp'i-tah pullira?
    What color-and skirt(typical Andean)? ("Is" and "the" are understood.)

27. **Akilinahpata pulliran pukaqa.** Akilina's skirt is red.
    Akilina-hpata pullira-n puka-qa.
    Akilina-of skirt(typical Andean)-her red-(emphatic particle). ("Is" is understood.)

28. **Chay q'epi yurah.** That "q'epi" is white.
    Chay q'epi yurah.
    That "q'epi" white. ("Is" is understood.)

29. **¿Pehpata chay yurah wasi?** Whose is that white house?/Whose white house is that? [**pi-** > **pe-**]
    ¿Pe-hpata chay yurah wasi?
    Who-of that white house? ("Is" is understood.)

30. **Chay yurah waseqa ñoqahpata.** That white house is mine. [**wasi** > **wase**]
    Chay yurah wase-qa ñoqa-hpata.
    That white house-(emphatic particle) I-of[mine]. ("Is" is understood.)

31. **¿Allinchu chay q'ellu kamisaqa?** Is that yellow shirt all right/fine/okay?
    ¿Alli-n-chu chay q'ellu kamisa-qa?
    Fine-(euphonic particle)-(question marker) that yellow shirt-(emphatic particle)? ("Is" is understood.)

32. **Arí, chay q'elluqa allillan.** Yes, that yellow one is fine.
    Arí, chay q'ellu-qa alli-lla-n.
    Yes, that yellow-(emphatic particle, here affixed to an adjective, making it a nouns, and thus conveying the idea of "one") fine-just-(euphonic particle). ("Is" is understood.)

D. DESCRIBING THINGS BY TASTE AND SMELL

33. **¿Imaynatah chay hilli kasan?** How is that broth?
    ¿Imayna-tah chay hilli kasa-n?
    How-and that broth/juice be-it?

34. **Ancha sumah.** It is very good.
    Ancha sumah.
    Very good. ("It is" is understood.)

Expansion:

"It is/They are very good."
"It is/They are very bad."

Ancha <u>sumah</u> kasa-n. It is very <u>good</u>.
Ancha <u>sumah</u> kasa-nku. They are very <u>good</u>.
Very good be-they.

mana <u>sumah</u> <u>bad</u>
not good
mana <u>allin</u> <u>bad</u>
not good

---

35. **¿Kay ch'uñu ancha hayachu kasan?**[6] Is this "chuño" very hot (spicy)?
    ¿Kay ch'uñu ancha haya-chu kasa-n?
    This "ch'uñu" very hot(spicy)/bitter/sour-(question marker) be-it?

Expansion:

Different tastes

¿Kay ch'uñu ancha haya-chu kasa-n? Is this "chuño" very hot (spicy)?

Ancha <u>haya</u>-chu kasa-n? Is it <u>very hot (spicy)/bitter/sour</u>?
Ancha <u>haya</u>-chu kasa-nku? Are they <u>very hot (spicy)/bitter/sour</u>?

<u>Misk'i</u> <u>sweet/flavorful</u>
<u>Kachi</u> <u>salty</u>
<u>Q'ayma</u> <u>insipid/without alcohol</u>

---

36. **Mana(n), ch'uñutarí ancha rupha tarini.** No, but I find the "chuño" very hot (temperature).
    Mana(-n), ch'uñu-ta-rí ancha rupha tari-ni.
    No(-emphatic particle), "ch'uñu"-(direct object marker)-but very burning hot[temperature] find-I.

Expansion:

Temperatures of food

Ch'uñu-ta ancha rupha tari-ni. I find the "chuño" very hot.

q'oñi hot
q'oñi-lla-ña just hot enough
hot-just-already
chiri cold
ancha chiri very cold
khata frozen

---

37. **¿Imaynalla kanka aycha q'apasan?**[7] How does the roast meat smell?
    ¿Imayna-lla kanka aycha q'apa-sa-n?
    How-just roast meat give smell/aroma-(progressive marker, "-ing")-it? ("The" is understood.)

38. **Sumah q'apasan.** It smells good.
    Sumah q'apa-sa-n.
    Good smell/give aroma-(progressive marker, "-ing")-it.

E. DESCRIBING THINGS BY PRICE AND VALUE

39. **¿Hayk'api(tah) windinkiri?** And how much is it (addressing the seller)?/And how much are they (addressing the seller)?
    ¿Hayk'a-pi(-tah) windi-nki-ri?
    How much-at(-and) sell-you(one person)-and/then(prolonging the question without adding any specific meaning). ("It" and "them" are understood.)

Expansion:

Various ways to inquire about prices

Addressing the seller:
¿Hayk'a-pi(-tah) windi-nki-ri? And how much is it (addressing the seller)?/And how much are they (addressing the seller)?
¿Hayk'a-pi(-tah) chay punchu-ta windi-nki-ri? And how much is that poncho (addressing the seller)?
How much-at(-and) that poncho-(direct object marker) sell-you(one person)-and/then(prolonging the question without adding any specific meaning)?

¿**Hayk'a-pi(-tah) chay punchu-s-ta windi-nki-ri?** And how much are those ponchos (addressing the seller)?
How much-at(-and) those poncho-s-(direct object marker) sell-you(one person)-and/then(prolonging the question without adding any specific meaning)?

Talking to others about the price:
¿**Hayk'a-pi(-tah) windi-nku-ri?** And how much is it (addressing someone other than the seller)?/And how much are they (addressing someone other than the seller)?
How much-at(-and) sell-they-and/then(prolonging the question without adding any specific meaning)? ("It" and "them" are understood.)
¿**Hayk'a-pi(-tah) chay punchu-ta windi-nku-ri?** And how much is that poncho (addressing someone other than the seller)?
How much-at(-and) that poncho-(direct object marker) sell-they-and/then(prolonging the question without adding any specific meaning)?
¿**Hayk'a-pi(-tah) chay punchu-s-ta windi-nku-ri?** And how much are those ponchos (addressing someone other than the seller)?
How much-at(-and) those poncho-s-(direct object marker) sell-they-and/then(prolonging the question without adding any specific meaning)?

Asking the seller or anyone else:
¿**Hayk'a-n chay?** How much is that?
How much-(euphonic particle)-that? ("Is" is understood.)
¿**Hayk'a-n chay-kuna (ka-nku)?** How much are those?
How much-(euphonic particle) that-(plural marker)[those] (be-they)?

¿**Hayk'a kwista-n?** How much does it cost?
How much cost-it?
¿**Hayk'a kwista-nku?** How much do they cost?
How much cost-they?

40. **Tawachunka pisupi windini.**[8] It is/They are 40 pesos (the seller speaking).
Tawa-chunka pisu-pi windi-ni.
Four-ten[Forty]-peso-at sell-I.

Expansion:

"It is 40 pesos."/"They are 40 pesos."
"It costs 40 pesos."/"They cost 40 pesos."

Tawa-chunka pisu-pi windi-ni. It is/They are 40 pesos (the seller speaking).
Tawa-chunka pisu. Aswan waratu-pi mana pi-pis windi-su-nki-man-chu. It is 40 pesos. Cheaper than that no one would sell it to you.
*Four-ten[Forty] peso. More cheap-at not who-any[**mana pi-pis** no one, nobody] sell-(triple marker for "he/she to you[one person would]")-(negative marker). ("It is" and "it" are understood.)*

Tawa-chunka pisu (ka-nku). They are 40 pesos.
Tawa-chunka pisu kwista-n. It costs 40 pesos.
Tawa-chunka pisu kwista-nku. They cost 40 pesos.

41. **¿Hayk'a pasahi kwista-n?** How much does a ticket cost?
    ¿Hayk'a pasahi kwista-n?
    How much passage/fare cost-it? ("A" is understood.)

42. **Uh wulitu ancha qolqe.** A ticket is a lot.
    Uh wulitu ancha qolqe.
    A ticket much money. ("Is" is understood.)

43. **¿Ancha qolqepi(tah) chayta windinkuchu?** Is that expensive (addressing someone other than the seller)?
    ¿Ancha qolqe-pi(-tah) chay-ta windi-nku-chu?
    Much money-at(-and) that-(direct object marker) sell-they-(question marker)?

Expansion:

"Is that/Are those expensive?"
"Is that/Are those inexpensive?"

¿Ancha qolqe-pi(-tah) chay-ta windi-nku-chu? Is that expensive (addressing someone other than the seller)?
¿Ancha qolqe-pi(-tah) chay-kuna-ta windi-nku-chu? Are those expensive (addressing someone other than the seller)?
Much money-at(-and) that-(plural marker)[those]-(direct object marker) sell-they-(question marker)?

Pisi qolqe inexpensive
Little money

---

44. **Mana(n), pisi qolqepi(tah) windinku.** No, it's inexpensive.
    Mana(-n), pisi qolqe-pi(-tah) windi-nku.
    No(-emphatic particle), little money-at(-and) sell-they.

45. **Chay util mana ancha qolqechu kwistan; pisi qolqe kwistan.** That hotel isn't expensive; it's inexpensive.
Chay util mana ancha qolqe-chu kwista-n; pisi qolqe kwista-n.
That hotel not much money-(negative marker) cost-it; little money cost-it.

46. **Kay punchu (ancha) chaninniyoh.** This poncho is worth a (whole) lot/is (very) valuable.
Kay punchu (ancha) chanin-ni-yoh.
This poncho (much) value-(euphonic particle)-with. ("Is" is understood.)

47. **¿Hayk'amanta qorpachawankiman?** For how much would you lodge me?/How much would you charge me to stay here?
¿Hayk'a-manta qorpa-cha-wa-nki-man?
How much-for guest-make(what the noun or adjective is to which it is attached)-me-(dual marker for "you[one person] would")?

Expansion:

"For how much would you (do something) for me?"/"How much would you charge me to (do something)?"

¿Hayk'a-manta <u>qorpa-cha</u>-wa-nki-man? For how much would you <u>lodge</u> me?/How much would you charge me to <u>stay here</u>?

<u>chay-ta</u> <u>rua</u> do that/make that (for)
that-(direct object marker) do/make
<u>kay-ta</u> <u>alli</u> fix this/repair this (for)
this-(direct object marker) fix/repair
<u>haqay-man</u> <u>pusa</u> take (me) there/guide (me) there
there-to guide/lead [Note: Although "me" is not is the phrase given here, it is used in the translation when it is substituted in the Model Sentence.]
<u>haqay-man</u> <u>pusa-wa-nki-man(-tah)</u> <u>kay-man</u> <u>pusa-mu-</u>...<u>-tah</u> take me there and bring me back here/guide me there and bring me back here
there-to guide/lead-me-(dual marker for "you[one person] would")(-and) here-to guide/lead-in this direction[bring back]...-and

---

48. **Tawachunka pisumanta.** For 40 pesos./Forty pesos.
Tawa-chunka pisu-manta.
Four-ten[Forty] peso-for.

F. DESCRIBING THINGS BY QUALITY

49. **¿Sumahchu haqay util?** Is that hotel good?
    ¿Sumah-chu haqay util?
    Good-(question marker) that(over there) hotel? ("Is" is understood.)

50. **Mana(n). Mana sumahchu.** No, it is bad./No, it's not good.
    Mana(-n). Mana sumah-chu.
    No(-emphatic particle). Not good-(negative marker). ("It is" is understood.)

G. DESCRIBING THINGS BY EASE AND DIFFICULTY

51. **¿Chayqa sasa ruaychu?** Is it hard to do that?/Is that hard to do?
    ¿Chay-qa sasa rua-y-chu?
    That-(emphatic particle) difficult do-(infinitive marker, "to")-(question marker)? ("Is" is understood.)

52. **Mana(n). Kay mana sasachu.** No. This is not hard./This is easy.
    Mana(-n). Kay mana sasa-chu.
    No(-emphatic particle). This not difficult-(negative marker). ("Is" is understood.)

NOTES

1. It was pointed out in Note 5 of Chapter 4 that with "how many," **hayk'a**, and with numbers, a following noun is singular rather than plural.
   ¿Hayk'a wawa-yoh ka-nki? How many children do you have?
   How many child-with be-you(one person)?
   Tawa wawa-yoh ka-ni. I have four children.
   Four child-with be-I.
   In the sentence dealt with here, a similar principle is followed because we are dealing with **ashkha** "many," "much," "abundant," an adjective of quantity, coupled with the idea of "to have" or "there is"/"there are". "That road has many curves (much curve)."/"There are many curves (There is much curve) on that road."
   Chay yan-pi ashkha llink'u tia-n. That road has many curves.
   That road-on many curve there be-it[there is/there are].)

2. As was seen before, a noun can be repeated to give a collective noun designating a group of the items indicated, as in **sach'a-sach'a**, "woods," "forest," from **sach'a**, "tree." Here is an example of a noun that is

repeated to create an adjective used to describe something that has an abundance of what that noun designates. **Chhapu**, "fringe," "frayed border," when doubled, **chhapu-chhapu**, is an adjective meaning "uneven," "irregular," and, with terrain, "rough."

3. Note that here in asking more than one person about their "q'epis," **q'epi** is in the singular because each person has only one.

4. Note that a noun preceded by a number is in the singular. Compare:
   kilu kilogram / **kilu-s** kilograms
   BUT
   tawa-chunka kilu forty kilograms
   four-ten[forty] kilograms

5. The word **winay**, "load," refers to a load in a sack to be carried by an animal. The contents of the sack will determine if it or how many like it can be carried by a llama.

6. **Ch'uñu**, frozen dried potato, which has high nutritive value, is commonly made with a variety of sour potatoes called **luki** (or **ruki**). The potatoes first are soaked in water, exposed to freezing night temperatures, then stomped upon or pressed to smash them. Finally they are dried in the open air. This process can be repeated to obtain the final product.

7. Note the difference between the verb **q'apa-y**, "to smell," as in "to give off an aroma," and **muski-y**, "to smell," which is for someone to use his or her sense of smell.
   Kanka aycha <u>sumah q'apa-n</u>. The roast meat <u>smells good</u>.
   Roast meat good smell-it. ("The" is understood.)
   Kanka aycha-ta <u>muski-ni</u>. <u>I smell</u> the roast meat.
   Roast meat-(direct object marker) smell-I. ("The" is understood.)

8. The monetary unit of Ecuador is the *sucre* (**sukri**), that of Peru the *inti* (**inti**) or *sol* (**sul**) (from the Spanish *sol*, "sun"), and of Bolivia the *peso (boliviano)* (**pisu**) (from the Spanish *peso*).

SECTION II

Model Sentences and Their Expansions

Chapter 8

This chapter deals with

A. Asking and Telling People's Names [Model Sentences 1-5]

B. Asking, Telling, and Pointing Out Who Someone Is [6-13]

C. Identifying People by Job, Role, or Position [14-15]

D. Identifying People by What They Are Doing [16-17]

E. Identifying People by Relationship [18-25]

A. ASKING AND TELLING PEOPLE'S NAMES

1. **¿Ima sutiyki?** What is your name?
   ¿Ima suti-yki?
   What name-your(one person)? ("Is" is understood.)

Expansion:

"What is your name?"
"What are your (more than one person) names?"

¿Ima suti-yki? What is your name?
¿Ima suti-ykicheh (ka-nku)?[1] What are your (more than one person) names?
What name-your(more than one person) (be-they)?

---

2. **Pidru(m) sutiy.** My name is Pedro.
   Pidru(-m) suti-y.
   Pedro(-particle of certainty or assurance) name-my. ("Is" is understood.)

Expansion:

"My name is . . ."
"Our names are . . ."

Pidru(-m) <u>suti-y</u>. <u>My name</u> is Pedro.
Pidru(-pis) Mariya-pis <u>suti-yku</u> (ka-nku). <u>Our (excluding the person[s] addressed) names are</u> Pedro and Maria.
Pedro(-and) Maria-and name-our(excluding the person[s] addressed) (be-they).

3. **¿Ima sutin?** What is his/her name?
   ¿Ima suti-n?
   What name-his/her? ("Is" is understood.)

Expansion A:

"What is his/her name?"
"What are their names?"

¿Ima <u>suti-n</u>? What <u>is his/her name</u>?
¿Ima <u>suti-n/suti-nku</u>?[2] What <u>are their names</u>?

Expansion B:

"What is (that person's) name?"
"What are (those people's) names?"

¿Ima <u>suti-n</u>? What is <u>his/her name</u>?

chay-pata suti-n that one's name
that one-of name-his/her
chay runa-hpata suti-n that man's/person's name
that man/person-of name-his
chay qhare-hpata suti-n that man's name (specifically a man, not just "person," which **runa** can mean) [**qhari** > **qhare**]
that man-of name-his

chay-kuna-pata suti-n/suti-nku those people's names
that-(plural marker)[those]-of name-his/her//name-their
chay runa-kuna-pata suti-n/suti-nku those men's/people's names
those man/person-(plural marker)[men/people]-of name-his//name their

4. **Pidru(m) sutin.** His name is Pedro.
   Pidru(-m) suti-n.
   Pedro(-particle of certainty or assurance) name-his. ("Is" is understood.)

Expansion A:

"His name is . . ."
"Their names are . . ."

Pidru(-m) <u>suti-n</u>. His name is Pedro.
Ruwirtu(-pis) Tirisa-pis <u>suti-n/suti-nku</u> (ka-nku). Their names are Roberto and Teresa.
Roberto(-and) Teresa-and name-his/her//name-their (be-they).

Expansion B:

"(This person's)/(That person's) name is . . ."

Pidru(-m) suti-n. His name is Pedro.

<u>Kay-pata</u> Pidru(-m) suti-n. This one's name is <u>Pedro</u>.
This one-of Pedro(-particle of certainty or assurance) name-his. ("Is" is understood.)

<u>chay-pata</u> Pidru(-m) that one's . . . Pedro
<u>haqay-pata</u> Pidru(-m) that one's (over there) . . . Pedro
<u>chay</u> wayna-hpata Ansilmu Sukari that young man's . . . Anselmo Sukari
<u>chay</u> sipas-pata Awrura Wayta that young woman's . . . Aurora Wayta

Expansion C:

"This one's/That one's/That one's (over there) name is . . ."

Pidru(-m) suti-n. His name is Pedro.

<u>Kay-qa</u>, Pidru suti-yoh. This one's name is Pedro.
This one-(emphatic particle), Pedro name-with. ("Is" is understood.)
<u>Chay-qa</u>, Tumas suti-yoh. That one's name is Tomás.
<u>Haqay-qa</u>, Akilinu suti-yoh. That one's (over there) name is Akilino.

5. ¿**Qanpatarí?** And yours (one person)?
   ¿Qan-pata-rí?
   You(one person)-of[yours]-and(with a contrastive nuance)?

B. ASKING, TELLING, AND POINTING OUT WHO SOMEONE IS

6. **¿Pi(tah) payqa?**[3] Who is he/she?
   ¿Pi(-tah) pay-qa?
   Who(-and) he/she-(emphatic particle)? ("Is" is understood.)

Expansion:

"Who is (the person pointed out or named)?"

¿Pi(-tah) pay-qa? Who is he/she?

chay that
chay qhare [qhari > qhare due to the following **-qa**] that man
chay warme [warmi > warme due to the following **-qa**] that woman
Lurinso [**Lurinsu** > **Lurinso** due to the following **-qa**] Lorenzo
Lurdis Lurdes

---

7. **Payqa Ruwirtu.**[4] He's Robert.
   Pay-qa Ruwirtu.
   He-(emphatic particle) Robert. ("Is" is understood.)

8. **¿Pikuna(tah) paykunaqa (kanku)?** Who are they?
   ¿Pi-kuna(-tah) pay-kuna-qa (ka-nku)?
   Who-(plural marker)(-and) he/she-(plural marker)[they]-(emphatic particle) (be-they)?

9. **Paykunaqa Ruwirtu(pis) Tirisapis (kanku).** They are Robert and Teresa.
   Pay-kuna-qa Ruwirtu(-pis) Tirisa-pis (ka-nku).
   He/She-(plural marker)[They]-(emphatic particle) Robert(-and) Teresa-and (be-they).

10. **¿Pi(tah) kamayoh?** Who is the one in charge?
    ¿Pi(-tah) kama-yoh?
    Who(-and) authority-with? ("Is" is understood.)

Expansion:

"Who is . . .?"

¿Pi(-tah) kama-yoh? Who is the one in charge?

patrun the landlord, proprietor

wayna q'epi-yoh the young man with the "q'epi"
young man "q'epi"-with ("The" is understood.)
Daniyela Kunturkanki Daniela Kunturkanki

11. **Payqa, chay.** He/She is that one (nearby).
    Pay-qa, chay.
    He/She-(emphatic particle), that one(nearby). ("Is" is understood.)

12. **¿Haqay warmi Mariya Kunturichu?** Is that woman over there Maria Kunturi?
    ¿Haqay warmi Mariya Kunturi-chu?
    That(over there) woman Maria Kunturi-(question marker)? ("Is" is understood.)

13. **Arí, haqay warmi Mariya Kuntureqa.** Yes, that woman certainly is Maria Kunturi. [**Kunturi** > **Kunture**]
    Arí, haqay warmi Mariya Kunture-qa.
    Yes, that woman (over there) Maria Kunturi-certainly. ("Is" is understood.)

C. IDENTIFYING PEOPLE BY JOB, ROLE, OR POSITION

14. **¿Qanchu wayk'oh kanki?** Are you the cook? [**wayk'u-** > **wayk'o-**]
    ¿Qan-chu wayk'o-h ka-nki?
    You(one person)-(question marker) cook-the one who be-you(one person)?

Expansion:

"Are you the (occupation or role/one who does something)?"

¿Qan-chu wayk'o-h ka-nki? Are you the cook? [**wayk'u-** > **wayk'o-**]

kay-pi trawaha-h the one who works here
here-in/at work-the one who
pusa-h the guide
guide/lead-the one who
awa-h the weaver
weave-the one who

15. **Chay runa kamacheh.** That man is the/a leader. [**-chi-** > **-che-**]
    Chay runa kama-che-h.
    That man command-make(what the meaning of the verb is)-the one who.
        ("Is" is understood.)

Expansion:

"That mán is (job, role, position)."
"Those men are (job, role, position)."

Chay runa <u>kama-che-h</u>. That man is <u>the/a leader</u>. [**-chi-** > **-che-**]
Chay runa-kuna <u>kama-che-h</u>-kuna (ka-nku). Those men are <u>the leaders</u>. [**-chi-** > **-che-**]

kama-yoh <u>the/a boss, the one in charge</u>
authority-with ("The one" is understood.)
llahta kama-yoh <u>the/a city father; the mayor</u>
town authority-with ("The one" is understood.)
(h)allp'a llank'a-h <u>the/a farmer</u>
land work-the one who
llama miche-h <u>the/a llama herder</u> [**michi-** > **miche-**]
llama herder/shepherd-the one who

D. IDENTIFYING PEOPLE BY WHAT THEY ARE DOING

16. **¿Pitah chay hamoh runa?** Who is that man who is coming? [**hamu-** > **hamo-**]
    ¿Pi-tah chay hamo-h runa?
    Who-and that come-the one who man? ("Is" is understood.)

Expansion:

"Who is . . . who . . . ?"
"Who are . . . who . . . ?"

¿Pi-tah <u>chay hamo-h runa</u>? Who is <u>that man who is coming</u>? [**hamu-** > **hamo-**]

<u>chay runa pi-chus hamu-sa-n</u> <u>that man who is coming</u> [optional construction to the one of the Model Sentence]
that man who-(particle that makes an interrogative pronoun a relative pronoun) come-(active [or present] participle marker, "-ing")-he

llama-man chahna-h wayna the young man who is loading the llama
llama-to load-the one who young man OR
wayna pi-chus llama-man chahna-sa-n the young man who is loading the llama
young man who-(particle that makes an interrogative pronoun a relative pronoun) llama-to load-(active [or present] participle marker, "-ing")-he

¿Pi-kuna-tah chay hamo-h-kuna runa-kuna (ka-nku)? Who are those men who are coming? [**hamu-** > **hamo-**]
Who-(plural marker)-and those come-the one who-(plural marker) man-(plural marker)[men] (be-they)?

chay runa-kuna pi-kuna-chus hamu-sa-nku those men who are coming [optional construction to the one of the sentence above]
those man-(plural marker)[men] who-(plural marker)-(particle that makes an interrogative pronoun a relative pronoun) come-(active [or present] participle marker, "-ing")-they

llama-man chahna-h-kuna wayna-kuna the young men who are loading the llama
llama-to load-the one who-(plural marker) young man-(plural marker)[young men] OR
wayna-kuna pi-kuna-chus llama-man chahna-sa-nku the young men who are loading the llama
young man-(plural marker)[young men] who-(plural marker)-(particle that makes an interrogative pronoun a relative pronoun) llama-to load-(active [or present] participle marker, "-ing")-they

17. **Chay hamoh runa amiguy Ransisku.** That man who is coming is my friend Francisco. [**hamu-** > **hamo**]
    Chay hamo-h runa amigu-y Ransisku.
    That come-the one who man friend(male)-my Francisco. ("Is" is undersood.)

Expansion:

Optional constructions for
"That man who is coming, . . ."
"That man who came, . . ."
"That man who will come, . . ."

Chay hamo-h runa amigu-y Ransisku. That man who is coming is my friend Francisco. [**hamu-** > **hamo**]

Chay runa pi-chus hamu-sa-n That man who is coming
That man who-(particle that makes an interrogative pronoun a relative pronoun) come(-progressive marker, "-ing")-he
Chay runa pi-chus hamo-rqa(n) That man who came [**hamu-** > **hamo**]
Chay runa pi-chus hamu-sah That man who will come

E. IDENTIFYING PEOPLE BY RELATIONSHIP

18. **Payqa, amiguy.** He is my friend.
    Pay-qa, amigu-y.
    He-(emphatic particle), friend-my. ("Is" is understood.)

Expansion:

"He is my friend."
"She is my friend."

"He is your friend."
"She is your friend." (and so on)

"They are my friends."
"They are your friends." (and so on)

Pay(-qa), amigu-y. He is my friend.

Pay, amigu-y. He is <u>my</u> friend.
Pay, amiga-y. She is <u>my</u> friend.
Pay-kuna, amigu-s ni-y (ka-nku). They are <u>my</u> friends (males or male[s] and female[s]).
He/She-(plural marker)[They], friend-s(males or male[s] and female[s])-(euphonic particle)-my (be-they).
Pay-kuna, amiga-s ni-y (ka-nku). They are <u>my</u> friends (females).

-yki your (one person)
-n his/her
-yku our (excluding the person[s] addressed)
-ncheh our (including the person[s] addressed)
-ykicheh your (more than one person)
-nku their

19. **Payqa, ñoqahapta amigay.** She is a friend of mine.
    Pay-qa, ñoqa-hpata amiga-y.
    She-(emphatic particle), I-of[of mine] friend(female)-my. ("Is" and "a" are understood.)

Expansion:

"She is a friend of mine."
"She is a friend of yours." (and so on)

"They are friends of mine."
"They are friends of yours." (and so on)

Pay-qa, ñoqa-hpata amiga-y. She is a friend of mine.
Pay-kuna-qa, ñoqa-hpata amiga-s-ni-y (ka-nku). They are friends (females) of mine.
He/She-(plural marker)[They]-(emphatic particle), I-of[of mine] friend-s(females)-(euphonic particle)-my (be-they).

qan-pata / -yki of yours (one person)
you(one person)-of[of yours] / -your(one person)
pay-pata / -n of his/of hers
he/she-of[of his/hers] / -his/her
ñoqayko-hpata / -yku of ours (excluding the person[s] addressed) [-yku- > -yko-]
we (excluding the person[s] addressed)-of[of ours] / -our(excluding the person[s] addressed)
ñoqancheh-pata / -ncheh of ours (including the person[s] addressed)
we (including the person[s] addressed)-of[of ours] / -our(including the person[s] addressed)
qan-kuna-hpata / -ykicheh of yours (more than one person)
you-(plural marker)-of[of yours] / -your(more than one person)
pay-kuna-hpata / -nku of theirs
he/she-(plural marker)[they]-of[of theirs] / -thei

20. **Payqa, ñoqahpata sispa aylluy.** He/She is a relative of mine by marriage.
Pay-qa, ñoqa-hpata sispa ayllu-y.
He/She-(emphatic particle), I-of[of mine] close-relative(dual construction for "relative by marriage")-my. ("Is" and "a" are understood.)

21. **¿Piniyki?** What relative of yours?
¿Pi-ni-yki?
Who-(euphonic particle)-your?

22. **Payqa, sispawawqey.** (a male speaking) He's my first cousin.
Pay-qa, sispa-wawqe-y.
He-(emphatic particle), close-brother(of a male)[first cousin]-my. ("Is" is understood.)

23. **Kayqa, Pidrohpata llahtamasin.** This is a fellow townsman of Pedro. [**Pidru > Pidro**]
Kay-qa, Pidro-hpata llahta-masi-n.
This-(emphatic particle), Pedro-of town-companion-his. ("Is" and "a" are understood.)

24. **¿Manachu wawqeyki Ruwirtu?** (to a male) Isn't he your brother Roberto?
¿Mana-chu wawqe-yki Ruwirtu?
*Not-(question marker, which follows **mana** in a negative question) brother(of a male)-your Robert? ("Is" and "he" are understood.)*

25. **Mana wawqeychu; sispawawqey.** (a male speaking) He's not my brother; he's my cousin.
Mana wawqe-y-chu; sispa-wawqe-y.
Not-brother(of a male)-my-(negative marker); close brother(of a male)[first cousin]-my. ("He" and "is" are understood.)

NOTES

1. Note that in this question and in an answer to it, found in the next Expansion, of Model Sentence 2, **suti**, "name," is used in the singular, as each person has one name.

    ¿Ima <u>suti-ykicheh</u> (ka-nku)? What are <u>your (more than one person) names</u>?
    What name-your(more than one person) (be-they)?
    Pidru(-pis) Mariya-pis <u>suti-yku</u> (ka-nku). <u>Our (excluding the person[s] addressed) names</u> are Pedro and Maria.
    Pedro(-and) Maria-and name-our(excluding the person[s] addressed) (be-they).

2. Remember, as was pointed out in Chapter 3, that in these and similar questions and answers, instead of **suti-nku**, "their name," **suti-n**, "its name," often is used.

3. Compare this question, "Who is he/she?" with "What is he/she?" from Chapter 1.

    ¿Pi-(tah) pay-qa? Who is he/she?
    Who(-and) he/she-(emphatic particle)? ("Is" is understood.)
    ¿Ima(-tah) pay-qa? What is he/she?
    What(-and) he/she-(emphatic particle)? ("Is" is understood.) OR
    ¿Ima(-tah) pay-rí? And what is he/she?
    What(-and) he/she-and(with a contrastive nuance)? ("Is" is understood.)

4. Compare "What is he/she?," "He is a student," and "Who is he/she?," "He is Robert."

> **¿Ima(-tah) pay-qa?** What is he/she?
> *What(-and) he/she-(emphatic particle)? ("Is" is understood.)*
> **Pay alumnu.** He is a student.
> *He student. ("Is" and "a" are understood.)*
> **Pay alumna.** She is a student.

> **¿Pi(-tah) pay-qa?** Who is he?
> *Who(-and) he/she-(emphatic particle)? ("Is" is understood.)*
> **Pay-qa Ruwirtu.** He's Robert.
> *He-(emphatic particle) Robert. ("Is" is understood.)*

In this second question/answer pair, the emphasis is on "he," "Who is he?," and "He is Robert," so the emphatic particle **-qa** is used with "he." However, a similar question and answer without any emphasis on "he" could also be used.

> **¿Pi(-tah) pay?** Who is he/she?
> *Who(-and) he/she? ("Is" is understood.)*
> **Pay, Ruwirtu.** He's Robert.
> *He, Robert. ("Is" is understood.)*

SECTION II

Model Sentences and Their Expansions

Chapter 9

This chapter deals with

A. Describing People by Physical Characteristics [Model Sentences 1-3]

B. Describing People by Age [4-5]

C. Describing People by Condition - Health and Feelings [6-32]

D. Describing People and Things by Making Comparisons [33-37]

A. DESCRIBING PEOPLE BY PHYSICAL CHARACTERISTICS

1. **¿Imaynatah pay?** What is he/she like?
   ¿Imayna-tah pay?
   How-and he/she? ("Is" is understood.)

Expansion:

"What is he/she like?"
"What are they like?"

> **¿Imayna-tah pay?** What <u>is he/she</u> like?
> **¿Imayna-tah pay-kuna (ka-nku)?** What <u>are they</u> like?
> *How-and he/she-(plural marker)[they] (be-they)?*

---

2. **Pidru suni.** Pedro is tall.
   Pidru suni.
   Pedro long[tall]. ("Is" is understood.)

3. **Mariya sumah chuhchayoh.**[1] Maria has beautiful hair. ("Has" - here, literally "is" - is understood.)
   Mariya sumah chuhcha-yoh.
   Maria beautiful hair-with. ("Is" is understood.)

163

Expansion A:

"(Different people) have/has beautiful hair."

Mariya sumah chuhcha-yoh. *Maria has beautiful hair.*

Ñoqa sumah chuhcha-yoh **ka-ni**. I have beautiful hair.
I beautiful hair-with be-I.

Qan .... **ka-nki** you have ...
You(one person) .... be-you(one person)
Pay he/she has ....
He/She ("Is" is understood.)
Ñoqayku .... **ka-yku** we (excluding the person[s] addressed) have ...
We(excluding the person[s] addressed) .... be-we(excluding the person[s] addressed)
Ñoqancheh .... **ka-ncheh** we (including the person[s] addressed) have ....
We(including the person[s] addressed) .... be-we(including the person[s] addressed)
Qan-kuna .... **ka-nki-cheh** you (more than one person) have ....
You-(plural marker) .... be-(dual marker for "you[more than one person]")
Pay-kuna .... **ka-nku** they have ....
He/She-(plural marker)[they] .... be-they

Expansion B:

"Maria has (physical characteristics)."

Mariya **sumah** **chuhcha**-yoh. Maria has <u>beautiful hair</u>.

suni chuhcha <u>long hair</u>
sumah ñawi[2] <u>beautiful eyes</u>
sumah uya <u>a pretty face</u>
pretty face ("A" is understood.)

B. DESCRIBING PEOPLE BY AGE

4. **¿Mashkha watayoh kanki?** How old are you?
   ¿Mashkha wata-yoh ka-nki?
   How many years-with be-you(one person)?

Expansion A:

Variant of "how many"

¿**Mashkha** wata-yoh ka-nki? <u>How</u> old are you?

Hayk'a How many

Expansion B:

"How old is/are (different people)?"

¿**Mashkha** wata-yoh **ka-nki**? How old <u>are you</u>? (**Hayk'a** could be used here as well.)

¿**Mashkha** wata-yoh **ka-nki-cheh**? How old <u>are you (more than one person)</u>?
How many year-with be-(dual marker for "you[more than one person]")?

¿**Mashkha** wata-yoh? How old <u>is he/she</u>?
How many year-with? ("Is he/she" is understood.)
¿**Mashkha** wata-yoh **(ka-nku)**? How old <u>are they</u>?
How many year-with (be-they)?

5. **Iskaychunkaiskayniyoh watayoh kani.** I'm 22 years old.
Iskay-chunka-iskay-ni-yoh wata-yoh ka-ni.
Two-ten[Twenty]-two-(euphonic particle)-with[Twenty-two] year-with be-I.

C. DESCRIBING PEOPLE BY CONDITION - HEALTH AND FEELINGS

6. ¿**Imaynallatah kasanki?**[3] How are you?
¿Imayna-lla-tah kasa-nki?
How-just-and-be-you(one person)?

Expansion:

Asking how different people are

¿**Imayna-lla-tah kasa-nki**? How <u>are you</u>?

kasa-nki-cheh <u>are you (more than one person)</u>

<u>kasa-n</u> is he/she
<u>Pidru</u> <u>kasa-n</u> is Pedro
<u>qosa-yki</u> <u>kasa-n</u> is your husband
<u>warmi-yki</u> <u>kasa-n</u> is your wife

<u>kasa-nku</u> are they
<u>Pidru(-pis)</u> <u>Tirisa-pis</u> <u>kasa-nku</u> are Pedro and Teresa
<u>wawa-yki-kuna</u> <u>kasa-nku</u> are your children
child-your(one person)-(plural marker)[your children] be-they

7. **Allillanpuni kasani.** I am very well.
   Alli-lla-n-puni kasa-ni.
   Well-just-(euphonic particle)-very be-I.

Expansion:

Telling that different people are very well

Alli-lla-n-puni <u>kasa-ni</u>. <u>I am</u> very well.

<u>kasa-n</u> he/she is
<u>Pidru</u> <u>kasa-n</u> Pedro is

<u>kasa-nku</u> they are
<u>Pidru(-pis)</u> <u>Tirisa-pis</u> <u>kasa-nku</u> Pedro and Teresa are
<u>wawa-y-kuna</u> <u>kasa-nku</u> my children are
child-my-(plural marker)[my children] be-they

<u>kasa-yku</u> we (excluding the person[s] addressed) are
<u>kasa-ncheh</u> we (including the person[s] addressed) are

8. **Mana(n) yallinyoh allinchu kasani, tatáy.** I'm not too well, sir.
   Mana(-n) yallin-yoh alli-n-chu kasa-ni, tatá-y.
   Not(-emphatic particle) excess-with well-(euphonic particle)-(negative marker) be-I, father[sir]-my.

9. **Qephnanayani.** I feel like (am on the verge of) throwing up./I'm about to throw up.
   Qephna-naya-ni.
   Vomit-feel like(be on the verge of)/be about to-I.

Expansion A:

"I feel like (am on the verge of) . . ."/"I am about to . . ."
"I feel like (want to) . . ."

Qephna-naya-ni. I feel like (am on the verge of) <u>throwing up</u>./I'm about to <u>throw up</u>. OR
Qephna-naya-wa-n. I feel like (am on the verge of) <u>throwing up</u>./I'm about to <u>throw up</u>.
Vomit-feel like(be on the verge of)/be about to-to me-it.
Puñu (from **puñu-y**, "to sleep") <u>sleeping</u>
Sama (from **sama-y**, "to rest") <u>resting</u>

Expansion B:

"(Different people) feel like throwing up."

Qephna-naya-<u>ni</u>. <u>I</u> feel like (am on the verge of) throwing up./<u>I</u>'m about to throw up. OR
Qephna-naya-<u>wa-n</u>.[4] <u>I</u> feel like (am on the verge of) throwing up./<u>I</u>'m about to throw up.
Vomit-feel like(be on the verge of)/be about to-to me-it.

-wa-yku <u>we (excluding the person[s] addressed)</u>
-(dual marker for "it to us[excluding the person(s) addressed]")
-wa-ncheh <u>we (including the person[s] addressed)</u>
-(dual marker for "it to us[including the person(s) addressed]")
-su-nki[5] <u>you (one person)</u>
-(dual marker for "it to you[one person]")
-su-nki-cheh[6] <u>you (more than one person)</u>
-(triple marker for "it to you[more than one person]")
-n pay-ta <u>he/she/it</u>
-it he/she-to[to him/her]
-n pay-kuna-ta <u>they</u>
-it he/she-(plural maker)[they]-to[to them]

10. **Ñoqa sinchi onqosqa kasani.** I am very sick.
    Ñoqa sinchi onqo-sqa kasa-ni.
    I very get sick-(past participle marker, "-ed")[sickened] be-I.

11. **Ruphayonqoyniyoh kasani.** I have a fever.
    Ruphay-onqoy-ni-yoh kasa-ni.
    Hot-sickness-(euphonic particle)-with be-I.

Expansion:

"I have (sickness)."

<u>**Ruphay-onqoy-ni-yoh**</u> kasa-ni. I have <u>a fever</u>.

Uma-nanay-ni-yoh a headache
Head-ache-(euphonic particle)-with ("A" is understood.)
Ch'oho-yoh a cough OR
Cough ("A" is understood.)
Ch'uhu-yoh a cough
Cough ("A" is understood.)
Suru(h)ch'i-sqa[7] soroche (Andean altitude sickness)
Afflict with altitude sickness-(past participle marker, "-ed")[afflicted]
Surump'i-sqa[8] light blindness
Afflict with light blindness-(past participle marker, "-ed")[afflicted]

12. **Q'ochawanchus hina kasani.** I may have sunstroke.
    Q'ocha-wan-chus hina kasa-ni.
    Sunstroke-with-maybe like be-I.

Expansion:

Different things someone may have or be suffering from

Q'ocha-wan-chus hina kasa-ni. I may have sunstroke.

Suru(h)ch'i soroche, Andean altitude sickness
Surump'i light blindness

---

13. **¿K'irisqachu kasanki?** Are you hurt?
    ¿K'iri-sqa-chu kasa-nki?
    Wound/Hurt-(past participle marker, "-ed")[Wounded/Hurt]-(question marker) be-you(one person)?

14. **Arí, k'irisqa kasani.** Yes, I am hurt.
    Arí, k'iri-sqa kasa-ni.
    Yes, wound/hurt-(past participle marker, "-ed")[wounded/hurt] be-I.

15. **¿Imanasorqatah?**[9] And what happened to you?
    ¿Imana-so-rqa-tah?
    What happen-(dual marker for "it did to you")-and?

16. **¿Imanaspa(yki)tah nanachikorqankiri?** And what were you doing when you hurt yourself/got hurt?/And how did you hurt yourself/get hurt? [**-ku-** > **-ko-**]
    ¿Imana-spa(-yki)-tah nana-chi-ko-rqa-nki-ri?
    What do-(invariable gerund marker, "-ing," used when the subject of the gerund is the same as that of the main verb)(-your[one person])-and hurt-make(what the meaning of the verb is)-self-did-you(one person) and/then(prolonging the question without adding any specific meaning)?

17. **Uh yana alqo khaniwarqa.**[10] A black dog bit me.
    Uh yana alqo khani-wa-rqa.
    A black dog bite-me-it did.

Expansion:

"(Different animals or plants) (did something to) me."

Uh yana alqo khani-wa-rqa. A black dog bit me.

Uh misi (OR **Uh michi**) / **rachi-wa-rqa** a cat / scratched me
Uh amaru / **khani-wa-rqa** a snake / bit me
Uh apasanka / **wach'i-wa-rqa** a big, poisonous spider / stung/bit me
Uh ch'uspi / **wach'i-wa-rqa** a fly/mosquito / bit/stung me
Uh llama / **thoqa-wa-rqa** a llama / spat on me
Uh phiña waka / **qatiri-wa-rqa** a ferocious bull/cow / chased me
A ferocious bull/cow / chase-me-it did
Uh khishka / **khishka-wa-rqa** a thorn / pricked me
A thorn / prick with thorn-me-it did
Uh kisa / **kisa-wa-rqa** a stinging nettle / pricked me
A stinging nettle / sting with nettles-me-it did
Ch'uspi-kuna / **wach'i-wa-rqa-nku** some flies/mosquitos / bit/stung me
Lachiwana-kuna / **wach'i-wa-rqa-nku** some bees / stung me
Lachiwana-kuna / **wach'i-ra-wa-rqa-nku** a swarm of bees / stung me
Bee-(plural marker) / sting-(marker denoting intensity of the action of the verb, when the action is performed by many in a relatively wide open space)-me-did-they

---

18. **¡Anchata llakikuni!** How sorry I am!
    ¡Ancha-ta llaki-ku-ni!
    Much-(adverb marker) cause sorrow-self-I[(to) myself]!

Expansion:

"I am sorry."

"We are sorry."

¡Ancha-ta llaki-ku-ni! I am very sorry.
¡Ancha-ta llaki-ku-yku! We are very sorry.
Much-(adverb marker)[Very] cause sorrow-selves-we(excluding the person[s] addressed)[to] ourselves].

19. **¿Imayki nanasasunki?** What hurts?
    ¿Ima-yki nana-sa-su-nki?
    What-your(one person) hurt-(progressive marker, "-ing")-(dual marker for "it [to] you")?

20. **Umay nanasawan.**[11] My head aches.
    Uma-y nana-sa-wa-n.
    Head-my hurt-(progressive marker, "-ing")-me-it.

21. **Ruk'ayta mana kuyuchinichu.**[12] I can't move my finger/toe.
    Ruk'a-y-ta mana kuyu-chi-ni-chu.
    Finger/toe-my-(direct object marker) not move-make(what the meaning of the verb is)-I-(negative marker).

Expansion:

"I can't move my . . ."

Ruk'a-y-ta mana kuyu-chi-ni-chu. I can't move my finger/toe.

Ruk'a[13] fingers/toes
Mamaruk'a thumb/big toe
T'upsina ruk'a index finger
Chawpiruk'a middle finger
Siwillina ruk'a ring finger
Sullk'aruk'a little finger
Maki arm/hand; arms/hands
Chaki leg/foot; legs/feet
Uma head

22. **Kay pichuskiy punkisqa kasan.** This (My) ankle is swollen.
    Kay pichuski-y punki-sqa kasa-n.
    This ankle-my swell-(past participle marker, "-ed")[swollen] be-it.

23. **Chakiychus p'akisqa hina kasan.** I think my leg/foot is broken.
    Chaki-y-chus p'aki-sqa hina kasa-n.
    Leg/Foot-my-maybe break-(past participle marker, "-ed")[broken]-like be-it.

Expansion:

"I think my leg/foot is broken."
"I think my leg/foot is twisted (sprained)."

Chaki-y-chus p'aki-sqa hina kasa-n. My leg/foot is broken.

q'ewi-sqa twisted (sprained)
twist-(past participle marker, "-ed")[twisted]

24. **Uh ruk'ay kuchuyoh.** My finger/toe is cut (has a cut).
    Uh ruk'a-y kuchu-yoh.
    A finger/toe-my cut-with. ("Is" is understood.)

25. **Ruk'ay q'eayoh kasan.** My finger/toe is infected.
    Ruk'a-y q'ea-yoh kasa-n.
    Finger/toe-my pus-with be-it.

26. **¿Sayk'usqa kasankichu?** Are you tired?
    ¿Sayk'u-sqa kasa-nki-chu?
    Tire-(past participle marker, "-ed?)[Tired] be-you(one person)-(question marker)?

27. **Arí, ancha sayk'usqa kasani.** Yes, I am very tired.
    Arí, ancha sayk'u-sqa kasa-ni.
    Yes, very tire-(past participle marker, "-ed")[tired] be-I.

28. **Samarinayani.** I feel like resting.
    Samari-naya-ni.
    Rest-feel like-I.

29. **Sayk'uniña purispa(y)wan.** I'm already tired of walking.
    Sayk'u-ni-ña puri-spa(-y)-wan.
    Tire-I-already walk-(invariable gerund marker, "-ing," used when the subject of the gerund is the same as that of the main very)(-my)-with.

Expansion:

"I'm already tired of (activity)."

Sayk'u-ni-ña puri-spa(-y)-wan. I'm already tired of walking.

llank'a-spa(-y)-wan of working
work-(invariable gerund marker, "-ing," used when the subject of the gerund is the same as that of the main verb)(-my)-with

lloq'a-spa(-y)-wan of climbing
climb-(invariable gerund marker, "-ing," used when the subject of the gerund is the same as that of the main verb)(-my)-with

30. **¡Samariy!** Rest! (addressing one person)
    ¡Samari-y!
    Rest-(command marker addressing one person)!

31. **Yarqay ñoqapah kan.**[14] I am hungry.
    Yarqay ñoqa-pah ka-n.
    Hunger I-for[for me] be-it[there is].

Expansion A:

"I am hungry/thirsty."
"I am hot/cold."

Yarqay ñoqa-pah ka-n. I am hungry.
Hunger I-for[for me] be-it[there is].

Ch'akiy thirsty
Thirst
Chiri cold
Ruphay hot
Heat

Expansion B:

Telling that different people are hungry

Yarqay ñoqa-pah ka-n. I am hungry.
Hunger I-for[for me] be-it[there is].

qan you (one person) (are)
pay he/she/it (is)
ñoqayku we (excluding the person[s] addressed) (are)
ñoqancheh we (including the person[s] addressed) (are)
qan-kuna you (more than one person) (are)
pay-kuna they (are)

32. **Chay runa sayk'usqa kasan.** That man is tired.
    Chay runa sayk'u-sqa kasa-n.
    That man tire-(past participle marker, "-ed")[tired] be-he.

> ### Expansion:
>
> "That man is tired."
> "That man is drunk."
> "That man is sober."
>
> **Chay runa <u>sayk'u-sqa</u> kasa-n.** That man is <u>tired</u>.
>
> <u>sayk'u-ri-sqa</u> a little tired
> *tire-(particle that softens the intensity of the action of the verb)-(past participle marker, "-ed")[a little tired]*
> **macha(-ri)-sqa** (a little) drunk
> **ch'aki sonqo** sober
> *dry heart*

D. DESCRIBING PEOPLE AND THINGS BY MAKING COMPARISONS

33. **Ñoqa qanhina sayk'usqa kasani.** I am as tired as you.
    Ñoqa qan-hina sayk'u-sqa kasa-ni.
    I you-like tire-(past participle marker, "-ed")[tired] be-I.

> ### Expansion:
>
> Examples of "(Someone or something is) as (something) as (someone or something else)."
>
> **Ñoqa qan-<u>hina</u> sayk'u-sqa kasa-ni.** I am <u>as</u> tired <u>as</u> you.
> **Q'epi-y q'epi-yki-<u>hina</u> llasa.** My "q'epi" is <u>as</u> heavy <u>as</u> your "q'epi."
> *"Q'epi"-my "q'epi"-your(one person)-like heavy. ("Is" is understood.)*
> **Kay ñan chay ñan-<u>hina</u> sumah.** This road is <u>as</u> good <u>as</u> that road.
> *This road that road-like good. ("Is" is understood.)*
> **Ayak'uchu Lima-<u>hina</u> karu kasa-n.** Ayacucho is <u>as</u> far as Lima.
> *Ayacucho Lima-like far be-it.*

34. **Chay kayhina kwistan.** That costs as much as this.
    Chay kay-hina kwista-n.
    That this-like cost-it.

35. **Ñoqa qanmanta (aswan) pisi sayk'usqa kasani.** I am less tired than you./I am not so tired as you.
Ñoqa qan-manta (aswan) pisi sayk'u-sqa kasa-ni.
I you-than (much) less tire-(past participle marker, "-ed")[tired] be-I.

Expansion:

Examples of "(Someone or something is) less (something) than/not so (something) as (someone or something else)."

Ñoqa qan-manta (aswan) pisi sayk'u-sqa kasa-ni. I am <u>less</u> tired <u>than</u> you./I am <u>not so</u> tired <u>as</u> you.
Q'epi-y q'epi-yki-manta (aswan) pisi llasa. My "q'epi" is <u>less</u> heavy <u>than</u> your "q'epi."/My "q'epi" is <u>not so</u> heavy <u>as</u> your "q'epi."
"Q'epi"-my "q'epi"-your-than (much) less heavy. ("Is" is understood.)

Kay ñan chay ñan-manta (aswan) pisi sumah. This road is <u>not so</u> good <u>as</u> that road./This road is <u>worse than</u> that road.
This road that road-than (much) less good. ("Is" is understood.)

---

36. **Kay sara chaymanta aswan kusay.** This corn is better than that.
Kay sara chay-manta aswan kusay.
This corn that-than more good/pleasant[better/more pleasant]. ("Is" is understood.)

Expansion:

More examples of "(Something is) . . .-er than (something else)."

Kay sara chay-manta aswan kusay. This corn is <u>better than</u> that.
Kay puka chay anqas-manta aswan sumah. This red one is <u>prettier than</u> that blue one.
This red one that blue one-than more pretty. ("Is" is understood.)
Llama-kuna uwiha-s-manta aswan hatun (ka-nku). Llamas are <u>bigger than</u> sheep.
Llama-(plural marker) sheep-(plural marker)-than more big[bigger] (be-they).

---

37. **¿Mayqentah sumahpuni.** Which is the best?
¿Mayqen-tah sumah-puni?
Which-and good-very? ("Is" is understood.)

Expansion:

More examples of the superlative, such as "the best"

¿**Mayqen-tah sumah-puni.** Which is the best?

mana sumah-puni the worst
not good-very

chanin-ni-yoh-puni the most expensive
value/price-(euphonic particle)-with-very
pisi chanin-ni-yoh-puni the least expensive/the cheapest
little value/price-(euphonic particle)-with-very OR
mana chanin-ni-yoh-puni the least expensive/the cheapest
not value/price-(euphonic particle)-with-very OR
chanin-ra-puni the least expensive/the cheapest
value/price-without-very

hatun-puni the biggest/the largest/the longest
big/large-very OR
suni-puni the biggest/the largest/the longest
big/large/long-very
huch'uy-puni the smallest/the shortest
small/short-very

sispa-puni the nearest/the closest
near/close-very
karu-puni the farthest
far-very

NOTES

1. There are several ways to say that someone has something. One is to say that different people are "with" whatever they have, as in
    Mariya sumah chuhcha-yoh. Maria has beautiful hair.
    Maria beautiful hair-with. ("Is" is understood.)
    (Ñoqa) sumah chuhcha-yoh ka-ni. I have beautiful hair.
    (I) beautiful hair-with be-I.
    Another way to say that someone has something is by using a construction with "there is" or "there are." For example:
    Mariya-hpata sumah chuhcha-n ka-n. Maria has beautiful hair.
    Maria-of beautiful hair-her be-it[there is].
    Mariya-hpata sumah chuhcha-n ka-pu-n. Maria has beautiful hair.
    Maria-of beautiful hair-her be-it-it[there is (it)].
    Mariya-hpata sumah chuhcha-n tia-n. Maria has beautiful hair.
    Maria-of beautiful hair-her be-it[there is].

Mariya-hpata sumah chuhcha-n tia-pu-n. Maria has beautiful hair.
Maria-of beautiful hair-her be-it-it[there is (it)].

Mariya-hpata sumah chuhcha-n tiya-n. Maria has beautiful hair.
Maria-of beautiful hair-her be-it[there is].

Mariya-hpata sumah chuhcha-n tiya-pu-n. Maria has beautiful hair.
Maria-of beautiful hair-her be-it-it[there is (it)].

Remember that the verb forms **ka-n, ti-an,** and **tiya-n** (the third-person singular of the present tense) from the verbs **ka-y, tia-y,** and **tiya-y,** respectively, mean "for there to be." There also are the verbs **ka-pu-y, tia-pu-y,** and **tiya-pu-y,** which mean "for there to be it/them (for someone)," with the idea of "(someone) has." For more on the constructions for "to have," see number 4. Possession, D. Quechua for "to have" in Section III: Quechua Grammar Notes.

2. **Ñawi** can mean both "eye" and "eyes." As can be seen in this Expansion, with parts of the body that are found in pairs, such as eyes, elbows, and feet, the singular form can be used for both the singular and the plural when speaking of those of a specific individual.
    Marya sumah ñawi-yoh. Maria has beautiful eyes.
    Maria beautiful eyes-with. ("Is" is understood.)

3. Remember that the verbs **ka-y** and **kasa-y,** "to be," are used in this book with different nuances. **Ka-y** is used to identify and with characteristics, traits, and qualities. **Kasa-y** is used for location, situations, and conditions. Compare Model Sentences 4 and 6. Since someone's age is considered an inherent characteristic, a form of **ka-y** is used in 4. How one feels is a condition, so a form of **kasa-y** is used in 6.

4. Note that in this expansion there is an example of each person as the object of a conjugated verb. For more on this, see number 16. Model for Verbs that Include (Pronominally) the Verbal Object "Me," 17. Model for Verbs that Include (Periphrastically and Pronominally) the Verbal Object "Us," 18. Model for Verbs that Include (Pronominally) the Verbal Object "You (One Person)," 19. Model for Verbs that Include (Periphrastically and Pronominally) the Verbal Object "You (More Than One Person)," and 20. Model for Verbs that Include (Only Periphrastically) the Verbal Objects "Him," "Her," and "Them" in Section III: Quechua Grammar Notes.

5. The construction **-su-nki** literally means "to you (one person)-he/she/it."

The usual subject ending in the present for "he," "she," and "it" is **-n**. One of the two options for the verb ending for the future tense for "we (including the person[a] addressed)," and for the "let's" command (as in "let's go") is **-su-n**. To avoid confusion with these forms, the present tense ending in the construction for "he/she/it to you (one person is changed to **-nki**, thus giving us the **-su-nki**, "he/she/it to you" as seen here.

6. This construction **-su-nki-cheh** literally means "to you (more than one person)-he/she/it." Just like the construction **-su-nki**, "to you (one person)-he/she/it" immediately above, **-su-nki-cheh** has the personal ending **-nki** instead of **-n** to avoid confusion with **su-n(cheh)**, one of the two options for the verb ending for the future tense for "we (including the person[s] addressed," and for the "let's" command (as in "let's go").

7. The symptoms of altitude sickness are headache, mild nausea, shortness of breath, sleepiness brought about by the thin air of high altitudes, and fatigue.

    The application of the word **suruchi**, which means "antimony," to the Andean altitude sickness came from the belief that the illness was caused by this metal, which is abundant in the Andes.

8. In the Andean high plateau of Peru and Bolivia, the brightness of the sun, especially that from its reflection on snow and ice, can cause light blindness that can last a day or more or even be permanent.

9. **¿Imana-so-rqa-tah?**, "What happened to you?," is from the verb **imana-y**, "to happen," "to occur," "to do." It is based on **ima**, "what," and the infix **-na-**, which here shows doubt.

10. With one exception (**urpi**, "dove"), all animals are considered masculine. To specifically designate the female of an animal, **china** precedes the noun.

    china alqo female dog

    To emphasize that the animal is a male, **orqo** precedes the noun.

    orqo alqo male dog

    To denote the male of animals whose name is borrowed from Spanish and ends in an "a," which would be the indication of a female animal, such as **waka**, "cow," and **uwiha**, "sheep," **kawra**, "goat," are often preceded by **orqo** to designate the male of the species.

    orqo waka bull

    orqo uwiha ram

    Urpi, "dove," is generally considered to be a female animal unless **orqo** precedes it, thus designating a male dove.

Note that in dealing with people, to designate a female, **warmi** precedes the noun, and to empasize reference to a male, **qhari** precedes the noun.

11. Note that here the progressive marker **-sa-**, "-ing," precedes the verbal object **-wa-**, "me." More frequently these two infixes are found in the opposite order, **-wa-sa-**.

12. When necessary to clarify if **ruk'a** means "finger" or "toe," **makiruk'a** (literally "finger digit") or **chakiruk'a** literally "foot digit") is used.

13. As was pointed out in Note 2 above, with parts of the body that are found in pairs, such as eyes, elbows, and feet, the singular form can be used for both the singular and the plural when speaking of those of a specific individual.

   ñawi-y my eye / my eyes
   chaki-y my foot / my feet

   Similarly, the singular form of nouns of parts of the body of which there are more than two can designate both the singular and plural of that item.

   kiru tooth / teeth
   k'ama molar / molars

   To indicate only one of a part of the body of which there is more than one, **uh**, or one of its variants, followed by the noun and the appropriate possessive marker to indicate the person involved may be used.

   Uh ñawi-y nana-wa-sa-n. An/One eye is bothering/hurting me./One of my eyes is bothering/hurting me.
   An/One eye-my hurt-(progressive marker, "-ing")-me-it is.
   Uh ñawi-n (pay-man) nana-sa-n. One of his/her eyes is bothering/hurting him/her.
   An/One eye-his/her (he/she-to[(to) him/her]) hurt-(progressive marker, "-ing")-it.
   [Note: It has been pointed out above that when "me," "us," "you (one person)," and "you (more than one person)" are objects of a verb, different constructions, usually including the insertion of the pronoun in the verb form, are used. When "him," "her," and "them" are the objects, a simple construction using **pay**, "him," "her," "it," (as in the last example above) and **pay-kuna**, "them," is used.]

   Uh kiru-y nana-wa-sa-n. A tooth is bothering/hurting me./One of my teeth is bothering/hurting me.
   A/One tooth-my hurt-(progressive marker, "-ing")-me-it.
   Uh kiru-n (pay-man) nana-sa-n. One of his/her teeth is bothering/hurting him/her.

A/One tooth-his/her (he/she-to[(to) him/her]) hurt-(progressive marker, "-ing")-it.

To indicate which part of the body of which there is a pair or more than two is involved, the noun is preceded by anything that can specify it, and is followed by the appropriate possessive marker to indicate the person.

Lloq'e ñawi-y nana-wa-sa-n. My left eye is bothering/hurting me.
Left eye-my hurt-(progressive marker, "-ing")-me-it.
Lloq'e ñawi-n (pay-man) nana-sa-n. His/Her left eye is bothering/hurting him/her.
Left eye-his/her (he/she-to[(to) him/her]) hurt-(progressive marker, "-ing")-it.

Mamaruk'a-y-ta mana kuyu-chi-ni-chu. I can't move my right thumb.
Thumb-my-(direct object maker) not move-make-I-(negative marker).
Mamaruk'a-n-ta mana kuyu-chi-n-chu. He/She can't move his/her right thumb.
Thumb-his/her-(direct object maker) not move-make-he/she-(negative marker).

To emphasize or clarify that both items of such pairs are being referred to, **purah, purahnin,** or **iskaynin,** "both," precedes the noun, which is followed by the appropriate possessive.

Purah ñawi-y nana-wa-sa-nku. Both (of my) eyes are bothering me/hurt.
Both eyes-my hurt-(progressive marker, "-ing")-me-they.
Purah ñawi-n (pay-man) nana-sa-nku. Both (of his/her) eyes are bothering him/her / hurt.
Both eyes-his/her (he/her-to [(to) him/her]) hurt-(progressive marker, "-ing")-they.

On the other hand, if one is referring in general to all the items designated by the noun, the usual plural construction with **-kuna** is used.

Ñawi-kuna riku-y-pah (ka-nku). Eyes are for seeing.
Eye-(plural marker) see-(infinitive marker, "to")-for (be-they).

14. There are different ways of expressing the idea of someone's physical condition such as being hungry and being thirsty.

   a. As seen earlier in the Expansion of Model Sentence 43 in Chapter 5, one is with the past participle of the verb showing the condition ([*verb stem*]-**sqa**, "-ed") followed by the appropriate form of **kasa-y**, "to be."
   Examples:

Yarqa-sqa kasa-ni. I am hungry..
Hunger-(past participle marker, "-ed")[Hungry] be-I.
Yarqa-sqa kasa-nki. You (one person) are hungry.
Yarqa-sqa. He/She/It is hungry.
and so on

b. A second way is seen here, in this Model Sentence, number 31, using **ka-n**, in its impersonal meaning, "there is," and literally saying "Hunger for (me) there is."
Examples:
Yarqay ñoqa-pah ka-n. I am hungry.
Hunger I-for[for me] be-it[there is][There is hunger for me].
Yarqay qan-pah ka-n. You (one person) are hungry.
Yarqay pay-pah ka-n. He/She/It is hungry.
and so on

c. The third way uses the verb, here, **yarqa-y**, "to cause hunger"; "to feel hunger," in a pronominal verbal construction for the first and second persons singular and plural ("I," "we"; "you (singular)," and "you (plural)," literally saying "it (causes hunger) to me, to us (excluding the person[s] addressed), to us (including the person[s] addressed); to you (one person), to you (more than one person)." (For the third persons singular and plural ("he/she/it" and "they"), the constructions are periphrastic, with **pay-ta** and **pay-kuna-ta**. See examples below.)

Examples of pronominal verbal constructions with **yarqa-y**, "to cause hunger," to say that "I," "we," you (one person)," and "you (more than one person)" are hungry:

Yarqa-wa-n. I am hungry
Causes hunger-me-it [It causes me hunger].
Yarqa-wa-yku. We (excluding the person[s] addressed) are hungry.
Causes hunger-(dual construction for "it [to] us[excluding the person(s) addressed]")[It causes us hunger].
Yarqa-wa-ncheh. We (including the person[s] addressed) are hungry.
Causes hunger-(dual construction for "it [to] us[including the person(s) addressed]")[It causes us hunger].
Yarqa-su-nki. You (one person) are hungry.
Causes hunger-(dual construction for "it [to] you [one person]")[It causes you hunger].)
Yarqa-su-nki-cheh. You (more than one person) are hungry.
Causes hunger-(triple construction for "it [to] you [more than one person]")[It causes to you hunger].)

[For pronominal verbal constructions with the objects "me," "us," "you (one person)," and "you (more than one person)," see numbers 16, 17, 18, and 19 respectively in Section III: Quechua Grammar Notes.]

Examples of periphrastic constructions (for the third persons, "he/she/it" and "they") with **yarqa-y**, "to cause hunger," to say that "he/she/it" and "they" are hungry:

Pay-ta yarqa-n. It makes him/her/it hungry.
He/She/It-(direct object marker)[Him/Her/It] causes hunger-it.[It causes him/her/it hunger.]
Pay-kuna-ta yarqa-n. It makes them hungry.
They-(direct object marker)[Them] causes hunger-it.[It causes them hunger.]

[For constructions with verbal objects "him/her/it" and "them," see number 20 in Section III: Quechua Grammar Notes.]

d. The fourth construction uses the double particle infix **-chi-ku-** (**-chi-** [make what the meaning of the verb is] and **-ku-**, "self," "selves") between the stem and ending of a regular, simple conjugation of the verb under consideration, here **yarqa-y** with its meaning "to feel hunger."

Yarqa-chi-ku-ni. I am hungry.
Feel hunger-make-myself-I.
Yarqa-chi-ku-nki. You (one person) are hungry.
Yarqa-chi-ku-n. He/She/It is hungry.
and so on

SECTION II

Model Sentences and Their Expansions

Chapter 10

This chapter deals with

A. The Time of Day [Model Sentences 1-13]

B. The Day of the Week [14-16]

C. The Month of the Year [17-19]

D. Dates [20-23]

A. THE TIME OF DAY

1. **¿Ima uraña(tah)?**[1,2] What time is it?
   ¿Ima ura-ña(-tah)?
   What hour-already(-and)? ("Is it" is understood.)

   ### Expansion:

   Various ways to ask "What time is it?"

   ¿Ima ura-ña(-tah)? What time is it?
   ¿Ima ura-s-ña(-tah) (ka-nku)?[3] What time is it?
   What hour-s-already(-and) (be-they)?

2. **La una.**[4,5] It is 1:00 (o'clock).
   La una.
   The one. ("It is" and "o'clock" are understood.)

   ### Expansion:

   Different ways to way "It is 1:00 (o'clock)."

   La una. It is 1:00 (o'clock).
   Una. It is 1:00 (o'clock).
   One. ("It is" and "o'clock" are understood.)

Una ura-n-ña. It is 1:00 (o'clock).
One hour-(euphonic particle)-already. ("It is" and "o'clock" are understood.)
Uh ura-n-ña.[6] It is 1:00 (o'clock).
One hour-(euphonic particle)-already. ("It is" and "o'clock" are understood.)

3. **Las dus. Las tris. Las kwaru. Las sinku. Las sis. Las siti. Las uchu. Las nuywi. Las dis. Las unsi. Las dusi.** It's two o'clock. It's three o'clock. It's four o'clock. It's five o'clock. It's six o'clock. It's seven o'clock. It's eight o'clock. It's nine o'clock. It's ten o'clock. It's eleven o'clock. It's twelve o'clock.
Two o'clock. Three o'clock. Four o'clock. Five o'clock. Six o'clock. Seven o'clock. Eight o'clock. Nine o'clock. Ten o'clock. Eleven o'clock. Twelve o'clock. ("It's" and "o'clock" are understood.)

Expansion:

Various ways to tell the hour from 2:00 (o'clock) on

Las dus. It is 2:00 (o'clock).

Dus ura-s-ña (ka-nku). It is 2:00 (o'clock).
Two hour-s-already (be-they).
Iskay ura(-s)-ña (ka-nku).[7] It is 2:00 (o'clock).
Two hour(-s) (be-they).

4. **Las dus sinku minutusniyoh (kanku).** It is 2:05.
Las dus sinku minutu-s-ni-yoh (ka-nku).
The two five minute-s-(euphonic particle)-with (be-they).

Expansion:

Various ways to express "It is 2:05." (Of course, different hours and a different number of minutes can be used following this same pattern.)

Las dus sinku minutu-s-ni-yoh (ka-nku). It is 2:05.
Dus ura-s sinku minutu-s-ni-yoh-ña (ka-nku) It is 2:05.
Two hour-s five minute-s-(euphonic particle)-with-already (be-they).
Iskay ura(-s) phisqa minutu(-s-ni)-yoh-ña (ka-nku) It is 2:05.
Two hour(-s) five minute(-s-[euphonic particle])-with-already (be-they).

5. **Las sinku midiyayoh (kanku).**[8] It is 5:30.
Las sinku midiya-yoh (ka-nku).
The five half-with (be-they).

Expansion:

Various ways to express the half hour

Las sinku <u>midiya-yoh</u> (ka-nku). It is 5:30.
Sinku ura-s <u>midiya-yoh-ña</u> (ka-nku). It is 5:30.
Five hour-s half-with-already (be-they).

trinta <u>minutu-s-ni-yoh-ña</u>
thirty minute-s-(euphonic particle)-with-already

Phisqa ura(-s) <u>kimsa-chunka minutu(-s-ni)-yoh-ña</u> (ka-nku).
Five hour(-s) three-ten[thirty] minute(-s-[euphonic particle])-with-already (be-they).

<u>khuskan-ura-yoh-ña</u>
half-hour-with-already

6. **Las sinku tawachunka minutu(sni)yoh (kanku).** It is 5:40.
   Las sinku tawa-chunka minutu(-s-ni)-yoh (ka-nku).
   The five four-ten[forty] minute(-s-[euphonic particle])-with (be-they).

Expansion:

"It is 5:40." (Of course, different hours and a different number of minutes can be used following this same pattern.)

Las sinku tawa-chunka minutu(-s-ni)-yoh (ka-nku). It is 5:40.
Phisqa ura(-s) tawa-chunka minutu(-s-ni)-yoh-ña (ka-nku). It is 5:40.
Five hour(-s) four-ten[forty] minute(-s-[euphonic particle])-with-already (be-they).
Iskay-chunka minutu(-s) sohta ura(-s)-pah pisi-nku. It is twenty to six.
Two-ten[Twenty] minute(-s) six hour(-s)-for lack-they.

7. **Qanchis ura(s)ña paqarinmanta.** It is 7:00 A.M.
   Qanchis ura(-s)-ña paqarin-manta.
   Seven hour(-s)-already morning-of. ("It is" is understood.)

8. **Kimsa ura(s)ña sukhamanta.** It is 3:00 P.M.
   Kimsa ura(-s)-ña sukha-manta.
   Three hour(-s)-already afternoon-of. ("It is" is understood.)

9. **Sohta ura(s)ña ch'isimanta.** It is 6:00 P.M.
   Sohta ura(-s)-ña ch'isi-manta.
   Six hour(-s)-already evening-of. ("It is" is understood.)

10. **(H)isqon ura(s)ña tutamanta.** It is 9:00 P.M.
    (H)isqon ura(-s)-ña tuta-manta.
    Nine hour(-s)-already night-of. ("It is" is understood.)

Expansion:

Telling time by indicating what occurs at that part of the day

Sut'iya-n-ña. It's dawn (approximately 6:00 A.M.).
Dawn/Become clear-it-already.
Inti p'utu-n-ña. The sun is coming up (approximately 6:00 A.M.).
Sun sprout/come out-it-already. ("The" is understood.)

Inti phawa-n-ña. The sun is already taking flight. [This can be either 6:00 A.M. or 10:00 A.M.]
Sun take flight-it-already. ("The" is understood.)

Akulli-y ura-ña. It's already time to break (time to rest, chewing coca leaves) (approximately 10:00 A.M.).
Chew coca leaves-(infinitive marker, "to") hour-already. ("It is" is understood.)
Yunta wata-y ura-ña. It's already time to tie the team of oxen or mules in order to plow (approximately 10:00 A.M.).
Team of oxen or mules tie-(infinitive marker, "to") hour-already. ("It is" and "the" are understood.)

Yunta wata-ra-y ura-ña. It's already time to untie the team of oxen or mules (approximately 4:00-4:30 P.M).
Team of oxen or mules tie-"un-"-(infinitive marker, "to") hour-already. ("It is" and "the" are understood.) OR
Yunta phaska-y ura-ña. It's already time to untie the team of oxen or mules (approximately 4:00-4:30 P.M.).
Team of oxen or mules untie-(infinitive marker,"-to") hour-already. ("It is" and "the" are understood.)

Inti yayku-n-ña. The sun is starting to set (approximately 6:00 P.M.).
Sun enter-it-already. ("The" is understood.)
Inti qhata-n-ña. The sun is setting (around or after 6:00 P.M.).
Sun cover-it-already. ("The" is understood.)
Inti paka-ku-n-ña. The sun is setting (around or after 6:00 P.M.).
Sun hide-self-it-already. ("The" is understood.)

11. **Khuskandiyaña.** It's noon.
    Khuskan-diya-ña.
    Half-day-already. ("It is" is understood.)

Expansion:

"It's noon."

Khuskan-diya-ña. It's noon.
Chawpi-diya-ña. It's noon.
Middle-day-already. ("It is" is understood.)
Chawpi-p'unchaw-ña. It's noon.
Middle-day-already. ("It is" is understood.)

---

12. **Khuskantutaña.** It's midnight.
    Khuskan-tuta-ña.
    Half-night-already. ("It is" is understood.)

Expansion:

"It's midnight."

Khuskan-tuta-ña. It's midnight.
Chawpi-tuta-ña. It's midnight.
Middle-night-already. ("It is" is understood.)

---

13. **Mikhuy pacha.** It's time to eat.
    Mikhu-y pacha.
    Eat-(infinitive marker, "to") time(occasion). ("It is" is understood.)

Expansion A:

"It's time to (do different things)."

Mikhu-y pacha. It's time to eat.

Sama-y to rest
Hatari-y to get up
Llohsi-y to leave

Expansion B:

"It's (different meal) time."

Mikhu-y pacha. It's time to eat.

Paqarin-mikhuy pacha. It's breakfast time.
Morning-eating time(occasion). ("It is" is understood.)
Khuskan-diya mikhuy lunch
Middle-day eating

Khuskan-sukha mikhuy mid-afternoon snack
Middle afternoon eating
Ch'isi mikhuy dinner
Evening eating OR
Tuta mikhuy dinner
Night eating

B. THE DAY OF THE WEEK

14. **¿Ima diyañatah?** What day is it?
    ¿Ima diya-ña-tah?
    What day-already-and? ("Is it" is understood.)

15. **Kunan diya lunis.** Today is Monday
    Kunan diya lunis.
    This day Monday. ("Is" is understood.)

Expansion:

"Today is Monday."

Kunan diya lunis. Today is Monday.

lunis diya Monday
Monday day

---

16. **Lunis. Martis. Mirkulis. Huywis. Wirnis. Sawaru. Dumingu.**
    Monday. Tuesday. Wednesday. Thursday. Friday. Saturday. Sunday.
    Monday. Tuesday. Wednesday. Thursday. Friday. Saturday. Sunday.

Expansion:

Quechua neologisms for the days of the week
[The names of the days given above are naturalized borrowings from Spanish.]

killachaw Monday
atichaw Tuesday
qoyllurchaw Wednesday
illapachaw Thursday
ch'askachaw Friday
k'uychichaw Saturday
intichaw Sunday OR
apuchaw Sunday

C. THE MONTH OF THE YEAR

17. **¿Ima killañatah?** What month is it?
    ¿Ima killa-ña-tah?
    What month(literally, moon)-already-and? ("Is it" is understood.)

18. **Iniru.**[9] (It is) January.
    Iniru.
    January. ("It is" is understood.)

Expansion:

"(It is) January."

Iniru. (It is) January.
Iniru-killa. (It is) January.
January-month. ("It is" is understood.)

---

19. **Iniru. Hiwriru. Marsu. Awril. Mayu. Hunyu. Hulyu. Awgustu. Sitimwri. Uktuwri. Nuwimwri. Disimwri.** It's January. It's February. It's March. It's April. It's May. It's June. It's July. It's August. It's September. It's October. It's November. It's December.
    January. February. March. April. May. June. July. August. September. October. November. December. ("It's" is understood.)

D. DATES

20. **¿Ima diya killahpata?** What day of the month is it?/What is the date today?
    ¿Ima diya killa-hpata?
    What day month-of? ("The" and "is it," and "is" and "the" are understood.)

21. **Wintisinku hulyu, mil nuwisintus nuwinta nuywi.** (It's) July 25, 1999.
    Wintisinku hulyu, mil nuwisintus nuwinta nuywi.
    Twenty-five July, thousand nine hundred ninety nine. ("It is" is understood.)

Expansion:

"(It's) July 25, 1999."
"(It's) July 25, 2000."

Anyone speaking of a year in all probability would use Quechua adaptations of Spanish numbers, and would follow the Spanish pattern of saying, for example, "one thousand nine hundred ninety-nine," and "two thousand." However, below are both the adaptations from Spanish and the Quechua for those same numbers.

Wintisinku hulyu, mil nuwisintus nuwinta nuywi. (It's) July 25, 1999.
Twenty-five July, thousand nine hundred ninety-nine. ("It is" is understood.)

Iskay-chunka-phisqa-yoh hulyu, waranqa (h)isqon-pachah (h)isqon-chunka-(h)isqon-ni-yoh wata. (It's) July 25, 1999.
Two-ten[Twenty]-five-with July, thousand nine-hundred nine-ten[ninety]-nine-(euphonic particle)-with year. ("It is" is understood.)

Wintisinku hulyu, dus mil. (It's) July 25, 2000.
Twenty-five July, two thousand. ("It is" is understood.)

Iskay-chunka-phisqa-yoh hulyu, iskay-waranqa wata. ("It's) July 25, 2000.
Two-ten[Twenty]-five-with July, two thousand year. ("It is" is understood.)

22. **Killa qallariypi.**[10] It is the beginning of the month.
Killa qallariy-pi.
Month beginning-at/during. ("It is," "the," and "of the" are understood.)

Expansion:

"It is the beginning of the month."
"It is the middle of the month."
"It is the end of the month."

Killa qallariy-pi. It is the beginning of the month.

Khuskan killa-pi. It is the middle of the month.
Half month-in/at/during. ("It is," "the," and "of the" are understood.) OR
Chawpi killa-pi. It is the middle of the month.
Half month-in/at/during. ("It is," "the," and "of the" are understood.)

Killa tuku(ku)y-pi. It is the end of the month.
Month end-in/at/during. ("It is," "the," and "of the" are understood.)

23. **San Anris diya.**[11] It's Saint Andrew's Day (November 30).
San Anris diya.
Saint Andrew day. ("It is" is understood.)

Expansion:

"It is (holiday)."

San Anris diya. It's Saint Andrew's Day (November 30).

Kantilarya Candlemas (February 2)
(from the Spanish "Candelaria," "Candlemas")
Santa Kurus Holy Cross (May 3)
Holy Cross
Tayta Sanyagu Saint James' (July 25)
Sir Santiago

NOTES

1. **Ura,** "hour," is a borrowing of the Spanish for "hour," *hora.* Similarly, the ways to ask and tell time are based on those used in Spanish. However, in rural areas, where watches or clocks are not generally used, time is judged by the position of the sun and expressed by the common activity for that time of day. Examples of this are seen in the Expansion of Model Sentence 10.

2. Constructions dealing with telling time, such as in this question, **¿Ima ura-ña(-tah)?,** "What time is it?," often include **-ña,** "already." The particle **-ta,** "at," can be used instead. However, in this book in dealing with the time of day, **-ña** is used for asking and telling time, while **-ta** is used for asking and telling "at" what time something happens, happened, or will happen.

3. In telling the time of day, both **ura,** "hour," and **ura-s,** "hours," may be used. Thus, "What time is it?" can be expressed by **¿Ima ura-ña(-tah)?,** *"What hour-already(-and)?,"* and **¿Ima ura-s-ña(-tah) (ka-nku)?,** *"What hour-s-already(-and) (be-they)?"*

4. In telling time, Quechua usually uses adaptations of Spanish numbers. For numbers in Quechua as well as the Quechua adaptations of Spanish numbers, see number 5. Cardinal Numbers in Section III: Quechua Grammar Notes.

5. The hour is told as in Spanish, by stating the number of the hour preceded by the Spanish "the" that accompanies feminine nouns (since *hora,* "hour," is feminine). If the hour is "one," the singular *la* is used; if the hour given is a higher number, *las* precedes it.

6. In this Expansion, in the first three sentences the adaptation of the Spanish for "one" (*una*), **una**, is used. In this and the following sentences, the Quechua for "one," **uh**, is used. Note that its variants **uj**, **uk**, **huh**, **huk**, and **hoq** can also be used.

7. Compare the following two ways to say "It is 2:00," one using **dus**, the adaptation of the Spanish number *dos*, "two," and one using the Quechua word for "two," **iskay**.
> **Dus ura-s-ña (ka-nku).** It is 2:00.
> *Two hour-s-already (be-they).*
> **Iskay ura(-s) (ka-nku).** It is 2:00.
> *Two hour(-s) (be-they).*

In the first sentence, Spanish influence is seen in both the number and the use of the plural for "hours," **ura-s**. In the second sentence, the Quechua for "two" is used, and there is a choice of the singular **ura**, "hour," or the plural **ura-s**, "hours." The use of the singular, **ura**, follows the Quechua grammatical usage of a singular noun after a number. In both sentences the plural verb form **ka-nku** is optional.

8. Here Quechua again adapts the Spanish time-telling pattern. The half hour is expressed with **midiya**, from the Spanish *media*, "half" (the feminine form to agree with *hora*, "hour," which is feminine), following the number of the preceding hour.
> **Las sinku midiya-yoh.** It is 5:30.
> *The five half-with. ("It is" is understood.)*

9. The ancient Quechua months, from new moon to new moon, were named according to typical weather conditions for that time of year or according to activities, mostly agricultural, that took place then. The ancient Quechua new year began in our month of June. Nowadays the Gregorian calendar is the one generally followed, and the names of the months are adaptations of the Spanish ones.

10. In many areas of the Quechuaphone world, mostly in those far from towns or cities, Quechua people do not often refer to dates or to the day of the month with much precision. They merely approximate the date by saying "at the beginning of the month," "at the middle of the month," or "at the end of the month."

11. The farther one goes away from areas of Spanish language influence, the more often one finds dates expressed by referring to the day on which a religious festivity or other observance is held.

At times **killa**, "month," is added to the name of the observance to indicate the month in which it falls.

> **Krus killa-pi trigu-ta wayra-chi-yku.** In (the month of) November we (excluding the person[s] addressed) winnow the wheat.
> *Holy Cross Day(May 3) month-in wheat-(direct object marker) blow-make(to have the action of the verb done)[winnow]-we(excluding the person[s] addressed).*

Similarly, there are constructions such as

> **Krus-manta uh killa ñawpah-ta ta(y)ta-y hamo-nqa.** A month before May 3 (Holy Cross Day) my father will come. [**hamu** > **hamo**]
> *Holy Cross Day(May 3)-of a/one month before-(adverb marker) father-my come-he will.*

SECTION II

Model Sentences and Their Expansions

Chapter 11

This chapter deals with asking and telling about

A. The Time, Day, Date, or General Time Period of an Event [Model Sentences 1-13]

B. The Duration of an Event [14-18]

C. The Frequency of an Event [19-20]

D. How Long Something Has Been Happening [21-22]

E. How Long Ago Something Happened [23-24]

F. The Weather [25-41]

A. THE TIME, DAY, DATE, OR GENERAL TIME PERIOD OF AN EVENT

1. **¿Ima ura(s)ta hamunki?** (At) what time are you coming?
   ¿Ima ura(-s)-ta hamu-nki?
   What hour(-s)-at(with an hour) come you(one person)?

Expansion A:

"What time is something happening/will something happen/did something happen?"

¿Ima ura(-s)-ta hamu-nki? (At) what time <u>are you coming/will you come</u>?

<u>**ri-nki**</u> <u>do you go</u>
go-you(one person)
<u>**ri-nki**</u> <u>will you go</u>
go-you(one person) will [Note that the present and future forms for "you (one person)" are the same.]

re-rqa-nki did you go [**ri-** > **re-**]
go-did-you(one person)

awtuwus chaya-mu-n is the bus getting here/does the bus get here
bus arrive-in this direction-it
awtuwus chaya-mo-nqa will the bus get here [**-mu-** > **-mo-**]
bus arrive-in this direction-it will
awtuwus chaya-mo-rqa did the bus get here [**-mu-** > **-mo-**]
bus arrive-in this direction-it did

Expansion B:

"What day/month/year are you coming?"

¿Ima ura(s)-ta hamu-nki? (At) what time are you coming?

Ima diya-ta (On) what day
What day-on
Ima killa-pi (In) what month
What month-in/during
Ima wata-pi[1] (In) what year
What year-in/during

2. **La unata.** At one o'clock.
   La una-ta.
   The one-at(with an hour). ("O'clock" is understood.)

Expansion A:

"At (time of day, on the hour)" using numbers

[Note: This phrase "At one o'clock" parallels "It is one o'clock." The difference is that in this Model Sentence "At one o'clock" and its Expansion, **-ta** is added to the basic time phrase, and replaces any **-ña**. (Compare this Expansion with that of Model Sentence 2 in Chapter 10, and see Note 2 in that chapter.) This same pattern can be followed with all phrases and sentences using the number of hours to express the time of day.]

La una-ta. At one o'clock.
Una-ta. At one o'clock.
One-at(with an hour). ("O'clock" is understood.)
Una ura-ta. At one o'clock.
One hour-at(with an hour). ("O'clock" is understood.)

Uh ura-ta. At one o'clock.
One hour-at(with an hour). ("O'clock" is understood.)

Expansion B:

Examples of "at (time of day between hours)"

La una-ta. At one o'clock.
Las dus sinku minutu-s-ni-yoh-ta. At 2:05.
The two five minute-s-(euphonic particle)-with-at(with an hour).
Iskay-chunka minutu(-s) pisi-nku sohta ura(-s)-pah-ta. At twenty to six.
Two-ten[Twenty] minute(-s) lack-they six hour(-s)-for-at(with an hour).
Chunka iskay-ni-yoh ura-ta. At twelve.
Ten two[Twelve]-(euphonic particle)-with hour-at(with an hour).

Expansion C:

Examples of "at (time of day)" without using numbers

Sut'iya-y-ta. At dawn (approximately 6:00 A.M.).
Dawn/Become clear-(infinitive marker, "to")-at(referring in general to an hour).
Inti yayku-y-ta. At the starting of the sun's setting (approximately 6:00 P.M.).
Sun enter-(infinitive marker, "to")-at(referring in general to an hour).

3. **Las dusta(chus) las tristachus.** At two or at three.
   Las dus-ta(-chus) las tris-ta-chus.
   The two-at(with an hour)(-either) the three-at(with an hour)-or.

4. **Chunka ura(s)ta paqarinmanta hamuni.** I am coming at 10:00 in the morning.
   Chunka ura(-s)-ta paqarin-manta hamu-ni.
   Ten hour(-s)-at(with an hour) morning-of come-I. ("The" is understood.)

Expansion:

"Monday morning/afternoon/evening/night"

Chunka ura(s)-ta paqarin-manta hamu-ni. I am coming at 10:00 in the morning.

Lunis paqarin-ta (on) Monday morning
Monday morning-on/during(with a period of time)

Lunis sukha-ta (on) Monday afternoon
Lunis ch'isi-ta (on) Monday evening
Lunis tuta-ta (on) Monday night

5. **Paqarinta hamuni.** I'm coming in the morning.
   Paqarin-ta hamu-ni.
   Morning-in/during(with a period of time) come-I. ("The" is understood.)

6. **Kunan paqarinta hamuni.** I am coming this morning.
   Kunan paqarin-ta hamu-ni.
   This morning-in/during(with a period of time) come-I.

Expansion:

"this morning"
"this afternoon"
"this evening"
"tonight"

"this week"
"this month"
"this year"

Kunan paqarin-ta hamu-ni. I am coming this <u>morning</u>.
Kay paqarin-ta hamu-ni. I am coming this <u>morning</u>.
This morning-in come-I.

sukha-ta afternoon
afternoon-in/during(with a period of time)
ch'isi-ta evening
evening-in/during(with a period of time)
tuta-ta night ["this night" = "tonight"]
night-in/during(with a period of time)

simana-pi[2] week
week-in/during(with a period of time)
killa-pi month
month-in/during(with a period of time)
wata-pi year
year-in/during(with a period of time)

7. **Kunan diyata rini.** I am going today.
   Kunan diya-ta ri-ni.
   This day[Today]-on/during(with a period of time) go-I.

Expansion:

"I am going today/tomorrow/the day after tomorrow/in two years/one of these days."

Kunan diya-ta ri-ni. I am going today.

Q'aya diya-ta tomorrow
Tomorrow day-on/during(with a period of time)
Q'aya-ta tomorrow
Tomorrow-on/during(with a period of time)
Minchha-ta the day after tomorrow/in two days
Minchha wata-ta in two years
Q'aya minchha-ta one of these days

8. **Q'aya simanata ripusah.** I will leave/I'm leaving next week.
   Q'aya simana-ta ripu-sah.
   Tomorrow week-in/during(with a period of time) leave-I will.

Expansion:

Variants of "next"

Q'aya simana-ta ripu-sah. I will leave/I'm leaving next week.

Hawa next *(with week, month, or year)*
Qhepa(n) next *(in order)*

9. **Awgustupi hamuni.** I am coming in August.
   Awgustu-pi hamu-ni.
   August-in/during(with a period of time) come-I.

10. **Awgustu ñawpahdiyapi hamuni.** I am coming on August 1.
    Awgustu ñawpah-diya-pi hamu-ni.
    August first-day-on come-I.

11. **Dus mil dis watapi hamusah.** I am coming/will come in 2010.
    Dus mil dis wata-pi hamu-sah.
    Two thousand ten year-in/during(with a period of time) come-I will.

12. **¿Hayk'ah llahtaykipata phistan?** When is your town's festival?
    ¿Hayk'ah llahta-yki-pata phista-n?
    When town-you(one person)-of[your] festival-its? ("Is" is understood.)

Expansion:

"When is (an event)?"

¿**Hayk'ah** **llahta-yki-pata phista-n**? When is your town's festival?

mirkadu diya market day
diaychaku-yki your birthday
birthday-your(one person)
qan-pata diya-yki your birthday
you(one person)-of[your] day-your(one person)

13. **Q'aya (diya) llahtaypata phistan.** Tomorrow is my town's festival.
    Q'aya (diya) llahta-y-pata phista-n.
    Tomorrow (day) town-my-of festival its. ("Is" is understood.)

Expansion:

"(Day) is/was (event)."

Q'aya (diya) llahta-y-pata phista-n. Tomorrow is my town's festival.
Kunan diya-qa ñoqa-hpata diyachaku-y. Today is my birthday.
This day[Today]-(emphatic particle) I-of[mine] birthday-my. ("Is" is understood.)
Huywis pay-pata diya-n ka-rqa. Thursday was his birthday.
Thursday he/she-of[his/her] day-his/her be-it was.

B. THE DURATION OF AN EVENT

14. ¿**Hayk'ahpacha kaypi kasanki?** Since when have you been here?
    ¿Hayk'ah-pacha kay-pi kasa-nki?
    When-since here-in/at be-you(one person)?

Expansion:

"Since when"

¿**Hayk'ah-pacha** kay-pi kasa-nki? Since when have you been here?

Mayk'ah-pacha Since when
When-since

15. **Qaynapacha kaypi kasani.** I have been here since yesterday.
    Qayna-pacha kay-pi kasa-ni.
    Yesterday-since here-in/at be-I.

16. **¿Hayk'ahta kaypi kasanki?** (For) how long are you going to/will you be here?
    ¿Hayk'ah-ta kay-pi kasa-nki?
    When-during(with a period of time) here-in/at be-you(one person)?

Expansion:

"(For) how long are you going to be here?"

¿Hayk'ah-ta kay-pi kasa-nki? (For) how long are you going to/will you be here?

Mayk'ah-ta (For) how long
When-during(with a period of time)

---

17. **Ashkha diyata kaypi kasasah.** I will be here (for) many days.
    Ashkha diya-ta kay-pi kasa-sah.
    Many day-during(with a period of time) here-in/at be-I will.

Expansion:

"I will be here (for) (amount of time)."

Ashkha diya-ta kay-pi kasa-sah. I will be here (for) many days.

uh diya-s-ta (for) a few days
some day-s-during(with a period of time)
tawa diya-ta (for) four days
four-day-during(with a period of time)
mana unay-ta-chu³ not (for) a long time
not long time-during(with a period of time)-(negative marker)

---

18. **¿Hayk'a unaypitah chayarqankicheh? ¿Tawa urapi?** How long did it take you (more than one person) to get there? Four hours?
    ¿Hayk'a unay-pi-tah chaya-rqa-nki-cheh? ¿Tawa ura-pi?
    How much time-in-and arrive/get there-did-(dual marker for "you[more than one person]")? Four-hour-in?

C. THE FREQUENCY OF AN EVENT

19. **¿Hayk'a kutita hayk'a unaypi Limaman rinki?** How often do you go to Lima?
    ¿Hayk'a kuti-ta hayk'a unay-pi Lima-man ri-nki?
    How many time(occasion)-on how much time-in Lima-to go-you(one person)?

20. **Sapa diya rini.** I go every day.
    Sapa diya ri-ni.
    Every day go-I.

Expansion:

Frequency of an activity

Sapa diya ri-ni. I go <u>every day</u>.

Kimsa kuti-ta uh killa-pi three times a month
Three time(occasion)-on one month-in
Sapa kuti-lla-n very often
Each time-just-(euphonic particle)
Kuti-kuna-ta sometimes
Time(occasion)-(plural marker)-at/on(with a period of time)

D. HOW LONG SOMETHING HAS BEEN HAPPENING

21. **¿Hayk'a unayta kaypi tiakunki?** How long have you been living here?
    ¿Hayk'a unay-ta kay-pi tiaku-nki?
    How much time-during(with a period of time) here-at live-you(one person)?

22. **Phishqa wataña kaypi tiakuni.** I have been living here for five years.
    Phishqa wata-ña kay-pi tiaku-ni.
    Five year-already here-in/at live-I.

E. HOW LONG AGO SOMETHING HAPPENED

23. **¿Hayk'a unayña kayman hamorqanki?** How long ago did you come here? [**hamu-** > **hamo-**]
    ¿Hayk'a unay-ña kay-man hamo-rqa-nki?
    How much time-already here-to come-did-you(one person)?

Expansion:

"How long ago did (different people) come here?"

¿Hayk'a unay-ña kay-man hamo-rqa-nki? How long ago <u>did you come</u> here? [hamu- > hamo-]

<u>**hamo-rqa-nki-cheh**</u> did you (more than one person) come [hamu- > hamo-]
come-did-(dual marker for "you[more than one person]")
hamo-rqa <u>did he/she/it come</u> [hamu- > hamo-]
come-he/she/it did
hamo-rqa-nku <u>did they come</u> [hamu- > hamo-]
come-did-they

24. **Kimsa uraña kayman hamorqani.** I came here three hours ago. [hamu- > hamo-]
    Kimsa ura-ña kay-man hamo-rqa-ni.
    Three hour-already here-to come-did-I.

F. THE WEATHER

25. **¿Kaypi anchata paramunchu?**[4] Does it rain a lot here?
    ¿Kay-pi ancha-ta para-mu-n-chu?
    Here-in/at much-(adverb marker) rain-(untranslatable infix usually used with verbs expressing natural phenomena when those talking consider themselves affected by them)-it-(question marker)?

Expansion:

"Does it rain/snow/freeze a lot here?"

¿Kay-pi ancha-ta <u>para-mu</u>-n-chu? Does it <u>rain</u> a lot here?

<u>rit'i-mu</u> <u>snow</u>
<u>qasa-mu</u> <u>freeze</u>

26. **Arí. Paqarinta wiñay paramun.** Yes. It always rains in the morning.
    Arí. Paqarin-ta wiñay para-mu-n.
    Yes. Morning-in/during(with a period of time) always rain-(untranslatable infix usually used with verbs expressing natural phenomena when those talking consider themselves affected by them)-it.

27. **¿Hayk'ah para(y) mit'a?** When is the rainy season?
    ¿Hayk'ah para(y) mit'a?
    When rain time(period)? ("Is" and "the" are understood.)

Expansion:

Asking when different seasons are

¿Hayk'ah para(y) mit'a? When is the <u>rainy</u> season?
¿Hayk'ah para(y) pacha? When is the <u>rainy</u> season?

ch'aki <u>dry</u>
chiri <u>cold</u>
rupha <u>hot</u>

tarpu-y <u>planting</u>
poqo-y <u>ripening</u>
aymura-y <u>harvest</u>

---

28. **Uh killamantawan.** Within one month.
    Uh killa-manta-wan.
    One month-from-with.

29. **¿Hayk'a unayta para(y) mit'a unan?** How long does the rainy season last?
    ¿Hayk'a unay-ta para(y) mit'a una-n?
    How much time-during(with a period of time) rain season last-it?

30. **Kimsa killata unan.** It lasts three months.
    Kimsa killa-ta una-n.
    Three month-during(with a period of time) last-it.

31. **¿Kunan diyata paramonqachu?** Will it rain today? [**-mu- > -mo-**]
    ¿Kunan diya-ta para-mo-nqa-chu?
    This day[Today]-on/during(with a period of time) rain-(untranslatable infix usually used with verbs expressing natural phenomena when those talking consider themselves affected by them)-it will-(question marker)?

32. **Paras ch'isita chayamonqa.**[5] They say (that) the rain will get here at dusk. [**-mu- > -mo-**]
    Para-s ch'isi-ta chaya-mo-nqa.
    Rain-(marker denoting that the information is secondhand) dusk-at/during(with a period of time) arrive-(in this direction)-it will. ("That" is understood.)

Expansion A:

"They say (that) . . . "

Para-s ch'isi-ta chaya-mo-nqa. They say (that) <u>the rain will get here at dusk</u>. [**-mu-** > **-mo-**]

Qasa-s kunan tuta-ta hamo-nqa. They say (that) <u>a freeze will come tonight</u>. [**-mu-** > **-mo-**]
Freeze-(marker denoting that the information is secondhand) this night[tonight]-at/during(with a period of time) arrive-it will. ("That" is understood.)

Orqo-kuna-s pata-n-pi rit'i-mo-nqa. They say (that) <u>it will snow on the top of the mountains</u>. [**-mu-** > **-mo-**]
Mountain-(plural marker)-(marker denoting that the information is secondhand) top-its-on snow-(untranslatable infix usually used with verbs expressing natural phenomena when those talking consider themselves affected by them)-it will. ("That" is understood.) OR

Orqo-s-si pata-n-pi rit'i-mo-nqa. They say (that) <u>it will snow on the top of the mountains</u>. [**-mu-** > **-mo-**]
Mountain-s-(marker denoting that the information is secondhand) top-its-on snow-(untranslatable infix usually used with verbs expressing natural phenomena when those talking consider themselves affected by them)-it will. ("That" is understood.)

Expansion B:

"They say (that) the (weather phenomenon) will get here tonight."

Para-s ch'isi-ta chaya-mo-nqa. They say (that) <u>the rain</u> will get here at dusk. [**-mu-** > **-mo-**]

Para-s kunan tuta-ta chaya-mo-nqa. They say (that) <u>the rain</u> will get here tonight. [**-mu-** > **-mo-**]
Rain-(marker denoting that the information is secondhand) this night[tonight]-at/during(with a period of time) arrive-(in this direction)-it will. ("That" is understood.)

<u>**Rit'i**</u> <u>snow</u>
<u>**Chhullunka**</u> <u>frost</u>
<u>**Qasa**</u> <u>freeze</u>

33. **Sinchita paramusan.** It's raining hard.
Sinchi-ta para-mu-sa-n.
Hard-(adverb marker) rain-(untranslatable infix usually used with verbs expressing natural phenomena when those talking consider themselves affected by them)-(progressive marker, "-ing")-it.

Expansion:

"It is (weather phenomenon)."

Sinchi-ta <u>para</u>-mu-sa-n. It's <u>rain</u>ing hard. OR
<u>Para</u>-yku-mu-sa-n. It's <u>rain</u>ing hard.
Rain-(marker used with a verb that is not one of motion or direction to indicate intensity)-(untranslatable infix usually used with verbs expressing natural phenomena when those talking consider themselves affected by them)-(progressive marker, "-ing")-it.

<u>wayra</u> <u>blow</u>
<u>chihchi</u> <u>hail</u>
<u>rit'i</u> <u>snow</u>
<u>phuyu</u> <u>cloud up</u> (When this is substituted above, **sinchi-ta** and **-yku-** convey the idea of "fast.")
<u>illari</u> <u>clear up</u> (When this is substituted above, **sinchi-ta** and **-yku-** convey the idea of "fast.")
<u>k'uychi</u> <u>a rainbow come out</u> (When this is substituted above, **sinchi-ta** and **-yku-** convey the idea of "brightly.")

34. **Chihchimun chihchimun.** It hails all the time.
Chihchi-mu-n chihchi-mu-n.
Hail-(untranslatable infix usually used with verbs expressing natural phenomena when those talking consider themselves affected by them)-it hail-(untranslatable infix usually used with verbs expressing natural phenomena when those talking consider themselves affected by them)-it. [Repetition of the verb shows frequency.]

35. **¿Qhonqhonnimusanchu?** Is it thundering?
¿Qhon-qhon-ni-mu-sa-n-chu?
(Noise thunder makes)-(noise thunder makes)-say-(untranslatable infix usually used with verbs expressing natural phenomena when those talking consider themselves affected by them)-(progressive marker, "-ing")-it-(question marker)?

Expansion:

"Is it thundering?"

¿**Qhon-qhon-ni-mu-sa-n-chu?** Is it thundering?
¿**Kunuñunu-mu-sa-n-chu?** Is it thundering?
Thunder-(untranslatable infix usually used with verbs expressing natural phenomena when those talking consider themselves affected by them)-(progressive marker, "-ing")-it-(question marker)?

36. **Arí, qhonqhonnimusanqa(tah) illapamusantah.** Yes, it is thundering and (it is) lightning.
    Arí, qhon-qhon-ni-mu-sa-n-qa(-tah) illapa-mu-sa-n-tah.
    Yes, (noise thunder makes)-(noise thunder makes)-say-(untranslatable infix usually used with verbs expressing natural phenomena when those talking consider themselves affected by them)-(progressive marker, "-ing")-it-(emphatic particle)(-and) lightning-(untranslatable infix usually used with verbs expressing natural phenomena when those talking consider themselves affected by them)-(progressive marker, "-ing")-it-and.

37. ¿**Kunan tutata qasamonqachu?** Will it freeze tonight? [**-mu-** > **-mo-**]
    ¿Kunan tuta-ta qasa-mo-nqa-chu?
    This night[Tonight]-on/during(with a period of time) freeze-(untranslatable infix usually used with verbs expressing natural phenomena when those talking consider themselves affected by them)-(progressive marker, "-ing")-it will-(question marker)?

38. **Mana(n). Kaypeqa manahayk'ah qasamonchu.** No. It never freezes here. [**-pi-** > **-pe-, -mu-** > **-mo-**]
    Mana(-n). Kay-pe-qa mana-hayk'ah qasa-mo-n-chu.
    No(-emphatic particle). Here-in/at-(emphatic particle) not-when[never] freeze-(untranslatable infix usually used with verbs expressing natural phenomena when those talking consider themselves affected by them)-it-(negative marker).

39. **Hatun tamya hamusan.** A big storm is coming.
    Hatun tamya hamu-sa-n.
    Big storm come-(progressive marker, "-ing")-it. ("A" is understood.)

40. **Q'aya (diya) pachaphuyumonqa.** It will be foggy tomorrow. [**-mu-** > **-mo-**]
    Q'aya (diya) pacha-phuyu-mo-nqa.
    Tomorrow (day) land-cloud-(untranslatable infix usually used with verbs expressing natural phenomena when those talking consider themselves affected by them)-it will.

41. **Anchata chirimusan.** It is very cold.
Ancha-ta chiri-mu-sa-n.
Much-(adverb marker) chill-(untranslatable infix usually used with verbs expressing natural phenomena when those talking consider themselves affected by them)-(progressive marker, "-ing")-it.

Expansion:

"It is very cold/hot."

Ancha-ta <u>chiri</u>-mu-sa-n. It is very <u>cold</u>.
Sinchi-ta <u>chiri</u>-mu-sa-n. It is very <u>cold</u>.
Strong-(adverb marker) chill-(untranslatable infix usually used with verbs expressing natural phenomena when those talking consider themselves affected by them)-(progressive marker, "-ing")-it.

<u>rupha</u> burning hot
burn
<u>q'oñi</u> hot
heat

NOTES

1. Note that we have used
    - **-ña** in asking and telling the hour, or the number of hours, days, weeks, months, years;
    - **-ta** in asking and telling "at" an hour, "in," "on," "at," or "during" a day or a part of a day, or "time(s) [occasions]," and
    - **-pi** in telling "in," "on," "at," "during" with a month, a part of a month, a date, a week, a season, and a year.

2. The most frequently used word for "week" is **simana**, borrowed from the Spanish *semana*. However, in some Quechuaphone areas **hunqahunah**, **qanchischaw**, and **qanchis p'unchaw unah** are used.

3. Often the Quechua words for "time," **unay** and **pacha**, are replaced by **timpu**, an adaptation of the Spanish *tiempo*, "time."

4. Verbs that signify atmospheric conditions can be personalized to show who is affected by them.
    For the first and second persons singular and plural ("I," "we"; "you [one person]," and "you [more than one person]") a pronominal construction can be used (see examples below and number 16. Model for Verbs that Include (Pronominally) the Verbal Object "Me," number 17. Model for Verbs that Include (Periphrastically and Pronominally) the

Verbal Object "Us," number 18. Model for Verbs that Include (Pronominally) the Verbal Object "You [One Person]," number 19. Model for Verbs that Include (Periphrastically and Pronominally) the Verbal Object "You [More Than One Person]" in Section III: Quechua Grammar Notes).

para-(mu)-y to rain

¿**Kay-pi ancha-ta para-mu-n-chu?** Does it rain here a lot?

Here-in/at much-(adverb marker) rain-(untranslatable infix usually used with verbs expressing natural phenomena when those talking consider themselves affected by them)-it-(question marker)?

Sinchi-ta para-mu-sa-n. It is raining hard.

Hard-(adverb marker) rain-(untranslatable infix usually used with verbs expressing natural phenomena when those talking consider themselves affected by them)-(progressive marker "-ing")-it.

Sinchi-ta para-mu-wa-sa-n. It is raining hard on me.

Hard-(adverb marker) rain-(untranslatable infix usually used with verbs expressing natural phenomena when those talking consider themselves affected by them)-on me-(progressive marker, "-ing")-it.

[Note that the use of a progressive form (with **-sa-**, "-ing," or one of its varaints; see number 12. Verbs Expressing Action or State of Being in Progress [Progressive Verbs] in Section III: Quechua Grammar Notes) is very common in verbal constructions dealing with weather.]

tutaya-y for night to fall

Tutaya-rqa(-n) Night fell.

Tutaya-wa-yko-rqa(-n). Night fell on us (excluding the person[s] addressed) [**-yku-** > **-yko-**).

Night fell-(dual marker for "it to us [excluding the persons[s] addressed]")-it did.

paqari-y for day to break, for it to dawn

¿**Qayna rit'i-spa paqare-rqa-chu?** Did it dawn snowing yesterday? More freely translated: Was it snowing at dawn yesterday?/Was it snowing when the sun came up yesterday? [**paqari-** > **paqare-**]

Yesterday snow-(invariable gerund marker, "-ing") dawn-it did-(question marker)?

¿**Qayna rit'i-spa paqari-so-rqa-chu?** Did it dawn snowing on you yesterday?/Was it snowing on you at dawn yesterday?/Was it snowing on you when the sun came up yesterday? (**-su-** > **-so-**)

> *Yesterday snow-(invariable gerund marker, "-ing") dawn-(dual marker for "it to you[one person] did)-(question marker)?*
>
> **¿Qayna rit'i-spa paqari-so-rqa-cheh-chu?** Did it dawn snowing on you (more than one person) yesterday?/Was it snowing on you (more than one person) at dawn yesterday?/Was it snowing on you (more than one person) when the sun came up yesterday? (**-su-** > **-so-**)
>
> *Yesterday snow-(invariable gerund marker, "-ing") dawn-(triple marker for "it to you[more than one person] did)-(question marker)?*
>
> [Note that while the English of the above examples is somewhat labored, the idea is clear, and this and similar Quechua constructions are very common.]

api wet, soaked

apicha-y to wet, to make wet

apiya-y to become wet, to get wet

> **Q'aya para-n apiya-so-nqa-cheh-sina.** Probably the rain will get you (more than one person) wet.
>
> *Tomorrow rain(-euphonic particle) get wet-(triple marker for "it to you [more than one person]")-probably/I think.*

For the third persons singular and plural ("he/she/it" and "they") a common periphrastic construction is used. (See examples below and number 20. Model for Verbs that Include (Only Periphrastically) the Verbal Objects "Him," "Her," and "Them" in Section III: Quechua Grammar Notes).

> **Pay-man sinchi-ta para-mo-rqa.** It rained hard on him/her. [-**mu-** > -**mo-**]
>
> *He/She-on[On him/her] hard-(adverb marker) rain-(untranslatable infix usually used with verbs expressing natural phenomena when those talking consider themselves affected by them)-it did.*
>
> **Pay-kuna-man tuta-ya-rqa.** Night fell on them.
>
> *He/She-(plural marker)[They]-on[On them] night-(to become what the stem to which it is attached is)-it did.*

5. To convey the idea of "they say," "one says," "it is said," the suffix **-s** (on a word ending in a vowel) or **-si** (on a word ending in a consonant) is used. For example:

> **Para-s ch'isi-ta chaya-mo-nqa.** <u>They say</u> (that) the rain will get here at dusk. [-**mu-** > -**mo-**]
>
> *Rain-(marker denoting that the information is secondhand) dusk-at(with period of time) arrive-(in this direction)-it will.*

Orqo-kuna-s pata-n-pi rit'i-mo-nqa. They say (that) it will snow on the top of the mountains.

Mountain-(plural marker)-(marker denoting that the information is secondhand) top-its-on snow-(untranslatable infix usually used with verbs expressing natural phenomena when those talking consider themselves affected by them)-it will. OR

Orqo-s-si pata-n-pi rit'i-mo-nqa. They say (that) it will snow on the top of the mountains.

Mountain-s-(marker denoting that the information is secondhand) top-its-on snow-(untranslatable infix usually used with verbs expressing natural phenomena when those talking consider themselves affected by them)-it will.

SECTION II
Model Sentences and Their Expansions

Chapter 12

This chapter deals with

A. Asking and Telling What Is Going On/Happening, Went On/Happened [Model Sentences 1-2]

B. Asking and Telling How Something Happened to Different People [3-4]

C. Wondering What To Do and Responding [5-7]

D. Asking What People Are Doing, When Present, with No Idea of What Is Going On, and Responding to Those Questions [8-9]

E. Asking and Telling What Activity People Do [10-13]

F. Asking and Telling What Activity People Are Doing [14-15]

G. Asking and Telling What Activity People Did [16-17]

H. Asking and Telling What Activity People Will Do [18-19]

I. Asking and Telling What Activity People Would Do [20-21]

J. Asking and Telling What People Are Doing the Way That They Are Doing Something [22-23]

K. Asking "What For" and "Why," and Telling "To (Activity)" and "Because" [24-27]

L. Asking and Telling How Something Is Done [28-30]

M. Asking and Telling When Something Will Happen or When Something Happens or Happened With Respect to Another Action [31-33]

A. ASKING AND TELLING WHAT IS GOING ON/HAPPENING, WENT ON/HAPPENED

1. **¿Imanantah?**[1] What is going on?/What is happening?
   ¿Imana-n-tah?
   Happen-it-and?

2. **¿Imanarqatah?** What happened?
   ¿Imana-rqa-tah?
   Happened-it did-and?

Expansion:

"What happened?"

¿Imana-rqa-tah? What happen<u>ed</u>?
¡¡Imana-sqa-tah!?[2] What happen<u>ed</u>!?
Happen-had[Had happened])(used to indicate surprise)-and!?

B. ASKING AND TELLING HOW SOMETHING HAPPENED TO DIFFERENT PEOPLE

3. **¿Imanaspa(yki)tah nanachikorqankiri?** How did you/How have you hurt yourself? [-ku- > -ko-]
   ¿Imana-spa(-yki)-tah nana-chi-ko-rqa-nki-ri?
   Do-(invariable gerund marker, "-ing," used when the subject of the gerund is the same as that of the main verb)(-your[one person])-and hurt-make(what the meaning of the verb is)-self-did-you(one person)-and/then(prolonging the question or statement without adding any specific meaning)?

4. **Llarq'ata p'itaspa(y)(lla) nanachikorqani.** I hurt myself jumping over the irrigation ditch. [-ku- > -ko-]
   Llarq'a-ta p'ita-spa(-y)(-lla) nana-chi-ko-rqa-ni.
   Irrigation ditch-(direct object marker) jump-(invariable gerund marker, "-ing," used when the subject of the gerund is the same as that of the main verb)(-my)(-just) hurt-make(what the meaning of the verb is)-self-did-I.

Expansion A:

"I (did something to myself) (doing something)."

Llarq'a-ta p'ita-spa(-y)(-lla) nana-chi-ko-rqa-ni. I hurt myself jumping over the irrigation ditch. [**-ku-** > **-ko-**]

T'anta-ta kuchu-spa(-y)(-lla) kuchu-ko-rqa-ni. I cut myself cutting bread. [**-ku-** > **-ko-**]

Bread-(direct object marker) cut-(invariable gerund marker, "-ing," used when the subject of the gerund is the same as that of the main verb)(-my)(-just) cut-self-did-I

T'uru-(n)ta puri-spa(-y)(-lla) llusk'a-ko-rqa-ni. I slipped walking through the mud. [**-ku-** > **-ko-**]

Mud-through walk-(invariable gerund marker, "-ing," used when the subject of the gerund is the same as that of the main verb)(-my)(-just) slip-self-did-I.

Expansion B:

"(Different people) hurt (themselves) jumping over the irrigation ditch."

Llarq'a-ta p'ita-spa(-y)(-lla) nana-chi-ko-rqa-ni. I did hurt (I hurt) myself jumping over the irrigation ditch. [**-ku-** > **-ko-**]

(-yki) ... rqa-nki you did
(-your[one person]) ... did-you(one person)

(-n) ... -rqa he/she/it did
(-his/her) ... he/she/it did

(-yku) ... rqa-yku we (excluding the person[s] addressed) did
(-our[excluding the person(s) addressed]) ... did-we(excluding the person[s] addressed)

(-ncheh) ... rqa-ncheh we (including the person[s] addressed) did
(-our[including the person(s) addressed]) ... did-we(including the person[s] addressed)

(-ykicheh) ... rqa-nki-cheh you (more than one person) did
(-your[more than one person]) ... did-(dual marker for "you[more than one person]")

(-nku) ... rqa-nku they did
(-their) ... did-they

C. WONDERING WHAT TO DO AND RESPONDING

5. **¿Imanasahmi?** What am I going to do? (asked in a quandary)
    ¿Imana-sah-mi?
    Do-I will-(particle of certainty or assurance)? ("What" is understood.)

> ### Expansion:
>
> "What am I going to do?" (asked in a quandary)
> "What are we going to do?" (asked in a quandary)
>
> **¿Imana-sah-mi?** What <u>am I going to do</u>? (asked in a quandary)
> **¿Imana-sahku?** What <u>are we (excluding the person[s] addressed) going to do</u>? (asked in a quandary)
> *Do-we(excluding the person[s] addressed) will? ("What" is understood.)*
> **¿Imana-su-n(cheh)?** What <u>are we (including the person[s] addressed) going to do</u>? (asked in a quandary)
> *Do-(dual marker for "we[including the person(s) addressed] will")? ("What" is understood.)*

6. **Imana-y-pas.** Do whatever you want.
   Imana-y-pas.
   Do-(command marker addressing one person)-any.

> ### Expansion:
>
> "Do whatever you want."
> "Do whatever you (more than one person) want."
>
> **Imana-y-pas.** Do whatever <u>you</u> want.
> **Imana-y-cheh-pas.** Do whatever <u>you (more than one person)</u> want.
> *Do-(dual command marker addressing more than one person)-any.*

7. **Hwanman rimasun(cheh).** Let's talk with Juan.
   Hwan-man rima-su-n(cheh).
   Juan-with talk-(dual marker for "let's").

D. ASKING WHAT PEOPLE ARE DOING, WHEN PRESENT, WITH NO IDEA OF WHAT IS GOING ON, AND RESPONDING TO THOSE QUESTIONS

8. **¿Imanasanki?** What are you doing (with no idea of what the person is doing)?
   ¿Imana-sa-nki?
   Do-(progressive marker, "-ing")-you(one person)? ("What" is understood.)

Expansion:

"What (are different people) doing?"

¿Imana-sa-nki? What are <u>you</u> doing (with no idea of what the person is doing)?

¿Imana-sa-nki-cheh? What are <u>you (more than one person)</u> doing (with no idea of what the people are doing)?
Do-(progressive marker, "-ing")-(dual marker for "you[more than one person]")? ("What" is understood.)

¿Imana-sa-n? What is <u>he/she</u> doing (with no idea of what the person is doing)?
Do-(progressive marker, "-ing")-he/she? ("What" is understood.)

¿Imana-sa-nku? What are <u>they</u> doing (with no idea of what the people are doing)?
Do-(progressive marker, "-ing")-they? ("What" is understood.)

[Remember that as long as the meaning allows it, any verb can be made progressive in any tense by inserting **-sa-** or one of its variants between the verb stem and ending. (See number 12. Verbs Expressing Action or State of Being in Progress [Progressive Verbs] in Section III: Quechua Grammar Notes.)]

9. **Yapusani.** I am plowing.
   Yapu-sa-ni.
   Plow-(progressive marker, "-ing")-I.

E. ASKING AND TELLING WHAT ACTIVITY PEOPLE DO

10. **¿Imata ruanki?**[3] What do you do?
    ¿Ima-ta rua-nki?
    What-(direct object marker) do-you(one person)?

11. **Llank'ani.** I farm/work the land.
    Llank'a-ni.
    Work(the land)-I.

12. **¿Imata llahtahpa phistanpi ruanku?** What do they do at the town festival?
    ¿Ima-ta llahta-hpa phista-n-pi rua-nku?
    What-(direct object marker) town-of festival-its-in/at do-they?

13. **Qhochukunku(tah), tusunku(tah), hawkankutah.** They gather together, they dance, and they have a good time.
    Qhochu-ku-nku(-tah), tusu-nku(-tah), hawka-nku-tah.
    Gather-selves-they(-and), dance-they(-and), have a good time-they-and.

F. ASKING AND TELLING WHAT ACTIVITY PEOPLE ARE DOING

14. **¿Imata ruasanki?** What are you doing/making?
    ¿Ima-ta rua-sa-nki?
    What-(direct object marker) do/make-(progressive marker, "-ing")-you(one person)?

15. **Uh punchuta awasani.** I'm weaving a poncho.
    Uh punchu-ta awa-sa-ni.
    A poncho-(direct object marker) weave-(progressive marker, "-ing")-I.

G. ASKING AND TELLING WHAT ACTIVITY PEOPLE DID

16. **¿Imata phistapi ruarqanki?** What did you do at the festival?
    ¿Ima-ta phista-pi rua-rqa-nki?
    What-(direct object marker) festival-in/at do-did-you(one person)?

17. **Takerqani.** I sang. [taki- > take-]
    Take-rqa-ni.
    Sing-did-I.

H. ASKING AND TELLING WHAT ACTIVITY PEOPLE WILL DO

18. **¿Q'aya (diya) kay urasta imata ruankichu?** What will you do tomorrow at this time?
    ¿Q'aya (diya) kay ura-s-ta ima-ta rua-nki-chu?
    Tomorrow (day) these hour-s-at(with an hour) what-(direct object marker) do-you(one person) will-(question marker)?

19. **Wallpasman qarasah.** I will feed the chickens.
    Wallpa-kuna-man qara-sah.
    Chicken-(plural marker)-to throw grain to fowl-I will.

Expansion:

"(Different people) will feed the chickens."

Wallpa-kuna-man qara-sah. I will feed the chickens.

qara-nki you (one person) will feed
qara-nqa he/she will feed
qara-sahku we (excluding the person[s] addressed) will feed OR
qara-sayku we (excluding the person[s] addressed) will feed OR
qara-sqa-yku we (excluding the person[s] addressed) will feed
qara-su-n(cheh) we (including the person[s] addressed) will feed
qara-nki-cheh you (more than one person) will feed
qara-nqa-nku they will feed

I. ASKING AND TELLING WHAT ACTIVITY PEOPLE WOULD DO

20. **¿Imata ruankiman?** What would you do?
    ¿Ima-ta rua-nki-man?
    What-(direct object marker) do-(dual marker for "you[one person] would")?

21. **Ch'isipah kutimuyman.** I would return here by evening.
    Ch'isi-pah kuti-mu-y-man.
    Evening-for return-in this direction-(dual marker for "I would").

Expansion:

"(Different people) would return here by evening."

Ch'isi-pah kuti-mu-y-man. I would return here by evening.

kuti-mu-wah you (one person) would return OR
kuti-mu-nki-man you (one person) would return
kuti-mu-n-man he/she/it would return
kuti-mu-yku-man we (excluding the person[s] addressed) would return
kuti-mu(-su)-ncheh-man we (including the person[s] addressed) would return
kuti-mu-wah-cheh you (more than one person) would return OR
kuti-mu-nki-cheh-man you (more than one person) would return
kuti-mu-nku-man they would return

[Remember that of the two forms for "you (one person) would" and "you (more than one person) would," **-wah** and **-wah-cheh** are more common, but when the conditional ending is preceded by the infix **-wa-** or **-su-**, the endings **-nki-man** and **-nki-cheh-man** are used instead.]

J. ASKING AND TELLING WHAT PEOPLE ARE DOING THE WAY THAT THEY ARE DOING SOMETHING

22. **¿Ima(tah) chay warmi hinasan?**[4] What is that woman doing (that way)?
    ¿Ima(-tah) chay warmi hina-sa-n?
    What(-and) that woman do like that-(progressive marker, "-ing")-she?

23. **T'antachasan.** She is making bread.
    T'anta-cha-sa-n.
    Bread-make(what the noun or adjective is to which it is attached)-(progressive marker, "-ing")-she.

K. ASKING "WHAT FOR" AND "WHY," AND TELLING "TO (ACTIVITY)" AND "BECAUSE"

24. **¿Imapah chayta ruasan?** What is he/she doing that for?
    ¿Ima-pah chay-ta rua-sa-n?
    What-for that-(direct object marker) do-(progressive marker, "-ing")-he/she?

25. **Millmata t'ahsaypah(tah) tullpuypahtah.** To wash and to dye the wool.
    Millma-ta t'ahsa-y-pah(-tah) tullpu-y-pah-tah.
    Wool-(direct object marker) wash cloth/clothing-(infinitive marker, "to")(-and) dye-(infinitive marker, "to") in order to-and.

26. **¿Imarayku chayta ruasankicheh?** Why are you (more than one person) doing that?
    ¿Ima-rayku chay-ta rua-sa-nki-cheh?
    What-for[Why] that-(direct object marker) do-(progressive marker, "-ing")-(dual marker for "you[more than one person]")?

27. **Kayta ruasayku kamiyunta allichayta munasqaykurayku.** We are doing this because we want/wanted to fix the truck.
Kay-ta rua-sa-yku kamiyun-ta alli-cha-y-ta muna-sqa-yku-rayku.
This-(direct object marker) do-(progressive marker, "-ing")-we(excluding the person[s] addressed) truck-(direct object marker) good-make(what the noun or adjective is to which it is attached)-(infinitive marker, "to")-(direct object marker) want-(past [or perfect] infinitive marker/particle used with a dependent verb for an action that is simultaneous to or prior to that of the main verb)-our(excluding the person[s] addressed)-for/because of.

Expansion A:

"We are doing this because (different people) want/wanted to fix the truck."

Kay-ta rua-sa-yku kamiyun-ta alli-cha-y-ta muna-sqa-yku-rayku.
We are doing this because we want/wanted [(because of) our (excluding the person[s] addressed) wanting/having wanted] to fix the truck.

muna-sqa-y I want/wanted [(because of) my wanting/my having wanted]
muna-sqa-yki you (one person) want/wanted [(because of) your (one person) wanting/ having wanted]
muna-sqa-n he/she/it wants/wanted [(because of) his/her/its wanting/having wanted]
muna-sqa-yku we (excluding the person[s] addressed) want/wanted [(because of) our (exluding the person[s] addressed) wanting/having wanted]
muna-sqa-ncheh we (including the person[s] addressed) want/wanted [(because of) our (including the person[s] addressed) wanting/ having wanted]
muna-sqa-ykicheh you (more than one person) want/wanted [(because of) your (more than one person) wanting/having wanted]
muna-sqa-nku they want/wanted [(because of) their wanting/having wanted]

Expansion B:

"We are doing this because (different people) are going (in the future) to Lima."

Kay-ta rua-sa-yku <u>kamiyun-ta</u> <u>alli-cha-y-ta</u> <u>muna-sqa-yku</u>-rayku.
We are doing this because <u>we want/wanted</u> [(because of) <u>our (exluding the person[s] addressed) wanting/having wanted] to fix the truck</u>.

Kay-ta rua-sa-yku <u>Lima-man</u> <u>ri-na-y</u>-rayku. We are doing this because <u>I am going (in the future) to Lima</u> [(because of) <u>my going (in the future) to Lima</u>].

This-(direct object marker) do-(progressive marker, "-ing")-we(excluding the person[s] addressed) Lima-to/toward go-(future infinitive marker/particle used with a dependent verb for an action that is in the future in relationship to that of the main verb)-my-for/because of.

<u>Lima-man</u> <u>ri-na-yki</u> <u>you (one person) are going (in the future) to Lima</u> [(because of) <u>your (one person) going (in the future) to Lima</u>].

Lima-to/toward go-(future infinitive marker/particle used with a dependent verb for an action that is in the future in relationship to that of the main verb)-your(one person)

<u>Lima-man</u> <u>ri-na-n</u> <u>he/she/it is going (in the future) to Lima</u> [(because of) <u>his/her/its going (in the future) to Lima</u>].

Lima-to/toward go-(future infinitive marker/particle used with a dependent verb for an action that is in the future in relationship to that of the main verb)-his/her/its

<u>Lima-man</u> <u>ri-na-yku</u> <u>we (excluding the person[s] addressed) are going (in the future) to Lima</u> [(because of) <u>our (excluding the person[s] addressed) going (in the future) to Lima</u>]

Lima-to/toward go-(future infinitive marker/particle used with a dependent verb for an action that is in the future in relationship to that of the main verb)-our(excluding the person[s] addressed)

<u>Lima-man</u> <u>ri-na-ncheh</u> <u>we (including the person[s] addressed) are going (in the future) to Lima</u> [(because of) <u>our (including the person[s] addressed) going (in the future) to Lima</u>]

Lima-to/toward go-(future infinitive marker/particle used with a dependent verb for an action that is in the future in relationship to that of the main verb)-our(including the person[s] addressed)

<u>Lima-man</u> <u>ri-na-ykicheh</u> <u>you (more than one person) are going (in the future) to Lima</u> [(because of) <u>your (more than one person) going (in the future) to Lima</u>]

Lima-to/toward go-(future infinitive marker/particle used with a dependent verb for an action that is in the future in relationship to that of the main verb)-your(more than one person)

Lima-man ri-na-nku they are going (in the future) to Lima [(because of) their going (in the future) to Lima]
Lima-to/toward go-(future infinitive marker/particle used with a dependent verb for an action that is in the future in relationship to that of the main verb)-their

L. ASKING AND TELLING HOW SOMETHING IS DONE

28. **¿Imaynalla chayta ruanku?** How do they do/make that?
    ¿Imayna-lla chay-ta rua-nku?
    How-just that-(direct object marker) do-they?

Expansion:

"How do they (do something)?"

¿Imayna-lla chay-ta rua-nku? How do they do/make that?

sara-ta wayk'u cook the corn
corn-(direct object marker) cook
punchu-s-ta rua make ponchos
poncho-s-(direct object marker) make

---

29. **Hinallatah.** Like this.
    Hina-lla-tah.
    Thus-just-and.

30. **Chayta awaspa(nku)(lla) ruanku.** They make that (by) weaving it.
    Chay-ta awa-spa(-nku)(-lla) rua-nku.
    That-(direct object marker) weave-(invariable gerund marker, "-ing," used when the subject of the gerund is the same as that of the main verb)(-their)(-just) do/make-they. ("It" is understood.)

Expansion A:

"By (doing something)."
Chay-ta awa-spa(-nku)(-lla) rua-nku. They make that (by) weaving it.

Awa-spa(-lla). By weaving it.

Maki-nku-wan awa weave by hand
Hand-their-with weave
Phushka spin OR
Qanqu spin

Kuchu cut OR
K'utu cut
Wayk'u cook OR
Yanu cook

Expansion B:

"Without (doing something)."

Chay-ta awa-spa(-nku)(-lla) rua-nku. They make that (by) weaving it.
Mana awa-spa(-lla). Without weaving.

wayk'u cook (it) OR
yanu cook (it)
t'impu boil (it)
kanka roast (it)
thehtichi fry (it)

M. ASKING AND TELLING WHEN SOMETHING WILL HAPPEN OR WHEN SOMETHING HAPPENS OR HAPPENED WITH RESPECT TO ANOTHER ACTION

31. **Chayamusaspa(nku) mikhonqanku.** They will eat when they get here. [**mikhu-** > **mikho-**]
Chaya-mu-sa-spa(-nku) mikho-nqa-nku.
Arrive-in this direction-(progressive marker, "-ing")-(invariable gerund marker, "-ing," used when the subject of the gerund is the same as that of the main verb)(-their) eat-(dual marker for "they will").

[Note that in Quechua the clause beginning with "when" must be first in the sentence.]

Expansion:

"They will eat when/before/after they get here."

Chaya-mu-sa-spa(-nku) mikho-nqa-nku. They will eat when they get here. [**mikhu-** > **mikho-**]

Mana-rah chaya-mu-sa-spa(-nku) before they get here
Not-yet[before] arrive-in this direction[get here]-(progressive marker, "-ing")-(invariable gerund marker, "-ing," used when the subject of the gerund is the same as that of the main verb)(-their)
Chaya-mu-sa-spa(-nku)-ña after they get here
Arrive-in this direction[get here]-(progressive marker, "-ing")-(invariable gerund marker, "-ing," used when the subject of the gerund is the same as that of the main verb)(-their)-already

[Note that in Quechua the clause beginning with "when," "before," and "after" must be first in the sentence.]

32. **Chayamusahtinku mikhusun(cheh).** We (including the person[s] addressed) will eat when they get here.
    Chaya-mu-sa-hti-nku mikhu-su-n(cheh).
    Arrive-in this direction[get here]-(progressive marker, "-ing")-(variable gerund marker, "-ing," used when the subject of the gerund is different from that of the main verb)-their eat-(dual marker for "we[including the person(s) addressed] will").

Expansion:

"We (including the person[s] addressed) will eat when/before/after they get here."

Chaya-mu-sa-hti-nku mikhu-su-n(cheh). We (including the person[s] addressed) will eat when they get here.

Mana-rah chaya-mu-sa-hti-nku before they get here
Not-yet[before] arrive-in this direction[get here]-(progressive marker, "-ing")-(variable gerund marker, "-ing," used when the subject of the gerund is different from that of the main verb)-their
Chaya-mu-sa-hti-nku-ña after they get here
Arrive-in this direction[get here]-(progressive marker, "-ing")-(variable gerund marker, "-ing," used when the subject of the gerund is different from that of the main verb)-their-already

33. **Kamiyunmanta uraykohina(y)qa urmakorqani.** On/While getting off the truck I fell. [**-ku-** > **-ko-**]
    Kamiyun-manta uray-ko-hina(-y)-qa urma-ko-rqa-ni.
    Truck-from lower-self-as(-my)-(emphatic particle) fall-self-did-I.

NOTES

1. **¿Imana-n-tah?** "What is going on?" is from the verb **imana-y**, "to happen," "to occur," "to do (something)." It is based on **¿ima?**, "what?," and **na**, which here shows doubt. It should be noted that when **imana-y** is used with the meaning "to do," it usually is in a question, and when no particular activity is visible or in mind.

   There is also a verb based on **-na-**, **na-y**, "to do," which is not used with great frequency. For example:

   ¡Kay-ta na-y! Do this!
   This-(direct object marker) do-(command marker addressing one person)!

   Na can also be used alone as a hesitation filler while the speaker is contemplating the next word, but it must have affixed to it the particle that would be affixed to the missing word, could the speaker think of it. For example:

   ¿Na-pi . . . Ururu-pi kasa-ncheh-ña? Are we in/at . . .er, uh . . . Oruro yet?
   Er/Uh-in/at . . . Oruro-in/at be-we(excluding the person[s] addressed)-already/yet?

2. The past perfect (pluperfect) tense, for example, "I <u>had</u> eaten," "you <u>had</u> eaten," and so on, in many Quechuaphone areas is used to indicate surprise about an action or state of being in the past just now discovered or to narrate or speak of actions, events, or states of being that were not witnessed by the speaker. Compare this sentence with the one above:

   ¿Imana-rqa-tah?, "What happened?," a simple question, with no exclamation marks,
   AND
   ¿¡Imana-sqa-tah!?, "What happened!?," a question with exclamation marks, indicating surprise

3. There are four verbs that mean "to do."
   (1) **Rua-y** (variants **ruwa-y** and **rura-y**) means "to do" in the sense of make, create, cause, act. This verb is generally used with an activity in mind. **¿Ima-ta <u>rua-nki</u>?**, "What do you do?"
   (2) **Imana-y**, which also means "to happen," "to occur," when used with the meaning "to do (something)" usually is in a question, and when no particular activity is visible or in mind. **¿<u>Imana-n</u>-tah?**, "What is going on?"
   (3) **Hina-y**, based on **hina**, "so," "thus," "like," is used in speaking of the way in which someone does something. **¿Ima-ta <u>hina-sa-nki</u>?**, "What are you doing like that?"
   (4) **Na-y**, a general verb for "to do," is not used with great frequency.

4. Remember that of the three verbs that mean "to do," each with its own use, **hina-y**, based on **hina**, "so," "thus," is used in speaking of the way in which someone does something.

SECTION II

Model Sentences and Their Expansions

Chapter 13

> **This chapter deals with**
>
> A. Wants, Being Glad, Being Sad [Model Sentences 1-16]
>
> B. Wonder and Surprise [17-20]
>
> C. Likes and Dislikes [21-28]
>
> D. Forgetting [29-30]
>
> E. Obligation [31-37]
>
> F. Intention [38-42]
>
> G. Ability [43-53]

A. WANTS, BEING GLAD, BEING SAD

1. **¿Imata munanki?** What do you want?
   ¿Ima-ta muna-nki?
   What-(direct object marker) want-you(one person)?

2. **Uh millma punchuta munani.** I want a wool poncho.
   Uh millma punchu-ta muna-ni.
   A wool poncho-(direct object marker) want-I.

Expansion:

"I want ... "

<u>Uh</u> <u>millma</u> <u>punchu</u>-ta muna-ni. I want <u>a wool poncho</u>.

<u>Q'oñi</u> <u>lawa</u> hot soup
<u>As</u> <u>t'anta</u> a little/some bread
<u>Aswan</u> <u>t'anta</u> more bread
<u>Aswan</u> a little more/some more
<u>Uh</u> <u>pisita-lla</u> just a little
A little bit-just

    Uh wan one more
    Lima-man kuti-y to go back to Lima
    Lima-to/toward go back/return-(infinitive marker, "to")
    Pidru-wan rima-y to talk with Pedro
    Pedro-with talk-(infinitive marker, "to")

3. **¿Mayqen punchuta munanki?** Which poncho do you want?
   ¿Mayqen punchu-ta muna-nki?
   Which poncho-(direct object marker) want-you(one person)?

4. **Mayqenllatapas.** Anyone.
   Mayqen-lla-ta-pas.
   Which-just-(direct object marker)-any.

5. **Punchuta awasasqan, chayta rantiyta munani.** I want to buy the poncho that she is weaving.
   Punchu-ta awa-sa-sqa-n, chay-ta ranti-y-ta muna-ni.
   Poncho-(direct object marker) weave-(progressive marker, "-ing")-(particle to form the passive [or past] participle for the present and past, used in a construction that in English is introduced by a relative pronoun, often "what," "that," or "which," when the verb denotes what someone or something did or is doing)-her[here, showing who is doing the weaving, "she"], that-(direct object marker) buy-(infinitive marker, "to")-(direct object marker) want-I.

Expansion:

"I want to buy the poncho that she is weaving."
"I want to buy the poncho that she wove/has woven."
"I want to buy the poncho that she weaves (in the future)/will weave."

Punchu-ta awa-sa-sqa-n, chay-ta ranti-y-ta muna-ni. I want to buy the poncho that she is weaving.

awa-sa-sqa-n that she wove/has woven
weave-(progressive marker, "-ing")-(particle to form the passive [or past] participle for the present and past, used in a construction that in English is introduced by a relative pronoun, often "what," "that," or "which," when the verb denotes what someone or something did or is doing)-her[here, showing who did the weaving, "she"], that-(direct object marker)

awa-sa-na-n that she weaves (in the future)/will weave
weave-(progressive marker, "-ing")-(particle to form the passive [or past] participle for the future, used in a construction that in English is introduced by a relative pronoun, often "what," "that," or "which," when the verb denotes what someone or something will do)-her[here, showing who will be weaving, "she"], that-(direct object marker)

[Remember: In these constructions (relative clause constructions), the one performing the action is indicated by a possessive particle affixed to the verb. If the one who is doing the action is to be clarified or emphasized, the appropriate noun or subject pronoun, with **-pah**, "for," attached precedes the verb, as in these examples:
pay-pah awa-sa-na-n that **she** weaves (in the future)/will weave
Maria-pah awa-sa-na-n that **Maria** weaves (in the future)/will weave]

6. **¿Mikhuyta munankichu?** Do you want to eat?
   ¿Mikhu-y-ta muna-nki-chu?
   Eat-(infinitive marker, "to")-(direct object marker) eat-you(one person)-(question marker)?

7. **Arí. Mikhuyta munani.** Yes. I want to eat.
   Arí. Mikhu-y-ta muna-ni.
   Yes. Eat-(infinitive marker, "to")-(direct object marker) want-I.

8. **Mana(n), mana mikhuyta munanichu.** No, I do not want to eat.
   Mana(-n), mana mikhu-y-ta muna-ni-chu.
   No(-emphatic particle), not eat-(infinitive marker, "to")-(direct object marker) want-I-(negative marker).

9. **Manarah mikhuyta munanichu.** I don't want to eat yet.
   Mana-rah mikhu-y-ta muna-ni-chu.
   Not-yet eat-(infinitive marker, "to")-(direct object marker) want-I-(negative marker).

10. **¿Imata ruayta munanki?** What do you want to do?
    ¿Ima-ta rua-y-ta muna-nki?
    What-(direct object marker) do-(infinitive marker, "to")-(direct object marker) want-you(one person)?

11. **Imallatapas.** Anything.
    Ima-lla-ta-pas.
    What-just-(direct object marker)-any.

12. **¿Imata ruasqayta munanki?** What do you want me to do (referring to an action in the present)?
    ¿Ima-ta rua-sqa-y-ta muna-nki?
    What-(direct object marker) do-(past [or perfect] infinitive marker/particle used with a dependent verb for an action that is simultaneous to or prior to that of the main verb)-my-(direct object marker) want-you(one person)?

Expansion:

"What do you want me to do (referring to the present)?"
"What do you want me to do (referring to the future)?"

¿Ima-ta rua-sqa-y-ta muna-nki? What do you want me to do (<u>referring to the present</u>)?
¿Ima-ta rua-na-y-ta muna-nki? What do you want me to do (<u>referring to the future</u>)?
What-(direct object marker) do-(future infinitive marker/particle used with a dependent verb for an action that is in the future in relationship to that of the main verb)-my-(direct object marker) want-you(one person)?

---

13. **Mikhusqaykita munani.** I want you to eat (referring to the present).
    Mikhu-sqa-yki-ta muna-ni.
    Eat-(past [or perfect] infinitive marker/particle used with a dependent verb for an action that is simultaneous to or prior to that of the main verb)-your(one person)-(direct object marker) want-I.

Expansion A:

"I want you to eat (referring to the present)."
"I want you to eat (referring to the future)."

Mikhu-sqa-yki-ta muna-ni. I want you to eat (<u>referring to the present</u>).
Mikhu-na-yki-ta muna-ni. I want you to eat (<u>referring to the future</u>).
Eat-(future infinitive marker/particle used with a dependent verb for an action that is in the future in relationship to that of the main verb)-your(one person)-(direct object marker) want-I.

Expansion B:

"I want (different people) to eat (referring to the present)."
"I want (different people) to eat (referring to the future)."

Mikhu-sqa-yki-ta muna-ni. I want you to eat (referring to the present).
Mikhu-na-yki-ta muna-ni. I want you to eat (referring to the future).

-n him/her
his/her
-yku us (excluding the person[s] addressed)
our(excluding the person[s] addressed)
-ncheh us (including the person[s] addressed)
our(including the persons[s] addressed)
-ykicheh you (more than one person)
your(more than one person)
-nku them
their

---

14. **¡Mayta kusikuni!** How glad I am!
    ¡May-ta kusi-ku-ni!
    How-(adverb marker) gladden-self-I!

15. **¡Mayta llakikuni!** How sad I am!
    ¡May-ta llaki-ku-ni!
    How-(adverb marker) sadden-self-I!

16. **¡Hamusqaykimanta mayta kusikuni!** How glad I am that you are coming/that you came!
    ¡Hamu-sqa-yki-manta may-ta kusi-ku-ni!
    Come-(past [or perfect] infinitive marker/particle used with a dependent verb for an action that is simultaneous to or prior to that of the main verb)-your(one person)-because of(used with a dependent verb that is dependent upon a verb that expresses sentiment) how-(adverb marker) gladden-self-I!

Expansion:

"How glad I am that (present or past action)!"
"How glad I am that (future action)!"

¡Hamu-sqa-yki-manta may-ta kusi-ku-ni! How glad I am that you are coming/came!

¡Hamu-sqa-yki-rayku may-ta kusi-ku-ni! How glad I am that you are coming/came!

-na-yki that you are coming/will come
(future infinitive marker/particle used with a dependent verb for an action that is in the future in relationship to that of the main verb)-your(one person)

B. WONDER AND SURPRISE

17. **¿Imachus? ¿I?** What must that be!? (expressing surprise and lack of knowledge)
¿Ima-chus? ¿I?
What-(question marker that shows wonder)? Huh?

18. **¿Imachus, a?** I don't know what that must be (responding in kind to a question that expresses surprise and lack of knowledge).
¿Ima-chus, a?
What-(question marker that shows wonder), (emphatic word)?

[Note that a question is used to answer the question in this particular exchange, showing wonder and lack of information on the part of both speakers. The only difference is the final tag.]

Expansion:

Asking and responding to:
"What must . . . !?"
"Where must . . . !?"
". . . do you suppose . . . ?"
"I wonder . . . ?"

¿Ima-chus? ¿I? What <u>must</u> that be? (<u>expressing surprise and lack of knowledge</u>)

¿Ima-chus, a? I <u>don't</u> <u>know</u> what that <u>must</u> be (<u>responding in kind to a question that expresses surprise and lack of knowledge</u>).

¿Ima-ta-chus rua-sa-nqa? ¿I? What <u>must</u> he be doing?/<u>I wonder</u> what he is doing.
What-(direct object marker)-(question marker that shows wonder) do-(progressive marker, "-ing")-he/she/it will(the future used to convey the idea of "must")? Huh?

¿Ima-ta-chus rua-sa-nqa, a? I <u>don't know</u> what he <u>must</u> be doing.
What-(direct object marker)-(question marker that shows wonder) do-(progressive marker, "-ing")-he/she/it will(the future used to convey the idea of "must"), (emphatic word)?

¿May-man-chus re-nqa? ¿I? I wonder where he is going./Where <u>must</u> he be going? [**ri- > re-**]
Where-to-(question marker that shows wonder) go-will he/she/it(the future used to convey the idea of "nust,")? Huh?

¿May-man-chus re-nqa, a? I wonder where he is going, too./I don't know where he must be going. [**ri-** > **re-**]
Where-to-(question marker that shows wonder) go-will he/she/it(the future used to convey the idea of "I wonder"/"I don't know . . . must"), (emphatic word)?

19. **¿Hamunchá?** Is he coming (showing doubt or surprise)?
    ¿Hamu-n-chá?
    Come-he-(question marker showing doubt or surprise)?

Expansion:

More examples of the use of **-chá** (showing doubt or surprise)

¿Hamu-n-chá? Is he coming (showing doubt or surprise)?

May-pi-chá kasa-n. I don't know where he/she/it is.
Where-in/at-(marker showing doubt or surprise that here conveys the meaning "I don't know") be-he/she/it.

¿Ima-tah chay? What is that?
What-and that? ("Is" is understood.)
¿Ima-chá? What (thing) (showing doubt or surprise)?
What-(question marker showing doubt or surprise)?

¿Ima-tah chay-kuna (ka-nku)? What are those?
What-and that-(plural marker)[those] (be-they)?
¿Ima-kuna-chá? What things (showing doubt or surprise)?
What-(plural marker)-(question marker showing doubt or surprise)?

¿Ima-pah-kay? What is this for?
What-for-this? ("Is" is understood.)
Ima-pah-chá. What must it be for?/I wonder what it is for./I don't know what it is for.
What-for-(marker showing doubt or surprise that here conveys the meaning "must," "I wonder" or "I don't know"). ("Is" and "it" are understood.)

---

20. **¡Qaninpa (diya) amiguy Antuniyu hamusqa!** My friend Antonio came the other day (showing surprise)!
    Qaninpa (diya) amigu-y Antuniyu hamu-sqa!
    The other day (day) friend-my Antonio came-had[had come](past perfect [pluperfect] tense used to show surprise in the past)!

C. LIKES AND DISLIKES

21. **¿Chay mikhunata gustankichu?**[1] Do you like that food?
    ¿Chay mikhuna-ta gusta-nki-chu?
    That food-(direct object marker) like-you(one person)-(question marker)?

22. **Arí, kay mikhunata anchata gustani.** Yes, I like this food a lot.
    Arí, kay mikhuna-ta ancha-ta gusta-ni.
    Yes, this food-(direct object marker) much-(adverb marker) like-I.

23. **¿Qanrí? ¿Gustankichu?** And you? Do you like it?
    ¿Qan-rí? ¿Gusta-nki-chu?
    You-and(with a contrastive nuance)? Like-you(one person)-(question marker)? ("It" is understood.)

24. **Arí, ñoqapis gustani.** Yes, I like it too.
    Arí, ñoqa-pis gusta-ni.
    Yes, I-also like-I. ("It" is understood.)

25. **Mana, mana gustanichu.** No, I don't like it.
    Mana, mana gusta-ni-chu.
    No, not like-I-(negative marker). ("It" is understood.)

26. **¿Wahkunatah? ¿Manachu gustanku?** And the others? Don't they like it?
    ¿Wah-kuna-tah? ¿Mana-chu gusta-nku?
    *The rest-(plural marker)[The others]-and? Not-(question marker, which follows **mana** in a negative question) like-they? ("It" is understood.)*

27. **Mana, paykunapis mana gustankuchu.** No, they don't like it either.
    Mana, pay-kuna-pis mana gusta-nku-chu.
    No, he/she-(plural marker)[they]-also not like-they-(negative marker). ("It" is understood.)

28. **¿Mayqenta gustanki?** Which do you like?
    ¿Mayqen-ta gusta-nki?
    Which-(direct object marker) like-you(one person)?

D. FORGETTING

29. **¡Ama qonqawaychu!** Don't forget me!
    ¡Ama qonqa-wa-y-chu!
    Not(used in a command) forget-me-(command marker addressing one person)-(negative marker)!

Expansion:

Commanding someone not to forget different people

¡Ama qonqa-wa-y-chu! Don't forget <u>me</u>!
¡Ama qonqa-wa-yku-y-chu! Don't forget <u>us</u>!
Not(used in a command) forget-(dual marker for "us[in a command, excluding the person(s) addressed]")-(command marker addressing one person)-(negative marker)!

¡(Pay-ta) ama qonqa-y-chu! Don't forget <u>him/her/it</u>!
(He/She/It)-(direct object marker)[Him/Her/It] not(used in a command) forget-(command marker addressing one person)-(negative marker)!

¡Pay-kuna-ta ama qonqa-y-chu! Don't forget <u>them</u>!
He/She/It-(plural marker)[They]-(direct object marker)[Them] not(used in a command) forget-(command marker addressing one person)-(negative marker)!

30. **¡Awtuwus wulituykita rantiymanta ama qonqakuychu!** Don't forget about buying your bus ticket!
    ¡Awtuwus wulitu-yki-ta ranti-y-manta ama qonqa-ku-y-chu!
    Bus ticket-your(one person)-(direct object marker) buy-(infinitive marker, "to")-about not(used in a command) forget-self-(command marker addressing one person)-(negative marker)!

Expansion A:

"Don't forget about . . .-ing"
"Don't forget to . . . "

¡Awtuwus wulitu-yki-ta ranti-<u>y-manta</u> <u>ama</u> <u>qonqa-ku-y-chu</u>! <u>Don't forget about</u> buy<u>ing</u> your bus ticket!

¡Awtuwus wulitu-s-ni-ykicheh-ta ranti-<u>y-manta</u> <u>ama</u> <u>qonqa-ku-y-cheh-chu</u>! <u>Don't forget (addressing more than one person) about</u> buy<u>ing</u> your (more than one person) bus tickets!
Bus ticket-s-(euphonic particle)-your(more than one person)-(direct object marker) buy-(infinitive marker, "to")-about not(used in a command) forget-selves-(dual command marker addressing more than one person)-(negative marker)!

¡Awtuwus wulitu-yki-ta ranti-<u>y-ta</u> <u>ama</u> <u>qonqa-y-chu</u>! <u>Don't forget to</u> buy your bus ticket!
Bus ticket-your(one person)-(direct object marker) buy-(infinitive marker, "to")-(direct object marker) not(used in a command) forget-(command marker addressing one person)-(negative marker)!

¡Awtuwus wulitu-s-ni-ykicheh-ta ranti-y-ta ama qonqa-y-cheh-chu!
Don't forget (addressing more than one person) to buy your (more than one person) bus tickets!
Bus ticket-s-(euphonic particle)-your(more than one person)-(direct object marker) buy-(infinitive marker, "to")-(direct object marker) not(used in a command) forget-(dual command marker addressing more than one person)-(negative marker)!

Expansion B:

"Don't forget about (something)."
"Don't forget (something)."

¡Awtuwus wulitu-yki-ta ranti-y-manta ama qonqa-ku-y-chu! Don't forget about buying your bus ticket!

¡Awtuwus wulitu-yki-ta ranti-y-ta ama qonqa-y-chu! Don't forget to buy your bus ticket!

¡Awtuwus wulitu-s-ni-ykicheh-ta ranti-y-manta ama qonqa-ku-y-cheh-chu! Don't forget (addressing more than one person) about buying your (more than one person) bus tickets!

¡Awtuwus wulitu-s-ni-ykicheh-ta ranti-y-ta ama qonqa-y-cheh-chu! Don't forget (addressing more than one person) to buy your (more than one person) bus tickets!

Wulitu-s the tickets
Ticket-s ("The" is understood.)
Phista the festival
Festival ("The" is understood.)

Hamu-y to come
Come-(infinitive marker, "to")
Mikhuna-ta apa-mu-y bringing food/to bring food
Food-(direct object marker) carry/take-in this direction[bring]-(infinitive marker, "to")

Q'aya (diya) para-mu-na-sa-n (The fact) that tomorrow it will be raining
Tomorrow (day) rain-(untranslatable infix usually used with verbs expressing natural phenomena when those talking consider themselves affected by them)-(future infinitive marker/particle used with a dependent verb for an action that is in the future in relationship to that of the main verb)-(progressive marker, "-ing")-its. ("That" is understood.)

E. OBLIGATION

31. **¿Imananatah?** What has to be done?/What should one do?/What do you (impersonal) have to do?
    ¿Imana-na-tah?
    Happen-(marker used with a verb that is used in conjunction with a verb, stated or understood, for "there is," "there was," and the like, to show obligation)-and? ("There is" is understood.)

32. **Trawahana.** One has to work./You (impersonal) have to work.
    Trawaha-na.
    Work-(marker used with a verb that is used in conjunction with a verb, stated or understood, for "there is," "there was," and the like, to show obligation). ("There is" is understood.)

33. **¿Imata ruanay (tian)?** What do I have to do?
    ¿Ima-ta rua-na-y (tia-n)?
    What-(direct object marker) do-(marker used with a verb that is used in conjunction with a verb, stated or understood, for "there is," "there was," and the like, to show obligation)-my (be-it[there is])?

34. **Trawahanayki (tian).** You have to work.
    Trawaha-na-yki (tia-n).
    Work-(marker used with a verb that is used in conjunction with a verb, stated or understood, for "there is," "there was," and the like, to show obligation)-your(one person) (be-it[there is]).

Expansion A:

"You have to/had to/will have to/would have to work."

Trawaha-na-yki (tia-n). You have to work.

[Note that in the present tense, as in the sentence above, **tia-n** is used, but in other tenses the third-person singular (the "he/she/it" form) of the appropriate tense of **ka-y** is used.]

Trawaha-na-yki ka-rqa. You had to work.
Trawaha-na-yki ka-sqa! You had to work (showing surprise)!
Trawaha-na-yki ka-nqa. You will have to work.

[Note that the future is not used very often; the present tense is used with future meaning.]

Trawaha-na-yki ka-n-man. You would have to work.

Expansion B:

"What (different people) have to do."

Trawaha-na-yki (tia-n). You have to work.

-y I
my
-yki you (one person)
your(one person)
-n he/she/it
his/her/its
-yku we (excluding the person[s] addressed)
our(excluding the person[s] addressed)
-ncheh we (including the person[s] addressed)
our(including the person[s] addressed)
-ykicheh you (more than one person)
your(more than one person)
-nku they
their

[Note: For all verb forms of obligation, see number 15. Model for Verbs Expressing Obligation, in Section III: Quechua Grammar Notes]

Expansion C:

"You have to (do different things)."

Trawaha-na-yki (tia-n). You have to work.

Llank'a work/farm
Ri go
Kuti return
Sama rest
Uh-ta rua do something
Something-(direct object marker) do

35. **Mana imata ruananchehchu (tian).** We don't have to do anything.
    Mana ima-ta rua-na-ncheh-chu (tia-n).
    No thing[Nothing]-(direct object marker) do-(marker used with a verb that is used in conjunction with a verb, stated or understood, for "there is," "there was," and the like, to show obligation)-our(including the person[s] addressed)-(negative marker) (be-it[there is]).

36. **¿Manachu las trista llohsinan (tian)?** Doesn't he have to leave at three?
   ¿Mana-chu las tris-ta llohsi-na-n (tia-n)?
   *Not-(negative marker, which follows **mana** in a negative question) the three-at leave-(marker used with a verb that is used in conjunction with a verb, stated or understood, for "there is," "there was," and the like, to show obligation)-his/her/its (be-it[there is]).*

37. **Mana(n), kunan diya mana llohsinan (tian)-chu.** No, he doesn't have to leave today.
   Mana(-n), kunan diya mana llohsi-na-n (tia-n)-chu.
   No(-emphatic particle), this day[today] not leave-(marker used with a verb that is used in conjunction with a verb, stated or understood, for "there is," "there was," and the like, to show obligation)-his/her/its (be-it[there is])-(negative marker).

F. INTENTION

38. **¿Imata ruah rinki?**[2] What are you going to do?
   ¿Ima-ta rua-h ri-nki?
   What-(direct object marker) do-(marker affixed to the stem of a verb that is the object of a verb of motion [to form the supine]) go-you(one person)?

39. **Mikhoh rini.** I am going to eat. [**mikhu-** > **mikho-**]
   Mikho-h ri-ni.
   Eat-(marker affixed to the stem of a verb that is the object of a verb of motion [to form the supine]) go-I.

Expansion:

Verbs of motion followed by an action

Mikho-h <u>ri</u>-ni. I am going to eat. [**mikhu-** > **mikho-**]

<u>Ripu</u> <u>go off, go away</u>
<u>Hamu</u> <u>come</u>
<u>Llohsi</u> <u>leave</u>
<u>Kuti</u> <u>return</u>
<u>Yayku</u> <u>come in/enter</u>

---

40. **¿Imapah hamunku?** What are they coming for?/What do they come for?
   ¿Ima-pah hamu-nku?
   What-for come-they?

41. **Mikhuypah hamunku.** They're coming (in order) to eat./They come (in order) to eat.
    Mikhu-y-pah hamu-nku.
    Eat-(infinitive marker, "to")-in order to come-they.

42. **Mikhusqaykupah hamunku.** They come/are coming/have come so that we can eat (referring to a simultaneous action).
    Mikhu-sqa-yku-pah hamu-nku.
    Eat-(past [or perfect] infinitive marker/particle used with a dependent verb for an action that is simultaneous to or prior to that of the main verb)-our(excluding the person[s] addressed)-in order to come-they.

Expansion:

"They come/are coming/have come so that we can eat (referring to a simultaneous action)."

"They came/were coming/had come so that we could eat (referring to a simultaneous action)."

"They come/are coming/have come so that we can eat (referring to a future action)."

Mikhu-sqa-yku-pah hamu-nku. They come/are coming/have come so that we can eat (referring to a simultaneous action).

Mikhu-sqa-yku-pah hamo-rqa-nku. They came/were coming/had come so that we could eat (referring to a simultaneous action). [hamu- > hamo-]

Eat-(past [or perfect] infinitive marker/particle used with a dependent verb for an action that is simultaneous to or prior to that of the main verb)-our(excluding the person[s] addressed)-in order to come-did-they.

Mikhu-na-yku-pah hamu-nku. They come/are coming/have come so that we can eat (referring to a future action).

Eat-(future infinitive marker/particle used with a dependent verb for an action that is in the future in relationship to that of the main verb)-our(excluding the person[s] addressed)-in order to/so that come-they.

G. ABILITY

43. **¿Ñoqaykuwan hamuyta atinkichu?** Can you come with us?
    ¿Ñoqayku-wan hamu-y-ta ati-nki-chu?
    We(excluding the person[s] addressed)-with[With us] come-(infinitive marker, "to")-(direct object marker) can-you(one person)-(question marker)?

44. **Mana(n). Mana atinichu, chaywanpis Karlus atin.** No. I can't, but Carlos can.
    Mana(-n). Mana ati-ni-chu, chay-wan-pis Karlus ati-n.
    No(-emphatic particle). Not can-I-(negative marker), that-with-still[but/nevertheless] Carlos can-he.

45. **¿Paykunamanta yanapayta mañayta atinkichu?** Can you ask them for help?
    ¿Pay-kuna-manta yanapay-ta maña-y-ta ati-nki-chu?
    He/She-(plural marker)[They]-from[From them] help-(direct object marker) ask for-(infinitive marker, "to")-(direct object marker) can-you(one person)-(question marker)?

46. **Mana(n), ñoqaqa mana atinichu, mana runasimita sumahta rimayta atisqayraykuchu.**
    No, I can't because I can't speak Quechua very well.
    Mana(-n), ñoqa-qa mana ati-ni-chu, mana runasimi-ta sumah-ta rima-y-ta ati-sqa-y-rayku-chu.
    No(-emphatic particle), I-(emphatic particle) not can-I-(negative marker), not Quechua-(direct object marker) good-(adverb marker)[well] speak-(infinitive marker, "to")-(direct object marker) can-(past [or perfect] infinitive marker/particle used with a dependent verb for an action that is simultaneous to or prior to that of the main verb)-my-for/because-(negative marker).

47. **¿Imarayku kaypi chay tukuy imakuna kasanku? ¿Imallapah (kanku)?** Why are all those things here? What are they for?
    ¿Ima-rayku kay-pi chay tukuy ima-kuna kasa-nku? ¿Ima-lla-pah (ka-nku)?
    What-for[Why] here-in/at those all thing-(plural marker) be-they? What-just-for (be-they)?

48. **Mana chay tukuy imakunawanqa mana awayta atinkumanchu.**
    Without all those things they wouldn't be able to weave.
    Mana chay tukuy ima-kuna-wan-qa mana awa-y-ta ati-nku-man-chu.
    *Not those all thing-(plural marker)-with[**mana . . . -wan** "without. . . "]-(emphatic particle) not weave-(infinitive marker, "to")-(direct object marker) able-(dual marker for "they would")-(negative marker).*

49. **Mana puñuyta atinichu.** I can't sleep./I haven't been able to sleep.
    Mana puñu-y-ta ati-ni-chu.
    Not sleep-(infinitive marker, "to")-(direct object marker) can/able-I-(negative marker).

Expansion:

"I haven't been able to . . . "

Mana puñu-y-ta ati-ni-chu. I haven't been able <u>to sleep</u>.

Pidru-ta riku-y to see Pedro
Pedro-(direct object marker) see-(infinitive marker, "to")
pay-kuna-ta uyari-y to hear them
he/she/it-(plural marker)[they]-(direct object marker)[them] hear-(infinitive marker, "to")
q'epi-y-ta tari-y to find my "q'epi"
"q'epi"-my-(direct object marker) find-(infinitive marker, "to")

50. **Mana puñuyta aterqanichu.** I couldn't (and didn't) sleep./I wasn't able to (and didn't) sleep. [**ati-** > **ate-**]
Mana puñu-y-ta ate-rqa-ni-chu.
Not sleep-(infinitive marker, "to")-(direct object marker) could/able-did-I-(negative marker).

51. **¿Maypi mikhuyta atikun?** Where can you (impersonal) eat?/Where can one eat?/Where is one able to eat?
¿May-pi mikhu-y-ta ati-ku-n?
Where-in/at eat-(infinitive marker, "to")-(direct object marker) can/able-for self-he/she?

Expansion:

"Where can you (impersonal) (do something)?"

¿May-pi mikhu-y-ta ati-ku-n? Where can you (impersonal) <u>eat</u>?/Where can one <u>eat</u>?/Where is one able <u>to eat</u>?

puñu-y <u>sleep/to sleep</u>
kirusin-ta ranti-y <u>buy kerosene/to buy kerosene</u>
kerosene-(direct object marker) buy-(infinitive marker, "to")

52. **Uchuta mana mikhuyta atinichu.** I can't eat chili pepper.
Uchu-ta mana mikhu-y-ta ati-ni-chu.
Chili pepper-(direct object marker) not eat-(infinitive marker, "to")-(direct object marker) can-I-(negative marker).

Expansion:

"I can't eat . . . "
"I can't drink . . . "

Uchu-ta mana mikhu-y-ta ati-ni-chu. I can't eat chili pepper.

Aycha meat
Khuchi-aycha pork
Pig-meat
Runtu-kuna eggs
Egg-(plural marker)

Lichi-ta mana uhya-y-ta ati-ni-chu. I can't drink milk.

Aqha chicha
Kafey coffee
Tragu liquor

53. **¿Q'epiyta kaypi saqeymanchu?** Could I leave my bag here?
    ¿Q'epi-y-ta kay-pi saqe-y-man-chu?
    "Q'epi"-my-(direct object marker) here-in/at leave-(dual marker for "I could")-(question marker)?

Expansion:

"Could I . . . ?"

¿Q'epi-y-ta kay-pi saqe-y-man-chu? Could I leave my bag here?

Kay-pi tiaku stay here
Here-in/at stay
Chay-pi puñu sleep there
There-in/at sleep
Qan-wan ri go with you
You(one person)-with go

NOTES

1. Present-day Quechua, like Spanish, does not have a verb that means "to like." It has borrowed the Spanish verb, *gustar*, which means "to appeal," giving Quechua the verb **gusta-y**.

   Some people express the idea that someone likes something by following the Spanish pattern, that is, saying that something appeals to someone. Others use **gusta-y** with the meaning "to like," so people can literally say that someone likes something.

   For the sake of simplicity, the easier construction, the one that literally says "you like . . . ," and so on, is the one used in the Model Sentences. However, following is the present tense of **gusta-y**, with the meanings "it appeals" and "they appeal." To construct other tenses, see number 16. Model for Verbs that Include (Pronominally) the Verbal Object "Me," number 17. Model for Verbs that Include (Periphrastically and Pronominally) the Verbal Object "Us," 18. Model for Verbs that Include (Pronominally) the Verbal Object "You (One Person)," and number 19. Model for Verbs that Include (Periphrastically and Pronominally) the Verbal Object "You (More Than One Person)," and number 20. Model for Verbs that Include (Only Periphrastically) the Verbal Objects "Him," "Her," and "Them" in Section III: Quechua Grammar Notes.

gusta-y to appeal

"It appeals to . . . "/. . . like(s) it.

Gusta-wa-n. It appeals to me./I like it.
Appeal-to me-it.
Gusta-su-nki. It appeals to you (one person)./You (one person) like it.
Appeal-(dual marker for "it to you[one person]").
Pay-man gusta-n. It appeals to him/her/it./He/She/It likes it.
He/She/It-to[to him/her/it] appeal-it.

Gusta-wa-yku. It appeals to us (excluding the person[s] addressed)./We(excluding the person[s] addressed) like it.
Appeal-(dual marker for "it to us[excluding the person(s) addressed]").
Gusta-wa-ncheh. It appeals to us (including the person[s] addressed)./We(including the person[s] addressed) like it.
Appeal-(dual marker for "it to us[including the person(s) addressed]").
Gusta-su-nki-cheh. It appeals to you (more than one person)./You (more than one person) like it.
Appeal-(triple marker for "it to you[more than one person]").
Pay-kuna-man gusta-n. It appeals to them./They like it.
He/She/It-(plural marker)[They]-to[to them] appeal-it.

"They appeal to . . . "/. . . like(s) them.

Gusta-wa-nku. They appeal to me./I like them.
Appeal-to me-they.
Gusta-su-nku. They appeal to you (one person)./You (one person) like them.
Appeal-(dual marker for "they to you[one person]").
Pay-man gusta-nku. They appeal to him/her/it./He/She/It likes them.
He/She/It-to[To him/her/it] appeal-they.

Gusta-wa-yku. They appeal to us (excluding the person[s] addressed)./We (excluding the person[s] addressed) like them.

Appeal-(dual marker for "they to us[excluding the person(s) addressed]").

Gusta-wa-ncheh. They appeal to us (including the person[s] addressed)./We (including the person[s] addressed) like them.

Appeal-(dual marker for "they to us[including the person(s) addressed]").

Gusta-su-nki-cheh. They appeal to you (more than one person)./You (more than one person) like them.

Appeal-(triple marker for "they to you[more than one person]").

Pay-kuna-man gusta-nku. They appeal to them./They like them.

He/She/It-(plural maker)[They]-to[to them] appeal-they.

2. The verbal stem plus **-h**, such as in **rua-h** (or its variants, **ruwa-h** or **rura-h**), has three functions.

   (a) One is that of the active participle, "the one who." For example:

   rua-h the one who does

   (b) Another is the equivalent of the Latin accusative supine (supine in "-um"). This form is used after a verb of motion, such as "go," to express intention. For example:

   ¿Ima-ta rua-h ri-nki? What are you going to do? (The idea of "you are going to, intending to do what?")

   What-(direct object marker) do-(marker affixed to the stem of a verb that is the object of a verb of motion [to form the supine]) go-you(one person)?

   Puri-ykacha-h llohsi-yku. We are going out for a walk/to take a walk/stroll.

   Walk-(marker indicating the action is done casually or intermittently)-(marker affixed to the stem of a verb that is the object of a verb of motion [to form the supine]) leave/go out-we(excluding the person[s] addressed).

   (c) The third is to replace the infinitive ending (**-y**) of any verb that is the object of the verbs **riku-y**, "to see," "to look at"; **qhawa-y**, "to look at," to see"; **uyari-y**, "to hear"; **saqe-y**, "to permit," "to allow"; and **kacha-y**, "to send." Compare:

   Take-h-ta uyari-ni. I hear singing.

   Sing-(marker affixed to the stem of a verb that is the object of "hear")-(direct object marker) hear-I.

   BUT

Taki-sqa-n-ta uyari-ni. I hear him singing.
Sing-(past [or perfect] infinitive marker/particle used with a dependent verb for an action that is simultaneous to or prior to that of the main verb)-his/her-(direct object marker)[him/her] hear-I.

SECTION II

Model Sentences and Their Expansions

Chapter 14

This chapter deals with

A. Direct Commands [Model Sentences 1-3]

B. "Let's" Commands [4-6]

C. Indirect Commands [7-8]

D. Warning [9-10]

E. Condition with "If" [11-13]

A. DIRECT COMMANDS

1. **¡Hamuy!** Come!
   ¡Hamu-y!
   Come-(command marker addressing one person)!

Expansion A:

"Come!" (addressing one person)
"Come!" (addressing more than one person)

¡Hamu-y! Come! (addressing one person)
¡Hamu-y-cheh! Come! (addressing more than one person)

Expansion B:

Ways of giving a different degree of strength to a direct command.

From the strongest to the weakest:

¡Hamu-na-yki-tia-n! Come! (addressing one person)
Come-(obligation marker)-your(one person)-be there-it[there is]!

249

¡Hamu-y! Come! (addressing one person)
Come-(command marker addressing one person)!

¡Hamu-nki! Come! (addressing one person)
Come-you(one person) will)!

¡Hamu-ri-y! Come! (addressing one person)
Come-(particle that softens the request/"please")-(command marker addressing one person)!

¡Hamu-ri-y a! Come! (addressing one person)
Come-(particle that softens the request/"please")-(command marker addressing one person) then!

¡Hamu-ri-lla-y a! Come! (addressing one person)
Come-(particle that softens the request/"please")-just-(command marker addressing one person) then!

¡Hamu-wah! Come! (addressing one person)
Come-you(one person) would! OR
¡Hamu-nki-man! Come! (addressing one person)
Come-(dual marker for you[one person] would)!

¡Hamu-ri-wah! Come! (addressing one person)
Come-(particle that softens the request/"please")-you(one person) would! OR
¡Hamu-ri-nki-man! Come! (addressing one person)
Come-please-(dual marker for you[one person] would)!

¡Hamu-ri-lla-wah! Come! (addressing one person)
Come-(particle that softens the request/"please")-just-you(one person) would! OR
¡Hamu-ri-lla-nki-man! Come! (addressing one person)
Come-please-just-(dual marker for you[one person] would)!

¿Hamu-ri-wah-chu? Come! (addressing one person)
Come-(particle that softens the request/"please")-you(one person) would-(question marker)? OR
¿Hamu-ri-nki-man-chu? Come! (addressing one person)
Come-please-just-(dual marker for you[one person] would)?

2. **¡Ama hamuychu!**[1] Don't come!
   ¡Ama hamu-y-chu!
   Not(used in a command) come-(command marker addressing one person)-(negative marker)!

Expansion:

"Come!" (addressing one person)
"Don't come!" (addressing one person)
"Come!" (addressing more than one person)
"Don't come!" (addressing more than one person)

¡Hamu-y! Come! (addressing one person)
¡Ama hamu-y-chu! Don't come! (addressing one person)

¡Qan, hamu-y! You (addressing one person), come!
You(one person), come-(command marker addressing one person)!
¡Qan, ama hamu-y-chu! You (addressing one person), don't come!
You(one person), not(used in a command) come-(command marker addressing one person)-(negative marker)!

¡Hamu-y-cheh! Come (addressing more than one person)!
¡Ama hamu-y-cheh-chu! Don't come (addressing more than one person)!

¡Qan-kuna, hamu-y-cheh! You (addressing more than one person), come!
You-(plural marker), come-(dual command marker addressing more than one person)!
¡Qan-kuna, ama hamu-y-cheh-chu! You (addressing more than one person), don't come!
You-(plural marker), not(used in a command) come-(dual command marker addressing more than one person)-(negative marker)!

3. **¡Pidru, t'antata aparimuy!** Pedro, please bring bread.
   ¡Pidru, t'anta-ta apa-ri-mu-y!
   Pedro, bread-(direct object marker) carry/take-(particle that softens the request/"please")-in this direction[please bring]-(command marker addressing one person).

B. "LET'S" COMMANDS

4. **¡Rina!** Let's go!
   ¡Ri-na!
   Go-("let's" command marker)!

Expansion A:

Variants of "Let's go!"

¡Ri-na! Let's go!
¡Ri-na-cheh! Let's go!
¡Ri-su-n! Let's go! (stronger)
¡Ri-su-n-cheh! Let's go! (stronger)

Expansion B:

"Let's (different actions)."

¡Ri-na(-cheh)! Let's go!
¡Ri-su-n(-cheh)! Let's go! (stronger)

Ripu go (off)/go (away)
Chaki-pi ri OR
Foot/Feet-on go
Chaki-manta-ri go on foot
Foot/Feet-(marker to indicate the way something is done) go
Re-rqo go quickly [**ri-** > **re-**]
Go quickly
Pay-kuna-ta uhyari listen to them
He/She-(plural marker)[They]-(direct object marker)[Them] hear/listen (to)
Wichari get on (bus/train/truck)

5. **¡Haku!** Come on!/Let's go! (not a verb, just an interjection)

Expansion:

Various expressions with **¡Haku!**, "Come on!"/"Let's go!"

¡Haku! Come on!/Let's go! (not a verb, just an interjection)
¡Haku(-cheh)! Come on!/Let's go!

¡Haku llohsi-na! Come on, let's go (leave)!
Come on, let's go let's go/leave-("let's" command marker)!
¡Haku mikhu-na! Come on, let's go eat!
¡Haku ripu-na! Come on, let's go!
¡Haku wasi-man! Come on, let's go home!
Come on house/home-to!
¡Haku wasi-y-man! Come on, let's go to my house!
Come on house/home-my-to!

6. **¡Ama rinachu!** Let's not go!
¡Ama ri-na-chu!
Not(used in a command) go-("let's" command marker)-(negative marker)!

C. INDIRECT COMMANDS

7. **¡Hamuchun!** Have him/her come!/Let him/her come! [Note that this "let" does not mean "permit" or "allow"; the idea is "let/have him/her come!," not someone else.]
¡Hamu-chu-n!
Come-(dual indirect command marker for "let him/her/it"/"have him/her/it")!

Expansion:

"Have/Let . . . come!"
"Have/Let . . . come in (the house)!"

¡Hamu-chu-n! Have him/her/it come!/Let him/her/it come!
¡Hamu-chu-nku! Have them come!/Let them come! [Note that this "let" does not mean "permit" or "allow"; the idea is "let/have them come!," not someone else.]
Come-(dual indirect command marker for "let them"/"have them")!
¡Pidru hamu-chu-n! Have Pedro come!/Let Pedro come!
Pedro come-(dual indirect command marker for "let him/her/it"/"have him/her/it")!

¡Wasi-man yayku-chu-n! Have him/her come in the house!/Let him/her come in the house!
House-in enter/come in-(dual indirect command marker for "let him/her/it"/"have him/her/it")!
¡(Pay-kuna) yayku-chu-nku! Have them come in!/Let them come in!
(He/She/It-[plural marker][They]) enter/come in-(dual indirect command marker for "let them"/"have them")!

---

8. **¡Ama hamuchunchu!** Don't have him/her come!
¡Ama hamu-chu-n-chu!
Not(used in a command) come-(dual indirect command marker for "let him/her/it"/"have him/her/it")-(negative marker)!

D. WARNING

9. **¡Pahtatah!** Watch out!/Careful!
   ¡Pahtatah!

Expansion:

Variant of "Watch out!"/"Careful!"

¡Pahtatah! Watch out!/Careful!
¡Pahtá! Watch out!/Careful! (showing annoyance, anger, or even a threat due to what someone is doing)

---

10. **¡Pahtatah urmakuwah!** Watch out, you could fall!/Careful, you could fall!
    ¡Pahtatah urma-ku-wah!
    Watch out/Careful fall-self-you(one person) could!

Expansion:

"Watch out, you could . . . "
"Careful, you could . . . "

¡Pahtatah urma-ku-wah! Watch out, you <u>could fall</u>!/Careful, you <u>could fall</u>!
¡Pahtatah urma-ku-wah-cheh! Watch out, you (more than one person) <u>could fall</u>!/Careful, you (more than one person) <u>could fall</u>!

chirma-ku get hurt
hurt-self
chay-ta p'aki break that
that-(direct object marker) break

E. CONDITION WITH "IF"

11. **Las dusta llohsispa(yke)qa, tutamanta ñawpahta mana chayankichu.**[2] If you leave at two, you won't/will not get there before dark. [**-yki-** > **-yke-**]

    Las dus-ta llohsi-spa(-yke)-qa, tuta-manta ñawpah-ta mana chaya-nki-chu.

    The two(o'clock)-at leave-(invariable gerund marker, "-ing," used when the subject of the gerund is the same as that of the main verb)-your[one person])-(emphatic marker used in this construction with -spa- to convey the idea of "if"), night-at(with part of a day) before-(adverb marker) not arrive-you(one person) will-(negative marker).

    [The same subject is doing the leaving and the arriving, so **-spa-** (that can be followed by a possessive, which is optional) is used. Compare this with sentence 12 below.]

Expansion:

"If you leave at two, you won't/will not get there before dark."
"If you left at two, you wouldn't get there before dark."

[Note that in these sentences, the same subject is doing both actions, so **-spa-** (that can be followed by a possessive, which is optional) is used.]

Las dus-ta llhosi-spa(-yke)-qa, tuta-manta ñawpah-ta <u>mana chaya-nki-chu</u>. If you leave at two, <u>you won't/will not get there</u> before dark. [**-yki-** > **-yke-**]

<u>mana chaya-wah-chu</u> (left)/you wouldn't get there

12. **Las dusta llohsehtiykoqa, tutamanta ñawpahta mana chayankichu.** If we leave at two, you won't/will not get there before dark. [**llohsi-** > **llohse-**, **-yku-** > **-yko-**]

    Las dus-ta llhose-hti-yko-qa, tuta-manta ñawpah-ta chaya-nki-chu.

    *The two(o'clock)-at leave-(variable gerund marker, "-ing," used when the subject of the gerund is different from that of the main verb)-our(excluding the person[s] addressed)-(emphatic marker used in this construction with **-hti-** to convey the idea of "if"), night-at(with part of a day) before-(adverb marker) not arrive-you(one person) will-(negative marker).*

    [Different subjects are doing the leaving and the arriving, so **-hti-** plus a possessive is used. Compare this with sentence 11 above.]

13. **Paramohtenqa, mana risahkuchu.**[4] If it rains, we won't/will not go. [-mu- > -mo-, -hti- > -hte-]
Para-mo-hte-n-qa, mana ri-sahku-chu.
*Rain-(untranslatable infix usually used with verbs expressing natural phenomena when those talking consider themselves affected by them)-(variable gerund marker, "-ing," used when the subject of the gerund is different from that of the main verb)-its-(emphatic marker used in this construction with **-hti-** to convey the idea of "if"), not go-we(excluding the person[s] addressed) will-(negative marker).*

Expansion:

"If it rains, we won't/will not go."
"If it rained, we wouldn't go."

Para-mo-hte-n-qa, mana ri-sahku-chu. If it rains, we (excluding the person[s] addressed) won't/will not go. [-mu- > -mo-, -hti- > -hte-]
Para-mo-hte-n-qa, mana ri-su-n(cheh)-chu. If it rains, we (including the persons[s] addressed) won't/will not go. [-mu- > -mo-, -hti- > -hte-]
. . . not go-(dual marker for "we[including the persons(s) addressed] will")-(negative marker)

mana ri-yku-man-chu we (excluding the person[s] addressed) wouldn't go
not go-(double marker for "we[excluding the person(s) addressed] would")-(negative marker)

mana ri(-su)-ncheh-man-chu we (including the person[s] addressed) wouldn't go
not go-(triple marker for "we[including the persons(s) addressed] would")-(negative marker)

NOTES

1. Note that one can also hear the negative command markers **ama** and **-chu** placed differently in a sentence, as in:
   ¡**Ama** chay-man ri-y-**chu**! Don't go there!
   ¡**Ama** chay-man-**chu** ri-y! Don't go there!
   ¡Chay-man **ama** ri-y-**chu**! Don't go there!

2. The particle **-spa**, affixed to the stem of a verb, forms the invariable gerund which is used to show a simulateous, consecutive, or conditional action that is secondary to that of the main verb in the sentence. The invariable gerund always has as its understood subject the same one as

the main verb, but an optional, redundant, possessive adjective for that subject may be affixed to the gerund. For example:

Simultaneous actions:

Llohsi-spa(-ykicheh), punku-ta wisq'a-nki-cheh. On leaving/When you (more than person) leave, you shut the door.

Leave-(invariable gerund marker, "-ing used then the subject of the gerund is the same as that of the main verb)(-your[more than one person]), door-(direct object marker)-shut-(dual marker for "you[more than one person]").

Consecutive actions:

Chaya-mu-sa-spa(-nku), mikho-nqa-nku. They will eat on arriving/ongetting here / when the arrive/when they get here. **[mikhu- > mikho-]**

Arrive-in this direction[get here]-(progressive marker, "-ing")-(invariable gerund marker, "-ing," used when the subject of the gerund is the same as that of the main verb)(-their), eat-(dual marker for "they-will").

Conditional action (the concept of "if" expressed with **-qa**):

Las dus-ta llohsi-spa(-nku)-qa, tuta-manta ñawpah-ta chaya-nqa-nku. If they leave at two, they will arrive there/get there before dark.

The two(o'clock)-at leave-(invariable gerund marker, "-ing," used when the subject of the gerund is the same as that of the main verb)(-their)-(emphatic marker used in this construction with -spa- to convey the idea of "if"), night-of before-(adverb marker) arrive-(dual marker for "they will").

It should be noted that in these constructions, the subject, tense, and mood of the main verb will dictacte the subject, tense, and mood of the verb of the dependent clause, with **-spa**. For example:

Chaya-mu-sa-spa, mikhu-ni. I eat on arriving/on getting here/when I arrive/get here.

Arrive-in this direction[get here]-(progressive marker, "-ing")-(invariable gerund marker, "-ing," used when the subject of the gerund is the same as that of the main verb), eat-I.

Chaya-mu-sa-spa, mikhu-nki. You (one person) hey eat on arriving/on getting here/when you (one person) arrive/get here.

Chaya-mu-sa-spa, mikhu-n. He/She/It eats on arriving/on getting here/when he/she/it arrives/gets here.

Chaya-mu-sa-spa, mikhu-yku. We (excluding the person[s] addressed) eat on arriving/on getting here/when we (excluding the person[s] addressed) arrive/get here.

Chaya-mu-sa-spa, mikhu-ncheh. We (including the person[s] addressed) eat on arriving/on getting here/when we (including the person[s] addressed) arrive/get here.

Chaya-mu-sa-spa, mikhu-nki-cheh. You (more than one person) eat on arriving/on getting here/when you (more than one person) arrive/get here.

Chaya-mu-sa-spa, mikhu-nku. They eat on arriving/on getting here/when they arrive/get here.

Chaya-mu-sa-spa, mikho-rqa-nku. They ate on arriving/on getting here/when they arrived/got here. [**mikhu-** > **mikho-**]
Arrive-in this direction[get here]-(progressive marker, "-ing")-(invariable gerund marker, "-ing," used when the subject of the gerund is the same as that of the main verb), eat-did-they.

Chaya-mu-sa-spa, mikho-nqa-nku. They will eat on arriving/on getting here/when they arrive/get here. [**mikhu-** > **mikho-**]
Arrive-in this direction[get here]-(progressive marker, "-ing")-(invariable gerund marker, "-ing," used when the subject of the gerund is the same as that of the main verb), eat-(dual marker for "they will").

Las dus-ta chaya-mu-sa-spa-qa, mikhu-nku-man. They would eat if they arrived (would arrive)/got (would get) here at two.
The two[Two o'clock]-at(with a period of time) arrive-in this direction[get here]-(progressive marker, "-ing")-(invariable gerund marker, "-ing," used when the subject of the gerund is the same as that of the main verb)-(emphatic marker used in this construction with -spa- to convey the idea of "if"), eat-(dual marker for "they would").

3. The infix **-hti-**, affixed to the stem of a verb, forms the variable gerund which is used to show a simulateous, consecutive, conditional, or causative action that is secondary to that of the main verb in the sentence. The subject of the variable gerund differs from that of the main verb, so the appropriate possessive adjective is affixed to indicate its subject . For example:

   Simultaneous actions:
   Llohse-hti-ykicheh, punku-ta wisq'a-ni. When you (more than person) leave/On your (more than one person) leaving, I shut the door. [**llohsi-** > **llohse-**]
   Leave-(variable gerund marker, "-ing," used when the subject of the gerund is different from that of the main verb)-your(more than one person), door-(direct object marker)-shut-I.
   Consecutive actions:

Chaya-mu-sa-<u>hti-nku</u>, mikhu-su-n(cheh). We (including the person[s] addressed) will eat when they get here.
Arrive-in this direction[get here]-(progressive marker, "-ing")-(variable gerund marker, "-ing," used when the subject of the gerund is different from that of the main verb)-their eat-(dual marker for "we[including the person(s) addressed] will").

Conditional action (the concept of "if" expressed with **-qa**):

Para-mo-<u>hte-n-qa</u>, mana ri-sahku-chu. If it rains, we (excluding the person[s] addressed won't/will not go. [**-mu-** > **-mo-, -hti-** > **-hte-**]
*Rain-(untranslatable infix usually used with verbs expressing natural phenomena when those talking consider themselves affected by them)-(variable gerund marker, "-ing," used when the subject of the gerund is different from that of the main verb)-its-(emphatic marker used in this construction with **-hti-** to convey the idea of "if"), not go-we(excluding the person[s] addressed) will-(negative marker).*

Causative:

Para-mo-<u>hti-n</u>, mana re-rqa-ncheh-chu. Because it rained, we (including the persons[s] addressed) did not go. [**-mu-** > **-mo-, ri-** > **re-**]
Rain-(untranslatable infix usually used with verbs expressing natural phenomena when those talking consider themselves affected by them)-(variable gerund marker, "-ing," used when the subject of the gerund is different from that of the main verb)-its-, not go-did-we(including the person[s] addressed)l-(negative marker).

4. In this section E. Condition With "If," there are three sentences using the particle **-qa** with the invariable gerund, **-spa**, and the variable gerund, **-hti-** to convey the idea of "if." It should be pointed out that there are additional ways to express the "if," using **-chus** or **chayqa**, the former affixed to a conjugated (finite) verb form, and the latter following one. For example:

Para-mu-n-chus, mana hamu-n-chu. If it rains, he doesn't come.
Para-mu-n-chus, mana hamo-nqa-chu. If it rains, he will not/won't come. [**hamu-** > **hamo-**]
Para-mu-n-chus, mana hamu-n-man-chu. If it rained, he wouldn't come.

Para-mu-n chayqa, mana hamu-n-chu. If it rains, he doesn't come.

Para-mu-n chayqa, mana hamo-nqa-chu. If it rains, he will not/won't come. [**hamu-** > **hamo-**]

Para-mu-n chayqa, mana hamu-n-man-chu. If it rained, he wouldn't come.

SECTION III

Quechua Grammar Notes

1. POSTPOSITIONS WITH THE FUNCTION OF PREPOSITIONS

The concepts expressed in English by prepositions ("from," "for," "to," and the like) are shown in Quechua by postpositions. For example:

from **llahta**, "town," we have:

llahta-pah	for the town, to the town
llahta-ta	to the town (indicating reaching there)
llahta-man	toward the town, to the town (in the direction of, headed for, or indicating reaching there)
llahta-manta	from the town
llahta-kama	over to the town, up to the town, down to the town, as far as the town
llahta-pi	in the town, at the town
llahta-neh-pi	around the town, somewhere in the town
llahta-(n)ta	through the town, around the town somewhere
llahta-rayku	for the town, because of the town

from **runa**, "man," we have:

runa llama-wan	the man with the llama (by, near it) (accompanying leading it)
runa llama-yoh	the man with the llama (he has/owns it)
runa mana llama-wan	the man without the llama (the one that isn't the person near the llama)
runa mana llama-yoh	the man without the llama (the one who doesn't have/own one)

and to express "of" (as well as "'s," and "s'") we have:

-h, -hta, -hpa or **-hpata**, used with words ending in a vowel

llahta-h	of the town, (the town's) OR
llahta-hta	of the town, (the town's) OR
llahta-hpa	of the town, (the town's) OR
llahta-hpata	of the town, (the town's)

AND

-pa, or **-pata**, used with words ending in a consonant

ñan-pa	-of the road, (the road's) OR
ñan-pata	-of the road, (the road's)

[Note that when the shorter form, **-pa**, is affixed to a noun that is followed by a noun with a possessive, **-pah**, "for," may be used instead. For example:
    fista Hwan-pa llahta-n-pata   Juan's town's festival OR
festival Juan-of[Juan's] town-his-of[his town's]
    fista Hwan-pah llahta-n-pata   Juan's town's festival]

2. PLURAL OF NOUNS

A. Formation of the plural of nouns with -kuna or with -s

To form the plural of a noun (to indicate more than one of what the noun designates), the original Quechua added the suffix **-kuna** to the singular form.

Today, while the plural of original Quechua nouns that end in a consonant (of which there are not many) is formed by adding **-kuna**, the plural of nouns that end in a vowel is formed in some areas by adding **-kuna**, in others, by influence of Spanish, by adding **-s**.

The plural of nouns borrowed/naturalized from Spanish that end in a vowel is formed by adding **-s**, and of those that end in a consonant by adding **-is**. For example:

llahta	town
llahta-kuna or **llahta-s**	towns

AND

waka	cow
waka-s	cows
awtuwus	bus
awtuwus-is	buses

B. Emphatic -ni- with plural nouns formed with -s

Any plural noun formed with **-s** (as happens with any word that ends in any consonant) requires the euphonic infix **-ni-** between it and any following suffix or infix that is a single consonant or that begins with **y-** or a double consonant combination not found in the alphabet. For example:

llahta-s-ni-n	its towns
llahta-s-ni-yoh	with towns
llahta-s-ni-nku	their towns

C. Position of affixes in plural nouns formed with -kuna

If the plural of a noun is formed with **-kuna**, any affix other than a possessive affix follows **-kuna**; the possessive must precede **-kuna**. For example:

ñan	road
ñan-kuna	road<u>s</u>

ñan-kuna-pi	on the road<u>s</u>
road-(plural marker)-in/on	
ñan-ni-nku-kuna	their road<u>s</u>
road-(euphonic particle)-their-(plural marker)	
ñan-ni-nku-kuna-pi	on their road<u>s</u>
road-(euphonic particle)-their-(plural marker)-in/on	

[In some Quechuaphone areas, nouns that form their plural with **-s**, by analogy with the construction with **-kuna**, have the possessive suffixes placed between a noun and the **-s** plural marker.]

llahta	town
llahta-s	town<u>s</u>
llahta-s-ni-nku	their towns OR
llahta-nku-s	their towns [less common]

3. ADJECTIVES

As in English, a descriptive adjective that directly modifies a noun (an attributive adjective) precedes the noun and does not change form. For example:

hatun llahta	large town
hatun llahta-kuna OR **hatun llahta-s**	large towns

An adjective that modifies a noun indirectly (a predicative adjective) with the connecting verb understood or stated follows the noun. Compare:

hatun llahta	large town
Llahta hatun.	The town is *(understood)* large.
hatun llahta-kuna (OR **hatun llahta-s**)	large towns
Llahta-kuna (OR **Llahta-s**) **hatun (ka-nku).**	The towns (are) large.

4. POSSESSION

A. Quechua for "my," your," and the like

Suffixes are used to show "my," "your (one person)," "his," "her," "its," "our," "your (more than one person)," and "their."

1. The following suffixes (two with variants, that are given in the notes below) are used with words ending in a vowel:

-y	my
-yki	your (one person)

-n	his, her, its
-yku	our (excluding the person[s] addressed)
-ncheh*	our (including the person[s] addressed)
-yki-cheh**	your (more than one person)
-nku	their

For example:
llahta-y	my town
llahta-nku	their town

*[Note: The form for "our (including the person[s] addressed)," **-ncheh**, has five variants:
- **-nchej**
- **-nchih**
- **-nchij**
- **-nchik**
- **-nchis**.]

[Note: The form for "your (more than one person)," **-yki-cheh, has five variants.
- **-yki-chej**
- **-yki-chih**
- **-yki-chij**
- **-yki-chik**
- **-yki-chis**

All forms may also be written as one word: **-ykicheh, -ykichej, -ykichih, -ykichij, -ykichik, -ykichis**.]

2. With words ending in a consonant the same suffixes given above for use with a word ending in a vowel are used, but the euphonic infix **-ni-** is inserted between that consonant and the possessive suffix. For example:

   ñan-ni-yku   our (excluding the person[s] addressed) roads
   road-(euphonic particle)-our

3. If the plural of a noun is formed with **-s**, the possessive, preceded by the euphonic infix **-ni-**, follows it. If the plural of a noun is formed with **-kuna**, the possessive must precede the **-kuna**. Compare:

   llahta-s-ni-nku   their towns
   town-s-(euphonic particle)-their
   ñan-ni-nku-kuna   their roads
   road-(euphonic particle)-their-(plural marker)

B. Quechua for "of," " 's," and "s "
   (This was also mentioned above in Quechua Grammar Note I. Postpositions with the Function of Prepositions.)

1. The following suffixes are used with words ending in a vowel: **-h, -hta, -hpa** or **-hpata,**
llahta-h	of the town, the town's OR
llahta-hta	of the town, the town's OR
llahta-hpa	of the town, the town's OR
llahta-hpata	of the town, the town's

2. The following suffixes are used with words ending in a consonant: **-pa** or **-pata.**
ñan-pa	of the road, the road's OR
ñan-pata	of the road, the road's

    [Note that when the shorter form, **-pa**, is affixed to a noun that is followed by a noun with a possessive, **-pah**, "for," may be used instead. For example:
    fista Hwan-pa llahta-n-pata   Juan's town's festival
    festival Juan-of[Juan's] town-his-of[his town's]
    OR
    fista Hwan-pah llahta-n-pata   Juan's town's festival]

C. Quechua for "mine," "of mine"; "yours," "of yours," and the like
  1. Possession with "mine," "of mine"; "yours (one person)," "of yours (one person)"; "his," "of his"; "hers," "of hers"; "its," "of its"; "ours," "of ours"; "yours (more than one person)," "of yours (more than one person)"; and "theirs," "of theirs" is expressed with the constructions such as "I-of."

      ñoqa-h OR **ñoqa-hta** OR **ñoqa-hpa** OR **ñoqa-hpata**
      mine, of mine

      qan-pa OR **qan-pata**
      yours (one person), of yours (one person)

      pay-pa OR **pay-pata**
      his, hers, its, of his, of hers, of its

      ñoqa-yko-h OR **ñoqa-yko-hta** OR **ñoqa-yko-hpa** OR **ñoqa-yko-hpata** [-yku- > -yko]
      ours (excluding the person[s] addressed), of ours (excluding the person[s] addressed)

      ñoqa-ncheh-pa OR **ñoqa-ncheh-pata**
      ours (including the person[s] addressed), of ours (including the person[s] addressed)

      qan-kuna-h OR **qan-kuna-hta** OR **qan-kuna-hpa** OR **qan-kuna-hpata**
      yours (more than one person), of yours (more than one person)

pay-kuna-h OR **pay-kuna-hta** OR **pay-kuna-hpa** OR **pay-kuna-hpata**
theirs, of theirs

For example:
¿**Qan-pata-chu kay-qa?**   Is this yours?
You(one person)-of[Yours]-(question marker) this-(emphatic particle)? ("Is" is understood.)
Chay-qa pay-pata.   That is hers.
That-(emphatic particle) he/she-of[his/hers]. ("Is" is understood.)

2. Often when the noun designating the thing possessed is expressed, it has the appropriate possessive suffix "my," "your," "his," and the like affixed. Compare:

pay-pa   his/hers/its
pay-pa wasi-n   his/her/its house
he/she/it-of[of his/of hers/of its] house-his/her/its
Mariya-hpa wasi-n   Maria's house
Maria-of[Maria's] house-her

D. Quechua for "to have"

Quechua has no verb for "to have." To convey this idea, different constructions can be used.

1. One way to say that people have something is to say that they are "with" whatever they have. For example:

Ñoqa wasi-yoh ka-ni.	I have a house.
I house-with be-I.	
Qan wasi-yoh ka-nki.	You (one person) have a house.
Pay wasi-yoh.	He/She/It has a house. ("Is" is understood.)
Ñoqayku wasi-yoh ka-yku.	We (excluding the person[s] addressed) have a house.
Ñoqancheh wasi-yoh ka-ncheh.	We (including the person[s] addressed) have a house
Qan-kuna wasi-yoh ka-nki-cheh.	You (more than one person) have a house.
Pay-kuna wasi-yoh (ka-nku).	They have a house.

2. The second way to say that someone has something is by using a construction with:

a. The person who has the thing(s) + "of"
b. The noun designating the thing(s) had + the appropriate possessive for "my," "your," "his/her/its," "our," "your," or "their," and
c. The verb for "there is/there are" (in Quechua one verb form is used for both), "there was/there were," or whatever tense is appropriate. Optionally the infix **-pu-**, "it," "them," can be included in the verb.

Ñoqa-hpata wasi-y ka(-pu)-n. I have a house.
I-of[Of mine] house-my be(-it)-it[there is (it)].

Qan-pata wasi-yki ka(-pu)-n. You (one person) have a house.
You(one person)-of[Of yours(one person)] house-your(one person) be(-it)-it[there is (it)].

Pay-pata wasi-n ka(-pu)-n. He/She/It has a house.
He/She/It-of[Of his/Of hers/Of its)] house-his/her/its be(-it)-it[there is (it)].

Ñoqayko-hpata wasi-yku ka(-pu)-n. We (excluding the person[s] addressed) have a house. [**ñoqayku** > **ñoqayko**]
We(excluding the person[s] addressed)-of[Of ours(excluding the person[s] addressed)] house-our(excluding the person[s] addressed) be(-it)-it[there is (it)].

Ñoqancheh-pata wasi-ncheh ka(-pu)-n. We (including the person[s] addressed) have a house.
We(including the person[s] addressed)-of[Of ours(including the person[s] addressed)] house-our(including the person[s] addressed) be(-it)-it[there is (it)].

Qan-kuna-hpata wasi-ykicheh ka(-pu)-n. You (more than one person) have a house.
You-(plural marker)[You(more than one person)-of[Of yours(more than one person)] house-your(more than one person) be(-it)-it[there is (it)].

Pay-kuna-hpata wasi-nku ka(-pu)-n. They have a house.
He/She/It-(plural marker)[They]-of[Of theirs] house-their be(-it)-it[there is (it)].

[It should be noted that the verb form **ka-n,** the third-person singular of the present tense of **ka-y,** "there to be," can be replaced with **tia-n** and **tiya-n,** from the verbs **tia-y,** and **tiya-y,** respectively, which also mean "for there to be." In some Quechuaphone areas, in tenses other than the present, these other two verbs are preferred over forms of **ka-y.** The construction with the infix **-pu-** can also be used with these two verbs.]

3. There is a third way to say "I have," "we have," "you (one person) have," and "you (more than one person) have."

The construction of the sentence is the same as that in 2. immediately above except for the verb form.

Here a more complex form (a pronominal verbal construction) is used, one that includes in the verb the object ("for me," "for us," "for you (one person)," and "for you (more than one person)" in "there is/there are it/them (referring to the item[s] possessed) for me / for us / for you (one person) / for you (more than one person)."
[In Section III. Quechua Grammar Notes see numbers
   11. Introduction to Complex Verbs,
   16. Model for Verbs that Include (Pronominally) the Verbal Object "Me,"
   17. Model for Verbs that Include (Periphrastically and Pronominally) the Verbal Object "Us, "
   18. Model for Verbs that Include (Pronominally) the Verbal Object "You (One Person)," and
   19. Model for Verbs that Include (Periphrastically and Pronominally) the Verbal Object "You (More Than One Person)."]

Ñoqa-hpata wasi-y ka-pu-wa-n.
I-of[Of mine] house-my be-it-for me-it[there is it for me].
I have a house.

Ñoqayko-hpata wasi-yku ka-pu-wa-yku. [ñoqayku > ñoqayko]
We(excluding the person[s] addressed)-of[Of ours(excluding the person[s] addressed)] house-our(excluding the person[s] addressed) be-it-(dual marker for "for us[excluding the person(s) addressed] it")[there is it for us (excluding the person[s]addressed)].
We (excluding the person[s] addressed) have a house.

Ñoqancheh-pata wasi-ncheh ka-pu-wa-ncheh.
We(including the person[s] addressed)-of[Of ours(including the person[s] addressed)] house-our(including the person[s] addressed) be-it-(dual marker for "for us[including the person(s) addressed] it")[there is it for us (including the person[s]addressed)].
We (including the person[s] addressed) have a house.

Qan-pata wasi-yki ka-pu-su-nki.

You(one person)-of[Of yours(one person)] house-your(one person) be-it-(dual marker for "for you[one person] it")[there is it for you (one person)]
You (one person) have a house.

Qan-kuna-hpata wasi-ykicheh ka-pu-su-nki-cheh.
Your-(plural marker)-of[Of yours(more than one person)] house-your(more than one person) be-it-(triple marker for "for you[more than one person]it "[there is it for you (more than one person)].
You (more than one person) have a house.

NOTE that for "he has," "she has," "it has," and "they have" verb forms do not include reference to the person. The constructions used are those given in 2. above

Pay-pata wasi-n ka-pu-n.
He/She/It-of[Of his/Of hers/Of its] house-his/her/its be-it-it[there is it].
He/She/It has a house.

Pay-kuna-hpata wasi-nku ka-pu-n.
He/She/It-(plural marker)[They-of][Of their] house-their be-it-it[there is it].
They have a house.

[In Section III. Quechua Grammar Notes see number 20. Model for Verbs that Include (Only Periphrastically) the Verbal Objects "Him," "Her," and "Them."]

5. CARDINAL NUMBERS

Following each number in Quechua (shown in bold face) is the Quechua adaptation of Spanish numbers. Note that in telling time and giving dates, the numbers borrowed/naturalized from Spanish are often used.

1 **uh** OR **uj** OR **uk** OR **hoq** OR **huk** OR **hoq**
una (used in saying "one o'clock")
2 **iskay**
dos
3 **kinsa** OR **kimsa**
tris
4 **tawa**
kwaru
5 **phishqa** OR **pisqa** OR **pichqa**
sinku

6 **sohta** OR **soqta** OR **suqta** OR **sojta**
   sis
7 **qanchis**
   siti
8 **pusah** OR **pusaq** OR **pusaj**
   uchu
9 **isq'on** OR **isqon** OR **isqun** OR **hisq'on**
   nuywi
10 **chunka**
   dis
11 **chunka-uh-ni-yoh** (literally: "ten-one[-euphonic particle]-with")
   unsi

[Note: All numbers larger than ten that are not multiples of ten are formed by attaching the suffix **-yoh**, "with," to a number ending in a vowel, and **-ni-yoh**, "(the required euphonic particle)-with," to one ending in a consonant.]

[Note: Any number larger than ten that includes a number lower than ten that has one or more variants (numbers one, three, five, six, eight, or nine) can use in its construction any of the variants. For example:
   15 **chunka-phishqa-yoh** OR
      chunka-pisqa-yoh OR
      chunka-pichqa-yoh OR
      kinsi]

12 **chunka-iskay-ni-yoh**
   dusi
13 **chunka-kimsa-yoh**
   trisi
14 **chunka-tawa-yoh**
   katursi
15 **chunka-phishqa-yoh**
   kinsi
16 **chunka-sohta-yoh**
   disisis
17 **chunka-qanchis-ni-yoh**
   disisiti
18 **chunka-pusah-ni-yoh**
   disiyuchu
19 **chunka-isq'on-ni-yoh**
   disinuywi

20 **iskay-chunka**
   winti
21 **iskay-chunka-uh-ni-yoh**
   wintiunu
22 **iskay-chunka-iskay-ni-yoh**
   wintidus
23 **iskay-chunka-kimsa-yoh**
   wintitris
29 **iskay-chunka-isq'on-ni-yoh**
   wintinuywi
30 **kimsa-chunka**
   trinta
31 **kimsa-chunka-uh-ni-yoh**
   trintayunu
40 **tawa-chunka**
   kwarinta
50 **phishqa-chunka**
   sinkwinta
60 **sohta-chunka**
   sisinta
70 **qanchis-chunka**
   sitinta
80 **pusah-chunka**
   uchinta
90 **isq'on-chunka**
   nuwinta
99 **isq' on-chunka-isq'on-ni-yoh**
   nuwintay-nuywi
100 **pachah**
   sintu / sin
101 **pachah-uh-ni-yoh**
   sintunu / sintuna
102 **pachah-iskay-ni-yoh**
   sintu dus
199 **pachah-isq'on-chunka-isq'on-ni-yoh**
   sintu nuwintay-nuywi
200 **iskay-pachah**
   dusintus / dusintas
300 **kimsa-pachah**
   trisintus / trisintas
351 **kimsa-pachah-phishqa-chunka-uh-ni-yoh**
   trisintus sinkwintayunu
500 **phishqa-pachah**

kiniyintus / kiniyintas
700 **qanchis-pachah**
sitisintus / sitisintas
999 **isq'on-pachah isq'on-chunka-isq'on-ni-yoh**
nwiwisintus nuwintay-nwiwi / nwiwisintas nuwintay-nuywi
1,000 **waranqa**
mil
2,000 **iskay-waranqa**
dus mil
5,555 **phishqa-waranqa phishqa-pachah phishqa-chunka-phishqayoh**
sinku mil kiniyintus sinkwintay-sinku
19,019 **chunka-isq'on-ni-yoh waranqa chunka-isq'on-ni-yoh**
disinuywi mil disinuywi

[Note that the only case in which a number has **-yoh** twice is when one precedes **waranqa**, "thousand," or **hunu**, "million."]

302,030 **kimsa-pachah-iskay-ni-yoh waranqa kimsa-chunka**
trisintus dus mil trinta / trisintas dus mil trinta
1,000,000 **hunu**
millun
2,000,000 **iskay-hunu**
dus millunis, **iskay**-millun

6. ORDINAL NUMBERS

Ordinal numbers (first, second, and so on) are formed by attaching **-ñeqe(n)** (the oldest and most authentic Quechua form), or one of its variants (**-ñaqe[n]** or **-ñiqe[n]**), or **-kah** to the corresponding cardinal number, or by affixing **-qhepa(n)** to the preceding corresponding cardinal number. For example:

first	**ñawpah(-ñeqe[n])**
second	**iskay-ñeqe(n)** OR **iskay-kah** OR **ñawpah-qhepa(n)**
third	**kimsa-ñeqe(n)** OR **kimsa-kah** OR **iskay-qhepa(n)**

7. NEGATION

Negative phrases and sentences are formed with two elements. The first element is **mana** or **ma**, "no," "not," used in statements, or **ama**, "no," "not," used in negative commands. This goes at the beginning of a phrase or sentence to be negated, or precedes the appropriate word that is to be negated, usually a verb, the word is then followed, or the phrase or sentence is then ended, with the untranslatable suffix **-chu**, which most frequently is affixed to the verb. In a question, the negative construction is **mana-chu**, and it introduces the question. For example:

Mana hamu-nku-chu.
Not come-they-(negative marker).
They do not come.
They are not coming.

Ma hamu-nku-chu.
Not come-they-(negative marker).
They do not come.
They are not coming.

¡Ama hamu-y-chu!
No(used in a command) come-(command marker addressing one person)-(negative marker)!
Don't come!

¿Mana-chu hamu-nku?
Not-(negative marker) come-they?
Aren't they coming?

8. QUESTIONS

Questions usually are formed by adding the interrogative suffix **-chu**, usually affixed to the verb and at the end of the sentence. For example:

¿Hamu-nki-chu?
Come-you (one person)-(question marker)?
Do you come?
Are you coming?

¿Chay-ta uyari-nki-chu?
That-(direct object marker) hear-you(one person)-(question marker)?
Do you hear that?
Are you hearing that?

Affixing **-chu** elsewhere in the sentence places emphasis on the word to which it is affixed.

¿Chay-ta-chu uyari-nki?

That-(direct object marker)-(question marker) hear-you(one person)?
Do you hear that? (emphasis on "that")
Are you hearing that? (emphasis on "that")

However, if the question begins with an interrogative word or is a very short one with no verb, **-chu** is not needed. For example:

¿Mayk'ah hamu-nki?
When come-you(one person)?
When do you come?
When are you coming?

¿Wah-kuna-tah?
The rest-(plural marker)[the others]-and?
And the others?

9. DIMINUTIVES

A diminutive, a word derived from another by the addition of a diminutive suffix, adds to the meaning of the base word one of many possible nuances. The meaning of the original word and the context in which the diminutive is used will provide the shade of meaning being conveyed by the diminutive. In addition to smallness in size, amount, or degree, a diminutive can also convey emphasis, intensity, precision, as well as friendliness, warmth, shortening of social distance, cuteness or charm, and, in a given context, even scorn..

The use of diminutives is extremely common in Quechua. Nouns, pronouns, adjectives, adverbs, and verbs all can have a diminutive construction.

A. The most authentic and common Quechua diminutive endings

The most authentic and common Quechua diminutive endings are the suffixs **-(n)cha** and **-(n)chu,** usually used today without the **n**.

t'ika	flower
t'ika-(n)cha	little flower
muyu	turn
muyu-(n)cha	little turn
wayna	young man
wayna-(n)cha	uncouth, loud mouth, worthless young man
para	rain
para-cha-wan	with little rain
Dani	Daniel
Dani-chu	Danny
Dani-cha	Danny

pisi	little (in amount)
pisi-cha	very little, a little bit
pay	he
pay-cha	he (showing closeness or affection); he himself (showing intensity)
q'omer	green
q'omer-cha	light green
mikhu-y	to eat
mikhu-cha-y	to eat a little, to snack

B. Additional diminutive suffixes.

   Quechua has the following additional diminutive suffixes:
   1. **-ku** and **-ka,** used with a given name or with a noun that shows family relationship

Husiy	Jose
Husiy-ku	Little Jose; Joey
Huli	Julia
Huli-ka	Juliette
mama	mother; in a given context, elderly lady
mama-ku	little old lady (showing affection)

   2. **-ita**, **-itu**, and **-situ**, borrowings from Spanish. For these diminitive endings, while personal and regional preferences could dictate something different, common constructions are as follows:
      a. for a word ending in **-a**, the **-a** is removed and replaced with **-ita**, unless the word refers just to a male, in which case **-itu** is used instead

t'anta	loaf of bread
t'ant-ita	small loaf of bread; roll
¡Mama! *(Mom)/Ma'am!*	Ma'am! (informal)
¡Mam-itá-y! *(Mommy-my)/Ma'am!*	Ma'am! (informal, with a greater degree of friendliness)
¡Wawa!	Baby!/Child!/(Little) boy!/(Little) girl!
¡Waw-itá-y! *Baby little-my!*	My little baby!/My little child!/My little boy!/My little girl! (with a greater degree of affection)
BUT	
¡Tata!	Sir! (informal)

(Dad)/Sir!	
¡Tat-itú-y!	Sir! (informal, with a greater
(Daddy-my)/Sir!	degree of friendliness)

b. for a word ending in **-o** or **-u**, that vowel is removed and replaced with **-itu**.

chohllo	ear of corn
chohll-itu	small ear of corn
mayu	river
may-itu	rivulet
alqo	dog
alq-etu [-ito- > -etu-]	little dog

c. for a word ending in a consonant, **-y,** or **-i, -situ** is affixed

ñan	road
ñan-situ	little road; path
¿Mayqen?	Which?
¿Mayqen-situ?	Exactly which one?
kay	this
kay-situ	exactly this, this very one
kay-pi	here
kay-pi-situ	right here
pisi	little (in amount)
pisi-situ	very little, a little bit

[Note: For a bi-syllabic word ending in **-n**, the diminutives **-ita, -itu,** or **-situ** may precede the **-n**.

kunan	now
kun-ita-n	right now OR
kunan-situ	right now
allin	fine, well
alli-situ-n	just fine, very well OR
allin-situ	just fine, very well]

10. MODEL FOR SIMPLE VERBS

Model verb: **uyariy** to hear

INFINITE FORMS

(Present) Infinitive

uyari-y to hear, hear; hearing (as a noun)
personalized forms: **uyari-y**-*(euphonic **ni**)-(possessive suffix)*
uyari-y-ni-y for me to hear, my hearing
uyari-y-ni-yki for you (one person) to hear, your (one person) hearing
uyari-y-ni-n for him/her/it to hear, his/her/its hearing
uyari-y-ni-yku for us (excluding the person[s] addressed) to hear, our (excluding the person[s] addressed) hearing
uyari-y-ni-ncheh for us (including the person[s] addressed), our (including the person[s] addressed) hearing
uyari-y-ni-ykicheh for you (more than one person) to hear, your (more than one person) hearing
uyari-y-ni-nku for them to hear, their hearing

Past (or Perfect) Infinitive

uyari-sqa to have heard, having heard; in context, often translated as: hear, heard, had heard
personalized forms: **uyari-sqa**-*(possessive suffix)*
uyari-sqa-y for me to have heard, my having heard
uyari-sqa-yki for you (one person) to have heard, your (one person) hearing, your (one person) having heard
uyari-sqa-n for him/her/it to have heard, his/her/its hearing, his/her/its having heard
uyari-sqa-yku for us (excluding the person[s] addressed) to have heard, our (excluding the person[s] addressed) hearing, our (excluding the person[s] addressed) having heard
uyari-sqa-ncheh for us (including the person[s] addressed) to have heard, our (including the person[s] addressed) hearing, our (including the person[s] addressed) having heard
uyari-sqa-ykicheh for you (more than one person) to have heard, your (more than one person) hearing, your (more than one person) having heard
uyari-sqa-nku for them to have heard, their hearing, their having heard

FUTURE INFINITIVE

uyari-na to hear (in the future), hearing (in the future)

personalized forms: **uyari-na-***(possessive suffix)*

uyari-na-y for me to hear (in the future), my hearing (in the future)

uyari-na-yki for you (one person) to hear (in the future), your (one person) hearing (in the future)

uyari-na-n for him/her/it to hear (in the future), his/her/its hearing (in the future)

uyari-na-yku for us (excluding the person[s] addressed) to hear (in the future), our (excluding the person[s] addressed) hearing (in the future)

uyari-na-ncheh for us (including the person[s] addressed) to hear (in the future), our (including the person[s] hearing (in the future)

uyari-na-ykicheh for you (more than one person) to hear (in the future), your (more than one person) hearing (in the future)

uyari-na-nku for them to hear (in the future), their hearing (in the future)

ACTIVE (OR PRESENT) PARTICIPLE (USED FOR THE PRESENT, PAST OR FUTURE)

uyare-h the one who hears, the one who used to hear, the one who was hearing, the one who heard, the one who will hear; listener [**uyari- > uyare-**]

uyare-h-kuna the ones who hear, the ones who used to hear, the ones who were hearing, the ones who heard, the ones who will hear; listeners [**uyari- > uyare-**]

personalized forms: **uyare-h-***(euphonic ni)-(possessive suffix)*
                     uyare-h-*(euphonic ni)-(possessive suffix)*-**kuna**

uyare-h-ni-y my listener [**uyari- > uyare-**]

uyare-h-ni-yki your (one person) listener [**uyari- > uyare-**]

uyare-h-ni-n his/her/its listener [**uyari- > uyare-**]

uyare-h-ni-yku our (excluding the person[s] addressed) listener [**uyari- > uyare-**]

uyare-h-ni-ncheh our (including the person[s] addressed) listener [**uyari- > uyare-**]

uyare-h-ni-ykicheh your (more than one person) listener [**uyari- > uyare-**]

uyare-h-ni-nku their listener [**uyari- > uyare-**]

uyare-h-ni-y-kuna my listeners [**uyari- > uyare-**]

uyare-h-ni-yki-kuna your (one person) listeners [**uyari- > uyare-**]

uyare-h-ni-n-kuna his/her/its listeners [**uyari- > uyare-**]

uyare-h-ni-yku-kuna our (excluding the person[s] addressed) listeners [**uyari- > uyare-**]

uyare-h-ni-ncheh-kuna our (including the person[s] addressed) listeners

[**uyari-** > **uyare-**]
uyare-h-ni-ykicheh-kuna your (more than one person) listeners [**uyari-** > **uyare-**]
uyare-h-ni-nku-kuna their listeners [**uyari-** > **uyare-**]

[Note that the Active (or Present) Participle has the variants, *(verb stem)*-**qe** and *(verb stem)*-**qi**, that may be found in more complex personalized constructions, often expanding or enriching their meaning. For example:
uyari-qe-y, my listener, **uyari-qe-y-kuna**, my listeners
uyari-qe-y-pah, for my listener, and **uyari-qe-y-kuna-pah**, for my listeners.

From:
ñawpa-y to move ahead, to go first, to precede
ñawpa-h the one or thing that goes first, precedes, moves ahead
ñawpa-h-ni-y the one or thing that goes before me, precedes me, goes ahead of me

ñawpa-qe the part that goes first, precedes
ñawpa-qe-y me (my face, my front); my presence
Ñawpa-qe-y-pi asi-n. He laughs in my presence (in front of me, in front of my face).]

[Note that the Active (or Present) Participle, mainly when used when referring to the job or a habit that a person has, and mostly in the Quechuaphone area where the language is in contact with Aymara, is constructed using the Active (or Present) Participle of that language: *(verb stem)*-**ri**. For example:
From **hampi-y** to heal, to cure
hampe-h healer [**hampi-** > **hampe-**]
hampi-ri healer

From **willaku-y** to complain
willako-h complainer [**willaku-** > **willako-**]
willaku-ri complainer]

PASSIVE (OR PAST) PARTICIPLE USED FOR THE PRESENT OR PAST

uyari-sqa heard; what is heard, what was heard
personalized forms: **uyari-sqa-***(possessive suffix)*
uyari-sqa-y what I hear, what I heard; what is heard by me, what was heard by me
uyari-sqa-yki what you (one person) hear, what you (one person) heard; what is heard by you (one person), what was heard by you (one person)
uyari-sqa-n what he/she/it hears, what he/she/it heard; what is heard by

him/her/it, what was heard by him/her/it

uyari-sqa-yku what we (excluding the person[s] addressed) hear, what we (excluding the person[s] addressed) heard; what is heard by us (excluding the person[s] addressed), what was heard by us (excluding the person[s] addressed)

uyari-sqa-nheh what we (including the person[s] addressed) hear, what we (including the person[s] addressed) heard; what is heard by us (including the person[s] addressed), what was heard by us (including the person[s] addressed)

uyari-sqa-ykicheh what you (more than one person) hear, what you (more than one person) heard; what is heard by you (more than one person), what was heard by you (more than one person)

uyari-sqa-nku what they hear, what they heard; what is heard by them, what was heard by them

---

PASSIVE (OR PAST) PARTICIPLE USED FOR THE FUTURE

[Note that this form is identical to the Future Infinitive.]

uyari-na heard (in the future); what is heard (in the future), what will be heard (in the future), what will have been heard (in the future)

personalized forms: **uyari-na**-*(possessive suffix)*

uyari-na-y what is heard by me (in the future), what will be heard by me (in the future), what will have been heard by me (in the future)

uyari-na-yki what is heard by you (one person) (in the future), what will be heard by you (one person) (in the future), what will have been heard by you (one person) (in the future)

uyari-na-n what is heard by him/her/it (in the future), what will be heard by him/her/it (in the future), what will have been heard by him/her/it (in the future)

uyari-na-yku what is heard by us (excluding the person[s] addressed) (in the future), what will be heard by us (excluding the person[s] addressed) (in the future), what will have been heard by us (excluding the person[s] addressed) (in the future)

uyari-na-ncheh what is heard by us (including the person[s] addressed) (in the future), what will be heard by us (including the person[s] hearing (in the future), what will have been heard by us (including the person[s] addressed) (in the future)

uyari-na-ykicheh what is heard by you (more than one person) (in the future), what will be heard by you (more than one person) (in the future), what will have been heard by you (more than one person) (in the future)

uyari-na-nku what is heard by them (in the future), what will be heard by them (in the future), what will have been heard by them (in the future)

INVARIABLE GERUND*

uyari-spa when (I, you [one person], he, she, it; we, you [more than one person], they [appropriate subject understood from context]) hear, on (my, your [one person], his, her, its; our, your [more than one person], their [appropriate subject understood from context]) hearing, hearing

optional (redundant) personalized forms: **uyari-spa***(-possessive suffix)*

uyari-spa-y when I hear, on my hearing

uyari-spa-yki when you (one person) hear, on yout (one person) hearing

uyari-spa-n when he/she/it hears, on his/her/itshearing

uyari-spa-yku when we (excluding the person[s] addressed) hear, on our (excluding the person[s] addressed) hearing

uyari-spa-ncheh when we (including the person[s] addressed) hear, on our (including the person[s] addressed) hearing

uyari-spa-ykicheh when you (more than one person) hear, on your (more than one person) hearing

uyari-spa-nku when they hear, on their hearing

> *[Note that this gerund is used when its subject and that of the main verb of the sentence are the same. That is why the personalization of the Invariable Gerund is not necessary and is redundant. As is pointed out above, if the possessive is not used, the form **uyari-spa** denotes the appropriate grammatical person(s), then distinguished by the context.]

VARIABLE GERUND (ALSO CALLED ADVERBIAL MOOD) (Possessive suffix to personalize the forms required to complete the meaning)*

uyare-hti-*(possessive suffix)* [**uyari-** > **uyare-**]

uyare-hti-y my hearing; when I hear, heard, used to hear, will hear [**uyari-** > **uyare-**]

uyare-hti-yki your (one person) hearing; when you (one person) hear, heard, used to hear, will hear [**uyari-** > **uyare-**]

uyare-hti-n his/her/its hearing; when he/she/it hears, heard, used to hear, will hear [**uyari-** > **uyare-**]

uyare-hti-yku our (excluding the person[s] addressed) hearing; when we (excluding the person[s] addressed) hear, heard, used to hear, will hear [**uyari-** > **uyare-**]

uyare-hti-ncheh our (including the person[s] addressed) hearing; when we (including the person[s] addressed) hear, heard, used to hear, will hear [**uyari-** > **uyare-**]

uyare-hti-ykicheh your (more than one person) hearing; when you (more than one person) hear, heard, used to hear, will hear [**uyari-** > **uyare-**]

uyare-hti-nku their hearing; when they hear, heard, used to hear, will hear [**uyari-** > **uyare-**]

*[Note that this gerund is used when its subject and that of the main verb of the sentence are different. That is why it is necessary to personalize the Variable Gerund to indicate its subject.]

SUPINE

uyare-h to hear (as object of a verb of motion) [**uyari-** > **uyare-**]

FINITE (CONJUGATED) FORMS

[Note that in conjugated verb forms, there are two forms for "we," one excluding the person(s) being addressed, and one including the person(s) being addressed.]

HABITUAL PRESENT AND IMMEDIATE PAST (PRESENT PERFECT)

I hear, I do hear, I am hearing (not a progressive); I just heard; I have heard; you hear, you do hear, etc.

[Note: The subject pronouns, "I," "you," and so on, are given below for this tense. Since the verb endings indicate the subject, these are used only for emphasis. In all of the rest of the conjugation patterns given they will be omitted.]

ñoqa uyari-ni I hear, I do hear, I am hearing; I just heard; I have heard

qan uyari-nki you (one person) hear, you (one person) do hear, you (one person) are hearing; you (one person) just heard; you (one person) have heard

pay uyari-n he/she/it hears, he/she/it does hear, he/she/it is hearing; he/she/it just heard; he/she/it has heard

ñoqayku uyari-yku we (excluding the person[s] addressed) hear, we (excluding the person[s] addressed) do hear, we (excluding the person[s] addressed) are hearing; we (excluding the person[s] addressed) just heard, we (excluding the person[s] addressed) have heard

ñoqancheh uyari-ncheh we (including the person[s] addressed) hear, we (including the person[s] addressed) do hear, we (including the person[s] addressed) are hearing; we (including the person[s] addressed) just heard, we (including the person[s] addressed) have heard

qankuna uyari-nki-cheh you (more than one person) hear, you (more than one person) do hear, you (more than one person) are hearing; you (more than one person) just heard; you (more than one person) have heard

paykuna uyari-nku they hear, they do hear, they are hearing; they just heard; they have heard

IMPERFECT (HABITUAL PAST)

I used to hear; you used to hear, etc.
I was hearing (not a progressive); you were hearing, etc.
I heard, you heard, etc.
I would hear (not a conditional) ; you would hear (not a conditional), etc
   [Note that all forms of this tense in this model verb have a sound change, **uyari- > uyare-**.]

uyare-h ka-ni* I used to hear, I was hearing (not a progressive), I heard, I would hear (not a conditional)

uyare-h ka-nki you (one person) used to hear, you (one person) were hearing (not a progressive), you (one person) heard, you (one person) would hear (not a conditional)

uyare-h* he/she/it used to hear, he/she/it was hearing (not a progressive), he/she/it heard, he/she/it would hear (not a conditional)

uyare-h ka-yku we (excluding the person[s] addressed) used to hear, we (excluding the person[s] addressed) were hearing (not a progressive), we (excluding the person[s] addressed) heard, we (excluding the person[s] addressed) would hear (not a conditional)

uyare-h ka-ncheh we (including the person[s] addressed) used to hear, we (including the person[s] addressed) were hearing (not a progressive), we (including the person[s] addressed) heard, we (including the person[s] addressed) would hear (not a conditional)

uyare-h ka-nki-cheh you (more than one person) used to hear, you (more than one person) were hearing (not a progressive), you (more than one person) heard, you (more than one person) would hear (not a conditional)

uyare-h ka-nku they used to hear, they were hearing (not a progressive), they heard, they would hear (not a conditional)

   *[Note that this tense consists of the Active (or Present) Participle of the conjugated verb, followed by the corresponding form of the Habitual Present of the verb **ka-y**, "to be," (**ka-ni**, **ka-nki**, etc.) as an auxiliary form, except for the 3rd person singular form (**ka-n**) that is omitted. (**Ka-n** is only used with its impersonal meanings "there is" and "there are.") Instead of using the present tense of **ka-y** in the formation of this tense, the preterite of **ka-y** (**ka-rqa-ni, ka-rqa-nki**, etc.) may be used. However, the forms with the habitual present are much more common.]

PRETERITE (FOR COMPLETED PAST ACTION), PRESENT PERFECT AND PAST PERFECT (PLUPERFECT)

I heard, I did hear; I have heard; I had heard; you heard, you did hear, etc.
   [Note that all forms of this model verb in this tense have a sound

change, **uyari-** > **uyare-**.]

uyare-rqa-ni I heard, I did hear; I have heard; I had heard

uyare-rqa-nki you (one person) heard, you (one person) did hear; you (one person) have heard; you (one person) had heard

uyare-rqa(-n) he/she/it heard, he/she/it did hear; he/she/it has heard; he/she/it had heard

uyare-rqa-yku we (excluding the person[s] addressed) heard, we (excluding the person[s] addressed) did hear; we (excluding the person[s] addressed) have heard; we (excluding the person[s] addressed) had heard

uyare-rqa-ncheh we (including the person[s] addressed) heard, we (including the person[s] addressed) did hear; we (including the person[s] addressed) have heard; we (including the person[s] addressed) had heard

uyare-rqa-nki-cheh you (more than one person) heard, you (more than one person) did hear; you (more than one person) have heard; you (more than one person) had heard

uyare-rqa-nku they heard, they did hear; they have heard; they had heard

[Note that instead of the Preterite marker **-rqa-**, some use only **-ra-**, omitting the **q**.]

FUTURE

I will hear, you will hear, etc.

uyari-sah I will hear

uyari-nki* you (one person) will hear

uyare-nqa he/she/it will hear [**uyari-** > **uyare-**]

uyari-sahku OR **uyari-sayku** OR **uyari-sqa-yku** we (excluding the person[s] addressed) will hear

uyari-su-n(cheh) we (including the person[s] addressed) will hear

uyari-nki-cheh* you (more than one person) will hear

uyare-nqa-nku they will hear [**uyari-** > **uyare-**]

*[Note that the forms for "you (one person)" and "you (more than one person)" in the future are identical to the correspondoing forms in the Habitual Present/Immediate Past (Present Perfect) tense. To avoid confusion between these two tenses, an adverb of time can be used. For example:
Yuya-yku-ta q'aya uyari-nki.
Tomorrow you will hear our idea.
Idea-our(excluding the person addressed)-(direct object marker) tomorrow hear you (one person) will.

Yuya-yku-ta tukuypacha uyari-nki.
You always hear our idea.
Idea-our(excluding the person addressed)-(direct object marker)always hear you (one person).]

CONDITIONAL (ALSO CALLED PAST [IMPERFECT] SUBJUNCTIVE)
I would hear, you would hear, etc.

uyari-y-man I would hear
uyari-wah* OR **uyari-nki-man** you (one person) would hear
uyari-n-man he/she/it would hear
uyari-yku-man we (excluding the person[s] addressed) would hear
uyari(-su)-ncheh-man we (including the person[s] addressed) would hear
uyari-wah-cheh* OR **uyari-nki-cheh-man** you (more than one person) would hear
uyari-nku-man they would hear

*[Note: The forms with **-wah** and **-wah-cheh** are used more often, but the ones with **-nki-man** and **-nki-cheh-man** are the only ones that can be used when **-wa-** ("me," "to me") is incorporated in the verb. For -wa-, see number 16. Model for Verbs that Include (Pronominally) the Verbal Object "Me."]

PRESENT PERFECT
I have heard, you have heard, etc.
The English present perfect ("I have . . .," "you have . . .," and so on) is expressed in Quechua by the <u>Habitual Present</u> or by the <u>Preterite</u> (see above).

PAST PERFECT (PLUPERFECT)
I had heard, you had heard, etc.
The simple idea of the English past perfect (pluperfect) ("I had . . .," "you had . . ," and so on) is usually expressed in Quechua by the <u>Preterite</u> (see above).

uyari-sqa-ni I had heard, I heard
uyari-sqa-nki you (one person) had heard, you (one person) heard
uyari-sqa he/she/it had heard, he/she/it heard
uyari-sqa-yku we (excluding the person[s] addressed) had heard, we (excluding the person[s] addressed) heard
uyari-sqa-ncheh we (including the person[s] addressed) had heard, we (including the person[s] addressed) heard

uyari-sqa-nki-cheh you (more than one person) had heard, you (more than one person) heard
uyari-sqa-nku they had heard, they heard

FUTURE PERFECT
I will have heard, you will have heard, etc.

uyari-sah ka-rqa I will have heard
uyari-nki ka-rqa you (one person) will have heard
uyare-nqa ka-rqa he/she/it will have heard [**uyari- > uyare-**]
uyari-sahku ka-rqa OR **uyari-sayku ka-rqa** OR **uyari-sqa-yku ka-rqa** we (excluding the person[s] addressed) will have heard
uyari-su-n(cheh) ka-rqa we (including the person[s] addressed) will have heard
uyari-nki-cheh ka-rqa you (more than one person) will have heard
uyare-nqa-nku ka-rqa they will have heard [**uyari- > uyare-**]

CONDITIONAL PERFECT (ALSO CALLED PLUPERFECT SUBJUNCTIVE)
I would have heard, you would have heard, etc.

uyari-y-man ka-rqa I would have heard
uyari-wah ka-rqa* OR **uyari-nki-man ka-rqa** you (one person) would have heard
uyari-n-man ka-rqa he/she/it would have heard
uyari-yku-man ka-rqa we (excluding the person[s] addressed) would have heard
uyari(-su)-ncheh-man ka-rqa we (including the person[s] addressed) would have heard
uyari-wah-cheh* OR **uyari-nki-cheh-man ka-rqa** you (more than one person) would have heard
uyari-nku-man ka-rqa they would have heard

> *[Note: The forms with **-wah** and **-wah-cheh** are used more often, but the ones with **-nki-man** and **-nki-cheh-man** are the only ones that can be used when **-wa-** ("me," "to me") is incorporated in the verb. See number 13. Model for Verbs that Include the Verbal Object "Me" for **-wa-**.]

DIRECT AND INDIRECT COMMANDS
hear; have him/her/ hear, have them hear; let him/her hear, let them hear; let's hear

uyari-y* hear (addressing one person)

uyari-y-cheh hear (addressing more than one person)

uyari-chu-n have him/her hear; let him/her hear
uyari-chu-nku have them hear; let them hear

uyari-na OR **uyari-na-cheh** let's hear OR **uyari-su-n(cheh)** (less strong in meaning than the others)

11. INTRODUCTION TO COMPLEX VERBS

Complex verbs are those that
- A. have incorporated in their forms one or more elements that expand the meaning of the simple, base verb in some fashion,
- B. include in their forms verbal object pronouns (pronominal constructions), or
- C. have a preceding or following periphrastic construction comprised of a personal pronoun with the appropriate direct or indirect object marker affixed to complete the complex verb construction

There are several categories of complex verbs:
- A. Verbs Expressing Action or State of being in Progress (Progressive Verbs)
- B. Verbs Expressing the Transformation of the Subject from one State to Another
- C. Verbs Expressing Transition of the Subject from one Condition or Situation to Another
- D. Verbs Expressing Obligation
- E. Verbs that Include (Pronominally or Periphrastically) an Object Pronoun, Direct or Indirect

    Verbs of this category are those that include, in both structure and meaning, the recipient of the action (direct object), and/or "whom," "to whom" or "for whom" the action is performed (indirect object). In form, they are either Pronominal Verbs, comprised of the simple forms of the base verb with verbal object pronoun particles included, or of a periphrastic construction, made up of a simple form of the base verb preceded or followed by a personal pronoun with the appropriate direct or indirect object marker affixed to complete the complex verb construction and its meaning.

    1) Non-Reflexive Verbs (verbs in which the subject and object are different from each other, as in "I hear you," for example)
        a. All forms of the verbs that include the object "me" or "you (one person)" are Pronominal Verbs.
        b. Verbs that include the object "us" or "you (more than one person)" are predonminantly pronominal, but have some periphrastic constructions as well.
        c. Verbs with the object "him," "her," "it," or "them" do not need to have the object expressed, but for clarification or emphasis it may be included by means of a periphrastic construction.

    2) Reflexive Verbs (verbs in which the subject and the object are the same, as in "I hear myself," for example)
        Reflexive Verbs are Pronominal Verbs, with the object -**ku-**, "self," "selves," affixed to the verb stem.

[Note: Pronominal Verbs can be replaced by periphrastic constructions, but the former are used much more frequently and are more proper Quechua than the latter.]

[Note: There are dual pronominal constructions, wherein a direct object (**-pu-**, "it" or "them") is inserted, followed by the particle indicating the person who is the object, here being an indirect object ("to whom" or "for whom" the action is performed).]

12. VERBS EXPRESSING ACTION OR STATE OF BEING IN PROGRESS (PROGRESSIVE VERBS)

To place emphasis on an action in progress, the equivalent of English "-ing," the progressive particle **-sa-** or one of its variants, **-chka-, -sha-, -shka-, -ska-, -skia-, -sia-,** and **-sya-,** used by personal or regional preference, is affixed to the stem of the verb.

Model verb: **uyarisay** to be hearing

> For example:
> **uyari-sa-y** "to be hearing," from the simple verb **uyari-y**, "to hear"
> **uyari-sa-ni** I am hearing (with emphasis on the action being in progress)
> **uyari-sa-rqa-ni** I was hearing (with emphasis on the action being in progress)
>
>> [Note: There is an exception in the position of **-sa-**. The verbal object pronoun **-wa-**, "me," (see 15. Model for Verbs that Include (Pronominally) the Verbal Object "Me" below) usually precedes it. Compare:
>> **uyari-wa-n** he hears me
>> **uyari-wa-sa-n** he is hearing me (with emphasis on the action being in progress)
>> **uyari-sa-wa-n** he is hearing me (with emphasis on the action being in progress)]
>
>> [Note: While **-sa-** has been used here for simplicity, any of the variants may be encountered in written Quechua. Of these progressive infixes, **-chka-** is the oldest and the most authentic form and the one from which all of the variants are derived.]

13. VERBS EXPRESSING TRANSFORMATION OF THE SUBJECT FROM ONE STATE TO ANOTHER

To express "to get," "to become," "to grow," "to go," "to end up" what the meaning of the verb is, the transformative infix **-ya-** is affixed to the stem of the simple, base verb.

To convey the idea of "to make (become)," "to cause (to become)" what the meaning of the verb is, the causative infix **-chi-** is affixed to the **-ya-** (**-ya-chi-**).

For example:
onqo-y to be sick
onqo-ya-y to get sick, to become sick
onqo-ya-chi-y to make (become, get) sick, to cause to become sick, to sicken

onqo-ni I am sick
onqo-ya-ni I get sick, I become sick
onqo-ya-chi-n it makes (become, get) sick, it sickens

onqo-rqa-ni I was sick
onqo-ya-rqa-ni I got sick, I became sick
onqo-ya-che-rqa(-n) it made (become, get) sick, it caused to become sick, it sickened [**chi-** > **che-**]

ñawsa-y to be blind
ñawsa-ya-y to go blind, to become blind
ñawsa-ya-chi-y to blind, to make (become, go) blind, to cause to become blind, to cause blindness

ñawsa-ni I am blind
ñawsa-ya-ni I go blind, I become blind
ñawsa-ya-chi-n it makes (become, go) blind, it causes to become blind, it causes blindness

ñawsa-rqa-ni I was blind
ñawsa-ya-rqa-ni I went blind, I became blind
ñawsa-ya-che-rqa(-n) it made (become, go) blind, it caused to become blind, it caused blindness [**chi-** > **che-**]

> [Note that another way of expressing this transformation of a subject is by using a construction with (*condition resulting from the transformation*)-**man tukuy**, "to end up toward (*condition resulting from the transformation*)"]

onqo-man tuku-y to get sick, to become sick, to end up sick
sickness-toward end up-(infinitive marker, "to")
onqo-man tuku-ni I get sick, I become sick, I end up sick
sickness-toward end up-I
onqo-man tuku-rqa-ni I got sick, I became sick, I ended up sick
sickness-toward end up-did-I

ñawsa-man tuku-y to go blind, to become blind, to end up blind
blind-toward end up-(infinitive marker, "to")
ñawsa-man tuku-ni I go blind, I become blind, I end up blind
blind-toward end up-I
ñawsa-man tuku-rqa-ni I went go blind, I became blind, I ended up blind
blind-toward end up-did-I

14. VERBS EXPRESSING TRANSITION OF THE SUBJECT FROM ONE CONDITION OR SITUATION TO ANOTHER

To form a verb expressing a change of the subject to a new condition or situation related to a noun, the double infix **-ya-pu-** (the transformative particle **-ya-**, "get," "become," "grow," "go," and **-pu-** or its variant **-po-** [**-pu-** > **-po-** before **-h**, **-hti-**, **-rqa-**, and **-nqa-**], used here as the verbal object pronoun "it," "them") is affixed to the noun, which becomes the stem of the new verb.

For example:
From **t'uru** mud
t'uru-ya-y to become mud, to get muddy
t'uru-ya-pu-y to become covered with mud, to get covered with mud
t'uru-ya-pu-n it becomes covered with mud, it gets covered with mud
t'uru-ya-po-rqa(-n) it became covered with mud, it got covered with mud [**-pu-** > **-po-**]

From **ñut'uhallp'a** dust
ñut'uhallp'a-ya-y to become dust
ñut'uhallp'a-ya-pu-y to become covered with dust, to get covered with dust, to get dusty
ñut'uhallp'a-ya-pu-n it becomes covered with dust, it gets covered with dust, it gets dusty
ñut'uhallp'a-ya-po-rqa(-n) it became covered with dust, it got covered with dust, it got dusty [**-pu-** > **-po-**]

15. MODEL FOR VERBS EXPRESSING OBLIGATION

Verbs of obligation are compound verbs whose forms consist of three elements:

   A. the Future Infinitive of the base verb (*[verb stem]*-**na**), the verb stem denoting the action or state of being that is to be the obligation,*
   B. the appropriate possessive marker, **-y** ("my"), **-yki** ("your [one person]"), **-n** ("his/her/its"), **-yku** ("our [excluding the person(s) addressed]"), **-ncheh** ("our [including the person(s) addressed]"), **-ykicheh** ("your [more than one person]"], **-nku** ("their"), affixed to this infinitive form to indicate the person who has the obligation,
   C. followed by the appropriate "he/she/it" form of the verb **ka-y**, "to be," except in two cases:
      1. the (Present) Infintive of Obligation, which stands alone, without a form of **ka-y**, and
      2. in the Habitual Present of Obligation, where the form **ka-n**, "it is," is omitted. Here, however **ti(y)a-n**, "there is," may optionally be used.

The Future of Obligation is not commonly used; the Habitual Present is used instead.

There are no commands in constructions of obligation.

*[Note that in the context of obligation, the Future Infinitive marker **-na** takes on the function of obligation marker, thus making of the *[verb stem]*-**na** construction the (Present) Infinitive of Obligation.]

Model verb: **uyarina** to have to hear

INFINITE FORMS

(PRESENT) INFINITIVE OF OBLIGATION

uyari-na* to have to hear; having to hear
personalized forms: **uyari-na**-*(possessive suffix)***

  *[Note that this Present Infinitive of Obligation (**uyari-na**), and the Future Infinitive of the base verb **uyari-y** (**uyari-na**) are identical.]
  **[Note that these personalized forms and those of the first option of the two in the Habitual Present of Obligation are identical.]

PAST (OR PERFECT) INFINITIVE OF OBLIGATION

uyari-na ka-sqa-n to have had to hear
personalized forms: **uyari-na**-*(possessive suffix)* **ka-sqa-n**

FUTURE INFINITIVE OF OBLIGATION
uyari-na ka-na-n to have to hear (in the future), having to hear (in the future)
personalized forms: **uyari-na-***(possessive suffix)* **ka-na-n**

ACTIVE (OR PRESENT) PARTICIPLE OF OBLIGATION
uyari-na ka-h the one who has to hear, used to have to hear, was having to hear, had to hear, will have to hear
uyari-na ka-h-kuna the ones who have to hear; used to have to hear, were having to hear, had to hear, will have to hear

PASSIVE (OR PAST) PARTICIPLE OF OBLIGATION
uyari-na ka-sqa what has to be heard; what had to be heard
personalized forms: **uyari-na-***(possessive suffix)* **ka-sqa**

INVARIABLE GERUND OF OBLIGATION*
uyari-na ka-spa(-n) having to hear, when (I, you [one person], he, she, it; we, you [more than one person], they [appropriate subject understood from context] have to hear, on (my, your [one person], his, her, its; our, your [more than one person], their [appropriate subject understood from context] have to hear
optional (redundant) personalized forms: **uyari-na-***(possessive suffix)* **ka-spa(-n)**

*[Note that this gerund is used when its subject and that of the main verb of the sentence are the same. That is why the personalization of the Invariable Gerund is not necessary and is redundant. As is pointed out above, if the possessive is not used, the form **uyari-na ka-spa(-n)** denotes the appropriate grammatical person(s), then distinguished by the context.]

VARIABLE GERUND OF OBLIGATION (ALSO CALLED ADVERBIAL MOOD)
(Possessive suffix to personalize the forms required to complete the meaning)*
uyari-na-*(possessive suffix)* **ka-hti-n**

*[Note that this gerund is used when its subject and that of the main verb of the sentence are different. That is why it is necessary to personalize the Variable Gerund to indicate its subject.]

SUPINE OF OBLIGATION

uyari-na ka-h to have to hear (as object of a verb of motion)

FINITE (CONJUGATED) FORMS

HABITUAL PRESENT AND IMMEDIATE PAST (PRESENT PERFECT) OF OBLIGATION

uyari-na-y OR **uyari-na-y ti(y)a-n** I have to hear; I have had to hear

uyari-na-yki OR **uyari-na-yki ti(y)a-n** you (one person) have to hear; you (one person) have had to hear

uyari-na-n OR **uyari-na-n ti(y)a-n** he/she/it has to hear; he/she/it had had to hear

uyari-na-yku OR **uyari-na-yku ti(y)a-n** we (excluding the person[s] addressed) have to hear; we (excluding the person[s] addressed) have had to hear

uyari-na-ncheh OR **uyari-na-ncheh ti(y)a-n** we (including the person[s] addressed) have to hear; we (including the person[s] addresssed) have had to hear

uyari-na-ykicheh OR **uyari-na-ykicheh ti(y)a-n** you (more than one person) have to hear; you (more than one person) have had to hear

uyari-na-nku OR **uyari-na-nku ti(y)a-n** they have to hear; they have had to hear

*[Note that the first option of the two here and the personalized forms of the (Present) Infinitive of Obligation are identical.]

IMPERFECT (HABITUAL PAST) OF OBLIGATION

uyari-na-y ka-h I used to have to hear, I was having to hear (not a progressive), I had to hear, I would have to hear (not a conditional)

uyari-na-yki ka-h you (one person) used to have to hear, you (one person) were having to hear (not a progressive), you (one person) had to hear, you (one person) would have to hear (not a conditional)

uyari-na-n ka-h he/she/it used to have to hear, he/she/it was having to hear (not a progressive), he/she/it had to hear, he/she it would have to hear (not a conditional)

uyari-na-yku ka-h we (excluding the person[s] addressed) used to have to hear, we (excluding the person[s] addressed) were having to hear (not a progressive), we (excluding the person[s] addressed) had to hear, we (excluding the person[s] addressed) would have to hear (not a conditional)

uyari-na-ncheh ka-h we (including the person[s] addressed) used to have to hear, we (including the person[s] addressed) were having to hear (not a progressive), we (including the person[s] addressed) had to hear, we (including the person[s] addressed) would have to hear (not a conditional)

uyari-na-ykicheh ka-h you (more than one person) used to have to hear, you (more than one person) were having to hear (not a progressive), you (more than one person) had to hear, you (more than one person) would have to hear (not a conditional)

uyari-na-nku ka-h they used have to hear, they were having to hear (not a progressive), they had to hear, they would have to hear (not a conditional)

PRETERITE (FOR COMPLETED PAST ACTION, PRESENT PERFECT AND PAST PERFECT (PLUPERFECT) OF OBLIGATION

uyari-na-y ka-rqa I had to hear; I have had to hear; I had had to hear

uyari-na-yki ka-rqa you (one person) had to hear; you (one person) have had to hear; you (one person) had had to hear

uyari-na-n ka-rqa he/she/it had to hear; he/she/it has had to hear; he/she/it had had to hear

uyari-na-yku ka-rqa we (excluding the person[s] addressed) had to hear; we (excluding the person[s] addressed) have had to hear; we (excluding the person[s] addressed) had had to hear

uyari-na-ncheh ka-rqa we (including the person[s] addressed) had to hear; we (including the person[s] addressed) have had to hear (not a progressive); we (including the person[s] addressed) had had to hear

uyari-na-ykicheh ka-rqa you (more than one person) had hear; you (more than one person) have had to hear; you (more than one person) had had to hear

uyari-na-nku ka-rqa they had to hear; they have had to hear (not a progressive); they had had to hear

FUTURE OF OBLIGATION

[Note: The forms of this tense are not commonly used. Those of the Habitual Present of Obligation are used instead.]

uyari-na-y ka-nqa I will have to hear

uyari-na-yki ka-nqa you (one person) will have to hear

uyari-na-n ka-nqa he/she/it will have to hear

uyari-na-yku ka-nqa we (excluding the person[s] addressed) will have to hear

uyari-na-ncheh ka-nqa we (including the person[s] addressed) will have to hear

uyari-na-ykicheh ka-nqa you (more than one person) will have to hear

uyari-na-nku ka-nqa they will have to hear

Conditional (Also Called Past [Imperfect] Subjunctive) of Obligation

uyari-na-y ka-n-man I would have to hear
uyari-na-yki ka-n-man you (one person) would have to hear
uyari-na-n ka-n-man he/she/it would have to hear
uyari-na-yku ka-n-man we (excluding the person[s] addressed) would have to hear
uyari-na-ncheh ka-n-man we (including the person[s] addressed) would have to hear
uyari-na-ykicheh ka-n-man you (more than one person) would have to hear
uyari-na-nku ka-n-man they would have to hear

Past Perfect (Pluperfect) of Obligation

uyari-na-y ka-sqa I had had to hear
uyari-na-yki ka-sqa you (one person) had had to hear
uyari-na-n ka-sqa he/she/it had had to hear
uyari-na-yku ka-sqa we (excluding the person[s] addressed) had had to hear
uyari-na-ncheh ka-sqa we (including the person[s] addressed) had had to hear
uyari-na-ykicheh ka-sqa you (more than one person) had had to hear
uyari-na-nku ka-sqa they had had to hear

Future Perfect of Obligation

uyari-na-y ka-nqa ka-rqa I will have had to hear
uyari-na-yki ka-nqa ka-rqa you (one person) will have had to hear
uyari-na-n ka-nqa ka-rqa he/she/it will have had to hear
uyari-na-yku ka-nqa ka-rqa we (excluding the person[s] addressed) will have had to hear
uyari-na-ncheh ka-nqa ka-rqa we (including the person[s] addressed) will have had to hear
uyari-na-ykicheh ka-nqa ka-rqa you (more than one person) will have had to hear
uyari-na-nku ka-nqa ka-rqa they will have had to hear

Conditional Perfect (Also Called Pluperfect Subjunctive) of Obligation

uyari-na-y ka-n-man ka-rqa I would have had to hear
uyari-na-yki ka-n-man ka-rqa you (one person) would have had to hear
uyari-na-n ka-n-man ka-rqa he/she/it would have had to hear
uyari-na-yku ka-n-man ka-rqa we (excluding the person[s] addressed) would have had to hear
uyari-na-ncheh ka-n-man ka-rqa we (including the person[s] addressed) would have had to hear,
uyari-na-ykicheh ka-n-man ka-rqa you (more than one person) would have had to hear
uyari-na-nku ka-n-man ka-rqa they would have had to hear

Direct and Indirect Commands

These forms do not exist here.

16. MODEL FOR VERBS THAT INCLUDE (PRONOMINALLY) THE VERBAL OBJECT "ME"

Model verb: **uyariway** to hear me

INFINITE FORMS

(Present) Infinitive

uyari-wa-y to hear me, hear me; hearing me, from the simple verb **uyari-y**, "to hear (See number 10. Model for Simple Verbs above.)

personalized forms: **uyari-wa-y-***(euphonic **ni**)-(appropriate possessive suffix)*

Past (or Perfect) Infinitive

uyari-wa-sqa to have heard me; in context, often translated as: hear me, heard me, had heard me

personalized forms: **uyari-wa-sqa-***(appropriate possessisve suffix)*

Future Infinitive

uyari-wa-na to hear me (in the future), hearing me (in the future)
personalized forms:
uyari-wa-na-*(appropriate possessisve suffix)* OR
uyari-na-wa-*(appropriate possessisve suffix)*

Active (or Present) Participle

uyari-wa-h the one who hears me, used to hear me, was hearing me, heard me, will hear me

uyari-wa-h-kuna the ones who hear me, used to hear me, were hearing me, heard me, will hear me

Passive (or Past) Participle

This form does not exist in this verb.

Invariable Gerund*

uyari-wa-spa when (you [one person], he, she, it; you [more than one person], they [appropriate subject understood from context]) hear me, on (your [one person], his, her, its; your [more than one person], their [appropriate subject understood from context]) hearing me

optional (redundant) personalized forms: **uyrai-wa-spa***(-appropriate* *possessisve suffix)*

*[Note that this gerund is used when its subject and that of the main verb of the sentence are the same. That is why the personalization of the Invariable Gerund is not necessary and is redundant. As is pointed out above, if the possessive is not used, the form **uyari-wa-spa** denotes the appropriate grammatical person(s), then distinguished by the context.]

VARIABLE GERUND (ALSO CALLED ADVERBIAL MOOD) (Possessive suffix to personalize the forms required to complete the meaning)*
uyari-wa-hti-yki-*(appropriate possessive suffix)*

*[Note that this gerund is used when its subject and that of the main verb of the sentence are different. That is why it is necessary to personalize the Variable Gerund to indicate its subject.]

SUPINE

uyari-wa-h to hear me (as object of a verb of motion) [**uyari- > uyare-**]

FINITE (CONJUGATED) FORMS

HABITUAL PRESENT AND IMMEDIATE PAST (PRESENT PERFECT)

uyari-wa-nki you (one person) hear, do hear, are hearing (not a progressive); just heard; have heard me

uyari-wa-n he/she/it hears, does hear, is hearing (not a progressive); just heard; has heard me

uyari-wa-nki-cheh you (more than one person) hear, do hear, are hearing (not a progressive); just heard; have heard me

uyari-wa-nku they hear, do hear, are hearing (not a progressive); just heard; have heard me

---

IMPERFECT (HABITUAL PAST)

uyari-wa-h ka-nki OR **uyare-h ka-wa-nki** you (one person) used to hear, were hearing (not a progressive), heard, would hear (not a conditional) me [**uyari > uyare**]

uyari-wa-h OR **uyare-h ka-wa-n** he/she/it used to hear, was hearing (not a progressive), heard, would hear (not a conditional) me [**uyari > uyare**]

uyari-wa-h ka-nki-cheh OR **uyare-h ka-wa-nki-cheh** you (more than one person) used to hear, were hearing (not a progressive), heard,

would hear (not a conditional) me [**uyari** > **uyare**]
uyari-wa-h ka-nku OR **uyare-h ka-wa-nku** they used to hear, hearing (not a progressive), heard, would hear (not a conditional) me [**uyari** > **uyare**]

PRETERITE (FOR COMPLETED PAST ACTION), PRESENT PERFECT AND PAST PERFECT (PLUPERFECT)

uyari-wa-rqa-nki you (one person) heard, did hear; have heard; had heard me

uyari-wa-rqa(-n) he/she/it heard, did hear; has heard; had heard me

uyari-wa-rqa-nki-cheh you (more than one person) heard, did hear; have heard; had heard me

uyari-wa-rqa-nku they heard, did hear; have heard; had heard me

FUTURE

uyari-wa-nki you (one person) will hear me
uyari-wa-nqa he/she/it will hear me
uyari-wa-nki-cheh you (more than one person) will hear me
uyari-wa-nqa-nku they will hear me

CONDITIONAL (ALSO CALLED PAST [IMPERFECT] SUBJUNCTIVE)

uyari-wa-nki-man* you (one person) would hear me
uyari-wa-n-man he/she/it would hear me
uyari-wa-nki-cheh-man* you (more than one person) would hear me
uyari-wa-nku-man they would hear me

*[Note: Of the two forms in the conditional for "you (one person)" and "you (more than one person)" the ones with **-nki-man** and **-nki-cheh-man** are the only ones that can be used when **-wa-** ("me," "to me") is incorporated. Those with **-wah** and **-wah-cheh** cannot be used here.]

PRESENT PERFECT

The English present perfect ("I have . . .," "you have . . .," and so on) is expressed in Quechua by the Habitual Present or by the Preterite (see above).

PAST PERFECT (PLUPERFECT)

The simple idea of the English past perfect (pluperfect) ("I had . . .," "you had . . ," and so on) is usually expressed in Quechua by the Preterite (see

above).
uyari-wa-sqa-nki you (one person) had heard, heard _me_
uyari-wa-sqa he/she/it had heard, heard _me_
uyari-wa-sqa-nki-cheh you (more than one person) had heard, heard _me_
uyari-wa-sqa-nku they had heard, heard _me_

Future Perfect

uyari-wa-nki ka-rqa OR **uyari-nki ka-wa-rqa** you (one person) will have heard _me_

uyari-wa-nqa ka-rqa OR **uyari-nqa ka-wa-rqa** he/she/it will have heard _me_

uyari-wa-nki-cheh ka-rqa OR **uyari-nki-cheh ka-wa-rqa** you (more than one person) will have heard _me_

uyari-wa-nqa-nku ka-rqa OR **uyare-nqa-nku ka-wa-rqa** they will have heard _me_ [**uyari-** > **uyare-**]

Conditional Perfect (also called Pluperfect Past Subjunctive)

uyari-wa-nki-man ka-rqa* OR **uyari-nki-man ka-wa-rqa** you (one person) would have heard _me_

uyari-wa-n-man ka-rqa OR **uyari-n-man ka-wa-rqa** he/she/it would have heard _me_

uyari-wa-nki-cheh-man ka-rqa* OR **uyari-nki-cheh-man ka-wa-rqa** you (more than one person) would have heard _me_

uyari-wa-nku-man ka-rqa OR **uyari-nku-man ka-wa-rqa** they would have heard _me_

*[Note: Of the two forms for "you (one person)" and "you (more than one person)" the ones with **-nki-man** and **-nki-cheh-man** are the only ones that can be used when **-wa-** ("me," "to me") is incorporated. Those with **-wah** and **-wah-cheh** cannot be used here.]

Direct and Indirect Commands

uyari-wa-y hear (addressing one person) _me_
uyari-wa-y-cheh hear (addressing more than one person) _me_

uyari-wa-chu-n have him/her hear; let him/her hear _me_
uyari-wa-chu-nku have them hear; let them hear _me_

17. MODEL FOR VERBS THAT INCLUDE (PERIPHRASTICALLY AND PRONOMINALLY) THE VERBAL OBJECT "US"

Model verb: **ñoqaykuta uyariy** to hear us

INFINITE FORMS

(Present) Infinitive (Periphrastic Construction)

ñoqayku-ta uyari-y to hear; hearing us (excluding the person[s] addressed)

ñoqancheh-ta uyari-y to hear; hearing us (including the person[s] addressed)

personalized forms: **ñoqayku-ta uyari-y**-*(euphonic **ni**)-(appropriate possessive suffix)*

                                 ñoqancheh-ta uyari-y-*(euphonic **ni**)-(appropriate possessive suffix)*

Past (or Perfect) Infinitive

uyari-wa-sqa-yku for you (one person), him, her, it; you (more than one person), them to have heard us (excluding the person[s] addressed), your (one person), his, her its; your (more than one person, their hearing us (excluding the person[s] addressed), your (one person), his, her its; your (more than one person, their having heard us (excluding the person[s] addressed)

uyari-wa-sqa-ncheh for you (one person), him, her, it; you (more than one person), them to have heard us (including the person[s] addressed), your (one person), his, her its; your (more than one person, their hearing us (including the person[s] addressed), your (one person), his, her its; your (more than one person, their having heard us (including the person[s] addressed)

Future Infinitive

uyari-wa-na-yku OR **uyari-na-wa-yku** for you (one person), him, her, it; you (more than one person), them to hear us (excluding the person[s] addressed) (in the future)

uyari-wa-na-ncheh OR **uyari-na-wa-ncheh** for you (one person), him, her, it; you (more than one person), them to hear us (including the person[s] addressed) (in the future)

ACTIVE (OR PRESENT) PARTICIPLE (periphrastic construction)

ñoqayku-ta **uyare-h** the one who hears, used to hear, was hearing, heard, will hear us (excluding the person[s] addressed) [**uyari-** > **uyare-**]

ñoqancheh-ta **uyare-h** the one who hears, used to hear, was hearing, heard, will hear us (including the person[s] addressed) [**uyari-** > **uyare-**]

ñoqayku-ta **uyare-h-kuna** the ones who hear, used to hear, were hearing, heard, will hear us (excluding the person[s] addressed) [**uyari-** > **uyare-**]

ñoqancheh-ta **uyare-h-kuna** the ones who hear, used to hear, were hearing, heard, will hear us (including the person[s] addressed) [**uyari-** > **uyare-**]

personalized forms:

ñoqayku-ta **uyare-h**-*(euphonic* **ni***)-(appropriate possessive suffix)* [**uyari-** > **uyare-**]

ñoqancheh-ta **uyare-h**-*(euphonic* **ni***)-(appropriate possessive suffix)* [**uyari-** > **uyare-**]

ñoqayku-ta **uyare-h**-*(euphonic* **ni***)-(appropriate possessive suffix)*-**kuna** [**uyari-** > **uyare-**]

ñoqancheh-ta **uyare-h**-*(euphonic* **ni***)-(appropriate possessive suffix)*-**kuna** [**uyari-** > **uyare-**]

PASSIVE (OR PAST) PARTICIPLE
This form does not exist in this verb.

INVARIABLE GERUND (periphrastic construction)*

ñoqayku-ta **uyari-spa** when (you [one person], he, she, it; you [more than one person], they [appropriate subject understood from context]) hear us (excluding the person[s] addressed), on (your [one person], his, her, its; your [more than one person], their [appropriate subject understood from context]) hearing us (excluding the person[s] addressed), and

ñoqancheh-ta **uyari-spa** when (you [one person], he, she, it; you [more than one person], they [appropriate subject understood from context]) hear us (including the person[s] addressed), on (your [one person], his, her, its; your [more than one person], their [appropriate subject understood from context]) hearing us (including the person[s] addressed)

optional (redundant) personalized forms:

ñoqayku-ta **uyari-spa***(-appropriate possessive suffix)*

ñoqancheh-ta **uyari-spa***(-appropriate possessive suffix)*

*[Note that this gerund is used when its subject and that of the main verb of the sentence are the same. That is why the personalization of the Invariable Gerund is not necessary and is redundant. As is pointed out above, if the possessive is not used, the forms **ñoqayku-ta uyari-spa** and **ñoqancheh-ta uyari-spa** denote the appropriate grammatical person(s), then distinguished by the context.]

VARIABLE GERUND (ALSO CALLED ADVERBIAL MOOD)

uyari-wa-hti-yku your (one person), his, her, its; your (more than one person), their hearing us (excluding the person[s] addressed), when you (one person), he, she, it; you (more than one person), they hear, heard, used to hear, will hear us (excluding the person[s] addressed)

uyari-wa-hti-ncheh your (one person), his, her, its; your (more than one person), their hearing us (including the person[s] addressed), when you (one person), he, she, it; you (more than one person), they hear, heard, used to hear, will hear us (including the person[s] addressed)

SUPINE (periphrastic construction)

ñoqayku-ta uyare-h to hear us (excluding the person[s] addressed) (as object of a verb of motion) [**uyari-** > **uyare-**]

ñoqancheh-ta uyare-h to hear us (including the person[s] addressed) (as object of a verb of motion) [**uyari-** > **uyare-**]

FINITE (CONJUGATED) FORMS

HABITUAL PRESENT AND IMMEDIATE PAST (PRESENT PERFECT)

uyari-wa-yku you (one person), he, she, it; you (more than one person), they hear, do hear, are hearing; just heard; have heard us (excluding the person[s] addressed)

uyari-wa-ncheh you (one person), he, she, it; you (more than one person), they hear, do hear, are hearing; just heard; have heard us (including the person[s] addressed)

IMPERFECT (HABITUAL PAST)

uyari-wa-h ka-yku OR **uyare-h ka-wa-yku** you (one person), he, she, it; you (more than one person), they used to hear, were hearing (not a progressive), heard, would hear (not a conditional) us (excluding the person[s] addressed) [**uyari** > **uyare**]

uyari-wa-h ka-ncheh OR **uyare-h ka-wa-ncheh** you (one person), he, she, it; you (more than one person), they used to hear, were hearing (not a progressive), heard, would hear (not a conditional) us (including the person[s] addressed) [**uyari** > **uyare**]

Preterite (for Completed Past Action), Present Perfect and Past Perfect (Pluperfect)

uyari-wa-rqa-yku you (one person), he, she, it; you (more than one person), they heard, did hear; have heard; had heard us (excluding the person[s] addressed)

uyari-wa-rqa-ncheh you (one person), he, she, it; you (more than one person), they heard, did hear; have heard; had heard us (including the person[s] addressed)

Future

uyari-wa-sahku OR **uyari-wa-sayku** OR **uyari-wa-sqa-yku** you (one person), he, she, it; you (more than one person), they will hear us (excluding the person[s] addressed)

uyari-wa-su-n(cheh) you (one person), he, she, it; you (more than one person), they will hear us (including the person[s] addressed)

Conditional (also called Past [Imperfect] Subjunctive)

uyari-wa-yku-man you (one person), he, she, it; you (more than one person), they would hear us (excluding the person[s] addressed)

uyari-wa(-su)-ncheh-man you (one person), he, she, it; you (more than one person), they would hear us (including the person[s] addressed)

Present Perfect

The English present perfect ("I have . . .," "you have . . .," and so on) is expressed in Quechua by the Habitual Present (see above) or by the Preterite (see above).

Past Perfect (Pluperfect)

The simple idea of the English past perfect (pluperfect) ("I had . . .," "you had . . ," and so on) is usually expressed in Quechua by the Preterite (see above).

uyari-wa-sqa-yku you (one person), he, she, it; you (more than one person), they had heard, heard us (excluding the person[s] addressed)

uyari-wa-sqa-ncheh you (one person), he, she, it; you (more than one person), they had heard, heard us (including the person[s] addressed)\

Future Perfect

uyari-wa-sahku ka-rqa OR **uyari-wa-sayku ka-rqa** OR **uyari-wa-sqa-yku ka-rqa** OR THE OPTIONAL CONSTRUCTIONS **uyari-sahku ka-wa-rqa** OR **uyari-sayku ka-wa-rqa** OR **uyari-sqa-yku ka-wa-rqa** you (one person), he, she, it; you (more than one person), they will have heard us (excluding the person[s] addressed) OR

uyari-wa-su-n(cheh) ka-rqa OR **uyari-su-n(cheh) ka-wa-rqa** you (one person), he, she, it; you (more than one person), they will have heard us (including the person[s] addressed)

Conditional Perfect (Also Called Pluperfect Subjunctive)

uyari-wa-yku-man ka-rqa OR **uyari-yku-man ka-wa-rqa** you (one person), he, she, it; you (more than one person), they would have heard us (excluding the person[s] addressed)

uyari-wa(-su)-ncheh-man ka-rqa OR **uyari(-su)-ncheh-man ka-wa-rqa** you (one person), he, she, it; you (more than one person), they would have heard us (including the person[s] addressed)

Direct and Indirect Commands

uyari-wa-yku hear us (excluding the person[s] addressed) (addressing one or more than one person); have him, her, it, them hear us (excluding the person[s] addressed); let him, her, it, them hear us (excluding the person[s] addressed)

[Note that this form is identical to the one for "you (one person), he, she, it; you (more than one person), they hear us (excluding the person[s] addressed) in the Habitual Present and Immediate Past (Present Perfect)]

uyari-wa-su-n(cheh) hear us (including the person[s] addressed) (addressing one or more than one person); have him, her, it, them hear us (including the person[s] addressed); let him, her, it, them hear us (including the person[s] addressed)

[Note that his form is identical to the one for "you (one person), he, she, it; you (more than one person), they will hear us (including the person[s] addressed)" in the Future.]

18. MODEL FOR VERBS THAT INCLUDE (PRONOMINALLY) THE VERBAL OBJECT "YOU (ONE PERSON)"

Model verb: **uyarisuy** to hear you (one person)

INFINITE FORMS

(PRESENT) INFINITIVE

uyari-su-y to hear you (one person), hear you (one person); hearing you (one person)
personalized forms: **uyari-su-sqa**-*(appropriate possessisve suffix)*

PAST (OR PERFECT) INFINITIVE

uyari-su-sqa to have heard you (one person); in context, often translated as: hear you (one person), heard you (one person), had heard you (one person)
personalized forms: **uyari-su-sqa**-*(appropriate possessisve suffix)*

FUTURE INFINITIVE

uyari-su-na to hear you (one person) (in the future), hearing you (one person) (in the future)
personalized forms:
uyari-su-na-*(appropriate possessisve suffix)* OR
uyari-na-su-*(appropriate possessisve suffix)*

ACTIVE (OR PRESENT) PARTICIPLE

uyari-so-h [-su- > -so-] the one who hears, used to hear, was hearing, heard, will hear you (one person)
uyari-so-h-kuna [-su- > -so-] the ones who hear, used to hear, were hearing, heard, will hear you (one person)

PASSIVE (OR PAST) PARTICIPLE]

This form does not exist in this verb.

INVARIABLE GERUND*

uyari-su-spa when (I, he, she, it; we, they [appropriate subject understood from context]) hear you (one person), on (my, his, her, its; our, their [appropriate subject understood from context]) hearing you (one person)

optional (redundant) personalized forms: **uyari-su-spa**(-*appropriate possessive suffix*)

*[Note that this gerund is used when its subject and that of the main verb of the sentence are the same. That is why the personalization of the Invariable Gerund is not necessary and is redundant. As is pointed out above, if the possessive is not used, the form **uyari-su-spa** denotes the appropriate grammatical person(s), then distinguished by the context.]

VARIABLE GERUND (ALSO CALLED ADVERBIAL MOOD) (Possessive suffix to personalize the forms required to complete the meaning)
uyari-so-hti-(*appropriate possessive suffix*)

*[Note that this gerund is used when its subject and that of the main verb of the sentence are different. That is why it is necessary to personalize the Variable Gerund to indicate its subject.]

SUPINE

uyari-so-h to hear you (one person) (as object of a verb of motion) [-su- > -so-]

FINITE (CONJUGATED) FORMS

HABITUAL PRESENT AND IMMEDIATE PAST (PRESENT PERFECT (*hear*) you (one person)

uyari-yki* I hear, do hear, am hearing; just heard; have heard you (one person); we hear, do hear, are hearing; just heard; have heard you (one person)**

uyari-su-nki* he/she/it hears, does hear, is hearing; just heard, has heard you (one person); they hear, do hear, are hearing; just heard; have heard you (one person)***

*[Note: Here and in all other tenses, the forms for "I hear you (one person)" and "we hear you (more than one person)" are identical, as are those for "he/she/it hears you (one person)" and "they hear you (more than one person)."]

[Note: Here and in all other tenses, if desired, to clarify that the subject is "we," **ñoqayku is used before the verb.]

***[Note: Here and in all other tenses, if desired, to clarify that the subject is "they," **paykuna** is used before the verb.]

IMPERFECT (HABITUAL PAST)
(hear) you (one person)

uyari-so-h ka-ni OR **uyare-h ka-yki** I used to hear, was hearing (not a progressive), heard, would hear (not a conditional) you (one person); we used to hear, were hearing (not a progressive), heard, would hear (not a conditional) you (one person) [**-su-** > **-so-**, **uyari-** > **uyare-**]

uyari-so-h OR **uyare-h ka-su-nki** he/she/it used to hear, was hearing (not a progressive), heard, would hear (not a conditional) you (one person); they used to hear, were hearing (not a progressive), heard, would hear (not a conditional) you (one person) [**-su-** > **-so-**, **uyari-** > **uyare-**]

PRETERITE (FOR COMPLETED PAST ACTION), PRESENT PERFECT AND PAST PERFECT (PLUPERFECT)
(hear) you (one person)

uyare-rqa-yki I heard, did hear, have heard, had heard you (one person); we heard, have heard, had heard you (one person) [**uyari-** > **uyare-**]

uyari-so-rqa(-n) OR **uyare-rqa(-n)-su-nki** he/she/it heard, did hear, has heard, had heard you (one person); they heard, did hear, have heard, had heard you (one person) [**-su-** > **-so-**, **uyari-** > **uyare-**]

FUTURE
(hear) you (one person)

uyari-sayki OR **uyari-sqa-yki** I will hear you (one person); we will hear you (one person)

uyari-so-nqa he/she/it will hear you (one person); they will hear you (one person) [**-su-** > **-so-**]

CONDITIONAL (ALSO CALLED PAST [IMPERFECT] SUBJUNCTIVE)
(hear) you (one person)

uyari-yki-man I would hear you (one person); we would hear you (one person)

uyari-su-nki-man he/she/it would hear you (one person); they would hear you (one person)

PRESENT PERFECT
The English present perfect ("I have . . .," "you have . . .," and so on) is

expressed in Quechua by the Habitual Present (see above) or by the Preterite (see above).

Past Perfect (Pluperfect)

The simple idea of the English past perfect (pluperfect) ("I had . . .," "you had . . ," and so on) is usually expressed in Quechua by the Preterite (see above).

(hear) you (one person)
uyari-sqa-yki I had heard you (one person); we had heard you (one person)
uyari-su-sqa he/she/it had heard you (one person); they had heard you (one person)

Future Perfect

(hear) you (one person)
uyari-sayki ka-rqa OR **uyari-sqa-yki ka-rqa** I will have heard you (one person); we will have heard you (one person)
uyari-so-nqa ka-rqa he/she/it will have heard you (one person); they will have heard you (one person) [su > so]

Conditional Perfect (also called Pluperfect Subjunctive)

(hear) you (one person)
uyari-yki-man ka-rqa I would have heard you (one person); we would have heard you (one person)
uyari-su-nki-man ka-rqa* he/she/it would have heard you (one person); they would have heard you (one person)

Indirect Commands

(hear) you (one person)
uyari-su-chu-n have/let him/her/it hear you (one person)
uyari-su-chu-nku have/let them hear you (one person)

19. MODEL FOR VERBS THAT INCLUDE (PERIPHRASTICALLY AND PRONOMINALLY) THE VERBAL OBJECT "YOU (MORE THAN ONE PERSON)"

Model verb: **qankunata uyariy** to hear you (more than one person)

INFINITE FORMS

(PRESENT) INFINITIVE (periphrastic construction)
qankuna-ta uyari-y to hear <u>you (more than one person)</u>; hearing <u>you (more than one person)</u>
<u>personalized forms</u>: **qankuna-ta uyari-y**-*(euphonic **ni**)-(appropriate possessive suffix)*

PAST (OR PERFECT) INFINITIVE
uyari-su-sqa-yki-cheh OR **uyari -sqa-su-yki-cheh** for me, him, her, it; us, them to have heard <u>you (more than one person)</u>, my, his, her, its; our, their hearing <u>you (more than one person)</u>, my, his, her, its; our, their having heard <u>you (more than one person)</u>

FUTURE INFINITIVE
uyari-su-na-yki-cheh OR **uyari-na-su-yki-cheh** for me, him, her, it; us, them to hear <u>you (more than one person)</u> (in the future)]

ACTIVE (OR PRESENT) PARTICIPLE (periphrastic construction)
qankuna-ta uyare-h the one who hears, used to hear, was hearing, heard, will hear <u>you (more than one person)</u> [**uyari-** > **uyare-**]
qankuna-ta uyare-h-kuna the ones who hear, used to hear, were hearing, heard, will hear <u>you (more than one person)</u> [**uyari-** > **uyare-**]

PASSIVE (OR PAST) PARTICIPLE]
This form does not exist in this verb.

INVARIABLE GERUND (periphrastic construction)*
qankuna-ta uyari-spa when (I, he, she, it; we, they [appropriate subject understood from context]) hear <u>you (more than one person)</u>, on (my, his, her, its; our, their [appropriate subject understood from context]) hearing <u>you (more than one person)</u>

optional (redundant) personalized forms: **qankuna-ta uyari-spa**(-*appropriate possessive suffix*)

> *[Note that this gerund is used when its subject and that of the main verb of the sentence are the same. That is why the personalization of the Invariable Gerund is not necessary and is redundant. As is pointed out above, if the possessive is not used, the form **qankuna uyari-spa** denotes the appropriate grammatical person(s), then distinguished by the context.]

VARIABLE GERUND (ALSO CALLED ADVERBIAL MOOD)* (pronominal and periphrastic construction)

uyari-so-hti-yki-cheh my, his.her, its; their hearing <u>you (more than one person)</u>, when I, he, she, it; they hear <u>you (more than one person)</u> [**-su-** > **-so-**]

> *[Note that this gerund is used when its subject and that of the main verb of the sentence are different. That is why it is necessary to personalize the Variable Gerund to indicate its subject.]

BUT

qankuna-ta uyare-hti-yku [**uyari-** > **uyare-**] our (excluding the persons addressed) hearing <u>you (more than one person)</u>, when we (excluding the persons addressed) hear <u>you (more than one person)</u>

SUPINE (PERIPHRASTIC CONSTRUCTION)

qankuna-ta uyare-h to hear <u>you (more than one person)</u> (as object of a verb of motion) [**uyari-** > **uyare-**]

FINITE (CONJUGATED) FORMS

HABITUAL PRESENT AND IMMEDIATE PAST (PRESENT PERFECT *(hear) you (more than one person)*

uyari-yki-cheh* <u>I</u> hear, do hear, am hearing; just heard; have heard <u>you (more than one person)</u>; <u>we (excluding the persons addressed)</u> hear, do hear, are hearing; just heard; have heard <u>you (more than one person)</u>**

uyari-su-nki-cheh* <u>he/she/it</u> hears, does hear, is hearing; just heard; has heard <u>you (more than one person)</u>; <u>they</u> hear, do hear, are hearing; just heard; have heard <u>you (more than one person)</u>***

> *[Note: Here and in all other tenses, the forms for "I hear you (more than one person)" and "we hear you (more than one person)" are identical, as are those for "he/she/it hears you (more than one person)"

and "they hear you (more than one person)."]
[Note: Here and in all other tenses, if desired, to clarify that the subject is "we," **ñoqayku is used before the verb.]
***[Note: Here and in all other tenses, if desired, to clarify that the subject is "they," **paykuna** is used before the verb.]

IMPERFECT (HABITUAL PAST)
(hear) you (more one person)

uyare-h ka-yki-cheh OR **qankuna-ta uyare-h ka-ni** I used to hear, was hearing (not a progressive), heard, would hear (not a conditional) you (more than one person); we (excluding the persons addressed) used to hear, were hearing (not a progressive), heard, would hear (not a conditional) you (more than one person) [**uyari-** > **uyare-**]

uyare-h ka-su-nki-cheh OR **qankuna-ta uyare-h** he/she/it used to hear, was hearing (not a progressive), heard, would hear (not a conditional) you (more than one person); they used to hear, were hearing (not a progressive), heard, would hear (not a conditional) you (more than one person) [**uyari-** > **uyare-**]

PRETERITE (FOR COMPLETED PAST ACTION), PRESENT PERFECT AND PAST PERFECT (PLUPERFECT)
(hear) you (more than one person)

uyare-rqa-yki-cheh I heard, did hear, have heard, had heard you (more than one person); we (excluding the persons addressed) heard, did hear, have heard, had heard you (more than one person) [**uyari-** > **uyare-**]

uyari-so-rqa-cheh OR **uyare-rqa-su-nki-cheh** he/she/it heard, did hear, has heard, had heard you (more than one person); they heard, did hear, have heard, had heard you (more than one person) [**-su-** > **-so-**, **uyari-** > **uyare-**]

FUTURE
(hear) you (more than one person)

uyari-sayki-cheh OR **uyari-sqa-yki-cheh** I will hear you (more than one person); we (excluding the persons addressed) will hear you (more than one person)

uyari-so-nqa-cheh he/she/it will hear you (more than one person); they will hear you (more than one person)

Conditional (Also Called Past [Imperfect] Subjunctive)

(hear) you (more than one person)

uyari-yki-cheh-man I would hear you (more than one person); we (excluding the persons addressed) would hear you (more than one person)

uyari-su-nki-cheh-man he/she/it would hear you (more than one person); they would hear you (more than one person)

Present Perfect

The English present perfect ("I have . . .," "you have . . .," and so on) is expressed in Quechua by the Habitual Present (see above) or by the Preterite (see above).

Past Perfect (Pluperfect)

The simple idea of the English past perfect (pluperfect) ("I had . . .," "you had . . ," and so on) is usually expressed in Quechua by the Preterite (see above).

(hear) you (more one person)

uyari-sqa-yki-cheh I had heard you (more than one person); we (excluding the persons addressed) had heard you (more than one person)

uyari-su-sqa-cheh OR **uyari-sqa-su-nki-cheh** he/she/it had heard you (more than one person); they had heard you (more than one person)

Future Perfect

(hear) you (more one person)

uyari-sayki-cheh ka-rqa OR **uyari-sqa-yki-cheh ka-rqa** I will have heard you (more than one person); we (excluding the persons addressed) will have heard you (more than one person)

uyari-so-nqa-cheh ka-rqa he/she/it will have heard you (more than one person); they will have heard you (more than one person) [**-su- > -so-**]

Conditional Perfect (Also Called Pluperfect Subjunctive)

(hear) you (more one person)

uyari-yki-cheh-man ka-rqa I would have heard you (more than one person); we (excluding the persons addressed) would have heard you (more than one person)

uyari-su-nki-cheh-man ka-rqa he/she/it would hear you (more than one person); they would hear you (more than one person)

Indirect Commands

(hear) you (more than one person)

qankuna-ta uyari-chu-n have/let him/her/it hear you (more than one person)

qankuna-ta uyari-chu-nku have/let them hear you (more than one person)

20. MODEL FOR VERBS THAT INCLUDE (ONLY PERIPHRASTICALLY) THE VERBAL OBJECTS "HIM," "HER," AND "THEM"

When the object of the verb is "him," "her," or "them" (direct object), or "(to) him," "for him," "(to) her," "for her," or "(to) them," "for them" (indirect object), the regular simple verb forms are used. These may be preceded by **pay** ("him"/"her"/"it") or **paykuna** ("them"), to which is affixed either **-ta**, the direct object marker, or **-man**, "to," here used as an indirect object marker.

For example:
Direct object ("whom" I hear)
(pay-ta) uyari-ni I hear him
(paykuna-ta) uyari-ni I hear them

(pay-ta) uyare-rqa-ni I heard him [**uyari-** > **uyare-**]
(paykuna-ta) uyare-rqa-ni I heard them [**uyari-** > **uyare-**]

Indirect object ("to whom" I give)
(pay-man) qo-ni I give (to) him
(paykuna-man) qo-ni I give (to) them

21. MODEL FOR VERBS IN WHICH THE SUBJECT AND THE OBJECT ARE THE SAME (REFLEXIVE VERBS)

A reflexive verb is one with the same subject and object. Compare:

"I hear you." "I" is the subject, "hear" is the verb, and "you" is the direct object. This is a non-reflexive construction, since the subject and object are different from each other.

"I hear myself." "I" is the subject, "hear" is the verb, and "myself" is the direct object. This is a reflexive construction since the subject and the object are the same person.

Most simple verbs can be made reflexive. This is done by adding an infix, usually **-ku-**, which when translatable usually is "self," "selves," or "for (one)self," "to (one)self." When **-ku-** is followed by **-h**, **-hti-**, **-rqa-** or **-nqa-** it becomes **-ko-**, and when followed by **-mu-**, **-pu-**, or **-mpu-** it becomes **-ka-**.

For example:
uyari-y to hear
uyari-ku-y to hear <u>oneself</u>

uyari-ni I hear
uyari-ku-ni I hear <u>myself</u>

maylla-y to wash
maylla-ku-y to wash <u>oneself</u>

maylla-mu-y to go to wash
maylla-ka-mu-y to go to wash <u>oneself</u> [-ku- > -ka-]

rua-y to do, to make
rua-pu-y to do it, to make it
rua-ka-pu-y to do it <u>for oneself</u>, to make it <u>for oneself</u> [-ku- > -ka-

QUECHUA – ENGLISH VOCABULARY

(-)a *(as a suffix[-a] or an independent word following what is being stressed; stressed in speech)* certainly, well, then, *emphatic word, often untranslatable, used to prolong, reinforce or add emphasis to what is being said*

(-)á *(as a suffix[-á] or an independent word following what is being stressed; stressed in speech)* certainly, well, then, *emphatic word, often untranslatable, used to prolong, reinforce or add emphasis to what is being said*

¿A? What?

Á, *(accented capital followed by a comma) interjection showing surprise or admiration about what follows the comma*

abasmut'i boiled fava beans served as a side dish

adiyús goodbye

agradisiy to thank

ahsu cotton petticoat

aka excrement

akana place to defecate

akakiti outhouse, latrine

akawasi outhouse, latrine

akay to defecate

akulliy to chew coca leaves

aliman German

Alimanya Germany

alkaldi mayor

alqo dog

alumna student *(a female)*

alumnu student *(a male)*

alwañil bricklayer, stone mason

alli(n) good, well

allichay to thank

allichu please

allillam fine *(well)*

allillan fine *(well)*

allin kah kind *(person)*, the one who is kind

allinchay to repair

allinkay kindness

allinsonqo very kind

allpaqa alpaca

allp'a land, soil, earth *(soil)*

allp'a llank'ah farmer, the one who farms, the one who works the land

ama *(used in a command)* do not, don't; *(used in prohibitions in conjunction with a form of the conditional)* not

amaru snake

amiga friend *(a female)*

amigu friend *(a male)*

ampi cotton

ancha much *(intensity)*, a lot *(intensity)*

anchata much, very

anqas blue

anta copper

antara pan pipes

añas skunk

añasqa admired

añathuya skunk

añay to admire

apa arm; space between arms in which one can carry something

apamuy to bring

apasanka big, poisonous spider

apah carrier, porter, the one

who carries, the one who takes *(carries, transports) (things)*
apay to take *(to carry) (things)*, to carry *(people)*; to wear *(as in clothing)*
api a kind of custard-like dessert
apiri llama driver
apu owner, boss; high dignitary
apuchaw Sunday
aqo sand
aqoaqo sandy
aqosapa sandy
aqha chicha *(made from corn)*
aqhachay to make chicha *(made from corn)*
aqhawasi tavern, *chichería (tavern)*, place where chicha is sold
arí yes
armakuna place to bathe; hot spring, baths
armay to bathe *(someone else)*
armakuy to bathe *(oneself)*, to take a bath
arus rice
as a little, some *(amount)*
as pisi a little less
asiriy smile; to smile
asiy laugh; to laugh
asllata just a little
asna bad smell
asnay to smell bad, to give off a bad smell
asnu donkey
astah carrier, carter, porter, the one who carries, the one who carts, the one who takes *(carries, transports) (things)*, the one who transports *(in parts; by repeated "trips")*
astawan a little more, some more
astay to carry, to cart, to take *(things)*, to transport *(in parts; by repeated "trips")*
aswan more; **aswan machu** older, oldest *(a male)*; **aswan paya** older, oldest *(a female)*; **aswan rukhu** older, oldest *(a male)*; **aswan sipas** younger, youngest *(a female)*; **aswan wayna** younger, youngest *(a male)*
ashkha many, much *(quantity)*
atichaw Tuesday
atikuy for one to be able, one can
atillcha friend
atiy to be able, can
atoh fox
awah weaver, the one who weaves
away to weave
awayu shawl
awgustu(killa) August
awril(killa) April
Awstralya Australia
awtu car
awtuñan paved road, roadway
awtuwus bus
aya cadaver, human remains
aycha meat; **aycha qhatu** butcher shop, meat market, meat stand/stall, place where meat is sold; **aycha wasi** house where meat is sold
aychata qhatoh butcher, the one who sells meat
ayllu family, relatives
aymuray harvest; to harvest

B
bandira flag
bañu latrine, bathroom
bola ball

CH
-(n)cha *diminutive marker*; make *(what the noun or adjective to which it is attached is) [in the formation of a verb]*
-chá *question marker showing doubt or surprise; affixed to an interrogative word to convey the meaning "I don't know"; marker expressing doubt or lack of knowledge*; maybe
chahnay to load
chahra farm, farm field, farmland, field, land
chahrah farmer, the one who farms, the one who works the land
chahray to farm
cha(n)ka thigh, thighs
chaki feet, foot; leg, legs
chaki moqo knee, knees
chakitahlla plow, foot plow (traditional Andean foot plow, a type of long-handled dibble with a flat end, close to which is a pedal for pressuring the tool with a foot. At times, somewhat higher up is a handle at right angles to the main one for the user to bend toward the ground, to guide and place pressure on the plow. This often is used to dig irrigation channels, to make holes for planting seeds, to loosen the soil.)
chakitahllay to perform farm tasks with a **chakitahlla**
chakitahllay to plow with a **chakitahlla**
challi astute, smart
challwa fish
challwah fisherman, the one who fishes
challwaqhatu fish stand/stall, place where fish is sold
challway to fish
chani(n) price, cost, value
chaninchay to appraise
chaninnah inexpensive, cheap
chaninnahpuni most inexpensive, cheapest
chani(n)yoh expensive, valuable
chanin(ni)yoh expensive, valuable
chanin(ni)yohpuni most expensive, most valuable
chaninra inexpensive, cheap
chaninrapuni least expensive, cheapest
chanta afterwards
chapi tin
chaskiy to receive
chawpi between, middle
chawpiruk'a middle finger
chawpidiya noon
chawpinchay to put in the middle, to put in between
chawpituta midnight
chay that *(nearby)*, that one *(nearby)*, those *(nearby)* those things *(nearby)*; there *(nearby)*
chayamuy to arrive *(here)*, to get here
chayanta tin
chayqa if *(following a*

conjugated verb form)
chayay to arrive *(there)*, to get there
chaykuna those *(nearby)*, those things *(nearby)*
chaynehpi around there *(nearby)*
chayqa if *(following a conjugated verb form)*
chaywanpis but, nevertheless
-chi make *(what the meaning of the verb is)*; to make *(to have the verb to which it is attached be done)*; *in combination with* **-ya-** (**-ya-chi**), to make [become], to cause [to become] *(what the meaning of the verb is)*; to allow *(what the meaning of the verb is)*, to permit *(what the meaning of the verb is)*
chicha alcoholic beverage made by fermenting corn
chihchi hail
chihchi(mu)y to hail
chinkay to lose; to get lost
chinpa across the way, the opposite bank of a river, irrigation ditch, gully, and the like; the other side of something that one is facing and that is difficult to reach, ahead *(of someone or something)*, facing, front, in front of *(someone or something)*
chinpachinakuy for one to go to the other side of a stream, being helped by the offered hand of the one staying behind, and then offering his or her hand to help the other person across
chinpachiy to bring near; to take something or to help someone to the other side of something that one is facing and that is difficult to reach *(as in the opposite bank of a river, irrigation ditch, gully)*
chinpakuy to approach, to get close, to get near
chinpay to go to the other side of something that one is facing and that is difficult to reach *(as in the opposite bank of a river, irrigation ditch, gully)*
chipana bracelet
chirawpacha spring *(season)*
chiri *(noun and adjective)* cold
chiri(ya)chiy to chill, to make cold
chiriy to be cold
chiripacha winter
chiri(mu)y for it to be cold *(weather)*
chiriy to chill
chiriyay to get cold
chirmakuy to get hurt
chirmay to hurt
chi(n)ruy to incline, to tilt, to tip
chompa sweater
-chu *negative marker; question marker; used to show affection, affixed to the given name of a male or to a noun referring to a male that shows family relationship*
-chu ... -chu either ... or ... *(in a question)*
-(n)chu *diminutive marker*
chufir driver *(of a vehicle)*
chuhcha hair, head of hair
chumpi sash worn by men

chunka ten
chunkaiskayniyoh twelve
chunkauhniyoh eleven
churay to put
churi son *(of a male)*
chu(w)a deep plate *(usually the bottom part of a gourd)*
-chus either, or; *affixed to a interrogative pronoun, makes of it a relative pronoun*; maybe; *question marker that shows doubt; question marker that shows wonder*
-chus ... -chus either ... or ... *(in an affirmative statement)*
chu(w)a deep plate *(usually the bottom part of a gourd)*
chuwi dry bean *(referring to a multiple variety that includes lima beans, butter beans, and kidney beans)*
chuwimut'i variety of dry beans, boiled and served as a side dish
¡Chuy! Hey! (very informal), Say there! (very informal)

CHH
chhapu frayed border
chhapuchhapu rough
chhicha shoe
chhichawasi shoe store
chhichay to make shoes, to repair shoes
chhichaykamayoh shoe repairman, shoemaker
chhika a little *(amount; intensity)*
chhikan size
chhulla dew
chhulla(mu)y for dew to appear
chhullunka frost
chhullunka(mu)y for there to be frost

CH'
ch'ahwa shouting
ch'ahway to shout
ch'aki dry; thirst; **ch'aki sonqo** sober
ch'akichay to dry
ch'akichiy to make dry; to make thirsty
ch'akipacha summer
ch'akisqa thirsty
ch'akiy thirst
ch'aphra underbrush
ch'aphrach'aphra full of underbrush
ch'aphsa underbrush
ch'aphsach'aphsa full of underbrush
ch'aqi soup consisting basically of ground corn or wheat, water, and meat
ch'arki sun-dried meat, jerky
ch'aska Venus *(planet)*
ch'askachaw Friday
ch'ete boy, child, young boy, youngster
ch'ihchu gray
ch'isi evening
ch'isi mikhuy dinner
ch'isiman in the evening *(before dark, without an hour given)*
ch'isimanta P.M. *(evening hours, after an hour is mentioned)*; in the evening *(before dark, after an hour is mentioned)*
ch'isiyay nightfall, dusk; to get dark (the day), to grow dark (the day), for night to fall

ch'iti boy, child, young boy, youngster
ch'oho cough; whooping cough
ch'ohoy to cough
ch'uchalli weak
ch'uhlla hut
ch'uhu cough; whooping cough
ch'uhuy to cough
ch'ullu cap *(colorful, native, conical-shaped, knit, wool cap with ear flaps)*
ch'uñu frozen, dried potatoes
ch'usah unoccupied, empty
ch'usahyachiy to empty
ch'uspi mosquito, fly
ch'uya clear *(said of water)*; without impurities *(said of water and of seeds)*
ch'uyay to purify *(said of water)*; to remove foreign objects *(from seeds)*

D

dis ten *(borrowing from Spanish, used in telling time)*
disimwri(killa) December
diya day
diyachaku birthday; Saint's Day
diyachakuy to celebrate a birthday; to celebrate a Saint's Day
Diyus God
Diyuspa wasin church
dumingu Sunday
dun don *(title of respect used with a man's first name)*
duña "doña" *(title of respect used with a married woman's first name)*
dus two *(borrowing from Spanish, used in telling time)*
dusi twelve *(borrowing from Spanish, used in telling time)*

G

gasulina gasoline; **gasulina qhatu** place where gasoline is sold
gustay to appeal, to like

H

-h of, 's, s' *(affixed to a word ending in a vowel)*; the one who *(affixed to the stem of a verb)*; marker affixed to the stem of a verb that is the object of a verb of motion (to form the supine); marker affixed to the stem of a verb that is the object of one of the following verbs: **rikuy**, "to see," "to look at"; **qhaway**, to look at," "to see"; **uyariy**, "to hear,""to listen (to)"; **saqey**, "to permit," "to let," "to allow"; and **kachay**, "to send"
¡Haku! Come on!, Let's go!
hak'u flour
hallp'a earth *(soil)*, land, soil; **hallp'a llank'ah** farmer, the one who farms, the one who works the land
hampeh healer; doctor, physician
hampi cure, medicine, remedy
hampikamayoh doctor, physician
hampiranteh pharmacist
hampiri healer
hampiwasi pharmacy
hampiy to heal, to cure; to prescribe remedies
hamuy to come
hanqa lame

hap'iy to grab, to grasp, to hold, to take (hold of)
Hapun Japan
haqay *(variants:* **chahay, chaqhay, anchahay**) that *(over there, farther away)*, that one *(over there, farther away)*, those *(over there, farther away)*, those things *(over there, farther away)*; there *(over there, farther away)*
haqaykuna those *(over there, farther away)*, those things *(over there, farther away)*
haqaynehpi around there *(farther away)*
hatariy to get up, to stand up
¡Hatari! Move aside., Move away., Get away from there.
hatun big, large; **hatun llahta** city, large town; **hatun wasi** multi-story building
hatunpuni biggest, largest
hatunllahtaruna man from the city
hawa outside; next *(week, month, year)*; after *(an action)*; part, place *(location)*; on, on top of, upon, above, over; high
hawanchay to put on top
hawapatan outside *(part of something)*
hawkay to have a good time
¿Hay? What? *(responding)*
hay niy to answer, to respond; **hay ñiy** to answer, to respond
haya bitter, hot *(spicy)*, sour
hayk'a how many, how much
hayk'ah when
hayt'a kick

hayt'ay to kick
hilli broth, juice
(-)hina like; thus; as *(used in comparison)* [Note: With a verb, it always goes at the end; in a construction with a noun, its location may vary.]
hinay to do in this way, to do in that way
hisp'akuy to urinate
hisp'ana place to urinate
hisp'ay to urinate
hisp'aykiti outhouse, latrine
hisp'aywasi outhouse, latrine
hisq'on nine
hisq'onchunka ninety
hisq'onpachah nine hundred
hiwriru(killa) February
hoqariy to lift, to pick up; to take (pilfer), to pilfer
hoq'o wet
hoq'oy to get wet
hoq'ochay to soak, to wet
-hpa of, 's, s' *(affixed to a word ending in a vowel)*
-hpata *(variants:* **-h, -hpa, -hta**) of, 's, s' *(affixed to a word ending in a vowel)*
-hta of, 's, s' *(affixed to a word ending in a vowel)*
-hti *variable gerund marker,* "-ing," *used when the subject of the gerund is different from that of the main verb*
huch'uy little, small, short
huch'uypuni littlest, smallest, shortest
huch'uysitu very little, very small, very short
huk'ucha mouse
hulyu(killa) July
humint'a tamale
hunu million

hunyu(killa) June
huq'ara deaf
hwywis Thursday

I

¿I? Heh?, Isn't that right?
ichaqa but, on the other hand, nevertheless
ichás maybe
ichhoh harvester
ichhuna sickle, scythe
ichhuy to reap, to harvest; to cut with a sickle or scythe
ilisya church
illapachaw Thursday
illari(mu)y to clear up *(weather)*
ima anything, something, thing; what, what thing
imachus the one that *(used with things)*
imamanaqa of course, why not
imanay to do; to happen, to occur
ima(lla)pas any *(with things)*, anything, something
ima(lla)pis any *(with things)*, anything, something
imarayku why
imaraykuchus because of, for *(because of)*
imaymana many things
imayna how
imayna manaqa of course
imilla girl
inhiñiru engineer
iniru(killa) January
inka Inca
Inlatira England
inles English (language)
inlis English (language)
inlisha church
inti sun; monetary unit of Peru

intisapa sunny
intichaw Sunday
iñaka mantilla; veil
iñirip'ata church *(denomination, congregation, religious group or community)*
iñiy belief; to believe
iru iron
iriru blacksmith
iskay two; **iskay kah** second; **iskay kutita** twice; **iskay qhepa(n)** third
iskaychunka twenty
iskaynin both
iskayñeqe(n) second
iskaypachah two hundred
iskwiyla school
isq'on nine
isq'onchunka ninety
isq'onpachah nine hundred
Istadus Unidus United States
-ita *diminutive marker (borrowing from Spanish)*
-itu *diminutive marker (borrowing from Spanish)*

K

-ka *diminutive marker*
kachamuy to bring, send *(in this direction)*
kachay to send *(when the object of **kachay** is a verb, the form used for that verb is the Active (or Present) Participle [verb stem-**h**])*
kachi salt; salty; **kachi churanacha** place to put salt, salt cellar, salt dish
kachikachi very salty
kachinchay to salt
kachinnay to make less salty, to put less salt

kachipay to make saltier, to add more salt
kachiykachiy to salt a little
kafiy coffee
-kah *particle affixed to a cardinal number to form the corresponding ordinal number [Note that "first," ñawpah(-ñeqe]n]), is an exception to this rule.]*
kahniyoh rich
kaka uncle *(brother of mother)*
kallpa strength
kallpasapa strong
-kama until; over to, up to, down to, to; authority *(in the given field or area)*; skill; exclusively, just (exclusively)
kamacheh leader, the one who leads
kamachiy to command, to order
kamay to command
kamayoh the one in charge, the one with skill; skillful
kamisa shirt
kamiyun truck
kan there is, there are
Kanada Canada
kancha enclosure; market
kanchay to make an enclosure
kanka roast
kankana spit for roasting
kankasqa roasted
kankay to roast
kapuy for there to be *(used in a construction with a verbal object pronoun to convey the idea of "to have," see numbers 16, 17, 18, and 19. in Section II: Quechua Grammar Notes)*

karpa tent
karpintiru carpenter
karta letter
karu far
karunchay to move *(something or someone)* away
karupuni farthest
karuruna stranger *(a male)*
karusipas stranger *(a young woman)*
karuwarmi stranger *(a woman)*
karuwayna stranger *(a young man)*
kasakuy to stay
kasay to be *(used here with condition, situation, and location)*
kastilla qowi rabbit *(in Bolivia)*
kastillanu Castilian, Spanish
kawallu horse
kay this, this one, these, these things; here; *makes an abstract noun of the adjective to which it is attached*
kay to be *(used here for identification, characteristics, and traits)*; for there to be
kaykuna these, these things
kaynehpi around here
kichasqa open *(opposite of "closed")*
kichay to open
kiki same
kilu kilogram
kilumitru kilometer
killa month, moon
killachaw Monday
killaku mean, stingy
kimsa three; **kimsa kah** third
kimsachunka thirty
kimsañeqe(n) third

kimsapachah three hundred
kinra border, edge, margin, side
kinsa three; **kinsa kah** third
kinsak'uchuhina triangular
kinsapachah three hundred
kiru tooth, teeth
kirusin kerosene; **kirusin qhatu** place where kerosine is sold
kisa stinging nettle
kiti place
kiti t'ahsana washing place *(on the bank of a river, etc.)* for clothes, hair, or anything else that can absorb water
-ku *(reflexive marker)* self, selves; d*iminutive marker*
kuchu cut
kuchuy to cut
kuka coca, coca leaf, coca shrub
kukuchu elbow, elbows
kukuli small dove, grey in color, with the eyes surrounded by bright blue circles
kulli purple
kulluna silo pit
kumarí friend *(a female) (from Spanish "comadre")*
¡Kumaríy! Friend! *(calling to a female) (from Spanish "comadre")*
kumpa friend *(a male)*
¡Kumparíy! Friend!, Pal! *(calling to a male) (from Spanish "compadre")*
-kuna *plural marker for nouns ending in a consonant; real plural marker for any Quechua noun, although in some Quechuaphone areas (mostly in Bolivia) usually replaced by* **-s** *on nouns ending in a vowel*
kunan now; this *(with day, part of a day, week, month, year)*; **kunan diya** today; **kunan pacha** right now
kunita(n) right now
kunka neck
kuntur condor
kurah older *(in rank, in age) (people)*, oldest *(in rank, in age) (people)*
kural corral
kurus cross
kusa *(adjective, adverb, and interjection used to show a very high degree of excellence)* good, great, wonderful, magnificent; well
kusay delicious, good *(things)*, pleasant *(things)*
kusaykusay stupendous
kusi happy
kusichiy to gladden, to cheer up
kusikuy to be glad
kusisqa happy
kutay to grind
kuti time(s) *(occasion)*
kutikunata sometimes
kutimuy to be back, to come back, to return *(here)*
kutiy to go back, to return *(there)*
kuyuchiy to move
kwaru four *(borrowing from Spanish, used in telling time)*
kwistay to cost

KH

khaniy to bite
kharkatiy to shake, to shiver
khata frozen
khirkinchu armadillo

khishka thorn
khishkay to prick
khuchi pig
khuchiaycha pork
khuska together; **khuska ... -wan** along ...
khuskan half,\; together; **khuskan diya mikhuy** lunch; **khuskan sukha mikhuy** mid-afternoon snack
khuskandiya noon
khuskantuta midnight

K'

k'acha good, beautiful, gorgeous, elegant, distinguished, regal, poised
k'achitu pretty
k'ama molar, molars
k'anchara lamp; fuel-burning lamp
k'ancharay to darken; to turn off the lights
k'anchay light, brightness; to illuminate; to shine; for there to be light
k'illimsa charcoal, coal; **k'illimsa qhatu** charcoal shop, place where charcoal is sold
k'irisqa hurt
k'iriy to hurt, to wound
k'iski narrow
k'ullu wood *(the trunk of a fallen tree)*
k'utuy to cut
k'uychi rainbow
k'uychichaw Saturday
k'uychi(mu)y for a rainbow to come out

L

la una one o'clock *(borrowing from Spanish)*
lachiwana bee
lachiwana misk'i honey
lapis pencil
laqha dark
lari fox
laru place, location, site
larupi next to
las dis ten o'clock *(borrowing from Spanish)*
las dus two o'clock *(borrowing from Spanish)*
las dusi twelve o'clock *(borrowing from Spanish)*
las kwaru four o'clock *(borrowing from Spanish)*
las nuiwi nine o'clock *(borrowing from Spanish)*
las sinku five o'clock *(borrowing from Spanish)*
las sis six o'clock *(borrowing from Spanish)*
las siti seven o'clock *(borrowing from Spanish)*
las tris three o'clock *(borrowing from Spanish)*
las uchu eight o'clock *(borrowing from Spanish)*
las unsi eleven o'clock *(borrowing from Spanish)*
lawa very thick soup; spicy porridge/soup made with corn, potatoes, onion, sometimes with meat, with lard, hot pepper, and salt
laway to prepare **lawa**
lichi milk; **lichi qhatu** place where milk is sold
lima qowi rabbit *(in Peru)*
liwru book
lunis Monday; **lunis diya**

Monday

LL

-lla just; just *(for emphasis)*; only
llahllay to plane, to trim *(wood)*
llahllaykamayoh carpenter; **llahllaykamayoh wasi** carpenter's shop
llahsa bronze
llahta city, town; **llahta kamayoh** city father, mayor
llahtamasi fellow townsman/ townswoman
llahwa spicy porridge/soup made with corn, potatoes, onion, sometimes with meat, with lard, hot pepper, and salt
llaway to prepare **llahwa**
llakeh sad
llakikuy to be sad, to be sorry, to cause oneself sorrow, to regret
llakisqa sad
llakiy to cause sorrow
llama llama
llanka clay
llank'ah farmer, the one who farms; worker *(mostly in farm fields)*, the one who works *(mostly in farm fields)*
llank'ay to farm *(to work the land)*, to work *(manual work, field work, traditional work of the Quechua people)*
llanthu shade
llanthusapa shady
llant'a firewood, wood *(for a fire)*
llant'ah firewood cutter, firewood seller
llant'ay to chop firewood; to gather firewood
llañu thin
llaqha dark *(in color)*
llarq'a irrigation ditch
llasa heavy
llasay to weigh
-lli *particle affixed to a noun to create a verb meaning "to put on" what the noun designates, or "to make [the noun] a part" of the person indicated (**-lli-ku** is used when the action is done to oneself or selves, **-lli-chi** when done to others)*
llihlla colorful woven shawl
llimp'i color
llink'u curve
llip'eh painter, the one who paints
llip'iy to paint
llohsiy to leave
lloq'achiy to make get on, to make climb on
lloq'ay to climb, to climb on *(implying that it is difficult to do)*, to get on *(implying that it is difficult to do)*
lloq'e left
llulla lie; liar
llullakuy to lie
llullay to deceive
llusk'a slippery
llusk'akuy to slip

M

-m *(affixed to a word ending in a vowel) assertive particle, particle of certainty or assurance, emphatic particle; euphonic particle*
ma no, not *(apocopation of* **mana***)*

machasqa drunk
machay to get drunk
machu old *(a male)*; **aswan machu** older, oldest *(a male)*
Machu Pihchu Machu Picchu *[Note: In the famous Machu Picchu ruins there are two peaks, the lower known as Machu (old) Pihchu, and the higher as Wayna (young) Pihchu. See pihchu.]*
mahchhiku lavatory *(place to wash hands)*
mahchhikuna wash basin or sink where one can wash up or wash anything that cannot absorb water
mahllu danger
mahllumahllu dangerous
maki hand, hands; arm, arms
makimoqo elbow, elbows
mal(l)ta of medium size
mallki tree (cultivated), fruit tree
mallki mallki grove, orchard
mallkichay to plant trees *[Note: Adding -cha-y to any noun designating a plant gives the idea of planting it.]*
mallkiyay for seed and saplings to grow into full-sized trees *[Note: Adding -ya-y to any noun designating a plant or animal gives the same idea of growing to maturity.]*
mama ma'am; mother
mamaruk'a thumb; big toe
mamáy ma'am; ¡**Mamáy**! Ma'am! *(informal)*
-man to, toward, in the direction of, headed for; into; during; to *(indirect object verb marker)*
. . . -man tukuy to become, to get, to go, to grow, to turn into, to end up *(showing transformation from one state to another)*
mana no, not; **mana(-tah) . . . -chu** neither . . . nor, not . . . or . . .; **mana . . . -wan** without . . . *(shows that the person is not accompanied by or does not have with him or her the noun to which -wan is attached)*, **mana . . . -yoh** *(indicates that the person does not have or is not wearing the item designated by the noun to which -yoh is attached; as appropriate to the noun to which -yoh is attached, may also indicate a physical condition, as in* "**mana wawayoh**," "*not with child*," "*not pregnant*"; "**mana suru(h)chiyoh**," "*without altitude sickness*")*; **mana** *[verb stem]*-**spa(lla)** without "*[verb]-ing*"; **mana allin** bad; **mana ima** nothing; **mana kahniyoh** poor; **mana pipas** no one, nobody, not anyone, not anybody; **mana pipis** no one, nobody, not anyone, not anybody; **mana qolqesapa** poor; **mana qolqeyoh** poor; **mana sasachu** easy; **mana sumah** bad, ugly; **mana ukhu** shallow
manahayk'ah never
manarah not yet

manchakuy to worry *(oneself)*
manchari(ku)y to be afraid
manka pot *(of clay)*
-manta of; from; about; for; because *(used with a dependent verb that is dependent upon a verb that expresses sentiment)*; at *(with a part of a day)*; than; within; *adverb marker that makes an adverb of an adjective, often "-ly" in English; marker to indicate the way something is done*
mante delicious, delightful *(referring to taste)*
mant'a floor throw, mat; table cover
mant'ay to spread out, to stretch out, to extend
manu loan *(of money)*
manukuy to borrow *(something consumable, such as money or food, that is to be returned with an equivalent; see* **mañay***) (with* **-manta** *affixed to the noun designating the one[s] doing the lending, with* **-ta** *affixed to the noun designating the item[s] being lent, and* **-man** *to the noun[s] designating the one[s] to whom it is/they are being lent)*
manuy to lend *(something consumable, such as money or food, that is to be returned with an equivalent; see* **mañay***) (with* **-manta** *affixed to the noun designating the one[s] doing the lending, with* **-ta** *affixed to the noun designating the item[s] being lent, and* **-man** *to the noun[s] designating the one[s] to whom it is/they are being lent)*
mañay to ask for *(something)*; to lend *(something that is to be returned as opposed to something consumable, such as money or food, that is to be returned with an equivalent; see* **manuy***) (with* **-manta** *affixed to the noun designating the one[s] doing the lending, with* **-ta** *affixed to the noun designating the item[s] being lent, and* **-man** *to the noun[s] designating the one[s] to whom it is/they are being lent)*; to borrow *(something that is to be returned as opposed to something consumable, such as money or food, that is to be returned with an equivalent; see* **manuy***) (with* **-manta** *affixed to the noun designating the one[s] doing the lending, with* **-ta** *affixed to the noun designating the item[s] being lent, and* **-man** *to the noun[s] designating the one[s] to whom it is/they are being lent)*
maran grinding stone, mortar *(platform used in grinding)*
marankiru molar, molars
maranuña a moon-shaped stone used as a pestle with a **maran**
marsu(killa) March
martis Tuesday

masa team (of two animals of the same species, often oxen or mules); pair of identical or similar items
masi companion, friend
mashkha how much, how many
matara rush *(plant)*
mate maté *(tea-like infusion)*
matey to drink maté
mathi dried gourd *(used as a drinking cup)*
mat'i forehead
mawk'a old *(deteriorated, out of style, in ruins)*
may where; how *(in an exclamation)*
maych'a healer *(with herbs)*
maystra teacher, professor *(a female)*
maystru teacher, professor *(a male)*
mayk'ah when
mayllaku lavatory *(place to wash hands)*
mayllakuna wash basin or sink where one can wash up or wash anything that cannot absorb water
mayllakuy to wash oneself
mayllay to wash *(anything that cannot absorb water)*
mayllapipas anywhere, any place, any old place
mayllapipis anywhere, any place, any old place
maynehpi whereabouts
mayninpi from time to time, once in a while, sometimes
maypi where
mayqen which
mayqenchus that, which, the one that, the one who
mayqen(lla)pas any *(with people, animals, things)*; anyone, anybody, anything; someone, somebody, something
mayqen(lla)pis any *(with people, animals, things)*; anyone, anybody, anything; someone, somebody, something
mayu river
mayu(killa) May
mesa table
-mi *(affixed to a word ending in a consonant)* assertive particle, particle of certainty or assurance, emphatic particle; euphonic particle
micheh herder, shepherd, the one who herds
michi cat
michiy to herd, to shepherd
mich'a greedy
midika doctor *(a female)*, physician *(a female)*
midiku doctor *(a male)*, physician *(a male)*
midiya half *(hour)* *(borrowing from Spanish, used in telling time)*
mihlla skirt
mihllay to carry something in a skirt *(by gathering up the hem in front and bringing it toward the waist to form a type of pocket)*
mikaniku mechanic
mikhuchiy to feed *(people)*, to serve food
mikhuna food, something to eat; meal; **mikhuna qhatu** grocery store, place where

groceries are sold; **mikhuna wasi** grocery store
mikhunakuna provisions, foodstuff
mikhunakunata qhatoh grocer, the one who sells groceries
mikhuy food, something edible; eating; to eat
mikhuywasi restaurant
mik'i damp, humid
millay too much, very
millma wool
-min *(variants:* **-mi, -m, -n***) particle used in a question to show some curiosity or doubt; assertive particle, particle of certainty or assurance, emphatic particle*
minchha in two days, the day after tomorrow, **minchha p'unchaw, minchha diya** in two days, the day after tomorrow, **minchha qanchischaw, minchha simana**, in two weeks, **minchha killa** in two months, **minchha wata** in two years
minutu minute
miqa wide
mirkadu market
mirkulis Wednesday
mischi cat
misi cat
misk'i flavorful; sweet; **misk'i q'eta** sweet, syrup-like or thicker byproduct of the making of chicha
mit'a season *(time period)*, time *(period)*
moqo joint
mosoh new

-mu *in this direction (used with verbs of motion);* to go to perform the action of the verb *(used with verbs not of motion); untranslatable infix usually used with verbs expressing natural phenomena when those talking consider themselves affected by them*
mulo mule
mulomasa team of mules
muhu grain
munay to want
muskiy to smell *(to use one's sense of smell)*
mut'i a very common boiled or steamed vegetable side dish *(of fava beans:* **abasmut'i***; of a variety of dry beans:* **chuwimut'i***; of corn kernels:* **saramut'i***; of lupine seeds:* **tarwimut'i***)*
mut'iy to boil or to steam the ingredients to prepare **mut'i**
muyu(y) round, circular, spherical; circle, circumference; turn, rotation
muyuy to encircle; to rotate, to revolve, to go in circles
muyuyhina round, spherical

N

-n *(affixed to a word ending in a vowel) assertive particle, particle of certainty or assurance, emphatic particle, euphonic particle;* his, her, its
-na *future infinitive marker; particle to form the passive [or past] participle for the future, used in a*

construction that in English is introduced by a relative pronoun, often "what," "that," or "which," when the verb denotes what someone or something will do); particle used with a dependent verb for an action that is in the future in relationship to that of the main verb; marker used with a verb that is used in conjunction with a verb, "there is," "there was," and the like, stated or understood, to show obligation ("to have to"); "-able," "-ible"; "let's" command marker; marker affixed to the stem of a verb to form a noun that designates the thing or place needed to carry out the action of the verb

na *hesitation filler while speaker contemplates the next word*

-naku *each other*

nanachikuy *to hurt oneself*

nanay *ache; to ache, to hurt*

nañaka *shoulder scarf*

napay *greeting, salutation*

napaykuy *to greet, to salute*

natah *crippled in the legs*

nay *to do, to make*

-naya *to feel like, to be about to, to be on the verge of (the meaning of the verb)*

-ncheh *(variants:* **-nchej, -nchih, -nchij, -nchik, -nchis***) our (including the person[s] addressed)*

-neh *(variants:* **-nih, -ñeh, -ñih,**

-ñek*) around; to, toward, in the direction of, headed for; more or less, approximately*

ni *no*

-ni *euphonic particle, required between a word ending in a consonant and a following particle that is a single consonant, or that begins with a* **y** *or a double consonant combination not found in the alphabet; affixed to a noun designating a plant or animal, denotes a place where a collection or abundance of what is expressed by the noun is (the origin of many place names, as in* **matarani** *[a place with an abundance of rushes (rush:* **matara***)])*

ni(-tah) . . . -chu *neither . . . nor (in a negative statement);* not . . . or . . . *(in a negative statement)*

ni ima *nothing, not anything*

ni ima(lla)pas *not anything*

ni ima(lla)pis *not anything*

nina *fire*

ninariy *to start the/a fire*

ninri *ear (outer ear), ears (outer ears)*

nipi *no one, nobody, not anybody, not anyone*

niy *to say, to tell*

niyta munay *to mean*

-nku *their*

-nnah *without*

-(n)ta *by; through; via*

-ntin *all*

-ntin *affixed to* **q'aya,** *tomorrow;* **qayna,** *yesterday;* **minchha,** *the day* after tomorrow; **qayninpa**, the day before yesterday, forms the idiomatic constructions **q'ayantin**, the following day, the next day; **qaynantin**, the day before, the preceding day; **minchhantin**, two days after tomorrow; and **qayninpantin**, two days before

-ntinta all through

nuwimwri(killa) November

nuiwi nine *(borrowing from Spanish, used in telling time)*

Ñ

ña already

-ña already *(used and often untranslated in asking and telling the hour, or the number of hours, days, weeks, months, years)*; *(affixed to a gerund)* after *(the action expressed by the verb)*

ñan path, road

ñaña sister *(of a female)*

ñawi eye, eyes

ñawpa ancient, antique, old *(historically)*

ñawpah before *(in time and location)*; **ñawpah-(ñeque[n])** first *(in order)*

ñawpaqe front; presence

ñawsa blind

ñawsaman tukuy to become blind, to go blind

ñawsay to blind; to be blind

ñawsayachiy to blind, to make (become, go) blind, to cause to become blind, to cause blindness

ñawsayay to become blind, to go blind

-ñeqe(n) *(variants:* **-ñaqe[n]**, **-ñiqe[n]***)* order *(hierarchy)*; *particle affixed to a cardinal number to form the corresponding ordinal number; the oldest and most authentic Quechua form of the three used to construct an ordinal number)* *[Note that in the formation of "first," **ñeqe(n)** can be used or omitted.]*

ñiy to say, to tell

ñiyta munay to mean

ñoqa *(variants:* **noqa, ñuqa, nuqa***)* I

ñoqahpata *(variants:* **noqahpata, ñuqahpata, nuqahpata**; *variants of the* **-hpata** *ending:* **-h, -hpa, -hta***)* *(I-of)* mine, of mine

ñoqancheh *(variants:* **ñuqancheh, noqancheh, nuqancheh**; *variants of the* **-ncheh** *ending:* **-nchih, -nchij, -nchik, -nchis***)* we *(including the person[s] addressed)*

ñoqanchehpata *(variants:* **ñuqanchehpata, noqanchehpata, nuqanchehpata**; *variant of the* **-pata** *ending:* **-pa***)* *(we[including the person[s] addressed)-of))* ours, of ours *(including the person[s] addressed)*

ñoqayku *(variants:* **ñuqayku, noqayku, noqayku**; *variants of the* **-hpata** *ending:* **-h, -hpa, -hta***)* we

(excluding the person[s] addressed)
ñoqaykohpata *(variants:* **ñuqaykohpata, noqaykohpata, nuqaykohpata**; *variants of the* **-hpata** *ending:* **-h, -hpa, -hta**) *(we[excluding the person(s) addressed]-of)* ours, of ours *(excluding the person[s] addressed)*
ñuk'u crippled in one hand
ñuñu breast, breasts; udder; mother's milk
ñuñuy to nurse, to breast feed, to suckle, to feed with mother's milk
ñut'uhallp'a dust
ñut'uhallp'ayapuy to become covered with dust, to get covered with dust, to get dusty
ñut'uhallp'ayay to become dust
ñut'uy to pulverize, to break into pieces, to crumble, to shred

O
onqo sickness
onqohkunawasi hospital
onqoman tukuy to become sick, to get sick
onqosqa sick
onqoy sickness; to be sick
onqoyay to become sick, to get sick
onqoyachiy to sicken, to make (become, get) sick, to cause to become sick, to cause sickness
oqa oca *(Oxalis tuberosa) (a variety of wood sorrel, cultivated for its edible tubers)*
orqo hill, mountain; male *(referring to animals and to plants that have only stamens)*; **orqo uywa** non-domesticated animal
orqoorqo hilly

P
-pa of, 's, s' *(affixed to a word ending in a consonant)*
-pacha right *(with adverbs of time or place)*; since
pacha earth *(planet),* world; place; time
pachah hundred
pachamanka barbecue *(gathering where barbecued meat is prepared)*, picnic
pachamankay to hold a barbecue or picnic; to feast, to banquet
pachamit'a season *(of the year)*
pachaphuyu fog
pagay to pay
paqo wool-bearing animals *(sheep, llamas, alpacas, vicunas or guanacos)*
-pah for; in order to
¡Pahtá! Careful! *(showing annoyance, anger or even a threat over what someone is doing)*; Watch out! *(showing annoyance, anger or even a threat over what someone is doing)*
¡Pahtatah! Careful!, Watch out!
pakay to hide
pakakuy to hide oneself; to set *(referring to the sun, moon, etc.)*

palla lady
pallacha young lady
pampa flat land, ground, prairie; floor
pana sister *(of a male)*
panpa flat land, ground, prairie; floor
¡Panpachaway! Excuse me! *(apologizing to one person)*
panpachay to flatten, to level; *(used idiomatically in apologizing)* to excuse, to pardon
pantalun *(singular)* pants, trousers *(modern style)*
pantay mistake; to make a mistake
paña right *(opposite of "left")*
papa potato
papil paper
paqarin early morning, morning; **paqarin mikhuy** breakfast
paqarinman in the morning *(without an hour given)*
paqarinmanta A.M., in the morning *(after an hour is mentioned)*
paqariy for day to break, for it to dawn
paraqunchuy rain storm
para(mu)y to rain
paratamya rain storm
para(y) rain
paraysapa rainy
parlay to speak, to talk
-pas any; although; even if; in spite of
-pas ... -pas ... and ... *(interchangeable with -tah ... -tah, except with verbs, when only -tah ... -tah can be used)*
pasahi fare, passage, ticket
pasay to come in *(used in commands to invite people to enter)*; to pass
pata bank *(of a river)*, shore; edge; top; up
-pata *(variant: -pa)* of, 's, s' *(affixed to a word ending in a consonant)*
patrun landlord, proprietor
pawu turkey
pay he, she, it
-paya *(affixed to the stem of a verb that is not one of motion)* often, frequently
paya old *(a female)*; **aswan paya** older, oldest *(a female)*
paykuna they
paykunahpata *(variants of the -hpata ending: -h, -hpa, -hta)* (they-of) theirs, of theirs
paypata *(variant of the -pata ending: -pa)* (he/she/it-of) his, of his; hers, of hers; its, of its
pehpata whose
pegay *(corruption of pihchay)* to chew coca leaves
perqa wall
perqakamayoh bricklayer, stone mason
perqay to make a wall, to wall
pi who
-pi at, in; on; in, at, during *(with a month, a part of a month, a date, a week, a year)*
pichana broom
pichay to sweep
pichi cat
pichus who, the one who
pichuski ankle, ankles
pihchay to chew coca leaves

pihchu wad of coca in someone's mouth that is noted by the protrusion it makes in the cheeks; hill in the northwest of the Cuzco, Peru, mountain range that resembles a coca wad being chewed *[Note: In the famous Machu Picchu ruins there are two peaks, the lower known as **Machu***(old)* **Pihchu**, and the higher as **Wayna** (young) **Pihchu**.]*
pili duck
pilti tin
piltikamayoh tinsmith
piltikamayoh wasi tinsmith's shop
piluta ball
pi(lla)pas any *(with people)*; anybody, anyone; somebody, someone
pi(lla)pis any *(with people)*, anybody, anyone; somebody, someone
pincha bathroom, lavatory, restroom, water closet, toilet; sewer
pintur painter
piñi necklace or any other adornment *(often one that hangs)*
pipas anybody, anyone; somebody, someone
pipis anybody, anyone; somebody, someone
pirwa barn *(an indigenous, rustic granary/barn)*
pirwakuy to store in a barn
-pis any; even if; although; in spite of; *affixed to an interrogative pronoun, and usually preceded by* **-lla-***, makes of it an indefinite pronoun*
-pis ... -pis ... and ... *(interchangeable with* **-tah ... -tah***, except with verbs, when only* **-tah ... -tah** *can be used)*
pisi a little, less, little *(amount)*; **pisi chanin(ni)yoh**, inexpensive, cheap; **pisi chanin(ni)yohpuni** least expensive, cheapest
piskatur fisherman
pisu peso *(monetary unit of Bolivia)*
plasa market; plaza
poqoy to ripen; ripening
-pu it, them
puhllay to play
puhyu spring *(of water)*
puhyuchay to dig a well
puka red
pulisia policeman
pullira "pollera" *(typical Andean skirt)*, skirt
punchu poncho
-puni very; always; of course, certainly, *intensive marker*, "certainly"; most *(with an adjective)*
punkisqa swollen
punkiy to swell
punku door
puñuna bed
puñuy sleeping, sleep; to sleep
puñuywasi hotel, hostel, place to lodge
puquypacha fall *(autumn)*, autumn
purah both
purahnin both
pureh traveler, the one who travels; walker, the one who

walks
pureh masi traveling companion
puriy to walk; to travel
purun barren; **purun pampa** barren prairie, paramo *(high, barren Andean plateau)*; **purun panpa** barren prairie, paramo *(high, barren Andean plateau)*
purutu dry bean *(referring to a multiple variety that includes lima beans, butter beans, and kidney beans)*
purwa crude, thick rope made of braided llama wool
purway to capture, to corral
pusah eight
pusah guide, the one who guides, leader, the one who leads
pusahchunka eighty
pusahpachah eight hundred
pusamuy to lead *(back, here) (used with people)*, to guide *(back, here) (used with people)*, to take *(to lead, to guide) (back, here) (used with people)*
pusay to lead *(there) (used mostly with people)*, to guide *(there) (used mostly with people)*, to take *(to lead, to guide) (there) (used mostly with people)*

PH

phankachu(w)a shallow flat plate *(usually the bottom part of a gourd)*
phapa(tu) hoof; shoe; **phapa(tu) qhatu** shoe store, place where shoes are sold
phapa(tu)kamayoh shoemaker, shoe repairman
pharmasiyutika pharmacist *(a female)*
pharmasiyutiku pharmacist *(a male)*
phaskay to untie
phaway to take flight, to fly; to run
phiña angry, ferocious; anger
phiñachiy to anger
phiñakuy anger; to be angry; to become angry; to get
phiñay to anger
phiri gritty dish made of wheat flour, barley, corn, salt, and lard
phishqa five
phishqachunka fifty
phishqapachah five hundred
phista festival
phuchu rather weak
phukuy to blow
phullu blanket
phushkay to spin
phusullu blister
phusullu(chi)y to blister *(to make a blister)*
phusullu(ya)y to become blistered
phusullusqa blistered
phutikuy to be sad, to be very sorry
phutisqa sad
phuyu cloud
phuyu(mu)y to cloud up

P'

p'acha clothing
p'acha(lli)y to wear *[Note that instead of the word for "clothing," **p'acha**, any article of clothing, such as*

poncho, **punchu***, can be substituted to convey the idea of wearing that item.]*
p'acha(lli)chiy to dress (someone) *[Note that instead of the word for "clothing,"* **p'acha***, any article of clothing, such as poncho,* **punchu***, can be substituted to convey the idea of putting on that item.]*
p'acha(lli)kuy to get dressed *[Note that instead of the word for "clothing,"* **p'acha***, any article of clothing, such as poncho,* **punchu***, can be substituted to convey the idea of putting on that item.]*
p'akisqa broken
p'akiy to break
p'aqo blond, blonde
p'enqakuy to be embarrassed, to be ashamed
p'itay to jump
p'uku clay plate
p'unchaw day; daytime, daylight time
p'unchay day; daytime, daylight time
p'unchayay for day to break, for it to dawn
p'utuy to come out, to sprout
p'uyñu jug

Q

-qa *emphatic particle; emphatic marker used to convey the idea of* "if"; *emphatic marker used to convey the idea of the non-existent* "one"; certainly; right *(emphatic); affixed to an adjective making it a noun and thus conveying the idea of* "one"; *emphatic particle affixed to* **-spa** *or* **-hti** *to convey the idea of* "if"; *said (referring the noun to which it is affixed)*
qallariy beginning; to begin
qallu tongue *(language and part of the body)*
qan *(variant:* **qam***)* you *(one person)*
qankuna *(variant:* **qamkuna***)* you *(more than one person)*
qankunahpata *(variant:* **qamkunahpata***; variants of the* **-hpata** *ending:* **-h***,* **-hpa***,* **-hta***) (you[more than one person]-of)* yours, of yours *(more than one person)*
qanpata *(variant:* **qampata***; variant of the* **-pata** *ending:* **-pa***) (you[one person]-of)* yours, of yours *(one person)*
qanchis seven; **qanchis p'unchaw unah** week
qanchischaw week
qanchischunka seventy
qanchispachah seven hundred
qaninpa (diya) the other day
qanqoy to spin
qaqa rock
qaqaqaqa rocky
qara leather
qaray to feed, to serve food
qarpay to irrigate
qasa(mu)y to freeze
qata blanket
qatiriy to chase
qaylla facing, in front of, in the presence of; near
qayllakuy to approach, to get close, to get near
qayna a prior time

qayna last *(with night, week, month, year)*; **qayna (diya)** yesterday, **qayna (p'unchaw)** yesterday
qaynantin the day before, the preceding day
qayninpa the day before yesterday, two days ago
qayninpantin two days before
qella(kay) lazy; laziness
qellakuy to be lazy
qellqa writing *(something written)*
qellqa(laqhe) letter
qellqarima reading
qellqarimay to read
qellqay to write
qenatawaqachiy to play the **qena** *(Andean reed flute)*
qepnay vomit; vomiting; to throw up, to vomit
qephnay vomit; vomiting; to throw up, to vomit
qocha lake
qolqe silver; money; **qolqe qhatu** silversmith's shop; **qolqe takah** silversmith
qolqesapa rich
qolqeyoh rich
qonqay to forget
qonqor(i) knee, knees
qonqoriy to kneel
qori gold
qorpa guest
qorpachakuy to lodge *(to stay)*, to stay
qorpachanawasi hotel, hostel, place to lodge
qorpachay to host, to lodge *(someone)*
qorpawasi guesthouse *(traditionally for llama drivers and for their llamas)*

qosa husband
qowi guinea pig
qoy to give
qoyllur star
qoyllurchaw Wednesday
qunchuy storm

QH
qhapah high class, illustrious, powerful, rich
qhari man; male (referring to a person); bold, daring; **qhari kuncha** nephew *(of a male)*; **qhari mulla** nephew *(of a female)*; **qhari siminisqa** fiancé; **(qhari) wawa** son *(of a female)*
qharimasi companion *(a male)*
qhasqo chest
qhata lid; roof
qhatay to cover
qhatiri herder, driver *(of animals)*, muleteer
qhati(ri)y to herd, to drive *(animals)*
qhatu market, stall, stand, place where something is sold
qhatudiya market day
qhatuy to sell, to market; to barter
qhaway to look at, to see *(when the object of qhaway is a verb, the form used for that verb is the Active (or Present) Participle [verb stem-h]*
qhelli dirt; dirty
qhellichay to dirty
qhena Andean reed flute
qhenatawaqachiy to play the qhena *(Andean reed flute)*
qhepa(n) behind
qhepakuy to stay

-qhepa(n) *particle used to form an ordinal number from "second" on ("first" is* **ñawpah[-ñeqe(n)]**)*, by affixing it to the preceding corresponding cardinal number*
qhepa(n) after; next *(week, month, year)*
qheshwa Quechua; temperate valley
qhocha lake
qhochu gathering
qhochukuy to gather together to have fun, to get together to have fun
qhon sound thunder makes
qhonqhonni(mu)y to thunder
qhoya mine *(of minerals)*
qhoyaruna miner

Q'

q'apay to smell *(to give off aroma)*
q'arachupa opossum
q'aya next *(week, month, year)*; **q'aya** a future time; **q'aya (diya)** tomorrow, **q'aya (p'unchaw)** tomorrow; **q'aya minchha** one of these days
q'ayantin the following day, the next day
q'ayma insipid; without alcohol
q'ea pus
q'eay to infect
q'ellu yellow
q'epi "q'epi," bundle, luggage, piece of luggage
q'epiy to carry something on one's back
q'eta (misk'i) sweet, syrup-like or thicker byproduct of the making of chichi
q'illay iron; **q'illay takah** blacksmith; **q'illay takana wasi** blacksmith's shop
q'ocha sunstroke
q'ochasqa afflicted with sunstroke
q'ochachiy to be afflicted with sunstroke
q'omer green
q'oñi hot; **q'oñi unu** hot water; tea, infusion of any kind, **q'oñi yaku** hot water; tea, infusion of any kind
q'oñichiy to make hot
q'oñi(mu)y for it to be hot *(weather)*
q'oñiy heat; to heat, to be hot
q'opa garbage, trash

R

-ra "un-" *(as in "untie")*; without; *marker denoting intensity of the action of the verb, when the action is performed by many in a relatively wide open space*
rachiy to scratch
-rah still; first, before
rakhu thick
rantiy to buy, to get *(to buy)*; to sell; to barter
raphi leaf
raphra wing
raphraykachay to flap *(wings)*
ratu a little while, minute *(figuratively)*, moment
-raya still is, still are *(affixed to an adjective or to the past participle of a verb, showing continuity of the state brought by the action of that verb)*

-rayku for *(because)*, because, because of
rehsinakuy to know each other; to meet *(someone for the first time)*
rehsiy to know
-ri and/then *(prolonging the question or statement without adding any specific meaning)*; marker indicating "to start"/"to begin" *to do the action indicated by the verb*; marker to soften the intensity of the action of the verb *(repetition of* **-ri** *emphasizes the softening)*; marker to soften the request/"please" *(repetition of* **-ri** *emphasizes the softening)*
-rí and *(with a contrastive nuance)*; but
rich'a(ri)chiy to wake *(someone)* up
rich'a(ri)y to wake *(oneself)* up
rihra shoulder; wing
rikhuriy to appear
rikuchiy to show
rikuy to see, to look at, to know (by sight) *(when the object of* **rikuy** *is a verb, the form used for that verb is the Active (or Present) Participle [verb stem-***h***])*
riloh watch
rimay to speak, to talk
rimapayay to chat
rinri ear *(outer ear)*, ears *(outer ears)*
rinriwal(l)qa earring
ripuy to go, to go away, to go off, to leave
ritriti bathroom, lavatory, restroom, water closet, toilet
rit'i snow
rit'iqunchuy snow storm
rit'i(mu)y to snow
rit'iysapa snowy
rit'itamya snow storm
riy to go
-rqo *(preceded by a verb stem)* quickly, suddenly, urgently
ruana job, occupation
ruay to do, to make; to build
ruht'u deaf
rukhu old *(a male)*; **aswan rukhu** older, oldest *(a male)*
ruk'a finger, fingers; **(chaki) ruk'a** toe, toes
rumi stone
rumisapa stony
runa man; people; person
runasimi Quechua
runayay for a child to grow to maturity
runtu egg
rupha burning, hot, very hot *(temperature)*
ruphachiy to heat, to make hot
ruphachikuy to get burned, to burn oneself
rupha(mu)y for it to be hot *(weather)*
ruphana llant'a firewood
ruphay sunlight; heat; hot; to burn, to heat
ruray to do, to make; to build
ruru fruit *(result, product)*
ruway to do, to make; to build

S

-s marker denoting that the information is second hand *(follows a vowel)*; plural marker used in some Quechuaphone areas for nouns ending in vowel

-sa- *(variants:* **-chka-**, **-sha-**, **-shka-**, **-ska-**, **-skia-**, **-sia-**, **-sya-***) progressive marker,* "-ing"; *followed by a preterite (past tense) ending, can give the idea of* "just did"
sach'a tree (uncultivated); shrub
sach'ara shrub
sach'asach'a woods, forest; forested
sahra bad, mean, evil
sahrapuni worst; meanest
sahta stew prepared with mashed ullucu *("Ullucus tuberosus," yellow Andean tuber used like potatoes)*, jerked beef, potatoes, and chili pepper
sakha wide
sallqa puna *(the Andean highlands)*
samanawasi hotel, hostel
samariy to rest
samay to rest
sanampa letter *(of the alphabet)*; sign
sani purple
sankhu gritty dish made of wheat flour, barley, corn, salt, and lard
-sapa with a big . . . ; with a lot of . . .
sapa each, every; **sapa kutillan** very often
sapa(lla) alone
sapayay to be alone, to be left alone
sapatiru shoemaker
saqey to leave (behind); **saqey** to permit, to let, to allow *(when the object of* **saqey** *is a verb, the form used for that verb is the Active (or Present Participle) [verb stem-***h***])*
saqerpariy to abandon
sara corn
saramut'i boiled or steamed corn kernels served as a side dish
sasa difficult, hard
sawaru Saturday
sayasqa steep
sayay to incline; to be standing; to stop
sayk'usqa tired
sayk'uy to tire
sayk'uyay to become tired, to get tired
senqa nose
-si *marker denoting that the information is second hand (follows a consonant)*
sihwa(na) whip
siki base, foot *(base)*; buttocks
sikuwa straw *("paja brava")*
sullk'aruk'a little finger; little toe
sillu fingernail, toenail
simana week
simi mouth; word; language
siminiy to promise
-sina I think that, it seems that, probably
sinchi hard, strong, too much
sinku five *(borrowing from Spanish, used in telling time)*
siñur sir
siñura ma'am; lady
siñuras ladies
siñuráy ma'am
sipas young *(a female)*; young lady, young woman *(15-20 years old)*
sipasita very young *(a female)*

sip'uy to fold
siray sewing; to sew
siraykamayoh tailor
siraywasi tailor's shop
sis six *(borrowing from Spanish, used in telling time)*
sispa close (to), near
sispa ayllu relative by marriage
sispakuy to get near
sispañaña first cousin *(female) (of a female)*
sispapana first cousin *(female) (of a male)*
sispapuni nearest, closest
sispatura first cousin *(male) (of a female)*
sispawawqe first cousin *(male) (of a male)*
siti seven *(borrowing from Spanish, used in telling time)*
sitimwri(killa) September
-situ *diminutive marker (borrowing from Spanish)*
siuh straight
siwi ring
siwillina ruk'a ring finger
siwulla onion
sohta six
sohtachunka sixty
sohtapachah six hundred
sonqo heart
sonqo(n)chay to be grateful for a favor
-spa *invariable gerund marker, "-ing," usually used when the subject of the gerund is the same as that of the main verb*
-sqa *past (or perfect) infinitive marker, "to have (past participle)"; particle to form the passive [or past] participle for the present and past, used in a construction that in English is introduced by a relative pronoun, often "what," "that," or "which," when the verb denotes what someone or something did or is doing; particle used with a dependent verb for an action that is simultaneous to or prior to that of the main verb*
-su *you (object of a gerund); you (object of an infinitive); part of a dual verbal ending that indicates "(the subject)" addresses the action "to you" See numbers 18. Model for Verbs that Include (Pronominally) the Verbal Object "You (One Person)," and 19. Model for Verbs that Include (Periphrastically and Pronominally) the Verbal Object "You (More Than One Person)" in Section III: Quechua Grammar Notes.*
su(w)a thief
su(w)ay to steal
suchi present, gift
sukri monetary unit of Ecuador
sukha afternoon
sukhaman in the afternoon *(without an hour given)*
sukhamanta in the afternoon *(after an hour is mentioned),* P.M. *(afternoon hours, after an hour is mentioned)*
sul monetary unit of Peru
suldadu soldier
sullk'a younger, youngest
sullk'aruk'a little finger; little toe

¡**Sullpa!** Thanks!
sullpay to thank
sumah pretty, beautiful, attractive, exquisite, good looking, handsome; pleasing, harmonious, good; well
sumahchay to make beautiful
sumahpuni most attractive, most beautiful, best looking, most handsome; best
sumwiru hat *(with a brim)*
suni big, large, long; tall
sunipuni biggest, largest; longest; tallest
sunk'a facial hair
suri breed of alpaca whose wool grows almost to the ground; nandu *(American ostrich)*
suru(h)chi soroche *(Andean altitude sickness)*
suru(h)chisqa afflicted with soroche *(Andean altitude sickness)*
suru(h)chiy to be afflicted with soroche *(Andean altitude sickness)*
surump'i light blindness
surump'isqa afflicted by light blindness
surump'iy to be afflicted with light blindness
suti name
sutichay to name, to give a name
sut'i light *(in color)*, visible, evident
sut'iyay to become clear, to dawn
su(w)a thief
su(w)ay to steal
suyay to wait

suyu area, department *(political division)*, district *(political division)*, region
swiku Swedish
Swisia Sweden

T

-ta at *(with an hour or referring in general to an hour)*; in, on, at, during *(with a period of time)*; marker for number of times; through *(as in -ntinta, "all through")*; direct object marker; to *(indicating reaching the place designated)*; adverb marker that makes an adverb of an adjective, often creating an adverb whose English equivalent ends in "-ly"
-(n)ta by; through; via
-tah *euphonic particle*
-tah ... -tah ... and ...
tahlla plow (simple, rustic)
tahllay to dig irrigation channels, to loosen the soil, to make holes for planting seeds, to plow (with a simple, rustic plow)
tahsa medium *(in size)*
takana hammer, to hit
takay to hammer
takeh singer, the one who sings
takiy song; to sing
tama flock, herd
tampuwasi hotel
tamya storm
tanta gathering, meeting
tantakuy to gather together, to get together, to meet *(to get together)*
tañu rampana truck

tapuy to ask
tarwi *(Lupinus mutabilis)* lupine seeds
tariy to find
tarpuy to sow, to plant
tarwimut'i boiled lupine seeds served as a side dish
¡Tata! *(shortened form of* **¡Tayta!**) Sir! *(informal)*
ta(y)ta father; sir; **ta(y)táy** sir, **¡Ta(y)táy!** Sir! *(somewhat formal)*
ta(y)tamama parents
tawa four
tawapachah four hundred
tawachunka forty
tawak'uchu hina rectangular, square
-ti *characterizer (as in* **wihsati** *pot-bellied from* **wihsa** *belly)*
ti(y)akuy to live, to reside; to stay; to sit, to sit down
ti(y)an there is, there are
ti(y)ana seat
ti(y)ay for there to be
tika adobe
tilihunu telephone
timpu time
tinkuy to find
titi lead
tiy tea
tiyariy to stand up
Tiyus God
Tiyuspa wasin church
tonqor(i) throat
tragu liquor
trawahah worker, the one who works
trawahay to work *(non-traditional [farming]); office work, and the like)*
trin train
trinta thirty *(borrowing from Spanish, used in telling time)*
tris three *(borrowing from Spanish, used in telling time)*
tropa flock, herd
tukuy all, everything; everybody, everyone
tukuy *[verb stem]-***h** *(Active [or Present] Participle)* to pretend to be the one who *[verb]*
tukuy (. . . -ta) to end (. . .), to finish (. . .); **. . .-man tukuy** to turn into . . ., to become . . ., to end up . . .
tullpuy to dye
tullu skinny
tupay to meet *(to encounter)*
tura brother *(of a female)*
turu bull
tusoh dancer, the one who dances
tusohkamayoh professional dancer
tusuku dance
tusuy to dance
tuta dark *(of the night)*, night
tuta mikhuy dinner
tutaman at night *(after dark, without an hour given)*
tutamanta at night *(after an hour is mentioned)*, P.M. *(after dark, after an hour is mentioned)*
tutayay for night to fall

TH
thalleh translator, the one who translates
thalliy to translate
thanta old, tattered, used, worn
thehtichisqa fried
thehtichiy to fry

thoqay to spit

T'

t'ahsakuna wash basin or sink where one can wash clothes, hair, or anything else that can absorb water
t'ahsana laundry
t'ahsay to wash clothes, hair, or anything else that can absorb water
t'ahsaykama a laundry
t'anta bread
t'antachay to make bread
t'antaqhatu bread stand/stall, place where bread is sold
t'antawasi bakery
t'asl(l)a flat, level, open *(referring to fields and the like)*
t'ika flower
t'ikay to flower
t'impusqa boiled
t'impuy to boil
t'inpu stew/boiled dinner *(a typical dish in the Cuzco, Peru, area that is made of different kinds of meats, bacon, cabbage, carrots, potatoes, garbanzos, rice, onions, frozen dried potatoes, and spices)*
t'ipana broach, pin *(broach)*
t'iu sand
t'iusapa sandy
t'iut'iu sandy
t'ohpiy to point, to point out (with something); to poke
t'ohriy to keep an eye on, to watch
t'oqo hole
t'upsina ruk'a index finger
t'upsiy to point, to point out (with something); to poke
t'uru mud
t'uruchay to make mud
t'urusapa muddy
t'uruyay to get muddy
t'uruyapuy to become covered with mud, to get covered with mud
t'uruyay to become mud
t'ustoh thresher *(person)*, the one who threshes
t'ustuna thresher *(instrument, machine)*
t'ustuna pata threshing floor
t'ustuy to thresh
t'utura high altitude lacustrine reed *(Scirpus riparius)*, the young shoots of which are used as food in Peru and Bolivia, and the reedy stems of which are used for making fences, boats (usually for one person), and floors; totora *(canoe-shaped boat, usually for one person, with rather high, pointed ends, made of bundles of the high altitude lacustrine reed [totora] seen on Lakes Titicaca and Poopó, and on some other Andean lakes)*

U

uchu eight *(borrowing from Spanish, used in telling time)*; chili pepper; meat dish characterized by a sauce of hot or bell pepper
uficina office
uh *(variants: uj, uk, huh, huk, hoq)* one, a, an, a few, some; another, one other; anybody, anyone, somebody,

someone, something
uh kutita once
uh qhepa(n) second
uhkuna some people
uhtawan again, once more
uhtawan niy to repeat
uhyana drinkable, potable; a drink, something to drink
uhyay drink; something drinkable; drinking; to drink
ukhu deep, inside, interior
ukhuna cotton petticoat
ukhunchay to put inside
uktuwri(killa) October
ulluku *(Ullucus tuberosus)* ullucu *or* ulluco *(yellow Andean tuber used like potatoes)*
uma head; top
umananay head ache
umayoh intelligent
umint'a tamal
una one *(borrowing from Spanish, used in saying "one o'clock")*
unay a long time, time
unay to last
unkhu undershirt
unsi eleven *(borrowing from Spanish, used in telling time)*
unu water
uña young animal
uñayoh pregnant *(animal)*
ura hour; below, down, under
uranchay to put *(something)* underneath
uray down
uraykuy to get off, to get down
urmakuy to fall down
urmay to fall
urpi dove
urpisonqo very kind
uspital hospital
usqhayta quickly
ususi daughter *(of a male)*
ushqay fast; haste; to be in a hurry
ushut'a rustic sandal
util hotel
utkhu cotton
uwiha sheep
uya face
uyarina ear *(inner ear)*, ears *(inner ears)*
uyariy to hear, to listen (to) *(when the object of* **uyariy** *is a verb, the form used for that verb is the Active (or Present) Participle [verb stem-*h*])*
uylla prayer
uyllapuy for someone to pray
uyllay to pray
uyllayma place to pray
uywa domesticated or domestic animal; **orqo uywa** non-domesticated animal
uywahampeh veterinarian
uyway to raise domesticated or domestic animals
uywayay for a domesticated or domestic animal to grow

W

wach'iy to bite, to sting
wah the other
wahcha needy, poor
wahkuna the others; the rest
waka cow, bull
wakamasa team of oxen
waleh fine, well
wallpa chicken
wallpasu(w)a turkey buzzard
wal(l)qa necklace or any other adornment *(often one that hangs)*

wal(l)qay to adorn with a necklace or any hanging adornment
wamira girl, young woman *(10-14 years old)*
wamra boy, young man *(10-14 years old)*
-wan with, with *(shows that the noun to which it is attached is in the company of the person)*
wanaku guanaco
wankar drum
wanp'u(y) boat, raft
wanp'uy to navigate, to raft
wantu stretcher
wañuchiy to kill
wañusqa dead
wañuy to die; for something to end
waqachiy to play a wind or stringed musical instrument
waqati child who cries a lot
waqay to cry; to chirp, to sing *(birds)*, to crow; for a musical instrument to make a sound; cry
wara *(singular)* pants, trousers *(typical of the rural areas)*
warak'a sling shot, sling to hurl stones
warak'ay to hurl with a sling
waranqa thousand
wariqolli candle
wariqolli qhatu place where candles are sold
warmi female, wife, woman
warmi churi daughter *(of a male)*
warmi kuncha niece *(of a male)*
warmi mulla niece *(of a female)*
warmi siminisqa fiancée
warmi siraykamayoh seamstress
(warmi) wawa daughter *(of a female)*
warmimasi companion *(a female)*
warmicha young woman
wasa back
wasi house; room *(area for a specific activity such as cooking)*; shop *(workshop)*, workshop
wask(h)a rope
wask(h)ay to lasso
wata year
wataray to untie
watay to tie
wateh(manta) again
wathi(y)a tubers and/or fruits roasted in a **wathi(y)a(na)**
wathi(y)a(na) earth oven *(a hole in the ground with hot clods of dirt)* for roasting tubers and/or fruits
wathi(y)ay to roast tubers and/or fruits in a **wathi(y)a(na)**
watoh seer, soothsayer, fortuneteller, the one who tells fortunes
watu string, cord, thin rope; strip of cloth used to tie something
watuchay to tie with a string, to tie with a cord, to tie with a thin rope
watuy to foretell, to tell someone's fortune
wawa baby, child *(male and female)*; little boy, little girl; **(qhari) wawa** son *(of a female)*; **(warmi) wawa**

daughter *(of a female)*
¡Waway! Little boy! *(in calling to the person)*, Little girl! *(in calling to the person)*; My boy! *(in calling to the person)*, My girl! *(in calling to the person)*
wawayoh pregnant *(person)*
wawqe brother *(of a male)*
wawqéy brother *(very friendly, used in addressing someone)*
wayaqa bag, sack
wayk'oh cook, the one who cooks
wayk'una wasi kitchen
wayk'uy to cook
waylla meadow, prairie; pastureland
wayna young *(a male)*; young man *(18-30 years old)* [Note: In the famous Machu Picchu ruins there are two peaks, the lower known as **Machu** (old) **Pihchu**, and the higher as **Wayna** (young) **Pihchu**. See *pihchu*.]
waynitu very young *(a male)*
wayq'u gorge, ravine
wayra(y) wind
wayra(y)qunchuy wind storm
wayrachiy to winnow
wayra(y)sapa windy
wayra(y)tamya wind storm
wayrahina(lla) light *(in weight)*
wayra(mu)y to blow *(referring to the wind)*
wayta wildflower
wayt'ay to swim
wayu fruit *(edible)*
wayuqhatu fruit stand/stall, place where fruit is sold
wayuwasi fruit store

wichariy to get on
wichay to get on *(implying that it is not difficult to do)*
wihch'uy to throw; to throw away; to squander
wihsa belly, stomach
wihsati pot-bellied
wihsuy to incline, to tilt, to tip
wik'uña vicuña
wilali milk; **wilali qhatu** dairy *(store)*, place where milk is sold, place where cheese is sold, place where dairy products are sold
willapi orange *(color)*
willakuy to complain
willay to inform, to let know, to tell
winay to bag, to sack; bag, sack, bundle *(of specific size and weight)*, load
winch'uy to throw out
windiy to sell
wiñay always
wiñay to grow *(increase in age or size)* *(people, animals, plants)*; to grow up
wira fat *(noun and adjective)*
Wiraqocha Viracocha, one of the names of the primary Inca deity *(see Note 4 in Chapter 2)*
wiraqocha man, gentleman; sir *(quite formal, used only by native speakers of Quechua when addressing urban residents or foreigners)*
wirnis Friday
wisk'acha vizcacha *(Andean rodent)*
wisk'achani place where vizcachas can be found
wisq'ay to close, to shut

wistidu dress
wulitu ticket
wutika pharmacy

Y

-y my; *command marker addressing one person*; *infinitive marker, "to"*; *(affixed to the name of a city or town)* to go to *(the city or town)*
-ya to become, to get, to grow, to go *(what the meaning of the stem of the verb to which it is attached is)*
-ya-chi to make to become, to get, to grow, to go *(what the meaning of the stem of the verb to which it is attached is)*
-ya-pu *affixed to the noun and followed by the appropriate verbal ending* creates a verb that expresses a change of the subject to a new state or condition related to the noun
yachacheh teacher, the one who teaches
yachachikuy to study
yachachiy to teach
yachakoh student
yachakuy to learn
yachay to know; knowledge
yachaywasi school
yaku water; tasteless, insipid
yallin excess, surplus
yallinyoh too
yan path, road
yana black, dark *(in color)*
yanapa help
yanapay to help
yanoh cook, the one who cooks
yanuna wasi kitchen
yanuy to cook
yapuna plow (any type)
yapuy to plow
yaqolla cloak
yarqachikuy to feel hunger
yarqay hunger; to cause hunger; to feel hunger
¡Yaw! Hey!, Say there! *(addressing one person) (very informal)*
¡Yawkuna! Hey!, Say there! *(addressing more than one person) (very informal)*
yawar blood
yawaray to bleed
yaya father
yayawki uncle *(brother of father)*
yaykumuy to come in, to enter this way *(in this direction)*
yaykuy to come in, to enter; to set *(used with the sun)*; to fit
-ykacha *marker used with a verb of motion indicating the action is done casually or intermittently*
-yki your *(one person)*
-ykicheh *(variants of the* **-cheh** *ending:* **-chej, -chih, -chij, -chik, -chis***)* your *(more than one person)*
-yku our *(excluding the person[s] addressed)*; *cordiality marker*; inside *(when used with verbs of motion)*; *marker used with a verb that is not one of motion or direction to indicate intensity*
-yoh with *(indicates the noun to which it is attached is owned by or being worn by the person mentioned; as*

appropriate to the noun to which it is attached, may also indicate a physical condition, as in **wawayoh**, *with child, pregnant;* **suru(h)chiyoh**, *with altitude sickness)*

yoqalla boy

-ysi to help *(to do the action of the verb to which stem it is attached)*

¡Yu! Hello!, Hi!, Hey! *(very informal)*, Say there! *(very informal)*

yunka semi-tropical valley on the eastern slopes of the Andes; warm valley on the western slopes of the Andes

yunta team of oxen

yura plant; bush, shrub

yurah white

yuru pitcher

yuyay to pay attention, to think about, to watch *(to pay attention)*

ENGLISH – QUECHUA VOCABULARY

A
A.M. paqarinmanta
a uh
abandon, to saqerpariy
able, to be atiy; **for one to be able** atikuy
"-able" -na
about -manta; **to think about** yuyay; **to be about to** *(the meaning of the verb)* -naya
above hawa
ache nanay; **to ache** nanay
across the way chinpa
add more salt, to kachipay
admire, to añay
admired añasqa
adobe tika
adorn with a necklace or any other hanging adornment, to wal(l)qay
adornment *(often one that hangs)* piñi, wal(l)qa
afflicted with light blindness surump'isqa, **afflicted with soroche** *(Andean altitude sickness)* suru(h)chisqa, **afflicted with sunstroke** q'ochasqa; **to be afflicted with light blindness** surump'iy, **to be afflicted with soroche** *(Andean altitude sickness)* suru(h)chiy, **to be afflicted with sunstroke** q'ochachiy
afraid, to be manchari(ku)y
after *(in order)* qhepa(n); **after** *(an action)* hawa; **the day after tomorrow** minchha, minchha p'unchaw, minchha diya; **two days after tomorrow** minchhantin

afternoon sukha; **in the afternoon** *(after an hour is mentioned)* sukhamanta, *(without an hour given)* sukhaman; **mid-afternoon snack** khuskan sukha mikhuy
afterwards chanta
again uhtawan, wateh(manta)
ago, two days qayninpa
ahead *(of someone or something)* chinpa
all -ntin; tukuy; **all through** -ntinta
allow, to saqey *(when the object of saqey is a verb, the form used for that verb is the Active (or Present) Participle [verb stem-h])*; **to allow** *(what the meaning of the verb is)* -chi
alone sapa(lla); **to be alone** sapayay; **to be left alone** sapayay
along ... khuska ... wan
alpaca allpaqa; **breed of alpaca whose wool grows almost to the ground** suri
already ña; *(used and often untranslated in asking and telling the hour, or the number of hours, days, weeks, months, years)* -ña
although -pas, -pis
always -puni; wiñay
an uh
ancient ñawpa
and *(with a contrastive nuance)* -rí; **and/then** *(prolonging the question or statement without adding any specific*

357

meaning) -ri; **... and ...**
(-pas) ... **-pas**,
(interchangeable with [-tah]
... **-tah**, *except with verbs,
when only* [-tah] ... **-tah**
can be used), **... and ...**
(-tah) ... **-tah**
Andean reed flute qhena
anger phiña, phiñakuy; **to
anger** phiñay, phiñachiy
angry phiña; **to be angry**
phiñakuy; **to become angry**
phiñakuy, **to get angry**
phiñakuy
**animal, domesticated and
domestic** uywa; **non-
domesticated animal** orqo
uywa; **young animal** uña
ankle, ankles pichuski
another uh
answer, to hay niy, hay ñiy
antique ñawpa
any -pas, -pis
any *(with people)* pi(lla)pas,
pi(lla)pis; *(with things)*
ima(lla)pas, ima(lla)pis;
*(with people, animals,
things)* mayqen(lla)pas,
mayqen(lla)pis
any old place mayqen(lla)pis,
mayqen(lla)pas
any place mayqen(lla)pis,
mayqen(lla)pas
anybody uh; pi(lla)pas,
pi(lla)pis, mayqen(lla)pas,
mayqen(lla)pis; **not
anybody** nipi
anyone uh; pi(lla)pas, pi(lla)pis,
mayqen(lla)pas,
mayqen(lla)pis; **not anyone**
nipi
anything ima, ima(lla)pas,
ima(lla)pis; mayqen(lla)pas,

mayqen(lla)pis; **not
anything** ni ima, ni
ima(lla)pas, ni ima(lla)pis
anywhere may(lla)pipas,
may(lla)pipis
appeal, to gustay
appear, to rikhuriy; **for dew to
appear** chhulla(mu)y
appraise, to chaninchay
approach, to chinpakuy,
qayllakuy
approximately -neh
April awril(killa)
area suyu
arm, arms maki
armadillo khirkinchu
around -neh; **around here**
kaynehpi, **around there**
(farther away) haqaynehpi,
(nearby) chaynehpi
arrive, to *(here)* chayamuy; **to
arrive** *(there)* chayay
as *(used in comparison)* [*Note:
With a verb, it always goes
at the end; in a construction
with a noun, its location may
vary.*] (-)hina
ashamed, to be p'enqakuy
ask, to *(a question)* tapuy; **to
ask for** *(something)* mañay
astute challi
at -pi; *(with an hour or
referring in general to an
hour)* -ta, *(with part of a
day)* -manta, -ta, *(with any
other period of time)* -ta
attention, to pay yuyay
attractive sumah; **most
attractive** sumahpuni
August awgustu(killa)
Australia Awstralya
authority *(in the given field or
area)* -kama

autumn puquypacha
away, to move *(something or someone)* karunchay

B

baby wawa
back wasa *(of something)*
back, to be kutimuy
bad mana allin, mana sumah; *(mean, evil)* sahra
bad smell asna
bag wayaqa, winay; **to bag** winay
bakery t'antawasi
ball, piluta
bank *(of a river)* pata
banquet, to pachamankay
barbecue *(gathering where barbecued meat is prepared)* pachamanka; **to hold a barbecue or picnic** pachamankay
barn *(an indigenous, rustic granary, barn)* pirwa; **to store in a barn** pirwakuy
barren purun; **barren prairie** purun pampa, purun panpa
barter, to qhatuy, rantiy
base siki
bath, to take a armakuy
bathe, to *(someone else)* armay; *(oneself)* armakuy
bathe, place to armakuna
bathroom pincha, bañu, ritriti
baths armakuna
be, to kay *(used here for identification, characteristics, and traits)*; kasay *(used here with condition, situation, and location)*; **to be able** atiy; **to be about to** *(the meaning of the verb)* -naya; **to be afflicted with light blindness** surump'iy, **to be afflicted with soroche** *(Andean altitude sickness)* suru(h)chiy, **to be afflicted with sunstroke** q'ochachiy; **to be afraid** manchari(ku)y; **to be alone** sapayay; **to be angry** phiñakuy; **to be ashamed** p'enqakuy; **to be back** kutimuy; **to be blind** ñawsay; **to be glad** kusikuy; **to be hot** q'oñiy; **to be cold** chiriy; **to be embarrassed** p'enqakuy; **to be grateful for a favor** sonqo(n)chay; **to be in a hurry** ushqay; **to be lazy** qellakuy; **to be left alone** sapayay; **to be on the verge of** *(the meaning of the verb)* -naya; **to be sad** llakikuy, phutikuy; **to be sick** onqoy; **to be sorry** llakikuy; **to be standing** sayay; **to be very sorry** phutikuy; **for it to be hot** *(weather)* rupha(mu)y q'oñi(mu)y; **for it to be cold** *(weather)* chiri(mu)y; **for there to be frost** chhullunka(mu)y; **for there to be light** k'anchay; **for one to be able** atikuy; **for there to be** kay, ti(y)ay; *(used in a construction with a verbal object pronoun to convey the idea of "to have," see numbers 16, 17, 18, and 19 in Section III: Quechua Grammar Notes)* kapuy
bean, variety of dry *(referring to a multiple variety that includes lima beans, butter beans, and kidney beans)*

purutu, chuwi
beautiful k'acha, sumah; **most beautiful** sumahpuni; **to make beautiful** sumahchay
because -rayku; *(used with a dependent verb that is dependent upon a verb that expresses sentiment)* -manta; **because of** imaraykuchus; -rayku
become, to *what the meaning of the stem of the verb to which it is attached is* **-ya**; *(showing transformation to a state or condition)* . . . -man tukuy; **to become angry** phiñakuy; **to become blind** ñawsayay, ñawsaman tukuy; **to become blistered** phusullu(ya)y; **to become clear** sut'iyay; **to become covered with dust** ñut'uhallp'ayapuy; **to become covered with mud** t'uruyapuy; **to become dust** ñut'uhallp'ayay; **to become mud** t'uruyay; **to become sick** onqoyay, onqoman tukuy; **to become tired** sayk'uyay; **to become what the meaning of the verb is** -ya *affixed to the stem of the verb*
bed puñuna
bee lachiwana
before ñawpah *(in time and location)*; -rah
begin, to qallariy; -ri *(marker indicating* **to start/to begin** *to do the action indicated by the verb)*
beginning qallariy
behind qhepa(n)

belief iñiy
believe to iñiy
belly wihsa
below ura
best sumahpuni; **best looking** sumahpuni
between chawpi; **to put in between** chawpinchay
big hatun; suni; **with a big . . .** -sapa; **big toe** mamaruk'a
biggest hatunpuni, sunipuni
birthday diyachaku; **to celebrate a birthday** diyachakuy
bite khaniy; wach'iy *(sting)*; **to bite** khaniy; wach'iy *(sting)*
bitter haya
black yana
blacksmith iriru, q'illay takah; **blacksmith's shop** q'illay takana wasi
blanket phullu, qata
bleed, to yawaray
blind ñawsa; **to blind** ñawsay, ñawsayachiy; **to be blind** ñawsay; **to become blind** ñawsayay, ñawsaman tukuy; **to go blind** ñawsayay, ñawsaman tukuy; **to make blind** ñawsayachiy
blindness, light surump'i; **afflicted by light blindness** surump'isqa; **to be afflicted with light blindness** surump'iy; **to cause blindness** ñawsayachiy
blister phusullu; **to blister** *(to make a blister)* phusullu(chi)y
blistered phusullusqa
blond p'aqo
blonde p'aqo
blood yawar

blow, to phukuy; *(referring to the wind)* wayra(mu)y
blue anqas
boat wanp'u(y); **canoe-shaped boat** *usually for one person, with rather high, pointed ends, made of high altitude lacustrine reed (Scirpus riparius)* (totora) *seen on Lakes Titicaca and Poopó, and on some other Andean lakes* t'utura
boil, to t'impuy; **to boil or to steam the ingredients to prepare "mut'i"** mut'iy
boiled t'impusqa; **boiled fava beans served as a side dish** abasmut'i; **boiled or steamed corn kernels served as a side dish** saramut'i; **boiled dinner/stew** *(a typical dish in the Cuzco, Peru, area that is made of different kinds of meats, bacon, cabbage, carrots, potatoes, garbanzos, rice, onions, frozen dried potatoes, and spices)* t'inpu; **boiled lupine seeds served as a side dish** tarwimut'i; **boiled variety of dry beans served as a side dish** chuwimut'i; **very common boiled or steamed vegetable side dish** *(of fava beans: "abasmut'i"; of a variety of dry beans: "chuwimut'i"; of corn kernels: "saramut'i"; of lupine seeds: " tarwimut'i")* mut'i
bold qhari
book liwru
border kinra; **frayed border** chhapu
borrow, to *(something consumable, such as money or food, that is to be returned with an equivalent; see* mañay*)* manukuy *(with* -manta *affixed to the noun designating the one[s] doing the lending, with* -ta *affixed to the noun designating the item[s] being lent, and* -man *to the noun[s] designating the one[s] to whom it is/they are being lent)*; *(something that is to be returned as opposed to something consumable, such as money or food, that is to be returned with an equivalent)* mañay *(see* manuy*) (with* -manta *affixed to the noun designating the one[s] doing the lending, with* -ta *affixed to the noun designating the item[s] being lent, and* -man *to the noun[s] designating the one[s] to whom it is/they are being lent)*
boss apu
both purah, purahnin, iskaynin
boy ch'ete, ch'iti, wamra *(10-14 years old)*, yoqalla, **little boy** wawa; **Little boy!** *(in calling to the person)* ¡Wawáy!; **My boy!** *(in calling to the person)* ¡Wawáy!
bracelet chipana
bread t'anta; **place where bread is sold** t'antaqhatu; **bread stall** t'antaqhatu; **bread stand** t'antaqhatu

break, to p'akiy; **to break into pieces** ñut'uy; **for day to break** paqariy, p'unchayay
breakfast paqarin mikhuy
breast, breasts ñuñu; **to breast feed** ñuñuy
bricklayer alwañil, perqakamayoh
brightness k'anchay
bring, to apamuy, kachamuy; **to bring near** chinpachiy
broach t'ipana
broken p'akisqa
bronze llahsa
broom pichana
broth hilli
brother *(of a female)* tura; *(of a male)* wawqe
build, to ruay, ruray, ruway
building, multi-story hatun wasi
bull turu, (orqo) waka
bundle q'epi; *(of specific size and weight)* winay
burn, to ruphay; **to burn oneself** ruphachikuy
burned, to get ruphachikuy
burning rupha
bus awtuwus
bush yura
but chaywanpis, ichaqa, -rí
butcher aychata qhatoh; **butcher shop** aycha qhatu
buttocks siki
buy, to rantiy
by -(n)ta

C

cadaver aya
can *(able)* atiy
Canada Kanada
candle wariqolli; **place where candles are sold** wariqolli qhatu
canoe-shaped boat *usually for one person, with rather high, pointed ends, made of high altitude lacustrine reed (Scirpus riparius)* (totora) *seen on Lakes Titicaca and Poopó, and on some other Andean lakes* t'utura
cap *(colorful, native, conical-shaped, knit, wool cap with ear flaps)* ch'ullu
capture, to purway
car awtu
Careful! ¡Pahtatah!; *(showing annoyance, anger or even a threat over what someone is doing)* ¡Pahtá!
carpenter karpintiru, llahllaykamayoh; **carpenter's shop** llahllaykamayoh wasi
carrier *(of things)* apah, *(of things)* astah
carry, to *(things)* apay, *(things)* astay; **to carry something in a skirt** *(by gathering up the hem in front and bringing it toward the waist to form a type of pocket)* mihllay; **to carry something on one's back** q'epiy
cart, to astay
carter astah
Castilian kastillanu
cat michi, mischi, misi, pichi
cause blindness, to ñawsayachiy, **to cause to become blind** ñawsayachiy; **to cause hunger** yarqay; **to cause sorrow** llakiy, **to cause oneself sorrow** llakikuy; **to cause sickness**

onqoyachiy, **to cause to become sick** onqoyachiy
celebrate a birthday, to diyachakuy
cellar, salt kachi churanacha
certainly (-)a *(as a suffix[-a] or an independent word following what is being stressed; stressed in speech)*, (-)á *(as a suffix[-á] or an independent word following what is being stressed; stressed in speech)*; -puni, -qa
charcoal k'illimsa, **place where charcoal is sold** k'illimsa qhatu
chase, to qatiriy
chat, to rimapayay
cheap chaninnah, chaninra, pisi chanin(ni)yoh
cheapest chaninnahpuni, chaninrapuni, pisi chanin(ni)yohpuni, mana chanin(ni)yohpuni
cheer up, to kusichiy
chest qhasqo
chew coca leaves, to akulliy, pihchay, pegay *(corruption of "pihchay")*
chicha *(made from corn)* aqha
chichería *(tavern)* aqhawasi
chicken wallpa
child ch'ete, ch'iti, *(male and female)* wawa, **child who cries a lot** waqati
chili pepper uchu
chill, to chiriy, chiri(ya)chiy
chirp, to waqay
chop firewood, to llant'ay
church ilisya, inlisha, Diyuspa wasin, Tiyuspa wasin; *(denomination, congregation, religious group or community)* iñirip'ata
circle muyu(y); **to go in circles** muyu(y)
circular muyu(y)
circumference muyu(y)
city llahta, hatun llahta; **city father** llahta kamayoh; **man from the city** hatunllahtaruna
clay llanka; **clay plate** p'uku; **clay pot** manka
clear *(said of water)* ch'uya
clear up, to *(weather)* illari(mu)y
clear, to become sut'iyay
climb, to lloq'ay; **to climb on** *(implying that it is difficult to do)* lloq'ay
cloak yaqolla
close sispa (near), qaylla (near), **close to** sispa, qaylla; **to get close** qayllakuy, chinpakuy
close, to wisq'ay
closest sispapuni
clothing p'acha
cloud phuyu; **to cloud up** phuyu(mu)y
coal k'illimsa
coca kuka; **coca leaf** kuka (raphi); **to chew coca leaves** pihchay, pegay *(corruption of "pihchay")*; **coca shrub** kuka (sach'ara)
coffee kafiy
cold *(noun and adjective)* chiri; **to be cold** chiriyay, **to get cold** chiriyay; **to make cold** chiri(ya)chiy; **for it to be cold** *(weather)* chiri(mu)y
color llimp'i
colorful woven shawl llihlla

Come on! ¡Haku!
come, to hamuy; **to come back** kutimuy; **to come in** yayku(mu)y, pasay; **to come out** p'utuy, **for a rainbow to come out** k'uychi(mu)y
command, to kamay, kamachiy
companion masi, *(a female)* warmimasi, *(a male)* qharimasi; **traveling companion** pureh masi
complain, to willakuy
condor kuntur
cook wayk'oh, yanoh; **to cook** wayk'uy; yanuy
copper anta
cord watu
corn sara
corn kernels, boiled or steamed, served as a side dish saramut'i
corral kural; **to corral** purway
cost chani(n)
cost, to kwistay
cotton ampi, utkhu; **cotton petticoat** ahsu, ukhuna
cough ch'oho, ch'uhu; **whopping cough** ch'oho, ch'uhu; **to cough** ch'ohoy, ch'uhuy
cousin, first *(female) (of a female)* sispañaña; *(female) (of a male)* sispapana; *(male) (of a female)* sispatura; *(male) (of a male)* sispawawqe
cover, to qhatay
covered with dust, to become ñut'uhallp'ayapuy; **to get covered with dust** ñut'uhallp'ayapuy
covered with mud, to become t'uruyapuy; **to get covered with mud** t'uruyapuy
cow waka
cries a lot, child who waqati
crippled in one hand ñuk'u; **crippled in the legs** natah
cross kurus
crow, to waqay
crumble, to ñut'uy
cry waqay; **to cry** waqay
cure hampi; **to cure** hampiy
curve llink'u
custard-like dessert, a kind of api
cut kuchu; **to cut** kuchuy, k'utuy; **to cut with a sickle or scythe** ichhuy
cutter, firewood llant'ah

D

dairy *(store)* wilali qhatu; **place where dairy products are sold** wilali qhatu
damp mik'i
dance tusuku; **to dance** tusuy
dancer tusoh; **professional dancer** tusohkamayoh
danger mahllu
dangerous mahllumahllu
daring qhari
dark *(in color)* llaqha, yana; **dark** *(of the night)* tuta
darken, to k'ancharay
daughter *(of a female)* (warmi) wawa; *(of a male)* ususi, warmi churi
dawn, to sut'iyay
day diya, p'unchaw, p'unchay; **the preceding day** qaynantin; **the day before** qaynantin; **the day before yesterday** qayninpa; **two days ago** qayninpa; **two days before** qayninpantin;

the other day qaninpa (diya); **the next day** q'ayantin; **the following day** q'ayantin; **the day after tomorrow** minchha, minchha p'unchaw, minchha diya
daylight time p'unchaw, p'unchay
daytime p'unchaw, p'unchay
dawn, for it to punchayay, paqariy
day to break, for punchayay, paqariy
dead wañusqa
deaf huq'ara, ruht'u
deceive, to llullay
December disimwri(killa)
deep ukhu; **deep plate** (*usually the bottom part of a gourd*) chu(w)a
defecate, to akay; **place to defecate** akana
delicious kusay, mante
delightful (*referring to taste*) mante
department (*political division*) suyu
dew chhulla; **for dew to appear** chhulla(mu)y
die, to wañuy
difficult sasa
dig a well, to puhyuchay; **to dig irrigation channels** tahllay
dinner ch'isi mikhuy, tuta mikhuy
dirt qhelli
dirty qhelli; **to dirty** qhellichay
dish (gritty) made of wheat flour, barley, corn, salt, and lard sankhu
dish, salt kachi churanacha
distinguished k'acha

district (*political division*) suyu
ditch, irrigation llarq'a
do, to imanay, ruway, ruray, ruay; nay; **to do in that way** hinay; **to do in this way** hinay; **do not** (*in a command*) ama
doctor hampeh, hampikamayoh, (*a female*) midika, (*a male*) midiku
dog alqo
domesticated or domestic animal uywa; **to raise domesticated or domestic animals** uyway
don (*title of respect used with a man's first name*) dun
"doña" (*title of respect used with a married woman's first name*) duña
donkey asnu
don't (*in a command*) ama
door punku
dove urpi; **small dove, grey in color, with the eyes surrounded by bright blue circles** kukuli
down ura(y); **down to** -kama; **to fall down** urmakuy; **to get down** uraykuy; **to sit down** ti(y)akuy
dress wistidu; **to dress (someone)** p'acha(lli)chiy [*Note that instead of the word for "clothing," p'acha, any article of clothing, such as poncho, punchu, can be substituted to convey the idea of putting on that item.*]
dressed, to get p'acha(lli)kuy [*Note that instead of the word for "clothing," p'acha, any article of clothing, such*

as poncho, punchu, *can be substituted to convey the idea of putting on that item.]*
dried gourd *(used as a drinking cup)* mathi; **frozen dried potatoes** ch'uñu
drink uhyana, uhyay; **to drink** uhyay; **to drink maté** matey
drinkable uhyana
drive, to *(animals)* qhati(ri)y
driver *(of a vehicle)* chufir; *(of animals)* qhatiri; **llama driver** apiri
drum wankar
drunk machasqa; **drunk, to get** machay
dry ch'aki; **to dry** ch'akichay; **to make dry** ch'akichiy
dry bean, variety of *(referring to a multiple variety that includes lima beans, butter beans, and kidney beans)* purutu, chuwi; **variety of dry beans, boiled and served as a side dish** chuwimut'i
duck pili
during *(a day, a part of a day, a time period)* -ta; *(with a month, a part of a month, a week, a season, and a year)* -pi
dusk ch'isiyay
dust ñut'uhallp'a; **to become dust** ñut'uhallp'ayay; **to become covered with dust** ñut'uhallp'ayapuy; **to get covered with dust** ñut'uhallp'ayapuy
dusty, to get ñut'uhallp'ayay
dye, to tullpuy

E

each sapa; **each other** -naku
ear, ears *(inner ear[s])* uyarina; *(outer ear[s])* ninri, rinri
early morning paqarin
earring rinriwal(l)qa
earth *(planet)* pacha; *(soil)* allp'a, hallp'a
earth oven *(a hole in the ground with hot clods of dirt)* **for roasting tubers and/or fruits** wathi(y)a(na)
easy mana sasachu
eat, to mikhuy
eating mikhuy
edge pata, kinra
edible, something mikhuy
egg runtu
eight pusah; *(borrowing from Spanish, used in telling time)* uchu; **eight hundred** pusahpachah; **eight o'clock** *(borrowing from Spanish)* las uchu
eighty pusahchunka
either *or* **or** -chus; **either ... or ...** *(in a question)* -chu ... -chu
elbow, elbows kukuchu, makimoqo
elegant k'acha
eleven chunkauhniyoh; *(borrowing from Spanish, used in telling time)* unsi; **eleven o'clock** *(borrowing from Spanish)* las unsi
embarrassed, to be p'enqakuy
empty ch'usah; **to empty** ch'usahyachiy
encircle, to muyuy
enclosure kancha; **to make an enclosure** kanchay
end, to tukuy; **to end (...)**

tukuy (. . . -ta); **to end up**
*(showing transformation
from one state to another)*
. . . -man tukuy; **for
something to end** wañuy
engineer inhiñiru
England Inlatira
English inles, inlis
enter, to yaykuy; **to enter this
way** *(in this direction)*
yaykumuy
even if -pas, -pis
evening ch'isi; **in the evening**
*(before dark, after an hour is
mentioned)* ch'isimanta,
*(before dark, without an
hour given)* ch'isiman
every sapa
everybody tukuy
everyone tukuy
everything tukuy
evident sut'i
evil sahra
excess yallin
exclusively -kama
excrement aka
excuse, to panpachay *(used
idiomatically in
apologizing)*; **Excuse me!**
(apologizing to one person)
¡Panpachaway!
expensive chani(n)yoh,
chanin(ni)yoh; **least
expensive** chaninrapuni; pisi
chanin(ni)yohpuni, mana
chanin(ni(yohpuni; **most
expensive**
chanin(ni)yohpuni
exquisite sumah
extend, to mant'ay
eye, eyes ñawi; **to keep an eye
on** t'ohriy, yuyay

F
face uya
facial hair sunk'a
facing chinpa, qaylla
fall *(autumn)* puquypacha
fall, to urmay
family ayllu
far karu
fare pasahi
farm chahra; **to farm** chahray,
(to do farm work) llank'ay
farm field chahra
farmer allp'a llank'ah; hallp'a
llank'ah; llank'ah; chahrah
farmland chahra
farthest karupuni
fast ushqay
fat *(noun and adjective)* wira
father ta(y)ta; yaya
**fava beans served as a side
dish, boiled** abasmut'i
feast, to pachamankay
February hiwriru(killa)
feed, to qaray, mikhuchiy; **to
breast feed** ñuñuy; **to feed
with mother's milk** ñuñuy
feel hunger, to yarqay
feel like, to *(the meaning of the
verb)* -naya
feet chaki
**fellow townsman/
townswoman** llahtamasi
female warmi; *(referring to
animals)* china
ferocious phiña
festival phista
few, a uh
fiancé qhari siminisqa
fiancée warmi siminisqa
field chahra
fifty phishqachunka
find, to tariy, tinkuy
fine allillam, allillan

fine waleh
finger, fingers ruk'a, **index finger** t'upsina ruk'a, **middle finger** chawpiruk'a, **ring finger** siwillina ruk'a, **little finger** sullk'aruk'a
fingernail sillu
finish, to tukuy; **to finish (. . .)** tukuy (. . . -ta)
fire nina; **to start the/a fire** ninariy
firewood llant'a, ruphana llant'a; **firewood cutter** llant'ah; **firewood seller** llant'ah
first *(before)* -rah; *(in order)* ñawpah(-ñeqe[n])
first cousin *(female) (of a female)* sispañaña; *(female) (of a male)* sispapana; *(male) (of a female)* sispatura; *(male) (of a male)* sispawawqe
fish challwa; **to fish** challway; **place where fish is sold** challwaqhatu; **fish stall** challwaqhatu; **fish stand** challwaqhatu
fisherman challwah, piskatur
fit, to yaykuy
five phishqa; **five** *(borrowing from Spanish, used in telling time)* sinku; **five hundred** phishqapachah; **five o'clock** *(borrowing from Spanish)* las sinku
flag bandira
flap, to *(wings)* raphraykachay
flat t'asl(l)a *(referring to fields and the like)* t'asl(l)a; **flat land** pampa, panpa
flatten, to *(used idiomatically in apologizing)* panpachay

flavorful misk'i
flight, to take phaway
flock tama
flock tropa, pampa
floor panpa; **floor throw** mant'a
flour hak'u
flower t'ika; **wildflower** wayta; **to flower** t'ikay
flute, Andean reed qhena
fly ch'uspi
fly, to phaway
fog pachaphuyu
fold, to sip'uy
following day, the q'ayantin
food mikhuna, mikhuy; **to serve food** mikhuchiy, qaray
foodstuff mikhunakuna
foot chaki; *(base)* siki
foot plow *(traditional Andean foot plow)* chakitahlla *(a type of long-handled dibble with a flat end, close to which is a pedal for pressuring the tool with a foot. At times, somewhat higher up is a handle at right angles to the main one for the user to bend toward the ground, to guide and place pressure on the plow. This often is used to dig irrigation channels, to make holes for planting seeds, to loosen the soil.)*
for *(because)* -rayku, *(because of)* imaraykuchus; -manta; -pah; **for a musical instrument to make a sound** waqay; **for a child to grow to maturity** runayay; **for a domesticated or domestic animal to grow** uywayay; **for seeds and**

saplings to grow into full-sized trees mallkiyay *[Note: Adding -ya-y to any noun designating a plant or animal gives the same idea of growing to maturity.]*; **for dew to appear** chhulla(mu)y; **for a rainbow to come out** k'uychi(mu)y; **for day to break** p'unchayay, paqariy; **for night to fall** tutayay, ch'isiyay; **for it to be hot** *(weather)* rupha(mu)y, q'oñi(mu)y; **for it to be cold** *(weather)* chiri(mu)y; **for there to be frost** chhullunka(mu)y; **for there to be light** k'anchay; **for one to be able** atikuy; **for one to go to the other side of a stream, being helped by the offered hand of the one staying behind, and then offering his or her hand to help the other person across** chinpachinakuy; **for someone to pray** uyllapuy; **for something to end** wañuy; **for there to be** kay, ti(y)ay; *(used in a construction with a verbal object pronoun to convey the idea of "to have," see numbers 16, 17, 18, and 19 in Section III: Quechua Grammar Notes)* kapuy
forehead mat'i
forest sach'asach'a
forested sach'asach'a
forget, to qonqay
foretell, to *(to tell someone's fortune)* watuy

fortuneteller watoh
forty tawachunka
four tawa; **four** *(borrowing from Spanish, used in telling time)* kwaru; **four hundred** tawapachah; **four o'clock** *(borrowing from Spanish)* las kwaru
fox atoh, lari
frayed border chhapu
freeze, to *(weather)* qasa(mu)y
frequently *(affixed to the stem of a verb that is not one of motion)* -paya
Friday ch'askachaw, wirnis
fried thehtichisqa
friend atillcha, *(a female) (borrowing from Spanish)* amiga, *(a male) (borrowing from Spanish)* amigu; *(a female) (from Spanish "comadre")* kumarí, *(a male)(from Spanish "compadre")* kumpa; *(companion)* masi; **Friend!** *(calling to a female) (from Spanish "comadre")* ¡Kumaríy!, **Friend!** *(calling to a male) (from Spanish "compadre")* ¡Kumparíy!
from -manta; **from time to time** mayninpi
front chinpa, ñawpaqe
frost chhullunka; **for there to be frost** chhullunka(mu)y
frozen khata; **frozen, dried potatoes** ch'uñu
fruit *(edible)* wayu; **place where fruit is sold** wayuqhatu; **fruit stall** wayuqhatu; **fruit stand** wayuqhatu; **fruit store** wayuwasi

fruit *(result, product)* ruru
fruit tree mallki
fry, to thehtichiy
fuel-burning lamp k'anchara
full of underbrush ch'aphsach'aphsa, ch'aphrach'aphra
fun, to gather together to have qhochukuy
future time, a q'aya

G

garbage q'opa
gasoline gasulina; **place where gasoline is sold** gasulina qhatu
gather firewood, to llant'ay; **to gather together** tantakuy; **to gather together to have fun** qhochukuy
gathering qhochu, tanta
gentleman wiraqocha
German aliman
Germany Alimanya
get, to *(to buy)* rantiy; **to get** *(showing transformation from one state to another)* . . . -man tukuy; **to get** *what the meaning of the verb is* -ya *affixed to the stem of the verb*; **to get angry** phiñakuy; **to get burned** ruphachikuy; **to get close** chinpakuy, qayllakuy; **to get cold** chiriyay; **to get covered with dust** ñut'uhallp'ayapuy; **to get covered with mud** t'uruyapuy; **to get dark** *(the day)* ch'isiyay; **to get down** uraykuy; **to get dressed** p'acha(lli)kuy *[Note that instead of the word for "clothing," p'acha, any article of clothing, such as poncho, punchu, can be substituted to convey the idea of putting on that item.]*; **to get drunk** machay; **to get dusty** ñut'uhallp'ayapuy; **to get here** chayamuy; **to get hurt** chirmakuy; **to get lost** chinkay; **to get muddy** t'uruyay; **to get near** qayllakuy; **to get off** uraykuy; **to get on** *(implying that it is difficult to do)* lloq'ay, *(implying that it is not difficult to do)* wichay; wichariy; **to get sick** onqoyay, onqoman tukuy; **to get there** chayay; **to get tired** sayk'uyay; **to get together** tantakuy; **to get together to have fun** qhochukuy; **to get up** hatariy; **to get wet** hoq'oy; **Get away from there.** ¡Hatari!
gift suchi
girl imilla; wamira; **little girl** wawa, **Little girl!** *(in calling to the person)* ¡Waway!; **¡My girl!** *(in calling to the person)* ¡Waway!
give, to qoy; **to give a name** sutichay; **to give off a bad smell** asnay
glad, to be kusikuy
gladden, to kusichiy
go, to riy; *(showing transformation from one state to another)* . . . -man tukuy; *what the meaning of the verb is* -ya *affixed to the*

stem of the verb; **to go away** ripuy; **to go back** kutiy; **to go to the other side of something that one is facing and that is difficult to reach** *(as in the opposite bank of a river, irrigation ditch, gully)* chimpay, chinpay; **to go blind** ñawsayay, ñawsaman tukuy; **to go in circles** muyuy; **to go off** *(away)* ripuy; **to go to** *perform the action of the verb (used with verbs not of motion)* -mu
God Diyus, Tiyus
gold qori
good alli(n); *(elegant, distinguished)* k'acha; *(adjective and interjection used to show a very high degree of excellence)* kusa, *(things)* kusay; sumah, **good looking** sumah; **to have a good time** hawkay
goodbye adiyús
gorge wayq'u
gorgeous k'acha
gourd, dried *(used as a drinking cup)* mathi
grab, to hap'iy
grain muhu
grasp, to hap'iy
grateful for a favor, to be sonqo(n)chay
gray ch'ihchu
great kusa *(adjective and interjection used to show a very high degree of excellence)*
greedy mich'a
green q'omer
greet, to napaykuy

greeting napay
grind, to kutay
grinding stone *(platform used in grinding)* maran
gritty dish made of wheat flour, barley, corn, salt, and lard sankhu
grocer mikhunakunata qhatoh
groceries, the one who sells mikhunakunata qhatoh; **place where groceries are sold** mikhuna qhatu
grocery store mikhuna qhatu, mikhuna wasi
ground pampa, panpa
grove mallki mallki
grow, to *(showing transformation from one state to another)* . . . -man tukuy; *what the meaning of the stem of the verb to which it is attached is* -ya; *(increase in age or size) (people, animals, plants)* wiñay; **to grow up** wiñay; **for a child to grow to maturity** runayay; **for a domesticated or domestic animal to grow** uywayay; **for seeds and saplings to grow into full-sized trees** mallkiyay *[Note: Adding -ya-y to any noun designating a plant or animal gives the same idea of growing to maturity.]*; **to grow dark** *(the day)* ch'isiyay
guanaco wanaku
guest qorpa; **guesthouse** *(traditionally for llama drivers and for their llamas)* qorpawasi

guide pusah; **to guide** *(back, here) (used with people)* pusamuy, *(there) (used mostly with people)* pusay
guinea pig qowi

H
hail chihchi; **to hail** chihchi(mu)y
hair chuhcha; **facial hair** sunk'a
half khuskan
hammer takana; **to hammer** takay
hand, hands maki; **on the other hand** ichaqa
handsome sumah, **most handsome** sumahpuni
happen, to imanay
happy kusisqa; kusi
hard sinchi, sasa
harmonious sumah
harvest aymuray; **to harvest** aymuray, *(with a sickle or scythe)* ichhuy
harvester *(with a sickle or scythe)* ichhoh
hat *(with a brim)* sumwiru
have, to *(used to convey the idea of "to have")* kapuy *(literally, "for there to be")*; **to have a good time** hawkay; **to gather together to have fun** qhochukuy; **to get together to have fun** qhochukuy; **to have to** -na *marker used with a verb that is used in conjunction with a verb, "there is," "there was," and the like, stated or understood, to show obligation (See number 15. Model for Verbs Expressing Obligation in Section III: Quechua Grammar Notes)*
he pay
head uma; **head ache** umananay; **head of hair** chuhcha
headed for -man, -neh
heal, to hampiy
healer hampeh, hampiri; *(with herbs)* maych'a
hear, to uyariy *(when the object of uyariy is a verb, the form used for that verb is the Active (or Present) Participle [verb stem-h])*
heart sonqo
heat q'oñiy, ruphay; **to heat** q'oñiy, ruphachiy, ruphay
heavy llasa
Heh? ¿I?
Hello! ¡Yu!
help yanapa; **to help** yanapay, *(to do the action of the verb to which stem it is attached)* -ysi; **to help someone or to take something to the other side of something that one is facing and that is difficult to reach** *(as in the opposite bank of a river, irrigation ditch, gully)* chinpachiy
her -n
hers, of hers paypata *(she-of)*
herd tama, tropa; **to herd** michiy; qhati(ri)y
herder micheh, qhatiri
here kay; **around here** kaynehpi
Hey! *(very informal)* ¡Chuy!, *(very informal)* ¡Yu!; *(addressing one person) (very informal)* ¡Yaw!, *(addressing more than one*

person) (very informal) ¡Yawkuna!
Hi! ¡Yu!
hide, to pakay; **to hide oneself** pakakuy
high hawa; **high class** qhapah; **high dignitary** apu
hill orqo; **hill in the northwest of the Cuzco, Peru, mountain range that resembles a coca wad being chewed,** pihchu *[Note: In the famous Machu Picchu ruins there are two peaks, the lower known as Machu (old) Pihchu, and the higher as Wayna (young) Pihchu.]*
hilly orqoorqo
his, of his paypata *(he-of)*; **his -** n
hit, to takay
hold, to hap'iy
hole t'oqo
honey lachiwana misk'i
hoof phapa(tu)
horse kawallu
hospital onqohkunawasi, uspital
host, to qorpachay
hostel puñuywasi, qorpachanawasi, samanawasi
hot q'oñi, rupha, ruphay; *(spicy)* haya; **very hot *(temperature)*** rupha; **to be hot** q'oñiy; **for it to be hot *(weather)*** rupha(mu)y, q'oñi(mu)y; **to make hot** q'oñichiy, ruphachiy; **hot spring** armakuna
hotel puñuywasi, qorpachanawasi, samanawasi, tampuwasi
hotel util
hour ura
house wasi; **house where meat is sold** aycha wasi
how imayna; **how** *(in an exclamation)* may; **how many** hayk'a, mashkha; **how much** hayk'a, mashkha
human remains *(cadaver)* aya
humid mik'i
hundred pachah
hunger yarqay; **to cause hunger** yarqay; **to feel hunger** yarqay, yarqachikuy
hurl with a sling, to warak'ay
hurry, to be in a ushqay
hurt k'irisqa; **to hurt** chirmay, k'iriy, nanay; **to hurt oneself** nanachikuy
husband qosa
hut ch'uhlla

I
I ñoqa; **I don't know** -chá *affixed to an interrogative word to convey this meaning*; **I think that** -sina
-ible -na
if *(following a conjugated verb form)* chayqa
if, even -pas
to illuminate k'anchay
illustrious qhapah
in -pi; *(a part of a day)* -ta; *(with a month, a part of a month, a week, a season, and a year)* -pi; **in order to** -pah; **in spite of** -pas, -pis; **in front of** chinpa, qaylla; **the one in charge** kamayoh; **in the morning** *(after an hour*

is mentioned) paqarinmanta; *(without an hour given)* paqarinman; **in the afternoon** *(after an hour is mentioned)* sukhamanta, *(without an hour given)* sukhaman; **in the evening** *(before dark, after an hour is mentioned)* ch'isimanta, *(before dark, without an hour given)* ch'isiman; **in the presence of** qaylla; **in the direction of** -man, -neh, **in this direction** *(used with verbs of motion)* -mu; **in two days** minchha, minchha p'unchaw, minchha diya; **in two weeks** minchha qanchischaw, minchha simana; **in two months** minchha killa; **in two years** minchha wata; **to come in** yaykumuy, yaykuy; **to do in that way** hinay; **to do in this way** hinay; **to enter this way** *(in this direction)* yaykumuy; **to put in between** chawpinchay; **to put in the middle** chawpinchay
Inca inka
incline, to sayay, chi(n)ruy, wihsuy
index finger t'upsina ruk'a
inexpensive chaninnah, chaninra, pisi chanin(ni)yoh, mana chanin(ni)yoh
infect, to q'eay
inform, to willay
infusion of any kind q'oñi unu, q'oñi yaku
inside ukhu; *(when used with verbs of motion)* -yku; **to put inside** ukhunchay
insipid q'ayma; yaku
instrument, for a musical instrument to make a sound waqay
intelligent umayoh
interior ukhu
into -man
iron q'illay, iru
irrigate, to qarpay
irrigation ditch llarq'a
Isn't that right? ¿I?
it pay; -pu; **it seems that** -sina
its, of its paypata *(it-of)*; **its** -n

J

January iniru(killa)
Japan Hapun
jerky ch'arki
job ruana
joint moqo
jug p'uyñu
juice hilli
July hulyu(killa)
jump, to p'itay
June hunyu(killa)
just -lla; *(for emphasis)* -lla; **just** *(exclusively)* -kama; **just a little** asllata
just did -sa- *followed by a preterite (past tense) ending can give this idea*

K

keep an eye on, to t'ohriy, yuyay
kerosine kirusin; **place where kerosine is sold** kirusin qhatu
kick hayt'a; **to kick** hayt'ay

kill, to wañuchiy
kilogram kilu
kilometer kilumitru
kind *(person)* allin kah; **very kind** allinsonqo, urpisonqo; **the one who is kind** allin kah
kindness allinkay
kitchen wayk'una wasi, yanuna wasi
knee, knees chaki moqo, qonqor(i)
kneel, to qonqoriy
know, to rehsiy, yachay; **to know** *(by sight)* rikuy; **I don't know** -chá *affixed to an interrogative word to convey this meaning*; **to let know** willay; **to know each other** rehsinakuy
knowledge yachay

L
lacustrine reed *(Scirpus riparius) (the young shoots of which are used as food in Peru and Bolivia, and the reedy stems of which are used for making fences, boats [usually for one person], and floors)* t'utura
ladies siñuras
lady palla, siñura; **young lady** *(15-20 years old)* sipas
lake qocha, qhocha
lame hanqa
lamp k'anchara, **fuel-burning lamp** k'anchara
land chahra, allp'a, **the one who works the land** chahrah, allp'a llank'ah, hallp'a llank'ah; hallp'a; **flat land** panpa, pampa

landlord patrun
language simi
large hatun, suni; **large town** hatun llahta
largest hatunpuni, sunipuni
lasso, to wask(h)ay
last *(with night, week, month, year)* qayna
last, to unay
latrine akakiti, akawasi, bañu, hisp'aykiti, hisp'aywasi
laundry t'ahsana, t'ahsaykama
laugh asiy; **to laugh** asiy
lavatory pincha, ritriti; *(place to wash hands)* mahchhiku, *(place to wash hands)* mayllaku
laziness qella(kay)
lazy qella(kay); **to be lazy** qellakuy
lead, to *(back, here) (used with people)* pusamuy; *(there) (used mostly with people)* pusay
lead titi
leader kamacheh, pusah
leaf raphi
learn, to yachakuy
least expensive chaninrapuni, pisi chanin(ni)yohpuni, mana chanin(ni)yohpuni
leather qara
leave, to llohsiy, ripuy; *(behind)* saqey
left lloq'e
leg, legs chaki
lend, to *(something consumable, such as money or food, that is to be returned with an equivalent* manuy *(see* mañay*) (with* -manta *affixed to the noun designating the one[s] doing*

the lending, with -ta *affixed to the noun designating the item[s] being lent, and* -man *to the noun[s] designating the one[s] to whom it is/they are being lent); (something that is to be returned as opposed to something consumable, such as money or food, that is to be returned with an equivalent* mañay *(see manuy) (with* -manta *affixed to the noun designating the one[s] doing the lending, with* -ta *affixed to the noun designating the item[s] being lent, and* -man *to the noun[s] designating the one[s] to whom it is/they are being lent)*
less pisi *(amount)*; **a little less as** pisi *(amount)*
let, to saqey; **to let know** willay
let's *command marker [verb stem]*-na; **Let's go!** ¡Haku!
letter qellqa(laqhe), karta; *(of the alphabet)* sanampa
level t'asl(l)a; **to level** panpachay
liar llulla
lid qhata
lie llulla; **to lie** llullakuy
lift, to hoqariy
light *(in color)* sut'i; *(illumination)* k'anchay, *(in weight)* wayrahina(lla); **light blindness** surump'i; **afflicted by light blindness** surump'isqa; **to be afflicted with light blindness** surump'iy; **for there to be** k'anchay
lights, to turn off the k'ancharay
like *[Note: With a verb, it always goes at the end; in a construction with a noun, its location may vary.]* (-)hina; **to like** gustay
liquor tragu
listen (to), to uyariy
little *(size)* huch'uy; *(amount)* pisi; **a little** *(amount)* as; *(amount)* pisi; *(amount; intensity)* chhika; **very little** huch'uysitu; **just a little** asllata; **a little less as** pisi; **a little more** astawan; **a little while** ratu; **little boy** wawa, **Little boy!** *(in calling to the person)* ¡Wawáy!; **little girl** wawa, **Little girl!** *(in calling to the person)* ¡Wawáy!; **little finger** sullk'aruk'a; **little toe** sullk'aruk'a
littlest huch'uypuni
live, to ti(y)akuy
llama llama; **llama driver** apiri; **crude, thick, braided llama wool rope** purwa
load winay; **to load** chahnay
loan *(of money)* manu
location laru
lodge, to *(someone)* qorpachay; **to lodge** *(to stay)* qorpachakuy; **place to lodge** puñuywasi, qorpachanawasi
long suni; **a long time** unay
longest sunipuni
look at, to qhaway *(when the object of* qhaway *is a verb, the form used for that verb is the Active (or Present) Participle [verb stem-*h*])*, rikuy *(when the object of* rikuy *is a verb, the form*

*used for that verb is the Active (or Present) Participle [verb stem-*h*]*)
loosen the soil, to tahllay
lose, to chinkay
lot, a *(intensity)* ancha; **with a lot of** -sapa
luggage q'epi
lunch khuskan diya mikhuy
lupine seeds *(Lupinus mutabilis)* tarwi
lupine seeds *(Lupinus mutabilis)*, **boiled, served as a side dish** tarwimut'i

M

ma'am mama, mamáy; siñura, siñuráy; ¡**Ma'am!** *(informal)* Mamáy!
Machu Picchu Machu Pihchu [*Note: In the famous Machu Picchu ruins there are two peaks, the lower known as* **Machu** *(old)* **Pihchu**, *and the higher as* **Wayna** *(young)* **Pihchu**. *See* **pihchu**.]
magnificent kusa *(adjective and interjection used to show a very high degree of excellence)*
make *(what the meaning of the verb is)* -chi; *(what the noun or adjective to which it is attached is)* [*in the formation of a verb*] -cha; **to make** ruay, ruray, ruway; nay; **to make a wall** perqay; **to make an enclosure** kanchay; **to make bread** t'antachay; **to make chicha** *(made from corn)* aqhachay; **to make shoes** chhichay; **to make less salty** kachinnay; **to make saltier** kachipay; **to make mud** t'uruchay; **to make a mistake** pantay; **to make climb on** lloq'achiy; **to make get on** lloq'achiy; **to make beautiful** sumahchay; **to make hot** q'oñichiy, ruphachiy; **to make cold** chiri(ya)chiy; **to make dry** ch'akichiy; **to make wet** hoq'ochay; **to make thirsty** ch'akichiy; **to make (become, go) blind** ñawsayachiy; **to make (become, get) sick** onqoyachiy; **for a musical instrument to make a sound** waqay
male *(referring to animals and to plants that have only stamens)* orqo; *(referring to a person)* qhari
man qhari, runa, wiraqocha; **man from the city** hatunllahtaruna; **young man** *(10-14 years old)* wamra, *(18-30 years old)* wayna
mantilla iñaka
many ashkha; **many things** imaymana
March marsu(killa)
margin kinra
market qhatu, mirkadu, plasa, kancha; **to market** qhatuy; **market day** qhatudiya
mat mant'a
maté *(tea-like infusion)* mate; **to drink maté** matey
May mayu(killa)
maybe ichás
maybe -chá, -chus
mayor llahta kamayoh, alkaldi

meadow waylla
meal mikhuna
mean killaku, sahra
mean, to niyta munay, ñiyta munay
meanest sahrapuni
meat aycha; **sun-dried meat** ch'arki; **meat market** aycha qhatu; **meat stall** aycha qhatu; **meat stand** aycha qhatu; **house where meat is sold** aycha wasi; **place where meat is sold** aycha qhatu; **the one who sells meat** aychata qhatoh
mechanic mikaniku
medicine hampi
medium *(in size)* tahsa
meet, to *(to get together)* tantakuy; *(to encounter)* tupay; *(someone for the first time)* rehsinakuy
meeting tanta
mid-afternoon snack khuskan sukha mikhuy
middle chawpi; **middle finger** chawpiruk'a; **to put in the middle** chawpinchay
midnight chawpituta, khuskantuta
milk wilali, lichi; **place where milk is sold** wilali qhatu, lichi qhatu; **to feed with mother's milk** ñuñuy; **mother's milk** ñuñu
million hunu
mine, of mine ñoqahpata *(I-of)*
mine *(of minerals)* qhoya
miner qhoyaruna
minute minutu; *(figuratively)* ratu
mistake pantay; **to make a mistake** pantay

molar, molars marankiru
moment ratu
monetary unit of Bolivia pisu, **of Ecuador** sukri, **of Peru** inti, sul
Monday killachaw, lunis, lunis diya
money qolqe
month killa
moon killa
moon-shaped stone used as a pestle with a maran maranuña
more aswan; **a little more** astawan; **some more** astawan
more or less -neh
morning paqarin; **in the morning** *(after an hour is mentioned)* paqarinmanta; *(without an hour given)* paqarinman
mortar *(platform used in grinding)* maran
mosquito ch'uspi
most *(with an adjective)* -puni; **most expensive** chanin(ni)yohpuni; **most valuable** chanin(ni)yohpuni
mother mama
mother's milk ñuñu; **to feed with mother's milk** ñuñuy
mountain orqo
mouse huk'ucha
mouth simi
Move aside.¡Hatari!, **Move away.**¡Hatari!
move, to kuyuchiy; **to move** *(something or someone)* **away** karunchay
much *(intensity)* ancha; *(quantity)* ashkha; **too much** millay, sinchi

mud t'uru; **to become mud** t'uruyay **to become covered with mud** t'uruyapuy; **to get covered with mud** t'uruyapuy
muddy t'urusapa; **to get muddy** t'uruyay
mule mulo
mules, team of masa; mulomasa
muleteer qhatiri
musical instrument, for a musical instrument to make a sound waqay
my -y; **My boy!** *(in calling to the person)* ¡Waway!; **My girl!** *(in calling to the person)* ¡Waway!

N

name suti; **to name** *(give a name)* sutichay
nandu *(American ostrich)* suri
narrow k'iski
navigate, to wanp'uy
near qaylla, sispa; **to get near** qayllakuy, chinpakuy, sispakuy
nearest sispapuni
neck kunka
necklace piñi, wal(l)qa; **to adorn with a necklace** wal(l)qay
needy wahcha
neither ... nor mana(-tah) ... -chu; *(in a negative statement)* ni(-tah) ... -chu
nephew *(of a female)* qhari mulla; *(of a male)* qhari kuncha
nettle, stinging kisa
never manahayk'ah
nevertheless ichaqa, chaywanpis
new mosoh
next *(week, month, year)* hawa, q'aya; *(in order)* qhepa(n); **next to** larupi; **the next day** q'ayantin
niece *(of a female)* warmi mulla; *(of a male)* warmi kuncha
night tuta; **at night** *(after an hour is mentioned)* tutamanta, *(after dark, without an hour given)* tutaman; **for night to fall** tutayay, ch'isiyay
nightfall ch'isiyay
nine hisq'on, isq'on; *(borrowing from Spanish, used in telling time)* nuiwi; **nine hundred** hisq'onpachah, isq'onpachah; **nine o'clock** *(borrowing from Spanish)* las nuiwi
ninety hisq'onchunka, isq'onchunka
no ma *(apocopation of* mana*)*, mana, ni
no one mana pipas, mana pipis, nipi
nobody mana pipas, mana pipis, nipi
non-domesticated animal orqo uywa
noon chawpidiya, khuskandiya
nor, neither ... mana(-tah) ... -chu
nose senqa
not mana, ma *(apocopation of* mana*)*; **not anybody** mana pipas, mana pipis, nipi; **not anyone** mana pipas, mana pipis, nipi; **not anything** ni ima; **not yet** manarah; **not ... or ...** mana(-tah) ...

-chu; **not ... or ...** *(in a negative statement)* ni(-tah) ... -chu
nothing ni ima, mana ima
November nuwimwri(killa)
now kunan; **right now** kunita(n), kunan pacha
nurse, to ñuñuy

O

oca *(Oxalis tuberosa) (a variety of wood sorrel, cultivated for its edible tubers)* oqa
occupation ruana
occur, to imanay
October uktuwri(killa)
of -manta
of *(affixed to a word ending in a vowel)* -h, -hpa, -hpata, -hta; *(affixed to a word ending in a consonant)* -pa, -pata; **of course** imamanaqa, imayna manaqa, -puni
off, to get uraykuy
office uficina
often *(affixed to the stem of a verb that is not one of motion)* -paya
often, (very) sapa kutillan
old thanta; *(a female)* paya; *(a male)* machu, rukhu; *(deteriorated, out of style, in ruins)* mawk'a; *(historically)* ñawpa
older *(in rank, in age) (people)* kurah; *(in age) (a female)* aswan paya; *(in age) (a male)* aswan machu, aswan rukhu
oldest *(in rank, in age) (people)* kurah; *(in age) (a female)* aswan paya; *(in age) (a male)* aswan machu, aswan rukhu
on -pi,-ta; *(a date)* -pi; *(a part of a month)* -pi; *(a day, "time[s]" or "occasion[s]")* -ta; **on** hawa, **on top of** hawa; **on the other hand** ichaqa; **to be on the verge of** *(the meaning of the verb)* -naya; **to get on** wichariy, *(implying that it is not difficult to do)* wichay; **to put on** *(an article of clothing)* [noun designating the article]-lli-y; **to put on top** hawanchay
once uh kutita; **once more** uhtawan; **once in a while** mayninpi
one uh; -qa *(affixed to an adjective making it a noun and thus conveying the idea of "one")*; -qa *(emphatic marker used to convey the idea of the non-existent "one")*; **one other** uh; **one can** atikuy; **the one in charge** kamayoh; **one o'clock** *(borrowing from Spanish)* la una; **one of these days** q'aya minchha
one that, the mayqenchus; *(used with things)* imachus
one who, the *(affixed to the stem of a verb)* -h; mayqenchus, pichus
onion siwulla
only -lla
open *(referring to fields and the like)* t'asl(l)a; kichasqa *(opposite of "closed")*
open, to kichay
opossum q'arachupa
opposite bank of a river,

irrigation ditch, gully, and the like chinpa
or *or* **either** -chus; **either . . . or . . .** *(in a question)* -chu . . . chu; **not . . . or . . .** *(in a negative statement)* ni(-tah) . . . -chu. mana(-tah) . . . -chu
orange *(color)* willapi
orchard mallki mallki
order, to *(to command)* kamachiy
ostrich, American (nandu) suri
other uh; **the other** wah; **the other day** qaninpa (diya); **the other side of something that one is facing and that is difficult to reach** chinpa; **on the other hand** ichaqa
others, the wahkuna
our *(excluding the person[s] addressed)* -yku; *(including the person[s] addressed)* -ncheh
ours, of ours *(excluding the person[s] addressed)* ñoqaykohpata *(we[excluding the person(s) addressed]-of)*; *(including the person[s] addressed)* ñoqanchehpata *(we[including the person(s) addressed]-of))*
out, to throw winch'uy
outhouse akakiti, akawasi, hisp'aykiti, hisp'aywasi
outside hawa; **outside** *(part of something)* hawapatan
over to -kama
owner apu
oxen, team of yunta

P
P.M. *(after dark, after an hour is mentioned)* tutamanta
paint, to llip'iy
painter llip'eh, pintur
pair of identical or similar items masa
panpipes antara
pants *(singular) (typical of the rural areas)* wara, *(singular) (modern style)* pantalun
paper papil
paramo *(high, barren Andean plateau)* purun pampa, purun panpa
pardon, to panpachay *(used idiomatically in apologizing)*
parents ta(y)tamama
part *(location)* hawa
pass, to pasay
passage pasahi
pastureland waylla
path ñan, yan
paved road awtuñan
pay, to pagay; **to pay attention** yuyay
pencil lapis
people runa
permit, to saqey *(when the object of* saqey *is a verb, the form used for that verb is the Active (or Present) Participle [verb stem-h])* **to permit** *(what the meaning of the verb is)* -chi
person runa
pestle *(moon-shaped stone used as a pestle with a maran)* maranuña
petticoat, cotton ahsu, ukhuna
pharmacist *(a female)* pharmasiyutika, *(a male)* hampiranteh

pharmacy hampiwasi, wutika
physician hampeh, hampikamayoh, *(a female)* midika, *(a male)* midiku
pick up, to hoqariy
picnic pachamanka; **to hold a barbecue or picnic** pachamankay
pilfer, to hoqariy
pig khuchi
pin *(broach)* t'ipana
pit, silo kulluna
pitcher yuru
place laru, pacha, kiti; hawa *(location)*; **place where something is sold** qhatu; **place where vizcachas can be found** wisk'achani
plane, to llahllay
plant yura; **to plant** *(to sow)* tarpuy; **to plant trees** mallkichay *[Note: Adding -cha-y to any noun designating a plant gives the idea of planting it.]*
plate, clay p'uku; **deep plate** *(usually the bottom part of a gourd)* chu(w)a; **shallow flat plate** *(usually the bottom part of a gourd)* phankachu(w)a
play, to puhllay
play a wind or stringed musical instrument, to waqachiy; **to play the qhena** *(Andean reed flute)* qhenatawaqachiy
plaza plasa
pleasant *(things)* kusay
please allichu; *(marker to soften the request/"please")* -ri *(repetition of -ri emphasizes the softening)*
pleasing sumah
plow *(any type)* yapuna; *(simple, rustic)* tahlla; *(traditional Andean foot plow)* chakitahlla *(a type of long-handled dibble with a flat end, close to which is a pedal for pressuring the tool with a foot. At times, somewhat higher up is a handle at right angles to the main one for the user to bend toward the ground, to guide and place pressure on the plow. This often is used to dig irrigation channels, to make holes for planting seeds, to loosen the soil.)*; **to plow** yapuy; *(with a simple, rustic plow)* tahllay; *(with a chakitahlla)* chakitahllay
point, to t'ohpiy, t'upsiy; **to point out** *(with something)* t'ohpiy, t'upsiy
poke, to t'ohpiy, t'upsiy
porridge/soup made with corn, potatoes, onion, sometimes with meat, with lard, hot pepper, and salt, spicy lawa, llahwa
poised k'acha
policeman pulisia
"pollera" *(typical Andean skirt)* pullira
poncho punchu
poor mana kahniyoh, mana qolqesapa, mana qolqeyoh, wahcha
pork khuchiaycha
porter apah, astah
pot *(of clay)* manka
pot-bellied wihsati
potable uhyana

potato papa; **potatoes, frozen, dried** ch'uñu
powerful qhapah
prairie pampa, panpa; waylla; **barren prairie** purun pampa, purun panpa
pray, to uyllay; **for someone to pray** uyllapuy; **place to pray** uyllayma; **prayer** uylla
preceding day, the qaynantin
pregnant *(animal)* uñayoh, *(person)* wawayoh
prepare lawa, to laway
prepare llahwa, to llahway
prescribe remedies, to hampiy
presence ñawpaqe
present *(gift)* suchi
pretend to be the one who [verb], to tukuy *[verb stem]* -h *(Active [or Present] Participle)*
pretty k'achitu, **pretty** sumah
price chani(n)
prick, to khishkay
prior time, a qayna
probably -sina
professional dancer tusohkamayoh
professor *(a male)* maystru, *(a female)* maystra
promise, to siminiy
proprietor patrun
provisions mikhunakuna
pulverize, to ñut'uy
puna *(the Andean highlands)* sallqa
purify, to *(said of water)* ch'uyay
purple kulli, sani
pus q'ea
put, to churay; **to put in between** chawpinchay; **to put in the middle** chawpinchay; **to put inside** ukhunchay; **to put on** *(an article of clothing)* [noun designating the article]-lli-y; **to put on top** hawanchay; **to put** *(something)* **underneath** uranchay; **to put less salt** kachinnay

Q

Quechua qheshwa, runasimi
quickly usqhayta, *[verb stem]* -rqo

R

rabbit *(in Bolivia)* kastilla qowi, *(in Peru)* lima qowi
raft wanp'u(y); **to raft** wanp'uy
rain para(y); **rain storm** paraqunchuy, paratamya; **to rain** para(mu)y
rainbow k'uychi; **for a rainbow to come out** k'uychi(mu)y
rainy paraysapa
rather weak phuchu
ravine wayq'u
read, to qellqarimay
reading qellqarima
reap, to ichhuy
receive, to chaskiy
rectangular tawak'uchu hina
red puka
reed, lacustrine *(Scirpus riparius) (the young shoots are used as food in Peru and Bolivia, and the reedy stems are used for making fences, boats [usually for one and floors)* t'utura
reed flute, Andean qhena; **to play the reed flute (qhena)** qhenatawaqachiy

regal k'acha
region suyu
regret, to llakikuy
relative by marriage sispa ayllu
relatives ayllu
remedies, to prescribe hampiy
remedy hampi
remove foreign objects, to *(from seeds)* ch'uyay
repair, to allinchay; **to repair shoes** chhichay, phapa(tu)y
repeat, to uhtawan niy
reside, to ti(y)akuy
respond, to hay niy, hay ñiy
rest, the wahkuna
rest, to sama(ri)y
restaurant mikhuywasi
restroom pincha, ritriti
return, to *(here)* kutimuy; *(there)* kutiy
revolve, to muyuy
rice arus
rich kahniyoh, qhapah, qolqesapa, qolqeyoh
right paña *(opposite of "left")*; **right** *(emphatic)* -qa; **right** *(with adverbs of time or place)* -pacha; **right now** kunan pacha, kunita(n)
ring siwi; **ring finger** siwillina ruk'a
ripen, to poqoy
ripening poqoy
river mayu
road ñan, yan
roadway awtuñan
roast kanka; **to roast** kankay; **to roast tubers and/or fruits in a wathi(y)a(na)** wathi(y)ay
roasted kankasqa
rock qaqa

rocky qaqaqaqa
roof qhata
room *(area for a specific activity such as cooking)* wasi
rope wask(h)a; **thick, crude rope made of braided llama wool** purwa; **thin rope** watu
rotate, to muyuy
rotation muyu(y)
rough chhapuchhapu
round muyu(y), muyuyhina
run, to phaway
rush *(plant)* matara
rustic sandal ushut'a

S

's *(affixed to a word ending in a vowel)* -h, -hpa, -hpata, -hta; *(affixed to a word ending in a consonant)* -pa, -pata
s' *(affixed to a word ending in a vowel)* -h, hpa, -hpata, -hta; *(affixed to a word ending in a consonant)* -pa, -pata
sack wayaqa, winay; **to sack** winay
sad llakisqa, phutisqa; **to be sad** llakikuy, phutikuy
said *(referring the noun to which it is affixed)* -qa
salt kachi; **to salt** kachinchay; **to salt a little** kachiykachiy; **to add more salt** kachipay; **to put less salt** kachinnay; **place to put salt** kachi churanacha; **salt cellar** kachi churanacha, **salt dish** kachi churanacha
saltier, to make kachipay
salty kachi, **very salty** kachikachi; **to make less**

salty kachinnay
salutation napay
salute, to napaykuy
same kiki
sand aqo, t'iu
sandal, rustic ushut'a
sandy aqoaqo, aqosapa, t'iut'iu
sandy t'iusapa
sash worn by men chumpi
Saturday k'uychichaw, sawaru
Say there! *(very informal)* ¡Yaw!
say, to niy, ñiy
scarf, shoulder nañaka
school yachaywasi, iskwiyla
scratch, to rachiy
scythe ichhuna; **to cut with a scythe or sickle** ichhuy
seamstress warmi siraykamayoh
season *(time period)* mit'a; *(of the year)* pachamit'a
seat ti(y)ana
second iskay kah, iskayñeqe(n); uh qhepa(n)
see, to rikuy *(when the object of rikuy is a verb, the form used for that verb is the Active (or Present) Participle [verb stem-h])*, qhaway *(when the object of qhaway is a verb, the form used for that verb is the Active (or Present) Participle [verb stem-h])*
seeds, lupine *(Lupinus mutabilis)* tarwi
seems that, it -sina
seer watoh
self *(reflexive marker)* -ku
sell, to qhatuy, windiy, rantiy
seller of firewood llant'ah
selves *(reflexive marker)* -ku

send, to *(in this direction)* kachamuy; **to send** kachay *(when the object of kachay is a verb, the form used for that verb is the Active (or Present) Participle [verb stem-h])*
September sitimwri(killa)
serve food, to qaray, mikhuchiy
set, to *(referring to the sun, moon, etc.)* pakakuy, yaykuy
seven qanchis, *(borrowing from Spanish, used in telling time)* siti; **seven hundred** qanchispachah; **seven o'clock** *(borrowing from Spanish)* las siti
seventy qanchischunka
sew, to siray
sewer pincha
sewing siray
shade llanthu
shady llanthusapa
shake, to kharkatiy
shallow mana ukhu
shawl awayu, **colorful woven shawl** llihlla
she pay
sheep uwiha
shepherd micheh
shepherd, to michiy
shine, to k'anchay
shirt kamisa
shiver, to kharkatiy
shoe chhicha, phapa(tu); **shoe repairman** chhichaykamayoh, phapa(tu)kamayoh; **shoe store** chhichawasi, phapa(tu) qhatu; **place where shoes are sold** phapa(tu) qhatu
shoemaker chhichaykamayoh, phapa(tu)kamayoh, sapatiru

shop *(workshop)* wasi; **blacksmith's shop** q'illay takana wasi; **butcher shop** aycha qhatu; **carpenter's shop** llahllaykamayoh wasi; **silversmith's shop** qolqe qhatu; **tailor's shop** siraywasi; **tinsmith's shop** piltikamayoh wasi
shore pata
short huch'uy; **very short** huch'uysitu
shortest huch'uypuni
shoulder rihra; **shoulder scarf** nañaka
shout, to ch'ahway
shouting ch'ahwa
show, to rikuchiy
shred, to ñut'uy
shrub sach'ara, sach'a, yura
shut, to wisq'ay
sick onqosqa; **to be sick** onqoy; **to become sick** onqoyay, onqoman tukuy; **to get sick** onqoyay, onqoman tukuy; **to make sick** onqo(ya)chiy
sicken, to onqoyachiy
sickle ichhuna; **to cut with a sickle or scythe** ichhuy
sickness onqo(y)
side kinra
side dish of boiled fava beans abasmut'i; **of a variety of boiled dry beans** chuwimut'i
sign sanampa
silo pit kulluna
sink or wash basin where one can wash clothes, hair, or anything else that can absorb water t'ahsakuna; **sink or wash basin where one can wash up or wash anything that cannot absorb water** mahchhikuna, mayllakuna
silver qolqe
silversmith qolqe takah; **silversmith's shop** qolqe qhatu
since -pacha
sing, to takiy, *(birds)* waqay
singer takeh
sir ta(y)ta, *(quite formal, used only by native speakers of Quechua when addressing urban residents or foreigners)* wiraqocha; siñur; **Sir!** *(informal)* ¡Tata! *(shortened form of* ¡Tayta!*)*; **Sir!** *(somewhat formal)* ¡Ta(y)táy!
sister *(of a female)* ñaña, *(of a male)* pana
sit (down), to ti(y)akuy
site laru
six sohta, *(borrowing from Spanish, used in telling time)* sis; **six hundred** sohtapachah; **six o'clock** *(borrowing from Spanish)* las sis
sixty sohtachunka
size chhikan
skill -kama; **the one with skill** kamayoh
skillful kamayoh
skinny tullu
skirt mihlla; pullira/"pollera" *(typical Andean skirt)*
skunk añas, añathuya
sleep puñuy; **to sleep** puñuy
sleeping puñuy
sling shot warak'a, **sling to hurl stones** warak'a; **to hurl with a sling** warak'ay

slip, to llusk'akuy
slippery llusk'a
small huch'uy; **very small** huch'uysitu; **small dove, grey in color, with the eyes surrounded by bright blue circles** kukuli
smallest huch'uypuni
smart challi
smell, bad asna; **to smell bad** asnay
smell, to *(to use one's sense of smell)* muskiy; **to smell** *(to give off aroma)* q'apay
smile asiriy; **to smile** asiriy
snack, mid-afternoon khuskan sukha mikhuy
snake amaru
snow rit'i; **snow storm** rit'iqunchuy, rit'itamya; **to snow** rit'i(mu)y
snowy rit'iysapa
soak, to hoq'ochay
sober ch'aki sonqo
soil allp'a, hallp'a
sold, place where something is qhatu
soldier suldadu
some as; uh; **some more** astawan; **some people** uhkuna
somebody uh; pi(lla)pas, pi(lla)pis; mayqen(lla)pas, mayqen(lla)pis
someone uh; pi(lla)pas, pi(lla)pis; mayqen(lla)pas, mayqen(lla)pis
something uh; ima, ima(lla)pas, ima(lla)pis; mayqen(lla)pas, mayqen(lla)pis; **something edible** mikhuy; **something to eat** mikhuna; **something to drink** uhyana
sometimes kutikunata, mayninpi
son *(of a female)* (qhari) wawa, *(of a male)* churi
song takiy
soothsayer watoh
soroche *(Andean altitude sickness)* suru(h)chi; **afflicted with soroche** suru(h)chisqa; **to be afflicted with soroche** suru(h)chiy
sorrow, to cause llakiy; **to cause oneself sorrow** llakikuy
sorry, to be very phutikuy
sound, for a musical instrument to make a waqay
sound thunder makes qhon
soup, very thick lawa, llahwa; **soup consisting basically of ground corn or wheat, water, and meat** ch'aqi; **spicy soup/porridge made with corn, potatoes, onion, sometimes with meat, with lard, hot pepper, and salt** lawa, llahwa
sour haya
sow, to tarpuy
space between arms in which one can carry something apa
Spanish kastillanu
speak, to rimay, parlay
spheric muyu(y)
spherical muyuyhina
spicy porridge/soup made with corn, potatoes, onion, sometimes with meat, with lard, hot pepper, and salt lawa, llahwa

spider, big, poisonous apasanka
spin, to phushkay, qanqoy
spit for roasting kankana
spit, to thoqay
spite of, in -pas, -pis
spread out, to mant'ay
spring *(season)* chirawpacha, *(of water)* puhyu
sprout, to p'utuy
squander, to wihch'uy
square tawak'uchu hina
stall qhatu; **bread stall** t'antaqhatu; **fish stall** challwaqhatu; **fruit stall** wayuqhatu; **meat stall** aycha qhatu
stand qhatu; **bread stand** t'antaqhatu; **fish stand** challwaqhatu; **fruit stand** wayuqhatu; **meat stand** aycha qhatu
stand up, to hatariy, tiyariy
standing, to be sayay
star qoyllur
start, to -ri *(marker indicating to start/to begin to do the action indicated by the verb)*; **to start the/a fire** ninariy
stay, to kasakuy, qhepakuy, qorpachakuy, ti(y)akuy
steal, to su(w)ay
steam, to, or to boil the ingredients to prepare "mut'i" mut'iy
steamed or boiled fava beans abasmut'i; **steamed or boiled corn kernels** saramut'i; **steamed or boiled lupine seeds** tarwimut'i; **steamed or boiled variety of dry beans** chuwimut'i; **very common steamed or boiled vegetable side dish** *(of fava beans: "abasmut'i"; of a variety of dry beans: "chuwimut'i"; of corn kernels: "saramut'i"; of lupine seeds: " tarwimut'i")* mut'i
steep sayasqa
stew, a kind of mut'i; **stew prepared with mashed ullucu** *("Ullucus tuberosus," yellow Andean tuber used like potatoes)*, **jerked beef, potatoes, and chili pepper** sahta; **stew/boiled dinner** *(a typical dish in the Cuzco, Peru, area that is made of different kinds of meats, bacon, cabbage, carrots, potatoes, garbanzos, rice, onions, frozen dried potatoes, and spices)* t'inpu
still -rah; **still is, still are** *(affixed to an adjective or to the past participle of a verb, showing continuity of the state brought by the action of that verb)* -raya
sting, to wach'iy
stinging nettle kisa
stingy killaku
string watu
strip of cloth used to tie something watu
stomach wihsa
stone mason perqakamayoh, alwañil
stone rumi; **moon-shaped stone used as a pestle with a maran** maranuña
stony rumisapa

stop, to sayay
store, fruit wayuwasi; **grocery store** mikhuna qhatu, mikhuna wasi
store in a barn, to pirwakuy
storm qunchuy, tamya
storm, rain paraqunchuy, paratamya; **snow storm** rit'qunchuy, rit'itamya; **wind storm** wayraqunchuy, wayra(y)tamya
straight siuh
stranger *(a male)* karuruna, *(a female)* karuwarmi, *(a young man)* karuwayna, *(a young woman)* karusipas
straw *("paja brava")* sikuwa
strength kallpa
stretch out, to mant'ay
stretcher wantu
strong kallpasapa, sinchi
student yachakoh, *(a female)* alumna, *(a male)* alumnu
study, to yachachikuy
stupendous kusaykusay
suddenly *[verb stem]*-rqo
suckle, to ñuñuy
summer ch'akipacha
sun inti
sun-dried meat ch'arki
sunlight ruphay
Sunday apuchaw, intichaw, dumingu
sunny intisapa
sunstroke q'ocha; **afflicted with sunstroke** q'ochasqa; **to be afflicted with sunstroke** q'ochachiy
surplus yallin
sweater chompa
Sweden Swisia
Swedish swiku
sweep, to pichay
sweet misk'i; **syrup-like or thicker byproduct of the making of chicha** misk'i q'eta, q'eta (misk'i)
swell, to punkiy
swim, to wayt'ay
swollen punkisqa

T
table mesa; **table cover** mant'a
take, to *(to carry) (things)* apay, astay; *(to lead, to guide) (there) (used mostly with people)* pusay; *(to lead, to guide) (back, here) (used with people)*, pusamuy; **to take to something or to help someone to the other side of something that one is facing and that is difficult to reach** *(as in the opposite bank of a river, irrigation ditch, gully)* chinpachiy; **to take** *(pilfer)* hoqariy; **to take (hold of)** hap'iy; **to take a bath** armakuy; **to take flight** phaway
talk, to rimay, parlay
tall suni
tallest sunipuni
tamal (h)umint'a
tasteless yaku
tattered thanta
tavern aqhawasi
tailor siraykamayoh; **tailor's shop** siraywasi
tea q'oñi unu, q'oñi yaku, tiy
teach, to yachachiy
teacher yachacheh, *(a female)* maystra, *(a male)* maystru
team (of two animals of the same species) masa; **team**

of mules mulomasa, **team of oxen** wakamasa, yunta
teeth kiru
telephone tilihunu
tell, to niy, ñiy, **to tell** willay; **to tell someone's fortune** watuy
tells fortunes, the one who watoh
temperate valley qheshwa
ten chunka, **ten** *(borrowing from Spanish, used in telling time)* dis; **ten o'clock** *(borrowing from Spanish)* las dis
tent karpa
than -manta
thank, to agradisiy, allichay, sullpay
Thanks! ¡Sullpa!
that *(nearby)* chay, *(over there, farther away)* haqay; **that one** *(nearby)* chay, *(over there, farther away)* haqay; mayqenchus
the one in charge kamayoh
the one that mayqenchus; *(used with things)* imachus
the one who *[verb stem]*-h; mayqenchus, pichus
the one with skill kamayoh
the others wahkuna
theirs, of theirs paykunahpata *(they-of)*
their -nku
them -pu
then (-)a *(as a suffix [-a] or an independent word following what is being stressed; stressed in speech); emphatic word, often untranslatable, used to prolong, reinforce or add emphasis to what is being said* (-)á *(as a suffix [-á] or an independent word following what is being stressed; stressed in speech);* **then/and** *(prolonging the question or statement without adding any specific meaning)* -ri
there *(nearby)* chay, *(over there, farther away)* haqay; **around there** *(nearby)* chaynehpi, *(farther away)* haqaynehpi; **for there to be** kay, ti(y)ay, *(used in a construction with a verbal object pronoun to convey the idea of "to have," see numbers 16, 17, 18, and 19 in Section III: Quechua Grammar Notes)* kapuy, **there is** kan, ti(y)an, **there are** kan, ti(y)an
these kay, kaykuna; **these things** kay, kaykuna
they paykuna
thick rakhu; **thick, crude rope made of braided llama wool** purwa
thief su(w)a
thigh, thighs cha(n)ka
thin llañu
thin rope watu
thing ima
things, many imaymana
think, to yuyay; **to think about** yuyay; **I think that** -sina
third kimsañeqe(n), kimsa kah, iskay qhepa(n)
thirst ch'aki(y)
thirsty ch'akisqa; **to make thirsty** ch'akichiy
thirty kimsachunka, **thirty**

(borrowing from Spanish, used in telling time) trinta
this *(with day, part of a day, week, month, year)* kay, kunan; **this one** kay
thorn khishka
those *(nearby)* chay, chaykuna, *(over there, farther away)* haqay, haqaykuna; **those things** *(nearby)* chay, chaykuna, *(over there, farther away)* haqay, *(over there, farther away)* haqaykuna
thousand waranqa
three kimsa, kinsa, *(borrowing from Spanish, used in telling time)* tris; **three hundred** kimsapachah, kinspachah; **three o'clock** *(borrowing from Spanish)* las tris
thresh, to t'ustuy
thresher *(instrument, machine)* t'ustuna, *(person)* t'ustoh
threshing floor t'ustuna pata
throat tonqor(i)
through -(n)ta, **through** *(as in -ntinta, "all through")* -ta, **all through** -ntinta
throw, to wihch'uy; **to throw away, to throw out** winch'uy; **to throw up** qep(h)nay
thumb, thumbs mamaruk'a
thunder (sound thunder makes) qhon; **to thunder** qhonqhonni(mu)y
Thursday illapachaw, hwywis
thus *[Note: With a verb, it always goes at the end; in a construction with a noun, its location may vary.]* (-)hina
ticket pasahi, wulitu

tie, to watay; **to tie with a string, cord, thin rope, or a strip of cloth** watuchay
tilt, to chi(n)ruy, wihsuy
time pacha, unay, timpu; *(occasion)* kuti; *(period)* mit'a; **a future time** q'aya, **a prior time** qayna; **from time to time** mayninpi; **times** *(occasions)*
tin chapi, pilti, chayanta
tinsmith piltikamayoh; **tinsmith's shop** piltikamayoh wasi
tip, to chi(n)ruy, wihsuy
tire, to sayk'uy
tired sayk'usqa
to *(indicating reaching the place designated)* -ta; *(infinitive marker)* -y; *(indirect object verb marker)* -man; -man, -kama; -neh
today kunan diya
toe, toes (chaki) ruk'a; **little toe** sullk'a ruk'a
toenail sillu
together khuska(n); **to gather together** tantakuy; **to get together** tantakuy
toilet pincha, ritriti
tomorrow q'aya (p'unchaw), q'aya (diya); **the day after tomorrow** minchha, minchha p'unchaw, minchha diya; **two days after tomorrow** minchhantin
tongue *(language and part of the body)* qallu
too yallinyoh; **too much** sinchi, millay
tooth kiru
top uma, pata; **to put on top** hawanchay

totora *(canoe-shaped boat, usually for one person, with rather high, pointed ends, made of lacustrine reed (Scirpus riparius)*, torota, seen on Lakes Titicaca and Poopó, and on some other Andean lakes) t'utura
toward -man; -neh
town llahta; **large town** hatun llahta
townsman, fellow llahtamasi
townswoman, fellow llahtamasi
train trin
translate, to thalliy
translator thalleh
transport, to *(in parts; by repeated "trips") (things)* astay
transporter *(in parts; by repeated "trips") (of things)* astah
trash q'opa
travel, to puriy
traveler pureh
traveling companion pureh masi
tree *(cultivated)* mallki, *(uncultivated)* sach'a
trees, to plant mallkichay *[Note: Adding -cha-y to any noun designating a plant gives the idea of planting it.]*
triangular kinsak'uchuhina
trim, to *(wood)* llahllay
trousers *(singular) (typical of the rural areas)* wara, *(modern style)* pantalun
truck tañu rampana, kamiyun
trunk of a fallen tree k'ullu
tubers and/or fruits roasted in a wathi(y)a(na) wathi(y)a

Tuesday atichaw, martis
turkey pawu
turkey buzzard wallpasu(w)a
turn muyu(y); **to turn** muyuy; **to turn into** *(showing transformation from one state to another)* . . . -man tukuy; **to turn off the lights** k'ancharay
twelve chunkaiskayniyoh, *(borrowing from Spanish, used in telling time)* dusi; **twelve o'clock** *(borrowing from Spanish)* las dusi
twenty iskaychunka
twice iskay kutita
two iskay, *(borrowing from Spanish, used in telling time)* dus; **two o'clock** *(borrowing from Spanish)* las dus; **two hundred** iskaypachah; **two days ago** qayninpa; **two days before** qayninpantin; **in two days** minchha, minchha p'unchaw, minchha diya; **in two weeks** minchha qanchischaw, minchha simana; **in two months** minchha killa; **in two years** minchha wata; **two days after tomorrow** minchhantin

U
udder ñuñu
ugly mana sumah
ullucu *or* **ulluco** *(yellow Andean tuber used like potatoes)* ulluku *(Ullucus tuberosus)*
un*(as in "untie")* –ra
uncle *(brother of father)* yayawki, *(brother of mother)*

kaka
under ura
underbrush, full of ch'aphrach'aphra, ch'aphsach'aphsa
underbrush ch'aphra, ch'aphsa
underneath, to put *(something)* uranchay
undershirt unkhu
United States Istadus Unidus
unoccupied ch'usah
untie, to phaskay, wataray
until -kama
up pata, **up to** -kama; **to end up . . .** -man tukuy
upon hawa
urgently *(verb stem]*-rqo
urinate, to hisp'akuy, hisp'ay; **place to urinate** hisp'ana
used thanta

V

valley (semi-tropical) on the eastern slopes of the Andes yunka; **warm valley on the western slopes of the Andes** yunka
valuable chani(n)yoh, chanin(ni)yoh; **most valuable** chanin(ni)yohpuni
value chanin
vegetable side dish, very common steamed or boiled *(of fava beans: "abasmut'i"; of a variety of dry beans: "chuwimut'i"; of corn kernels: "saramut'i"; of lupine seeds: " tarwimut'i")* mut'i
veil iñaka
Venus *(planet)* ch'aska
verge of, to be on the *(the meaning of the verb)* -naya

very anchata, millay, -puni; **very hot** *(temperature)* rupha; **very kind** allinsonqo, urpisonqo; **very little** huch'uysitu; **very often** sapa kutillan; **very salty** kachikachi; **very short** huch'uysitu; **very small** huch'uysitu; **very young** *(a female)* sipasita, *(a male)* waynitu; **to be very sorry** phutikuy
veterinarian uywahampeh
via -(n)ta
vicuña wik'uña
Viracocha Wiraqocha, one of the names of the primary Inca deity (see Note 4 in Chapter 2)
visible sut'i
vizcacha *(Andean rodent)* wisk'acha
vomit qephnay, qepnay
vomiting qephnay, qepnay

W

wad of coca in someone's mouth that is noted by the protrusion it makes in the cheeks pihchu
wait, to suyay
wake *(oneself)* **up, to** rich'a(ri)y; **to wake** *(someone)* **up** rich'a(ri)chiy
walk, to puriy
walker pureh
wall perqa; **to make a wall** perqay
want, to munay
warm valley on the western slopes of the Andes yunka
wash basin or sink where one can wash clothes, hair, or

anything else that can absorb water t'ahsakuna; **wash basin or sink where one can wash up or wash anything that cannot absorb water** mahchhikuna, mayllakuna; **to wash clothes, hair, or anything else that can absorb water** t'ahsay; **to wash anything that cannot absorb water** mayllay; **to wash oneself** mayllakuy

washing place *(on the bank of a river, etc.)* **for clothes, hair, or anything else that can absorb water** kiti t'ahsana

watch riloh

watch, to *(to keep an eye on)* t'ohriy, *(to pay attention to, to keep an eye on)* yuyay

Watch out! ¡Pahtatah!; *(showing annoyance, anger or even a threat over what someone is doing)* ¡Pahtá!

water unu, yaku

water closet pincha, ritriti

way, to do in that hinay, **to do in this way** hinay

we *(excluding the person[s] addressed)* ñoqayku *(variants:* ñuqayku, noqayku, noqayku; *variants of the* -hpata *ending:* -h, -hpa, -hta*);* *(including the person[s] addressed)* ñoqancheh *(variants:* ñuqancheh, noqancheh, nuqancheh; *variants of the* -ncheh *ending:* -nchih, -nchij, -nchik, -nchis*)*

weak ch'uchalli; **rather weak** phuchu

wear, to p'acha(lli)y *[Note that instead of the word for "clothing," p'acha, any article of clothing, such as* poncho, punchu, *can be substituted to convey the idea of wearing that item.]*

weave, to away

weaver awah

Wednesday qoyllurchaw, mirkulis

week qanchis p'unchaw unah, qanchischaw, simana

weigh, to llasay

well (-)a *(as a suffix [-a] or an independent word following what is being stressed; stressed in speech)*, (-)á *(as a suffix [-á] or an independent word following what is being stressed; stressed in speech)*; alli(n), sumah, waleh; kusa *(adverb and interjection used to show a very high degree of excellence)*

well *(of water)* puhyu; **to dig a well** puhyuchay

wet hoq'o; **to get wet** hoq'oy; **to wet** hoq'ochay

what ima; **what thing** ima; **What?** ¿A?; **What?** *(responding)* ¿Hay?

when hayk'ah, mayk'ah

where may, maypi

whereabouts maynehpi

which mayqen, mayqenchus

while, once in a mayninpi

whip sihwa(na)

white yurah

who pi, pichus

whopping cough ch'oho, ch'uhu

whose pehpata
why imarayku; **why not** imamanaqa
wide miqa, sakha
wife warmi
wildflower wayta
wind wayra(y); **wind storm** wayra(y)qunchuy, wayra(y)tamya
windy wayra(y)sapa
wing rihra, raphra
winnow, to wayrachiy
winter chiripacha
with -wan; *(shows that the noun to which it is attached is in the company of the person)* -wan; *(indicates the noun to which it is attached is owned by or being worn by the person mentioned; as appropriate to the noun to which it is attached, may also indicate a physical condition, as in "wawayoh," "with child," "pregnant"; "suru(h)chiyoh," "with altitude sickness")* -yoh; **with child** *(pregnant [person])* wawayoh
with a lot of . . . -sapa
with a big . . . -sapa
within -manta
without -ra; .-nah; . . mana . . . -wan *(shows that the person is not accompanied by or does not have with him or her the noun to which -wan is attached)*, mana . . . -yoh *(indicates that the person does not have or is not wearing the item designated by the noun to which -yoh is attached; as appropriate to the noun to which -yoh is attached, may also indicate a physical condition, as in "mana wawayoh," "not with child," "not pregnant"; "mana suru(h)chiyoh," "without altitude sickness")*; **without alcohol** q'ayma; **without impurities** *(said of water and of seeds)* ch'uya; **without "[verb stem]-ing"** mana *[verb stem]*-spa(lla)
woman warmi; **young woman** warmicha, *(10-14 years old)* wamira, *(15-20 years old)* sipas
wonderful kusa *(adjective and interjection used to show a very high degree of excellence)*
wood *(for a fire)* llant'a, *(the trunk of a fallen tree)* k'ullu
woods sach'asach'a
wool millma
wool-bearing animals *(sheep, llamas, alpacas, vicunas or guanacos)* paqo
word simi
work, to *(manual work, field work, traditional work of the Quechua people)* llank'ay
worker *(mostly in farm fields)* llank'ah, trawahah
works *(mostly in farm fields)*, **the one who** llank'ah; **the one who works the land** chahrah, hallp'a llank'ah; **the one who works** trawahah
workshop wasi
world pacha
worn thanta
worry *(oneself)*, **to** manchakuy
worst sahrapuni

wound, to k'iriy
woven shawl, colorful llihlla
write, to qellqay
writing *(something written)* qellqa(laqhe)

Y

year wata
yellow q'ellu
yes arí
yesterday qayna (p'unchaw), qayna (diya); **the day before yesterday** qayninpa
you *(one person)* qan, *(more than one person)* qankuna; *(object of a gerund)* -su; *(object of an infinitive)* -su
young *(female)* sipas, *(male)* wayna *[Note: In the famous Machu Picchu ruins there are two peaks, the lower known as **Machu** (old) **Pihchu**, and the higher as **Wayna** (young) **Pihchu**. See pihchu.]*; **very young** *(a female)* sipasita, *(a male)* waynitu
younger sullk'a, *(a female)* aswan sipas, *(a male)* aswan wayna
youngest sullk'a, *(a female)* aswan sipas, *(a male)* aswan wayna
youngster ch'ete, ch'iti
your *(one person)* -yki, *(more than one person)* -ykicheh
yours, of yours *(one person)* qanpata *(you[one person] -of)*, *(more than one person)* qankunahpata *(you[more than one person]-of)*

About the Authors

Judith Noble and Jaime Lacasa, who received their doctorates from Louisiana State University and Iowa State University respectively, taught for nearly forty years in the Department of Foreign Languages and Literatures at Iowa State before they retired. Authors of textbooks and reference books in the field of Spanish language and culture, they turned the focus of their work to the Quechua language, which resulted in their writing *Introduction to Quechua, Language of the Andes*.

CPSIA information can be obtained
at www.ICGtesting.com
Printed in the USA
LVHW03s2103060818
586120LV00038BA/2163/P